# MOTOR RACING
# HEROES
## The Stories of 100 Greats
### ROBERT NEWMAN

VELOCE

For post publication news, updates and
amendments relating to this book visit:

www.veloce.co.uk/books/V4748

# www.veloce.co.uk

First published in May 2014 by Veloce Publishing Limited, Veloce House, Parkway Farm Business Park, Middle Farm Way, Poundbury, Dorchester DT1 3AR, England.
Fax 01305 268864 / e-mail info@veloce.co.uk / web www.veloce.co.uk / www.velocebooks.com.
ISBN: 978-1-845847-48-1 UPC: 6-36847-04748-1 © 2014 Robert Newman and Veloce Publishing. All rights reserved. With the exception of quoting brief passages for the purpose of review, no part of
this publication may be recorded, reproduced or transmitted by any means, including photocopying, without the written permission of Veloce Publishing Ltd. Throughout this book logos, model names
and designations, etc, have been used for the purposes of identification, illustration and decoration. Such names are the property of the trademark holder as this is not an official publication. Readers with
ideas for automotive books, or books on other transport or related hobby subjects, are invited to write to the editorial director of Veloce Publishing at the above address. British Library Cataloguing in
Publication Data – A catalogue record for this book is available from the British Library. Typesetting, design and page make-up all by Veloce Publishing Ltd on Apple Mac. Printed in India by Replika Press.

# MOTOR RACING
# HEROES
## *The Stories of 100 Greats*
### ROBERT NEWMAN

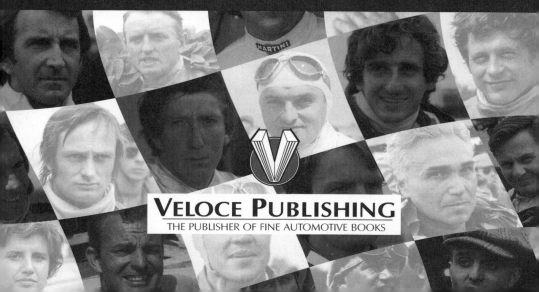

## VELOCE PUBLISHING
### THE PUBLISHER OF FINE AUTOMOTIVE BOOKS

# Contents

# Introduction

## The Birthday Card

I WAS A KID in Melbourne, Australia, when I first got hooked on motor sport. It was the Mercedes-Benz W196 'Streamliner' that did it. I had never seen such a beautiful car, with its flowing lines of pure 1950s elegance. It made everything else around it seem obsolete. And it was driven by two men who would feature strongly in my life many years later, not that I knew it at the time. Like the rest of the world, I just followed the adventures of Juan Manuel Fangio and Stirling Moss as they gave their own personal impression of a train, Moss usually glued to Fangio's tail with little more than a fag paper between them.

Many years later, Stirling told me that Alfred Neubauer, the Mercedes-Benz team boss, once said he shouldn't drive so close to the back of Fangio's car and asked, 'What happens if he goes off?' Stirling replied drily, 'He doesn't go off.' Their performance in the 'Streamliner' and open-wheel W196s in 1955 took my breath away.

Instead of spending my weekly paper round money on *Captain Marvel* and *Superman* comics, I soon started to invest in *Motor Sport* magazine, and devoured Denis Jenkinson's reports on the European Grand Prix scene.

Times and people's outlooks change, never more so – as far as I was concerned – than when my parents decided to return to the UK after emigrating to Australia straight after the Second World War. That decision was a huge blow for me back in 1956.

Little did I know I had started on a long journey that would involve Fangio, Moss, Phil Hill, Luigi Villoresi, Sir Jack Brabham, Nigel Mansell,

Innes Ireland, Karl Kling, Nelson Piquet, Roy Salvadori and rally greats like Markku Alén and Sandro Munari.

So we left our home in the Melbourne suburb of Hawthorn and returned to my birthplace, Ashford, Kent, where I became a junior journalist on the *Kentish Express*. I qualified through the National Council for the Training of Journalists programme and thought about the Big Smoke – that's what we provincial kids used to call London back then – and I started looking around for a job in the city. I found one in 1965, when I became press officer of Pirelli Limited, the international tyre group's British subsidiary.

A couple of years into the job, I discovered that Fangio had been contracted to do promotional work for Pirelli in Milan and that he was coming to Britain. So after checking with the Italian HQ, I called Innes Ireland, sports editor of *Autocar* magazine and winner of the 1961 US Grand Prix, and invited him to interview Fangio. Innes drove us from central London to Heathrow Airport in his Lotus Elan and there we waited in the VIP lounge with not one but two members of the Argentine embassy – it's not every day that you get to meet your country's national hero – to interpret for us, as Fangio spoke no English.

About 20 minutes later an immaculately tailored, powerfully built man well into his 50s was ushered into the lounge. I noticed right away that he had a presence, an almost royal aura, about him that I hadn't encountered in anyone else. But the five-times Formula 1 World Champion immediately embraced Ireland and chatted to him through one of the embassy officials as if the winner of that one solitary Grand Prix was his friend and equal.

The interview went fine. Fangio was quietly spoken in that slightly high-pitched voice of his, never interrupted, was the essence of courtesy and answered Ireland's questions fully. He gave an uncluttered statement of his views, nothing more, nothing less.

After the interview Fangio was whisked off to Claridges, the top people's London hotel, in a sleek Mercedes-Benz. I didn't see him again until 1986 at the launch of my book *With Flying Colours*, an illustrated history of motor racing.

The great champion had agreed to travel halfway around the world from his home in Buenos Aires to be guest of honour at our book's London launch. As he entered the presentation room, a Life Guards' trumpet fanfare blared out and, to a man, all 450 people in the audience stood. That was the effect

Fangio had on everyone. And when it was his turn to speak, this is what he said, 'When I came to Europe with my team in 1948 nobody knew Fangio, but Pirelli gave me tyres for my racing cars. That is why I am here today.'

The packed room echoed with thunderous applause, after which lunch was served. Fangio liked *With Flying Colours*, so I suggested we should commemorate his 80th birthday, which was five years away, with one of our illustrated books. He seemed to like the idea. 'It is possible,' he said with characteristic caution. In the end, we agreed that I should send him my proposals for the book and he would discuss them with his business associates.

Before that second encounter with Fangio I had worked with Stirling Moss several times. On one occasion we went to the group's test facility in Milan so that he could drive a Porsche 911 for a television programme segment being made about one of our new products.

So I thought, what if... A few days later, after about an hour spent answering his searching questions, Moss agreed to put his name to the book as co-author with motor racing historian Doug Nye, and we shook hands on the deal. By the way, a handshake is the only 'contract' that ever existed between Stirling and me in the 20 years that we worked together.

There had been no news from Fangio on whether or not he would allow us to produce his book, so I sent him a fax telling him that Stirling Moss had agreed to be its co-author. A few hours later along came his reply, saying he was thrilled his old teammate had agreed to co-author the book and immediately approved the whole project. I replied thanking him and promising him the best birthday card he had ever had – the book.

A few weeks later, in April 1990, it seemed like disaster had struck. Stirling hobbled into the Schlossgarten Hotel in Stuttgart on crutches with his right leg in plaster. He had been knocked off his scooter by a car in central London and broken his leg. After a couple of weeks in hospital Moss, a professional to his fingertips, could move about on his crutches sufficiently well to travel to the Mercedes-Benz test track for the book's first photo shoot with Fangio and Karl Kling (their 1955 teammate) and two open-wheel W196 cars.

After the photographic session and lunch with the full 1955 Mercedes driver line-up, Fangio and we began our 200-mile journey to the old Nürburgring in a shiny new 500 SE lent to us for the journey, me driving.

To say I was nervous about chauffeuring the great champion is a massive understatement. But we eased our way through Stuttgart's evening traffic without much difficulty, Juan with a vaguely uneasy expression on his face.

We stopped off for soft drinks at an autobahn service area, and on the way back to the car Fangio said in his near-perfect Italian, 'I have a good idea, I'll drive, you navigate.' I couldn't get rid of the car keys fast enough; I was going to be driven by the five-times Formula 1 World Champion.

Within minutes we were cruising towards the 'Ring at a steady 125mph in the outside lane of the derestricted German motorway, my hero just sitting there with the fingertips of his right hand at six o'clock on the steering wheel, whistling quietly under his breath.

But even at the age of 78 that famous driving precision was still there when an ancient Borgward Isabella suddenly lurched out in front of us at less than half our speed. It seemed an accident was imminent. But Fangio's hands flew to the ten-to-two position on the wheel, he did some lively cadence braking and in seconds we were sitting behind the old car doing 50mph ourselves. The Isabella eventually swung back into the centre lane and Fangio immediately floored the accelerator, where it stayed for the next 100 miles.

Once we were in the hotel at the 'Ring news of Juan's arrival travelled fast, and everyone wanted to meet him. The 'Ring's museum curator wanted him to visit his display of cars, pens and scruffy bits of paper were thrust at him, all of which he autographed. But the person he most enjoyed talking to was an elderly Spanish waiter who remembered that Fangio always asked for room 29 in the old hotel – now demolished and rebuilt – because it was the one with an en suite bathroom. After the stress of a day's racing, Fangio enjoyed a long, invigorating soak in his private bathtub.

The morning after our arrival we went off to the old Nürburgring so that Fangio could be reunited with the Maserati 250F in which he won the 1957 German Grand Prix and his fifth world title. The idea was for him to drive the car and for my photographer, Phil Sayer, to hang out of the back of an estate car taking pictures of Juan at the wheel. Trouble was the pedigree racing car and driver kept going faster than the estate car, so the job took longer than expected.

But with the shots in the can, Fangio told me to climb aboard the 500 SE; he wanted to drive the full circuit again. What followed was his running commentary on how he set ten consecutive lap records that day in August 1957 in his successful attempt to overtake the Ferraris of Mike Hawthorn and Peter Collins, who thought they had the race in the bag.

Fangio showed me the humps from which the Maserati literally took off, corners where he drifted through at perilous speeds in hot pursuit of the two Englishmen. He called out the rpm and gear changes he had used at just about every bend and confessed he went into every corner – all 172 of them on the 14.17-mile track – in a higher gear than usual. He grinned mischievously as he said he'd never driven like that before or since. '*Troppo pericoloso,*' he remarked – too dangerous.

Juan kept chuckling as the memories came flooding back, especially one from the evening after the race when his chief mechanic, Guerino Bertocchi, took him after dinner to see his decidedly agricultural Maserati 250F with its front air intake clogged up with earth and grass.

A week later the book's art director Derek Forsyth, photographer Phil Sayer and I met Fangio in Monte Carlo so that we could take pictures of him at the principality's famous Grand Prix. It turned out to be a long haul, because, as we photographed him on that hot sunny day in the organised chaos of the cramped pits we couldn't move more than a pace or two without JMF being stopped by admirers, autograph hunters and friends. But eventually we got away and I hailed a cab; we were expected at the palace.

The late Prince Rainier had invited us to his castle for drinks: so while thousands of spectators sat comfortably in the stands wearing their shorts and T-shirts, Fangio and I were suffocating in shirts, ties and smartly pressed suits as the taxi pulled up outside the prince's turreted home.

When I explained who we were, the uniformed guards at the front gate snapped to attention and their commander pressed a discreetly hidden button under his desk. In seconds, the prince's press secretary was at my right elbow, ready to lead us across the courtyard to a gilded reception room. His Serene Highness, silver haired and impeccably dressed, was a gracious host and, after drinks and the obligatory photographs on the battlements, showed us around his stunning vintage car collection.

As we walked through the prince's packed, temperature-controlled underground garage, I 'accidentally' let slip that the Automobile Club de Monaco couldn't find time in its pre-race schedule for Fangio to drive a borrowed Ferrari 250 GT California Spider around the circuit on a couple of laps of honour, one with my photographer and one with me.

With a wave of the prince's right hand, the press secretary quietly left us, and our tour continued. Later, as we took the sun with the prince in the grounds of his castle home, the press chief returned and whispered in Rainier's ear.

'If you gentlemen would like to be at the club's offices in half an hour, Mr Fangio will be most welcome to drive two laps of the circuit,' said the Prince in his upmarket Italian.

After the photographer jumped out of the Ferrari, it was my turn to be driven around the elegant Monaco Grand Prix city circuit on race day by the great Formula 1 champion. The applause of the fans lining the route competed with the snarling exhaust note of the 250 GT as Juan entered into the spirit of things and gave the crowd what was, to him, a modest sample of the driving precision for which he was world famous. The casino, Mirabeau, station hairpin, Tabac, Ste Devote … magic.

Ayrton Senna won that year's Monaco Grand Prix in a McLaren MP4/5B-Honda and, at the celebration dinner that night, he dedicated his victory to his motor racing hero, Juan Manuel Fangio. When JMF told me of Senna's gracious gesture the next morning at breakfast, he was clearly moved.

After visiting friends in Europe, Juan returned to Argentina. My team and I were to join him there, but before he left he gave us carte blanche to photograph anything in or out of his amazing museum in Balcarce, about 200 miles south-west of Buenos Aires.

Balcarce's single claim to fame is that it produced, almost literally, the man Stirling Moss and lesser experts regard as the greatest motor racing driver of all time. The town provided financial support for Juan and his brother Toto as they worked in their tiny garage – still owned by the Fangio family – to convert a series of innocuous vehicles, including a taxi, into international race winners. Once, the citizens of Balcarce even had a whip-round to raise enough money for the Fangio brothers to buy a new car that they then converted into a South American road race winner. Another time they ran a raffle.

Juan never forgot the generosity of the people of Balcarce. That's why he insisted on his museum, which houses hundreds of his trophies, honours and racing cars, being established in his home town instead of in Buenos Aires. The museum building, which is visited by busloads of people from the big city, is six storeys high. When I was there, instead of lifts and escalators it had a kind of slightly inclined track that wound its way up the inside of the structure from the ground floor to the sixth, with stop-offs at interim floors crammed with exhibits.

Although I adored the W196 Streamliner on loan from Mercedes-Benz in Stuttgart, the star exhibit for me was the 110mph 1947 Negrita, a mongrel of a car built by Toto Fangio using a six-cylinder Second World War Guerrero truck engine. It was ugly, but it won that year's Rosario Grand Prix and symbolised better than most the mechanical ingenuity and talent of the Fangio brothers.

Throughout our stay Juan was generosity itself. We were allowed to take out and photograph any car we wished – including the Streamliner. He even returned to his Buenos Aires home and rummaged through the memorabilia in his cellar to find us more old pictures, which he and his chauffeur – who hardly ever drove him – carried from their car to our room in the museum the next day.

By the end of nine days we had taken more than enough photographs and it was time for us to return to Europe. But just as we were ready to leave for our hotel 40 miles away in Mar del Plata for the last time, Fangio walked into the museum. He invited us to dinner at his Balcarce family home, a rare honour. Dinner turned out to be an Argentine *asado*, a huge feast of barbecued meat, bread, salad and wine – lots of wine.

As I sipped a potent aperitif, vast racks of beef sizzled in a glass-fronted barbecue against a wall that had to be at least 30ft long. Then the door to the huge dining room opened and in walked José Froilán González. So after the Fangio sisters and Toto emerged from their barbecue room, I dined in the company of the first man to win a World Championship Formula 1 race for Ferrari. More magic.

It was a delightful evening, but the next day we started our journey back to Europe to pull the book together and plan its international launch and Juan Manuel Fangio's 80th birthday party.

By March 1991 the book was ready and its launch had been planned. The first phase was a press unveiling of *Fangio: a Pirelli Album* at the Mercedes-Benz showroom in Piccadilly, London. Sir Tim Rice, chairman of the publishers and the other half of the hit musical duo with Andrew Lloyd Webber, hosted the proceedings.

Stirling gave an eloquent appreciation of his Mercedes-Benz teammate and both he and Juan Manuel responded to press questions for about an hour. After a light lunch the two stars of the day slipped away to get some rest before the emotional night that lay ahead.

The big night was dinner with a live TV show in the Dorchester Hotel's ballroom, attended by 400 people. Guests included Nigel Mansell, Tony Brooks, Phil Hill, Sir Jack Brabham, John Surtees and Geoff Duke. The elegant room was 'decorated' with an Alfa Romeo 158 (the car in which Fangio won his first world title), a Maserati 250F (in which he won his fifth world title) and a W196 open-wheeler (in which he won his third and fourth world titles).

After dinner, the fun began with a fanfare by the Queen's Life Guards. Murray Walker was our master of ceremonies and, with the help of film inserts plus leading motor sport journalist and businessman Barrie Gill interviewing some of the guests, Murray told Fangio's story. In interviews, Brooks, Hill, Surtees, Brabham, Mansell and others all contributed their favourite stories about Juan, although Nigel simply paid tribute to the great champion and said of he and his young colleagues, 'We're just out there trying to do today what he did all those years ago.'

After the show, Moss spoke with affection of his friend Juan, and then it was Fangio's turn.

His speech was in Italian and I had the honour of interpreting for him; me, the kid from Melbourne who had idolised him from 13,000 miles away 40 years earlier! He started by saying that, with his job, he didn't expect to become 80 years old in the first place. Then he regaled his audience with one hilarious motor racing story after another. It was a performance that got what it deserved: a standing ovation.

At the end of it all there was one more thing left to do. I stood, said a few words, then presented my hero with the first copy of his illustrated biography. My inscription on the inside front cover read, 'To Juan, with congratulations on your 80th. This was the birthday card I promised you two years ago. With admiration, Bob Newman.' It was my turn to feel a little emotional.

I felt a little emotional on numerous occasions when writing this book.

Here, we have more than a century of heroes, men and women of exceptional courage, determination, an insatiable hunger for excitement and success, all of whom branded their eras with their own identities in such dramatic ways.

But what makes them motor racing heroes and heroines? Racing drivers pull off feats we can only dream about. After that, we do. You and me. By the way our minds process their superhuman accomplishments.

We're all different, you, me and everyone else. We've been brought up differently, in different countries, states, counties, provinces, towns, homes and schools, all with their different traditions and ways of looking at things. We've all had different childhoods, developed different values. And when we were young, we were exposed to the top drivers of our day at a time when we were at our most impressionable. Young people tend to carry over into adult life the impressions that other people, places and, yes, racing drivers make on them. So in a way there's no cut-and-dried answer to what makes a hero or heroine, except that we do, for myriad tangled reasons.

This book tries to explain why these 100 men and women are my motor racing heroes. You may not agree with my choices – it's all subjective, of course – so there's only one thing for it: read the book and decide for yourself.

Certainly, I didn't reach my conclusions lightly. What you're about to read is the result of months of research, often in dark, dusty corners long-since forgotten, in the records of the sport from that very first Grand Prix win by Ferenc Szisz near Le Mans on a 120-mile circuit in June 1906 driving a Renault AK, right through to Michael Schumacher's ground-breaking seven Formula 1 world titles.

The whole idea came about around ten years ago when my friend Casey Annis, publisher of *Vintage Racecar Journal*, wanted to revamp the magazine and asked his writers to come up with ideas for columns. Mine was 'Heroes,' and it has been running in VRJ, one hero at a time, ever since. With a great deal more research, the idea turned into this book of 100 heroes, but even that doesn't say it all as far as my personal experiences are concerned.

For instance, I haven't said a word about putting the boot on the other foot. The time I drove Gigi Villoresi around California in the very Ferrari 340 America in which he won the 1951 Mille Miglia. Or tyre-smoking my way around Spain's Jarama circuit in a 7-series BMW with mischievous triple F1 World Champion Nelson Piquet at the wheel. Or chatting to a worried

Roy Salvadori in an out-of-the-way garage in Reims as he peered into the guts of his Lola-Climax the night before the 1962 GP of France. Or trying to interpret from German into English and Italian between Karl Kling, Fangio and Moss. Or high jinks with Stirling Moss and Murray Walker in Singapore. Or a celebrity tour of South Africa as Juan Manuel Fangio's interpreter.

Could all that be the basis of another book, I ask myself?

*Robert Newman*
*Dorga, Italy*

---

### Dedication
For Els, James and Lindsey, with love.

---

# Alboreto, Michele

KEN TYRRELL ONCE SAID that, contrary to what had been written about him, he had no special talent for spotting good racing drivers. 'If they're quick, they're good,' he growled. So was that all there was to it? Lap times? Whatever it was, he ended up employing the likes of Sir Jackie Stewart, Jody Scheckter, Ronnie Peterson and Michele Alboreto.

Take Alboreto, for instance. He had just become the 1980 European Formula 3 Champion when one of Ken's spies pointed out the courteous Italian. The lad seemed promising, so Ken offered him three 1981 races in Tyrrell's number two car alongside Eddie Cheever. Michele qualified his Tyrrell 010-Ford 17th in the first race at Imola and that was good enough for Ken.

He signed Alboreto to a three-year contract, although his cars – still powered by normally aspirated Ford Cosworth engines – were struggling against their turbocharged brethren. Even Ferrari, which had not always been quick to adopt new developments in the past, fielded a turbo for the first time in 1981, while Michele was to persevere with the venerable Cosworth for another two seasons.

Alboreto was born near Milan, Italy, two days before Christmas 1956. He started out in Formula Monza in 1976, won the 1979 Italian Formula 3 Championship and 12 months later the European title in a March 803-Alfa Romeo. In 1981 Michele's smooth driving style endeared him to Tyrrell, who was slow to switch to turbos. Lack of power and reliability meant Alboreto qualified low on the grid and retired six times that year. But, a talented and persistent young man, he gave every race his best shot and eventually scored World Championship points with a fourth place in the 1982 Grand Prix of Brazil. He came fourth again at Long Beach and then got himself on the podium by coming third in the Tyrrell 011-Ford at Imola, a sixth in France and a fifth before his home crowd at Monza: a points scoring build-up to his first Formula 1 win in the last event of the season at Caesar's Palace, Las Vegas. It was an oddball event, held on a 2.27-mile temporary course on the Las Vegas Strip that was riddled with sharp corners. Just the thing for cars without turbos, which outran the boosted big guns with their turbo lag, although Alain Prost and René Arnoux in the works Renault RE30Bs began pulling away from the field early in the 75-lap GP. But Arnoux's car retired with engine problems and Prost's Renault was vibrating so much that Michele caught and passed him to lead his first Grand Prix and then win it, even though John Watson in a McLaren MP4/1C-Ford was closing in on him towards the end.

He amassed 25 points that year and earned himself equal seventh place in the championship with Patrick Tambay.

Tyrrell still stuck to the normally aspirated Ford Cosworth for 1983, while all around him were switching to turbos: blower pioneers Renault, Ferrari, Brabham, Alfa Romeo, McLaren-Porsche, Williams and even newcomer Spirit all boasted the new form of engine and set about trying to tame its notorious throttle lag. It was the driving finesse of Michele Alboreto that still enabled Tyrrell to give a reasonable account of itself, despite its engine disadvantage.

In fact, the gritty Italian put up an incredible performance to beat the turbo-powered cars and win a nail-biter of a Grand Prix at Detroit. Nelson Piquet led the race for the first nine laps in the Brabham-BMW turbo, but René Arnoux passed him and held on to the lead in the blown Ferrari 126C2B until he retired and Piquet took command again. But Alboreto in the turboless Tyrrell 011 overtook the Brazilian, who was slowing, nine laps from the end, and held the lead until the chequered flag to win Tyrrell's last victory and score the Ford Cosworth engine's 155th and last success.

Since Arturo Merzario's departure 11 years earlier, the Italian press had been pestering Enzo Ferrari to sign an Italian driver. The Great Man liked Michele's driving style and quiet, pleasant demeanour: the youngster reminded the legendary constructor of another of Formula 1's fine gentlemen, Wolfgang von Trips. So Ferrari sent his emissary, Franco Gozzi, to an awards ceremony in Britain being attended by Michele to give the young driver the nod for 1984. Alboreto liked driving for Tyrrell, but he was clearly flattered by Ferrari himself sending Gozzi to London with the proposition and they immediately agreed terms.

The young Milanese qualified his first factory Ferrari 126C4 on the front row of the grid at Rio de Janeiro, although he retired with mechanical problems and then came a lowly 11th in South Africa. But he was spectacular at Zolder. He won the first pole position of his career qualifying for the 1984 Grand Prix of Belgium, which he then led for all 70 of its laps to become the first Italian to win in a Ferrari Formula 1 car since Ludovico Scarfiotti in the 1966 Grand Prix of Italy.

Then followed a whole series of retirements due to turbocharger problems, until Alboreto took sixth at Monaco, after which he went back to retiring again. A fifth in Britain, a third in Austria, a second at Monza, second and fastest lap in Germany and a fourth in Portugal all contributed to the 30.5 points that got him to fourth place in the championship.

In 1985 it looked liked Michele would become World Champion in the Ferrari 156/85, with which he dominated the first half of the season. He would have won at Monaco had it not been for a puncture, but he still took second and set the fastest lap: later, he won in Canada and Germany. After that the Ferrari lost its competitive edge, and a series of lowly finishes and retirements meant he scored little or nothing. That gave Alain Prost the chance to squeak past Alboreto and loosen the title from the Italian's grasp. After that results were thin on the ground, and Michele left Maranello at the end of 1988.

He joined Tyrrell briefly and produced a third in Mexico before an argument with Ken over sponsorship caused him to depart abruptly to drive the seriously underdeveloped Lola LC89-Lamborghini. His career was winding down as he continued to grace a series of uncompetitive cars with his class and talent: Arrows, Footwork, Lola, Scuderia Italia and Minardi, all certain contenders for a place at the back of the grid where the sun doesn't shine.

Disillusioned by Formula 1 and a failed attempt at the 1996 Indianapolis 500, Michele gravitated to sports car racing and delighted his friends and fans by winning the 1997 24 Hours of Le Mans in a Porsche WSC95 with Tom Kristensen and another Ferrari refugee, Stefan Johansson. Then he won the 2000 Petit Le Mans at America's Road Atlanta, sharing an Audi R8 with Allan McNish and Dindo Capello, and after that the 2001 12 Hours of Sebring in an R8 partnered by Capello and Laurent Aiello.

But Michele Alboreto's renaissance came to an end on 24 April 2001. He died after an accident due to tyre failure while testing an Audi A8 at Germany's Lausitzring.

# Amon, Chris

THERE WAS NEVER ANY doubt that Chris Amon was an exceptional talent. Mauro Forghieri, Ferrari's chief designer for almost 20 years, put him in the same sparsely populated category as the legendary Jim Clark. But even though he was in Formula 1 for 14 years and a works Ferrari driver for three of them, Chris never won a World Championship Grand Prix. Why? Circumstances, bad luck, mechanical ills, pit mistakes, coincidence, misfortune, all of those.

In his 96 Grands Prix, he won the pole position five times, took podium positions 11 times and won 83 Formula 1 World Championship points. But he never won a world title GP.

He was so unlucky that Mario Andretti once remarked that if Chris became an undertaker, people would stop dying.

From humble beginnings in Bulls, on New Zealand's North Island, Amon showed promise in a 2.5-litre Cooper-Climax at Sandown Park in 1963, when he was spotted by Reg Parnell, who invited the 19-year-old to test-drive a Lola-Climax F1 at Goodwood. Amon felt really at home in the car and was soon making top six finishes in lesser events, like the Glover Trophy and Aintree 200.

Chris' career rumbled on in uncompetitive cars for a while until he won the 1966 24 Hours of Le Mans with Bruce McLaren in a Ford GT40 – a victory that earned him an invitation to join Ferrari for 1967; and, not unreasonably, the young New Zealander felt he was on his way to the top. Lorenzo Bandini crashed at the chicane during the year's Grand Prix of Monaco and died soon afterwards. A sickened Chris was forced to continually pass the blazing wreckage of his team leader's car, before eventually driving his Ferrari 312 into third place. He scored a fourth in Holland and another third in the Grand Prix of Belgium at Spa-Francorchamps, where his more experienced teammate Mike Parkes crashed and seriously fractured his right leg. So with Ludovico Scarfiotti in the doldrums, Chris lowered himself gingerly into the hot seat as Ferrari's number one driver at the tender age of 24. He fought some memorable F1 battles with the Brabham-Repcos of 'Black Jack' Brabham and Denny Hulme and the Lotus 49s of Jim Clark and Graham Hill, but he never won. A couple of thirds in the British and German Grands Prix were the best he could do.

And then the New Zealander was inflicted with the freakish bad luck that would never leave him alone. He was catching the two 49s at Watkins Glen when his oil pressure went and Clark managed to shuffle across the line to win, despite broken rear suspension.

In Mexico, the last race of the season, Chris shared the front row of the grid with the Scot, whom he chased with a vengeance – and then ran out of fuel just before the end.

The 1968 Tasman Cup series proved a shot in the arm for the unlucky Amon, who won Pukekohe and Levin before Jim Clark's Lotus 49T snapped up victories at Wigram, Surfers' Paradise, Warwick Farm and Sandown Park to win the series. But anyone who saw Jim and Chris cover 55 nose-to-tail laps at Sandown could not help but conclude that, on his day, Amon was a match for the Scot. Clark won by just a tenth of a second from the New Zealander.

Amon came fourth behind the Lotus-Fords of Clark and Hill and Jochen Rindt's Brabham-Repco on New Year's Day at Kyalami, but his bad luck kicked in again at the 1968 Grand Prix of Spain, which he started from pole and was leading when his fuel pump blew a fuse on lap 58. He was way ahead of John Surtees in the Honda at Spa when he was baulked by Jo Bonnier's dawdling McLaren-BRM and ended up behind Big John. And that wasn't the worst of it: the Honda sent a stone flying through his radiator and sent Chris into retirement. Amon chose the wrong tyres for a wet French Grand Prix and his differential went at the Nürburgring. At Monza he was lying second when his Ferrari slipped on oil and crashed badly. He was leading by one minute in Canada when his transmission broke.

The circus moved Down Under again for the Tasman Cup at the end of 1968 and Chris got a major morale boost. He won the series in the Ferrari 246T with victories at Pukekohe, Levin, Lakeside and Sandown Park. But glory in Oz and NZ did not translate into glory in Europe. The new V12 in his 1969 Ferrari 312 turned out to be less powerful than the 1968 unit and the best Amon could do was a third at Zandvoort. The rest was a mishmash of mechanical failures and repeated retirements.

Things got so bad that Ferrari temporarily withdrew from F1 to develop the 312B and Chris signed for the fledgling March, a disastrous decision. Jacky Ickx won the Grands Prix of Austria and Canada in the new Ferrari 312B and Amon's March 701 did not come good until mid-season, when he scored seconds in Belgium and France: still no victory, though. But he did win the non-championship International Trophy race at Silverstone by ten seconds from Jackie Stewart in another March.

Chris left March for Matra at the end of 1971. The car's chassis was brilliant but the engine was not, although he did have a lucky win in the non-championship (again) Grand Prix of Argentina. He really looked like he was going to do it in the 1972 Grand Prix of France, which he led until he had a puncture on lap 19. He got back into the race in eighth place, put in an amazing drive to work his way up to an eventual third and set the race's fastest lap of 2min 53.9sec in the process, but there he stayed until the end, preceded by winner Jackie Stewart in a Tyrrell 003-Ford and Emerson Fittipaldi driving a Lotus 72D-Ford.

Next, Chris made an even worse career decision, this time to replace Nanni Galli at the Pederzani brothers' Tecno for 1973. The car was a 'home-made' 12-cylinder PA 123/6, but it did not make its debut until the fifth Grand Prix of the year at Zolder, where Chris' fantastic talent was more responsible than the car in coming sixth to score Tecno's one and only point in Formula 1. Amon had had enough by the Italian Grand Prix in September, so he left Tecno to drive a third Tyrrell 005-Ford in Canada and the USA, but had very little to show for it at season's end.

By the end of 1973 Amon firmly believed that the only way to get out of his downward spiral was to build his own car, but the pale blue Amon AF1 was hopelessly under-financed. Its best performance was to qualify 20th but not even start at Monaco. So Chris jacked that in and drove a BRM P201 in Canada and the United States, but that was a flop too. And all that a few rides got him in Morris Nunn's Ensign N175 and N176 in 1975 and 1976 was a fifth place in the Spanish GP, before Amon decided to retire and move back to New Zealand in 1977.

# Andretti, Mario

MARIO ANDRETTI IS A motor racing galaxy, not just a star – a man who is so talented and incredibly versatile that he has won more in the sport than anyone else on the planet. Like, for instance, the 1978 Formula 1 World Championship for drivers, the 1965, 1966 and 1969 Indycar Championships, the 1984 CART Championship and the 1979 International Race of Champions (aka IROC).

Those are just the main headings under which his achievements can be neatly filed. They happen to include victory in 12 F1 Grands Prix between 1971 and 1978, seven World Sports Car Championship races including three 12 Hours of Sebring, 33 Indycar races among them the Indianapolis 500, 19 CART wins and a NASCAR victory at the 1967 Daytona 500. He even went drag racing and won the 1969 Pike's Peak hillclimb. In all, Mario entered 879 races, won 111 of them and took 109 pole positions.

Mario's is a breathtaking list of accomplishments to which *nobody* else can lay claim. And to think that all of this might never have happened.

Mario and his twin brother Aldo were born to Rina and Luigi Andretti in the Italian town of Montona, not far from Trieste, where they built their own wooden soap-box cars and raced them through the streets. Three years later the Andrettis moved to Lucca amid the gentle Tuscan hills, and it was near there that Mario had his first glimpse of top class motor racing. He rode his bicycle to the Rome–Brescia stretch of the 1954 Mille Miglia and watched winner Alberto Ascari flash by in the Lancia D24. From that moment on the boy was sold on motor racing.

Fortunately for the sport, the Andretti family emigrated to the United States in 1955 and settled in Nazareth, Pennsylvania, where the twins worked in their uncle's garage. They put their hard-earned money into a Hudson Hornet Sportsman stock car and, unknown to their parents, took turns racing it on oval dirt tracks near their home. By the end of 1961 Mario had won 21 out of a possible 45 modified stock car events.

But Andretti's sights were firmly fixed on single-seater racing, and he got in on the ground floor in the early '60s by racing ¾-size midgets. He competed in about 100 events in 1963 alone, and pulled off the remarkable feat of winning three races at two different tracks on that year's Labour Day afternoon – one at Flemington, New Jersey, and two at Hatfield, Pennsylvania.

He got into United Racing Club sprint cars in 1964 – the year he became a naturalised American citizen – and was competing in them when he also moved into Indycar racing. His first event in the championship was at the New Jersey State fairground at Trenton, where he started 16th and came 11th. The late Clint Brawner, a great talent spotter, saw Mario perform at Terra Haute, Indiana, and knew he had found a promising new driver. Mario finished 11th in the Indycar Championship that year, but much better was to come.

The following year, Andretti won his first Indycar race, the Hoosier Grand Prix on the road circuit of the Indianapolis Raceway Park. He came a stunning third in the Indianapolis 500 driving the Brawner Hawk and was named 'Rookie of the Year.' He won his first Indycar Championship in 1965, at just 25 years old the youngest driver to have done so at the time. He won the Indycar Championship again a year later, when he also took pole in the Indy 500, but lost a wheel on lap 59. He came second in the championship in 1967 and 1968 but regained the title in 1969, when he achieved his great ambition of winning the Indianapolis 500. Between 1966 and 1969 he won 29 of USAC's 85 championship races.

In 1968 Mario had his first crack at Formula 1 at Watkins Glen, where he started from pole position in a Lotus 49B but retired with mechanical problems. The following year his hectic Indycar schedule only permitted him three Grands Prix, which earned him three retirements. In 1970 he moved to an uncompetitive March 701, but his best score was third at Jarama, Spain. Things looked up in 1971, when Mario switched to the legendary Ferrari 312B and set the fastest lap and won the South African GP at Kyalami. When his US schedule allowed he drove for Ferrari throughout that year; in 1972 he came eighth in the F1 Drivers' Championship. But it was a much different story in endurance racing: partnered by Jacky Ickx, he won the 1972 6 Hours of Daytona, the 12 Hours of Sebring, the 1000 Kilometres of Brands Hatch and the 6 Hours of Watkins Glen, all in the 312P, to help Ferrari win the year's World Sports Car Championship.

Mario drove the disappointing Maurice Philippe-designed, Ford-powered Parnelli VPJ4 with poor results until the USGP West of March 1976, when he was forced to retire. After that he switched to Lotus, but Colin Chapman's cars were unsuccessful that year. The American stuck it out, though, and was eventually rewarded with a pole and victory in an extremely wet Grand Prix of Japan.

Andretti stayed on with the Hethel team for 1977, when he won four GPs in the Lotus 78 wing car.

He fired a shattering warning shot when he won the first round of the 1978 championship in Argentina, but he was up against some stiff opposition, much of it from his own teammate Ronnie Peterson. But, driving the Lotus 79, Andretti succeeded in adding the Belgian, Spanish, French, German and Dutch GPs to his tally to win the Formula 1 World Championship with 64 points, 13 ahead of runner-up Peterson.

The American spent another two season with Lotus, but not much came of them, so he switched to Alfa Romeo for 1981; but its 179C produced a similarly disappointing story.

That was it for Mario in F1, except for guesting in a Williams at Long Beach and an injured Didier Pironi at Ferrari, thrilling the Italian *tifosi* witless with pole and third place in the 1982 Grand Prix of Italy at Monza driving the 126 C2.

After all that F1 success, Andretti went back to racing full time in the United States in 1982 and came third in the CART/PPG Championship. He joined Newman/Haas Racing in '83 and took its Lola T700-Cosworth to victory at Elkhart Lake and Las Vegas. A year later, driving a Lola T800-Cosworth, he started from pole nine times out of 16 and won his fourth CART title.

Mario's son Michael won his first CART/PPG race in a March 86C-Cosworth at Long Beach in 1986, although dad was down in fifth place. Michael went on to take second place in the championship that year. The youngster joined Mario at Newman/Haas in 1989, with Michael winning at Toronto and a couple of weeks later at Michigan. He won the CART/PPG Championship in 1991.

Mario's last IndyCar win was in the Newman/Haas Lola 93/00-Ford at the Phoenix International Raceway on 4 April 1993, when he was well over 53 years old and the oldest recorded winner of a CART/PPG event. His last season was in 1994: it was christened 'The Arrivederci Tour,' in which he competed in his 407th and last Indy race in September of that year.

The 24 Hours of Le Mans has never been kind to the Andrettis, but it was not for want of trying. In 1966 Mario and Lucien Bianchi shared a Holman Moody Ford MkII, but that fizzled out when the car dropped a valve six hours into the race. The next year he campaigned a Ford MkIV GT40 for Holman Moody, but his front brakes locked and he crashed. He partnered son Michael in a Mirage M12 Ford in 1982 and they qualified eighth, only to find their car was not allowed to run because it did not comply with the technical regulations. But 12 months later they finished third with Philippe Alliot in a Porsche 956. The Andrettis returned to La Sarthe in 1988 with a third crew member, Mario's nephew John Andretti, and they drove their works Porsche 962 into sixth.

After retiring from full-time racing Mario still had a yen to win Le Mans, so back he came in 1995 to join Bob Wollek and Eric Helary in a Courage C34-Porsche, which they took to second place. He tried again in 1996 and came 13th, then retired in 1997. His definitive goodbye to Le Mans came in 2000, when he finished 16th in a Panoz LMP-1 Roadster-S.

Mario received many honours during and since his outstanding career, one of them Italy's highest civilian award of *Commendatore dell'Ordine al Merito Della Repubblica Italiana*, on 23 October 2006.

# Arnoux, René

BORN IN PONTCHARRA IN the Grenoble Arrondissment of France, René Arnoux learnt his trade the hard way as he fought for the European Formula 2 Championship against tough nuts like future Formula 1 World Champion Keke Rosberg, double Can-Am Champion Patrick Tambay, Indy 500 winners Danny Sullivan and Eddie Cheever and FIA-GT Champion Klaus Ludwig. He got to within one point of his objective in Tico Martini's Mk19-Renault in 1976, winning at Pau, Enna and Estoril, only to lose the title by that single point to Jean-Pierre Jabouille.

But the little ex-mechanic nailed the championship a year later in a Martini Mk22-Renault with victories at Silverstone, Pau again and Nogaro as well as taking three seconds, to win the title with 52 points to Cheever's 40.

Tico Martini tried his hand at Formula 1 in 1978 with his self-designed Mk23 powered by a Ford DFV V8, and took René with him. But the car only started in four Grands Prix and the best Arnoux could do with it was to come ninth in Belgium. So René switched to Team Surtees for the last two races of the season, but was only able to claim ninth place with the TS20 in the USGP at Watkins Glen and retired the car in Canada.

Renault had begun to make its mark in F1 in 1978, when Jabouille came fourth at Watkins Glen in the RS01, so they recruited his old F2 sparring partner Arnoux and the pair of them went off in search of the team's first Grand Prix victory. But the Régie's first win by Jean-Pierre in an RE10 in the 1979 Grand Prix of France at Dijon was completely eclipsed by some sensational but wheel-banging fun and games between René in the Renault and Gilles Villeneuve in his works Ferrari 312T4 as they fought every inch of the way for second place. They banged their tyres together at Grand Prix speeds at least six times a lap for the last six laps, but Gilles eventually got the better of Arnoux and came second to Jabouille – with René third just 1/25th of a second behind him. It was one of the most spectacular yet spine-chillingly dangerous clashes Formula 1 fans had ever seen, but the spectators and world television audience loved it. Even today Jabouille agrees that the Renault turbo's first win is still obscured by memories of the two young lions' wheel-banging escapade. Seconds in the Grands Prix of Great Britain at Silverstone and the United States at Watkins Glen took René to eighth in the 1979 Formula 1 World Championship.

Michel Tetu's Renault V6 turbo engine still lacked reliability in the RE20 during 1980, but Arnoux was able to cajole it into doing good things when it was alive and kicking. René set the fastest lap time of 2min 27.311sec on the 4.893-mile Interlagos high-altitude circuit, which favoured the turbocharged cars in the Grand Prix of Brazil. But Jean-Pierre Jabouille took pole and led the race for more than half distance before having to retire with turbo trouble. René, who had not qualified well in sixth place on the grid, was running second, so he took over the lead and held it for the last 15 laps to score his first F1 victory. He and Jean-Pierre hogged the front row of the grid at the next Grand Prix of South Africa at Kyalami, where it was more of the same: Jabouille led for 61 of the race's 78 laps but had to retire again, which let Arnoux through to score his second successive Grand Prix win. But that was it. There were pole positions and fastest laps for both drivers throughout the season, but the fragile RE20 just could not finish races on a regular basis, which is why René came a lowly sixth in the drivers' championship table and Renault third in the constructors' with 54 points, 41 down on title winners Williams.

Alain Prost replaced Jabouille at Renault in 1981 and that put René somewhat in the shade. Alain proved to be faster if less spectacular than his fellow countryman and managed to coax the inconsistent RE30B to victories in France, Holland and Italy, while all Arnoux could do was collect an array of low placings and retirements.

The same thing happened in 1982, when Alain won the first two Grands Prix of the season in South Africa and Brazil in the Renault RE30B, while René collected three pole positions but unimpressive race results. He got the fright of his life during the first lap of the Grand Prix of Holland, when his brakes suddenly disappeared as he charged down the main straight of the Zandvoort circuit; he scrubbed off most of his speed by a series of spins and retired. Then he was involved in an accident at the GB GP, but things looked up when he won the Grand Prix of France in the RE30B, to everyone's delight except Prost's. Alain was in second place and claimed Arnoux went against team orders for not handing him the win on a plate, as he was best placed in the championship at the time. René made it clear he thought there were no team orders and that he was free to race his own race.

René took second place in the German GP before his second win of the season in the GP of Italy at Monza, the day after which it was announced that he was about to realise every racing driver's dream and join Ferrari in 1983.

Once again, Ferrari had an all-French driving team, as Patrick Tambay had taken over from the late Gilles Villeneuve and René took Didier Pironi's place after his crippling accident when qualifying for the 1982 Grand Prix of Germany. If he hadn't made such a slow start to the season, Arnoux may well have won the 1983 Formula 1 World Championship instead of Brazilian Nelson Piquet in the Brabham-BMW. Third at Long Beach and Imola were the only respectable results Arnoux turned in until 12 June, when he won in Canada, then in Germany and Holland, where he thrust his way up through the field from tenth place on the grid. That plus seconds in Austria and Italy were still not enough to head off Piquet, who took the title from second-placed Prost with Arnoux third.

The 1984 season was less than spectacular for Ferrari, with newcomer Michele Alboreto scoring Maranello's only victory in Belgium. The best René could do in an erratic year was seconds at Imola and Dallas and thirds in Belgium and Monaco, to end up sixth in the World Championship. So there was ferment in the Ferrari camp as 1985 got under way and, with the Italian press screaming for blood, Arnoux became the sacrificial lamb: he was fired to make way for Sweden's Stefan Johansson after just one race. Arnoux did not compete in Formula 1 again until the following year, by which time he had joined Jacques Lafitte at Ligier for four undistinguished years, before leaving the circus to the likes of Prost, Mansell, Senna et al.

# Ascari, Alberto

ALBERTO ASCARI AND HIS works Lancia D50 plunged into Monte Carlo harbour at 120mph after missing the chicane in the 1955 Grand Prix of Monaco. Even as the ex-World Champion struggled to free himself from the cockpit of the sinking red car, frogmen were ready to dive in and haul him to safety. They dragged him to the surface and unceremoniously heaved him into their small rescue boat, shaken, gasping for breath and incredulous – but glad to be alive. Before being rushed to hospital, he insisted that the divers returned to the depths and extract his lucky blue helmet from the sunken Lancia. A morbidly superstitious man, Ascari always refused to drive a racing car without his indispensible headgear. Soaked, badly shaken and with a severely bruised back, he still had to have it with him as he bobbed about in the little boat – although many would doubt the helmet's powers after such an episode.

That sky blue helmet spelt peace of mind to Alberto, who first sat in the cockpit of a racing car when he was six years old, on his dad Antonio's lap in an Alfa Romeo P2 at the 1924 Grand Prix of France. That peace of mind and his brilliance had paid off handsomely until the Monte Carlo dunking, by which time 37-year-old Alberto had won much more than his father: two world titles in Ferrari 500 F2s, 18 Grands Prix – 13 of them world title events, including a record run of nine successive championship GP wins – the 1953 1000 Kilometres of the Nürburgring in a Ferrari 375 MM and the 1954 Mille Miglia driving a Lancia D24.

Alberto moped around his Milan apartment for a few days after his frightening Monaco accident. On the Thursday, four days after his watery plunge, his friend and pupil Eugenio Castellotti invited him to nearby Monza to watch the young ascending star test a Ferrari 750 Sport to help take Ascari's mind off the Monaco debacle.

With mixed feelings, Alberto drove from his Milan home to the famous circuit, scene of three of his previous accidents and many triumphs. By chance he called in at the track's bar, where he found his ever-jovial best friend Gigi Villoresi, who helped lift his spirits.

Of course, Ascari had no intention of driving a racing car that day, because he was not carrying his indispensible blue helmet. Its leather chinstrap had snapped during the Monaco accident, so Alberto had taken it to a local cobbler to be repaired. There would be no question of Ascari driving a racing car without his blue helmet, Castellotti thought.

Eugenio had just come in after 25 laps in the open-top Ferrari and was pleased to see his friend in the pits.

Ascari had been mulling over the question of if and when he would get back into a racing car and knew he would have to do so. But, clearly, he had come unprepared to drive that morning.

Yet, just before 1:00pm on that day in May, the unthinkable happened. Alberto asked his young friend if he could drive the Ferrari 750 Sport for a few laps to see how it affected his sore back. For a few seconds, Castellotti was speechless. The short, thickset champion had obviously made a spur-of-the-moment decision that was completely alien to his super-cool, calculating character. He even asked Eugenio if he could borrow the youngster's helmet and goggles. The request of an entirely different man, not the Alberto Eugenio knew. But what could Castellotti do? He glanced at an alarmed Gigi Villoresi and, after a moment's hesitation, had no choice but to hand over the gear.

With Castellotti's white helmet perched uneasily on his head, Alberto slid behind the wheel of the unpainted Ferrari, pulled down the borrowed goggles and accelerated off down pit lane, then out on to the track.

Ascari warmed up on the first lap, but on the second he was getting into the groove. On the third, Castellotti, Villoresi and the Ferrari mechanics saw the car fly past the pits; then they heard the raucous Ferrari engine suddenly cut out. After that, a fleeting silence, followed by a series of metallic bangs – like someone kicking an empty oil drum. Then nothing.

Their minds madly trying to rationalise what they had heard, Castellotti, Villoresi and the mechanics ran to the scene at the back of the circuit; they stopped in their tracks at the Vialone corner.

The battered 750 was upside down and Ascari was lying on his back nearby, his breathing shallow. Castellotti and Villoresi quickly knelt down next to the prostrate champion, but seconds later they heard him exhale one last time before he died.

Castellotti and Villoresi were beside themselves with grief.

The time was 1:13pm on 26 May 1955, precisely 29 years and 10 months after Alberto's father Antonio, an Alfa Romeo works driver, had crashed during the 1925 Grand Prix of France at Montlhéry and died soon afterwards.

Italy was deeply shocked by the death of its great hero. Enquiries were set up, investigations conducted, but the cause of the accident that killed Alberto Ascari was never established. It happened on a deserted part of the track during an unscheduled, unofficial test drive. No witnesses came forward.

The rhetorical question in the press was whether or not Ascari was more seriously upset than anyone had imagined by his high-speed dive into Monte Carlo harbour. Or was his car hit by a freak blast of wind that knocked it off course? Did Alberto swerve to avoid a clandestine spectator who had decided to cross the track? Or did one of the rabbits or hares, for which Monza is well known, suddenly scamper across the track, spook Ascari and make him change course abruptly?

The Ferrari 750 was badly bent, but found to be in good mechanical condition: yet nobody has ever come up with a convincing explanation for the death of Italy's great World Champion.

Alberto was a Monza accident 'veteran.' His first came within an ace of burning him to death as a petrol filler tube broke away and soaked him with fuel. In the second, his feet became entangled with his Ferrari 375's extended brake pedal and the car accelerated wildly, spun at high speed and threw him out. The third was while he was leading the 1953 Grand Prix of Italy in a Ferrari 500 F2 and came upon an unexpected slow back-marker and, as he tried to avoid it, spun and was T-boned by Onofre Marimon's Maserati 250F.

It's possible that the dive into Monte Carlo harbour and fragments of the Monza accidents flashed through Alberto's mind. Certainly, he knew he would have to put himself to the test to gauge whether or not he still had the stomach for top-level motor racing. But he obviously had no intention of doing so at Monza on 26 May – otherwise he would have ensured the cobbler had repaired his helmet's chinstrap.

So why did he summon all his strength of character, which was considerable, to overcome his qualms about driving a racing car so soon after the Monaco disaster? What made him break a lifetime of superstition, buckle on Castellotti's helmet and drive the unpainted, open racing car to his death?

That is the Ascari mystery, to which there may never be a satisfactory answer.

# Ascari, Antonio

HIS CONTEMPORARIES CALLED HIM a *Garibaldino*, a term they reserved for the best of their select band. Like Giuseppe Garibaldi, the patriot who kicked the Austrians and French out of Italy with his thousand volunteers in the mid-19th century, Antonio Ascari was a courageous and determined fighter. He was the one who always got the corners right, trying lap after lap to take his car as close as possible to the extreme limit of adhesion. In fact, Arturo Mercanti – the driving force behind the Monza Autodrome, and the race director of the 1924 Grand Prix of Italy at the circuit – sent an enraged note to the Alfa Romeo pits during the GP, saying, 'If Ascari continues to take the corners in this dangerous way to himself and the other drivers, I shall be forced to stop him.' But Antonio kept up his knife-edge performance in the factory Alfa Romeo P2, and won the race by 16 minutes!

Antonio Ascari was born in 1888 at Bonferraro di Sorga, near Mantua, Italy. A foolish prank got him expelled from school, so the young Antonio went to work in a local blacksmith's forge. There, he often worked on the racing bicycles of Giuseppe and Arturo Nuvolari – the latter an Italian cycle-racing champion – the father and uncle respectively of Tazio Nuvolari, later to become one of the greatest racing drivers the world has ever known.

But while the Nuvolaris worked their land in the Mantuan countryside, Antonio's father, who was a wheat salesman, wanted more for his family, so he moved them to Milan in the early 20th century. Antonio graduated in agricultural engineering but thought the work dull, so after the First World War he opened an Alfa Romeo dealership in Milan; and he bought a 1914 Fiat Grand Prix 4500, which he entered for his first motor sport event – the 1919 Parma-Poggio di Berceto hillclimb – and won. Enzo Ferrari also made his motor racing debut in the same event, but could only manage 11th overall in his CMN 15/20.

Four weeks later, Ascari went in for the 1919 Targa Florio – his first race, rather than just a hillclimb – with the big Fiat, and was up there among the leaders until one of the tortuous circuit's thousands of hairpins foxed him and he skidded off the muddy track and down into a deep ravine and out of the race, injuring himself and his riding mechanic Giacomo Menini. It was not an auspicious performance – except that those sage talent-spotters at Alfa Romeo saw something others did not in this shortish, athletically built dealer of theirs, and he became an Alfa Corse driver.

Some of the Alfa bosses must have regretted their choice after a while, because 1920–22 yielded slim pickings, and their man even hurt himself in a crash at Mugello in 1922.

Meanwhile, Ascari's business flourished, and he was appointed Alfa's concessionaire for the entire Lombardy area. He also had an influence on the development of the company's products and it was under his guidance that the 1920 Alfa Romeo ES Sport was developed and built as both a racer and a road car. The racing version went on to win the 1921 and 1922 Coppa Del Garda races.

But Antonio eventually got into the groove and started to win races. His first victory was in the 1923 Circuito di Cremona in an Alfa Romeo RLTF. He should have won that year's Targa Florio, too, but his factory RL broke down while he was leading and within sight of the finish line. He quickly repaired the car with the help of two spectators, whom he allowed to board his Alfa RLS/3.0 and cross the finish line with them in apparent victory. But a race official told him to reverse back to his breakdown spot, drop off his helpers and finish the race again. In the meantime, though, Ugo Sivocci caught the frustrated Antonio as his helpers were getting out of the car, shot past Ascari in his works RL and took the win. Antonio's only consolation was to have set the race's fastest lap of 41min 10.45sec over the 67.12-mile route.

It happened again in the 1924 Targa Florio, where Ascari was firmly in the lead in an uprated 3.6-litre Alfa Romeo RLTF. This time he was only a few hundred yards from victory when the engine of the big Alfa seized and the car went into a spin. Antonio and his mechanic, Giulio Ramponi, jumped out and stuck in the starter handle, but the engine would not turn – so they pushed the 1000kg car over the finish line with the help of some spectators, but Christian Werner flew past them to win the race for Mercedes-Benz, and Ascari was disqualified for accepting outside help.

A month later, though, he won his first major race, the 1923 Circuit of Cremona, and recorded the event's fastest lap.

Antonio became the first man to race Vittorio Jano's new 140hp Alfa Romeo P2, in which he won the 1924 Circuito di Cremona. But luck deserted him yet again at the year's Grand Prix de l'ACF at Lyon as his P2 broke down while he was in the lead with only 30 of the race's 503 miles to go.

But it was a very different story in the 1924 Grand Prix of Italy at Monza. Antonio and his P2 dominated the race from start to finish to score a home win in every sense – Lombardy car, Lombardy driver, Lombardy track – with a fastest lap of 3min 43.6sec as the cherry on the cake.

Motor sport's governing body the AIACR introduced its World Championship of Grand Prix Racing in 1925 and Ascari immediately set Alfa Romeo on the road to the title by winning the opening counter, the Grand Prix of Belgium and Europe at Spa-Francorchamps, the first time the country had held a national GP. Once again Antonio set a fastest lap for the 9.31-mile circuit of 6min 51.2sec. He covered the 502 miles at an average speed of 74.859mph and won from his second-placed teammate Giuseppe Campari by almost 22 minutes!

The 1925 Grand Prix of France was scheduled for 26 July, just under a month after Antonio's triumph at Spa. Ascari and the P2 shot straight into the lead again and were up front on lap 23 when he made a small and rare mistake, clipped a fence post and over-corrected a skid before the P2 became ensnared in a mass of roadside picket fencing. The car slowly overturned and fatally injured Ascari, who died in an ambulance on the way to hospital.

The other two P2s were withdrawn by Alfa, shattered by the loss of its great driver. At the end of the race, winners Robert Benoist and Alberto Divo drove their Delage to the scene of the accident and lay their victory garlands on the spot where Antonio had lain mortally injured. Ironically, neither of the French drivers had set the race's fastest lap; that was achieved by the late Antonio Ascari with a time of 6min 52sec.

Antonio was buried at the Cimitero Monumentale in Milan, where seven-year-old Alberto Ascari, future double World Champion, held Giulio Ramponi's hand and cried his heart out.

# Benoist, Robert

## Grover-Williams, William
## and Wimille, Jean-Pierre

## Heroes at War

TEARS STREAMED DOWN A thousand faces in the Bois de Boulogne in Paris on 9 September 1945. Tears for the absent French men and women who had been murdered by the Nazis. Tears for the torture, deprivation and humiliation the living had suffered under the cruel subjugation of the Third Reich's forces of occupation.

The Second World War had ended four months earlier, and motor racing was about to make its contribution to helping the French people find their way back to peacetime existence. The sport was also set to honour three of its own, including Robert Marcel Charles Benoist. It was almost one year to the day since the Grands Prix and 24 Hours of Le Mans winner had been executed by the Nazis, and one of the day's races was named after him.

Many had expected the Continent's first post-war race to be a Victory in Europe Day Grand Prix, staged in the flattened centre of Berlin. But France had decided to blare out the song of victory in its own, decidedly less devastated capital instead, and, at the same time, reinstate itself at the centre of world motor sport. The three races that graced the Bois de Boulogne that day in late 1945 may have been of a more modest stamp than a full-blown

GP, their grids made up of a hotchpotch of pre-war cars, but they were the first to be held in post-war Europe and were an impassioned salute to the heroes of the French Resistance.

The three had won an impressive list of Grands Prix and other major races before the war. But, as destiny would have it, they came together in the early 1940s under very different circumstances: as officers of the French arm of the Special Operations Executive, the fabled SOE.

Only one of the trio escaped the Gestapo's net. The Nazis tortured and then murdered the other two. One was the gallant Benoist, who was hung in Buchenwald, a concentration camp not far from Leipzig, Germany, on 12 September 1944. The other was William Charles Frederick Grover-Williams, born in 1903 in the Montrouge area of Paris of a British father and a French mother. He is believed to have been shot by the SS on a death march out of Sachsenhausen concentration camp, near Berlin, in the spring of 1945.

The survivor, but no less courageous, was Jean-Pierre Wimille. After the liberation of Paris in 1944 he joined the Free French Air Force: his commanding officer had given him special permission to race in the Bois de Boulogne on 9 September, but his reprieve did not last long. He died four years later, practising in a 1430cc Simca-Gordini for the 1949 General Perón Grand Prix near Buenos Aires, Argentina.

Old racing cars had been dusted off – literally – for the end-of-war races, having been winkled out of hiding places that had kept them safe from Gestapo and SS witch-hunts. Soon they were to bellow their own victorious battle cry along roads a stone's throw from where columns of Wehrmacht had so mockingly swaggered into Paris in June 1940. Roads on which French men and women had been shot in August 1944, cut down by Nazi snipers fighting a rearguard action as the Allies closed in to liberate the French capital.

A 2.8km circuit had been cobbled together in the Bois de Boulogne for French motor racing's emotional wake. Three races were scheduled to take place, and their *raison d'être* was set out in a properly printed programme, which included brief biographies and photographs of the drivers they honoured. The very names of the races tore at the hearts of all who read them: there was the Coupe Robert Benoist for cars of up to 1500cc, the Coupe de la Liberation for up to 2000cc entries and the Coupe des Prisonniers for cars of over 2000cc. The competing drivers were the lucky ones: they had survived the Nazi carnage. And they turned up in the Bois de Boulogne that day to celebrate their deliverance in the best way they knew how. Racing.

Robert Benoist's motor racing career encompassed rallying, Grand Prix and endurance events. He was born in Rambouillet, Ile de France, in 1895, so he was old enough to enlist for the First World War, serving first as an infantryman and later as a fighter pilot over Verdun.

Benoist became a works Delage driver in 1924 and placed third in the season's first Grand Prix in his native France, at the wheel of a 2LCV in which he beat people of the calibre of Louis Wagner, Henry Segrave and René Thomas. He won the French GP the following year in a similar car – with the help of fellow works Delage driver Albert Divo – after a tragic race that claimed the life of Italy's great Antonio Ascari: and Robert came second in the Grand Prix of San Sebastian. But after a couple of honourable placings in 1926, Benoist's biggest year was 1927, just as Grover-Williams was getting started. Robert won the period's motor racing's grand slam – the French, Spanish, Italian and British Grands Prix – for Delage in its 15S8 and put up the fastest lap in three of them. The French Government awarded him the Legion of Honour to mark his remarkable performance.

After the financial collapse of Delage, Benoist raced for Bugatti in 1928 and took a second in San Sebastian again. The following year he drove for Alfa and won the 24 Hours of Spa for them, co-driven by Portello factory stalwart Attilio Marinoni. But that was it for a while: Robert quit racing until 1934, when he made his comeback in a Bugatti. He won the Picardie Grand Prix and placed fourth in both the Grands Prix of France and Belgium in a T59. But by this time the German Government-backed Mercedes-Benz and Auto Union teams were beginning to make their presence felt in a campaign that would progressively crush the opposition.

Benoist's biggest comeback success was with his protégé and a man who would play a major role in his life during the war, Jean-Pierre Wimille. In 1937 the two won a wet 24 Hours of Le Mans together driving a Bugatti T57G 'tank,' after which Benoist retired from motor racing for good at the age of 42 and retreated to his country home in Auffargis, just outside Paris.

On the outbreak of the First World War in 1914, William Grover-Williams and his family moved to Monte Carlo. A lover of all things mechanical, William raced motorcycles before returning to Paris in 1919. There he got himself a job as chauffeur to the famous portrait painter and Irish peer

Sir William Orpen – later to become an art advisor to Winston Churchill, Britain's Second World War prime minister – driving and maintaining Orpen's black Rolls Royce.

It was not long before motor racing beckoned, and the young chauffeur began to enter himself for events as 'W Williams.' He won the 1928 Grand Prix of France in a Bugatti T35C under that simplification of his name when he was just 25 years old. Later, Grover-Williams acquired a T35B and had it painted in what is now British racing green. In 1929 he won the first-ever Grand Prix of Monaco in that car, soundly beating the great Rudolf Caracciola, who was admittedly struggling with an unwieldy and thirsty Mercedes-Benz SSK.

Grover-Williams also married his boss' beautiful Belgian model and live-in girlfriend Yvonne Aubicq, the year he won in Monte Carlo. The couple lived in a house in Paris, but they also bought a seaside home in the French coastal town of La Baule, on the Bay of Biscay. Each year La Baule staged its own Grand Prix and 'W Williams' won it three times in succession from 1931. That was the year he also won the Belgian Grand Prix at Spa-Francorchamps, driving a Bugatti T51 with Caberto Conelli. The best he and the 51 could do in 1932, though, was a sixth in the French GP, won by Tazio Nuvolari in a works Alfa Romeo P3. After that Grover-Williams continued to race spasmodically, but his motor sport career gradually wound down.

Almost 13 years Benoist's junior and five years younger than 'W Williams,' Wimille began his top echelon racing career driving a Bugatti 37A in the 1930 Grand Prix of France on the 16km Circuit de Morlaas, not far from Pau. J-P went out with supercharger trouble after a couple of laps, but Grover-Williams set the fastest time of the day in his 35C before he also retired. Victories for Jean-Pierre followed in lesser events, like the La Turbie hillclimb and the Grands Prix of Lorraine and Oran, and in 1934 he also won the Algerian GP in a Bugatti T59.

The paths of Benoist and Wimille would often cross in pre-war motor racing before Robert's 1937 retirement, with Wimille taking fourth and his mentor sixth driving Bugatti T59s in the 1935 Grand Prix of Spain. But the younger man's first big victory came in the 1936 Grand Prix of France at Montlhéry, where he won with wealthy industrialist Raymond Sommer in a Bugatti 'tank.' Four Delahaye 135s followed their T57G across the line, and they were pursued by Grover-Williams in sixth place in another 'tank,' which he shared with Pierre Veyron. Wimille scored other victories in smaller races at the Marne, Deauville, Comminges, Pau and even the Coupe de Paris, but his best results were still to come in Alfa Romeos after the Second World War, except for the 1937 24 Hours of Le Mans, won with his friend Benoist.

Grover-Williams, Benoist and Wimille became friends during the carefree days of pre-war motor racing. But their relationship was soon to take a much more dangerous turn, which would end in death for two of them.

After the Germans blitzkrieged their way into France and marched into Paris on 24 June 1940, Grover-Williams and Benoist escaped to Britain, like many French citizens. There they ended up as members of the London-based Special Operations Executive and were trained as secret agents. Soon after completing their courses, the two were parachuted back into France to bolster French Resistance activities.

Grover-Williams was dropped in first, with a brief to build a network of sabotage cells and parachute drop reception units in the Paris area. Benoist followed: he linked up with Grover-Williams and, as well as running their destabilisation operations against the Nazis, the two retrieved weapons from night drops in the Rambouillet woods. Fraught with danger though it was, they transported the arms to Robert's Auffargis home on the outskirts of the city, where the firearms would be sorted, stored and later distributed to Underground fighters.

In late June 1942 Benoist met his friend Wimille and asked the 34-year-old to join him as a member of the Resistance. In turn, Jean-Pierre recruited his beautiful wife Christiane, who was once on the French national ski team. She would barely escape from the Nazis with her life.

An informer betrayed the network in June 1943 and Robert's home was raided by the SS. Information from the same traitor led to Grover-Williams being picked up and taken to the French capital's infamous Gestapo headquarters at 82–84 Avenue Foch, just down the road from the Arc de Triomphe. He was interrogated and brutally tortured, but told his tormentors nothing. So they transferred him to Sachsenhausen concentration camp. In the spring of 1945, with the Allies advancing, the SS were ordered to close the camp and move their sick, starved, skeletal prisoners towards the German coast. There they were to be embarked on old ships and then drowned by scuttling the vessels. They were not moved by truck or train, but had to walk as best they could. Many prisoners had no shoes or boots at all, so they were made to trudge through rain, ice and snow in bare feet: the luckier ones shuffled along with their feet bound in rags, still scant protection from cavernous blisters and sores. Diseased and weak from malnutrition, most collapsed on the way, utterly exhausted. So their SS guards shot them where they lay: including Grover-Williams, it is believed.

Jean-Pierre Wimille joined the French Armée de l'Air as Hitler's rhetoric turned to armed belligerence, but he was demobilised after France's defeat in June 1940. Then 32, Wimille spent his time working on a car of his own design, until Benoist asked him to join the Resistance in Paris. J-P was lucky and escaped arrest during the SS raid on Robert's Auffargis home. He lived to fight another day.

Benoist was not so fortunate. The Gestapo caught him in Paris two weeks later, but as he was being driven to Avenue Foch for interrogation he jumped from the moving car and disappeared. He immediately contacted the French Underground and, with its help, was smuggled back to Britain. But he was parachuted into France again in October 1943 and ran a special SOE operation for four months before making his way back to England again.

Robert's British sojourn did not last long. A month later he was dropped back into France with a 29-year-old French woman named Denise Bloch, who had been recruited by the SOE in Lyons. Benoist contacted Jean-Pierre again and asked him and others to join his new sabotage network, which became operational just in time for D-Day. To help undermine the Germans' defence against the Allied landings in Normandy on 6 June 1944, Benoist, Wimille, Denise Bloch and others attacked a number of targets in the port of Nantes and blew them to pieces.

Twelve days later, as the Allies were establishing their foothold on the Continent, Robert Benoist was arrested in Paris and this time there was no escape. He was taken to the notorious Fresnes prison, where he was harangued and tortured: the Gestapo even told him he could see his sick and elderly mother if he talked, but that was a lie. She was either dead or had been arrested and sent to a concentration camp. Her crime? Her son was in the French Resistance. Still refusing to speak under the most agonising torture, the heroic Frenchman was transported to Buchenwald on 17 August and hung there in an underground execution chamber 23 days later.

The remainder of Benoist's team was trapped in a house not far from the capital. The building, in Sermaise, was surrounded by the Gestapo and SS. Even so, Wimille was able to clamber out of a window, jump into a stream and make for a clump of trees at the back of the property, where he stayed until the Nazis had gone. But his companions, including Denise Bloch, were taken away.

Denise was first taken to the feared Gestapo headquarters in Avenue Foch, where she too was interrogated and tortured. After that she was transported to Ravensbruck women's concentration camp, southeast of Hamburg, Germany, where she was executed and her body burnt to ashes in the camp's ovens.

The Gestapo also arrested Wimille's wife, but she was luckier. Christiane was sent to Fresnes and was about to be transported to Ravensbruck women's concentration camp, which would have ended in her certain death. But that day, by sheer chance, a relative of hers in the Red Cross was giving out meagre sandwiches in the prison's exercise yard to the inmates assembling for the journey to Ravensbruck. He slipped her into his van, gave her a Red Cross coat and told her to help distribute the sandwiches until the prisoners left for Germany. When her fellow inmates had been shipped off to the death camp, Christiane quietly left the prison in the van with her Red Cross benefactor.

The emotion-charged series of three races in the Bois de Boulogne took place one year almost to the day after Robert Benoist was murdered in Buchenwald; just months after William Grover-Williams is believed to have been shot by the SS and Denise Bloch had been killed and cremated at Ravensbruck. It is little wonder that sorrow weighed so heavily on the hearts of the spectators in Paris that chilly autumn day. Among them was Ettore Bugatti, whose cars had been driven to victory by all three Frenchmen, and who had turned up in his huge Royale coupé to add a little opulence to the bitter-sweet proceedings.

The site for the three 1945 Coupe des Prisonniers races had been carefully chosen: it was just across from what is now the Periphérique Extérieur, a stone's throw from the eastern end of the Avenue Foch. Entries included Philippe Etancelin in his old Alfa Romeo Monza, Raymond Sommer with a works Talbot, Maurice Trintignant and a Tipo 51 Bugatti, Eugene Chaboud, Georges Grignard and Louis Villeneuve of Delahaye fame,

Henri Louveau in a Maserati 4CL and Wimille in a works-entered 4.7-litre Tipo 59/50B unsupercharged Bugatti, the company's last single-seater.

The Coupe Robert Benoist was won by Amédée Gordini in a car he built out of Fiat and Simca components; the Coupe de la Liberation went to Louveau and his Maserati. Fittingly, the winner of the Coupe des Prisonniers was none other than the one that got away: Jean-Pierre Wimille.

By comparison, the day was, perhaps, a modest tribute to such great sacrifice, but it was deeply sincere homage paid by motor racing to the extreme courage and fortitude of the men and women of the French Resistance, including three of its own.

The names of Captain Robert Benoist and Captain William Grover-Williams are now recorded on the Roll of Honour of the Special Operations Executive monument at Valençay, near Tours. And a memorial was erected to Jean-Pierre Wimille in the Bois de Boulogne – on the Coupe des Prisonniers road circuit, not far from the hated 82–84 Avenue Foch.

*Note*

This remarkable story is as accurate as the results of my extensive research allow. Many records concerning the French Resistance, William Grover-Williams and Robert Benoist have either been lost, are incomplete, remain secret or were destroyed by the Nazis as the Allies closed in on them. For instance, SOE records say Grover-Williams was killed at Sachsenhausen in March 1945; other sources that he was shot by an SS guard on the march out of the death camp. While researching his outstanding novel *Early One Morning* (Headline Book Publishing, 2002) author Rob Ryan uncovered the story of a man named Georges Tambal, who closely resembled Williams, was an expert on racing cars and whose date of birth was the same as Grover-Williams' – 16 January 1903. Tambal is said to have moved into the Normandy farmhouse owned by Yvonne, the driver's wife, after the war. Yvonne, a leading dog breeder, died in 1973 and the mysterious 'Georges Tambal' was killed in a road accident a decade later.

Robert Benoist was hanged with piano wire – a slow and agonising death – by the SS at Buchenwald on 12 September 1944.

# Bandini, Lorenzo

MILAN WAS IN MOURNING the first time I visited the cathedral city in the late spring of 1967. In fact, all of Italy hung its collective head in sadness at the loss of one of its favourite sons. *'Bandini è Morto'* declared the northern industrial town's daily newspaper, the *Corriere della Sera*, and many ordinary people went about their business wearing black armbands or lapel pins. They were in mourning for Lorenzo Bandini, whose suffering had mercifully come to an end at last. It had been three days since he had been terribly burned before being pulled from the acrid wreckage of his Ferrari, which had crashed as he attempted to reclaim the lead in the 1967 Grand Prix of Monaco from eventual winner Denny Hulme.

Bandini may never have had the stuff of champions, but he was still the best Italian Formula 1 driver of his decade. He was also a modest, easygoing man, full of good will and enthusiasm for his sport, a man of generous disposition that led Ferrari's tyrannical motor sport director Eugenio Dragoni to push him around as if he were a domestic servant. Lorenzo was also an eternal number two, who was pitchforked into the team leader's role in 1967 after John Surtees suddenly left Ferrari. The Italian paid for his promotion with his life, trying too hard to be worthy of the number one spot.

Born in Barce, Libya, on 21 December 1935, Bandini left his family home in Florence at 15 and went to work in a Milan garage. His boss, Goliardo Freddi, whose daughter Margherita Lorenzo later married, loaned him a Lancia Appia coupé, which he drove to a 2000cc Grand Touring class win in a tame 1958 Mille Miglia, a shadow of its former self after the 1957 crash disaster. Encouraged by that unexpected success, Bandini moved on to Formula Junior and became a factory driver at Stanguellini, for whom he won the 1959 Grand Prix of Freedom in Cuba. Impatient to take the huge step from Formula Junior to Formula 1, Lorenzo signed with Scuderia Centro Sud in 1960 to drive one of Mimmo Dei's outdated Cooper-Maseratis. His elevation to the really big time came after his victory in the 1961 4 Hours of Pescara, the fifth and last round in the season's World Sports Car Championship, driving a 3-litre 250 Testa Rossa with Giorgio Scarlatti. The win clinched the title for Maranello.

Bandini was briefly recruited by Ferrari for 1962, just four years after his very first motor race, at a time when the team was still reluctant to take on Italian drivers, but was dropped to make way for Willy Mairesse in 1963. The good-natured Lorenzo made his disconsolate way back to Scuderia Centro Sud, who were running factory-supported BRMs by then. But Willy crashed in the Grand Prix of Germany and Bandini was brought back into the Ferrari fold.

A better sports racing car driver than an F1 talent, Lorenzo came second in the 1963 12 Hours of Sebring in a Ferrari 250P co-driven by Mairesse and Sicilian school headmaster Nino Vaccarella. He repeated that performance in the season's Targa Florio, sharing a Dino 196P with Mairesse and Ludovico Scarfiotti, before he and Ludovico won the highly prestigious 24 Hours of Le Mans in a 250P – all key performances that helped make Ferrari World Sports Car Champions again. And Bandini had been steadily piling up points in the Italian Championship, which he had won for the first time by the end of the season.

Lorenzo's sole Formula 1 win came on the bumpy Zeltweg circuit in the 1964 Grand Prix of Austria driving a Dino 156, and he rounded off that season with thirds in the Grands Prix of Italy and Mexico, where he helped engineer John Surtees' World Championship victory. That took the self-effacing Italian to equal fourth with BRM's Richie Ginther in the title table. Meanwhile, Bandini continued to be a top runner in sports racers: he came third with Surtees in the season's 12 Hours of Sebring and 24 Hours of Le Mans in a Ferrari 330P, and second with the British Champion in the 12 Hours of Reims in a 250LM, to help Ferrari win yet another World Sports Car Championship.

After an earlier homologation squabble with the organisers of the Targa Florio, Enzo Ferrari surprised everyone by sending three 275Ps to Sicily for the 1965 race. Two of them retired with mechanical trouble, but the Bandini-Vaccarella car did not miss a beat. The lone factory Ferrari covered ten laps or 446.4 miles of the Piccolo Circuito delle Madonie at an average 63.59mph to take an extremely popular all-Italian victory.

Formula 1 did not go so well for Bandini that year. The best he could do was come second in a 158 at Monaco in this last year of the 1.5-litre formula. And 1966, the first year of the 3-litre cars, was not much better: Lorenzo took a creditable second at Monaco again and came third in the 156/246 to team leader Surtees' victory in a new 312 in Belgium. He did, however, win the Italian Championship again.

But 1967 started well. In early February, Bandini and young Chris Amon roundly beat the Ford GT40s on their home ground by winning the 24 Hours of Daytona in the legendary Ferrari 330P4. That was the day the cars from Maranello crossed the finish line three abreast to take the first three places in the American classic and produce one of the most iconic images ever to come out of motor racing. In a similar car a couple of months later, Bandini-Amon put Porsche – Ferrari's other arch-rival – in its place by winning the 1000 Kilometres of Monza, to the accompaniment of whoops of joy from a deliriously happy home crowd.

Ferrari did not compete in the first Grand Prix of 1967 at Kyalami, South Africa, so its maiden event of the year was the 25th Grand Prix of Monaco in the ultra-chic fairy-tale principality. Lorenzo qualified well and got himself on to the front row of the grid with pole-sitter Jack Brabham. And when Louis Chiron dropped the flag with his inimitable flourish to start the race it was Bandini's Ferrari 312 number 18 that leapt into the lead and held it for the first lap, until Denny Hulme in the other Brabham-Repco came calling and took command. The race was running its course on the tight little city circuit until over the halfway mark, when Lorenzo started slashing Denny's lead dramatically: but it was exhausting work and the Italian eased off again. With 18 of its 100 laps to go, Bandini went into the harbour chicane too fast. His 312 hit the wooden barriers, upended, rolled over, caught fire and slithered upside down for 35 yards with Bandini trapped inside it. Marshals attacked the flames with extinguishers, convinced Lorenzo had been thrown out of the car. It took them over three minutes to tame the blaze and when they did they were horrified to find Bandini still strapped into the 312. He was eventually extricated from the cockpit with appalling burns and internal injuries, to which he succumbed in a Monte Carlo hospital at 3:36pm on 10 May 1967.

# Barnato, Woolf

WOOLF BARNATO IS THE man with a perfect score. He entered the 24 Hours of Le Mans three times and won it three times, in 1928, 1929 and 1930, driving his own beloved Bentley cars. It is a record that still stands today, despite many attempts to break it over the last 80-odd years.

In fact, Bentleys dominated Le Mans from 1924 until 1930, winning the race five times out of seven. Ettore Bugatti famously described the large, rather crude-looking cars as 'the fastest trucks in the world.' But that was only sour grapes, because although his cars competed in the very first Le Mans in 1923, a Bugatti did not win the race until 14 years later, driven by future French Resistance heroes Robert Benoist and Jean-Pierre Wimille.

Barnato was an all-rounder. Not only did he race cars with such success, he was also a first-class cricketer, a heavyweight boxer, a superb horseman and hunter and a medal-winning powerboat racer.

More than anything else, Barnato was rich. Very rich. His father Barney, who was a business associate of Cecil Rhodes, after whom Rhodesia was named, made his money in the diamond mines of Kimberley in South Africa. But as he and his family – including two-year-old Woolf – returned to Britain by luxury liner, Barney inexplicably threw himself overboard and was never seen again.

So Woolf became a baby millionaire. He went to the exclusive Charterhouse School and then on to Trinity College, Cambridge, before being commissioned into the Royal Field Artillery. Barnato made it through the First World War and was demobilised at its end as a captain.

In the 1920s Woolf became a leader of the 'Bentley Boys,' a clique of young men who could afford the big, powerful cars made by Walter Owen ('WO') Bentley, and would race them on circuits and public roads as the whim took them. The cars were remarkable for the period; they may look ungainly today, but they had an advanced engine with aluminium pistons, twin spark ignition, an overhead camshaft that worked four valves per cylinder, a single cast cylinder block and head and dry sump lubrication.

Most of the Bentley Boys were rich, loved champagne, fast cars, exotic parties and beautiful women, and called Barnato 'Babe,' an ironic reference to his muscular heavyweight build. But multi-millionaire Woolf went one better than any of them. Inspired by the John Duff-Frank Clement victory in a 3-litre Bentley Sports at the 1924 Le Mans – the pair came fourth in the very first Le Mans in 1923 – Barnato became the majority shareholder in WO's company in 1925 and chairman that same year, providing a much needed injection of cash that its creator invested in the development of his new six-cylinder 6½-litre generation of cars. The rest went into a project on which Barnato was keen but WO was dead set against. This was the supercharged version of the 4½-litre or Blower Bentley, an idea dreamed up by Sir Henry 'Tim' Birkin. But the wily old boss was right and the car's poor durability turned it into a failure on the circuits.

The six-cylinder, which made its first appearance in 1925, had all the advanced technological and mechanical engine components of the 3-litre, but put out a lot more power. A high performance version made its debut in 1928 and was called the 6.5-litre Speed Model, but that was soon condensed to the Speed Six.

Woolf began racing Bentleys at Brooklands that same year, and shared the driving with Duff when the pair established a new 24-hour record in a Bentley Sport by averaging 95.03mph at Montlhéry.

As Bentley Motors Ltd chairman, Barnato supported WO's racing programme, which centred on annual trips to Le Mans for the 24-hour race, and he was thrilled when Sammy Davis and Benjy Benjafield won the 1927 high-speed marathon.

In 1928 chairman Barnato decided he would compete at Le Mans with his friend Bernard Rubin, another fabulously wealthy Bentley Boy, whose money came from farming and pearl fishing interests in Australia. Their car was a 4½-litre prototype, but it ended up touch and go because the car's chassis frame cracked on the last of the 10.73-mile laps; that pulled out the radiator's top hose and drained the cooling water. Barnato, his heart in his mouth, was as gentle as he dared be with the car and managed to get it across the finish line to take the win – with the engine red hot and the temperature gauge jammed over to the right of maximum!

The brand new Bentley Speed Six, with its immense power, speed and reliability, gave Barnato and Sir Tim a much easier time in 1929. They were in command from start to finish and the Barnato-Birkin car led four Bentleys home in the first four places, the other three 4.4-litre cars.

Woolf had roamed France for some time, wallowing in the exquisite luxury the country's top hotels had to offer. In March 1930 he was regaling friends with lusty tales of his racing exploits at a dinner party aboard a friend's yacht moored in Cannes harbour, when one of the diners changed the subject slightly. He wondered whether or not it would be possible to race the superfast Blue Train from St Raphael to Calais, the cross-Channel ferry port on the French coast. Barnato became all fired up, thinking that if he did so in a Bentley Speed Six the company would have a publicity field day. He was so confident that he wagered £200 on his probable success and went one further. He said that he could reach his London club in the time the Blue Train took to get to Calais.

The bet and the race were on. So the next day as *Le Train Bleu* hissed and puffed its way out of Cannes railway station, Woolf and his relief driver, accomplished yachtsman Dale Bourne, set off on their dramatic journey.

Woolf had not won two 24 Hours of Le Mans for nothing by this time. He telegraphed ahead and had service and refuelling areas set up along the route, which were run like Le Mans pit stops. It was not an easy race on the French *routes nationales* of over 80 years ago, but the Speed Six could charge on while the train was making its obligatory stop at Marseilles. The Bentley was hampered by rain, fog, a misplaced service area for which they lost time searching, and a cross-channel boat ride to Dover, from which they made their last 80-mile dash to London.

After 700 miles of racing, Barnato parked his muddy Bentley outside the Conservative Club in St James,' London, a day later at 3:20 pm, four minutes before *Le Train Bleu* pulled into Calais railway station.

Bentley Motors entered three Speed Sixes, and Birkin – who had set up his own team – three Blowers for the 1930 Le Mans. One of Birkin's cars did not start and the others retired from the race, bearing out WO's earlier scepticism. But the Sixes triumphed, the win going to Barnato and Glen

Kidson, a First World War submariner, while second place went to the other Speed Six driven by Frank Clement and Richard Watney.

And that was it. Immediately afterwards Bentley Motors retired from motor racing and Barnato announced he would do likewise.

# Biondetti, Clemente

DESCRIBING CLEMENTE BIONDETTI AS colourful is like saying the 88-storey Petronas Towers in Kuala Lumpur, Malaysia, are quite high. Unpredictable, imaginative, irascible, gentle, gruff, fascinating, stubborn, generous, outspoken, he was all of those things. He was also the only man to win the Mille Miglia four times, an extraordinary feat of skill, concentration and raw courage.

Born in 1898, Biondetti grew up to be a headstrong young man who did not like compromises, preferred everything to be straightforward and hated to be pushed around just a little more than he hated snobbery. He was forthright to the point of seeming brusque, yet underneath that jagged exterior there was a kind and gentle person, as well as the greatest road racer of his day.

From an early age Clemente loved speed. He started racing motorcycles in 1924 and rode for Norton before progressing to four wheels – none of which sat well with his mother. She was saddened and disappointed that, instead of working with his brothers in the building trade, he had decided to become what she considered a sort of hare-brained playboy, risking his life racing bikes, then cars. But he kept her sweet by saying that one day he would buy her a beautiful house and take her out in his expensive new car; and that is just what he did.

But not for some time to come. Biondetti came from a working class family, so he did not have the kind of money possessed by some of his wealthy opposition, like Count Antonio Brivio or his pal Count Carlo Felice Trossi. He first competed in the Mille Miglia in 1936 and showed the world what to expect in the years ahead: he came fourth in a sports-car-bodied Alfa Romeo Tipo B P3 Grand Prix racer entered by Scuderia Ferrari, finishing just over 15 minutes behind his best friend Carlo Pintacuda, the race won by Brivio.

An odd couple those two, because the diminutive Pintacuda was the quintessence of the Hollywood matinee idol, all immaculately slicked back hair, Errol Flynn good looks and smart clothes: Biondetti's ponderous features and dishevelled appearance made him look like a peasant whose clothes were well-worn hand-me-downs.

Good looks or peasant's features, tailor's dummy or rumpled ruffian, the two of them dominated the Mille Miglia in the mid-to-late 1930s. Pintacuda scored two victories, a second and a third in the four races of 1935–38, and when Biondetti chalked up the first of his four wins in 1938 in an Alfa Romeo 8C 2900C it was his friend Carlo Pintacuda who took second place, 2½ minutes behind him, in another Alfa.

Clemente's first Mille Miglia victory was given little publicity as he was a sworn enemy of the ruling Fascists, and they knew it; the black shirts put the word out and their puppet editors all but ignored the Florentine's success, turning it into a mute victory. Biondetti, who should have become a national hero that year, was furious.

Public opinion was outraged for another reason. During the 1938 Mille Miglia, a Lancia Aprilia cannoned off a railway level crossing in Bologna and tore into the crowd, killing three adults and seven children, so the Fascists banned the race. There was no Mille Miglia in 1939, but a race of sorts did take place in 1940. It was called the Grand Prix of Brescia, a watered-down affair aimed at minimising public outcry, and was run over nine laps of a 103-mile Brescia–Cremona–Mantua–Brescia triangle. Clemente was in a six-cylinder, 2443cc Alfa Romeo 6C 2500B, but the best he could do was to come fourth again, while victory went to BMW 328 driver Baron Huschke von Hanstein, whose overalls were emblazoned with the insignia of the Nazi SS. War had come to the Mille Miglia.

As the hostilities had stopped motor racing in its tracks, Clemente Biondetti decided he had better rearrange his life. First, he hid his Norton and Harley Davidson motorbikes in a remote barn amid the gently rolling hills of his native Tuscany; then he set about organising a new source of income. He and Pintacuda went into a business the rough-hewn Florentine grew to love: they bought and sold paintings. Little could be further from Biondetti's panel-beater appearance than the sophisticated world of art, but he was captivated by it and remained an art lover until his dying day.

Clemente also joined the partisans – the Italian resistance – and fought the hated Axis forces and their collaborators until they were defeated.

In 1947, with the Fascists no longer in power, the press did justice to Biondetti's second Mille Miglia win for Alfa Romeo: he became a national hero at last. But it happened in an odd way. Clemente had no money and no car until he travelled by train to Brescia on the off-chance and was asked by Emilio Romano to drive his detuned 1938 Alfa Romeo 2900 Berlinetta in the event. Biondetti drove a canny race, taking it easy at first but getting into a quick rhythm to eventually overtake race leader Tazio Nuvolari, whose Cisitalia was delayed, to win by over 16 minutes.

Clemente had established himself as a top road racer: in both 1948 and 1949 he won the Mille Miglia and the Targa Florio for Ferrari. He was making good money too, but he spent a lot. He used to say, 'Money is either round to roll around or paper so that it can fly. It should never stick to your hands.' And it never did.

Between races, Biondetti did not really do much. He would prepare as well as he could for his races. Perhaps he would call in at Pasquino Ermini's workshop and socialise with the mechanics. Later, he set up his own workshop, where he employed three men and a boy; the lad was Michele Cortini, who became Clemente's riding mechanic in one of the three XK120s entered by Jaguar for the 1951 Mille Miglia. Unfortunately they retired when the XK's water hose burst.

Biondetti had no head for business. He was a racing driver, not a businessman. In fact, he never really had a job apart from driving racing cars, but he did become involved in a number of projects. He started a restaurant – which later burnt down – called *La Beffa* ('The Practical Joke'), in Via Bolognese, Florence, from which his friends would catch a brief glimpse of him competing in the Mille Miglia; he bought and sold property as well as paintings; he had his own workshop; he tried to build a car of his own design, but it was a disaster. The prototype had an engine made up of eight Norton cylinders, all in line. Not surprisingly, it never worked properly – everything went its own way and sounded like metallic madness.

There was no Mille Miglia glory to be had in 1952, when Biondetti's works Ferrari caught fire while refuelling at Siena. Nor was there much in 1953, when he could only manage eighth in his factory Lancia D20. But, with fatal illness tightening its deadly grip on him, Clemente's fourth place in 1954 in a Ferrari 275S was the equivalent of a healthy man's victory. He came in little more than 49 minutes behind the winner, Alberto Ascari, having maintained an average of 82mph for 12hr 15min 36sec, just over 15 minutes behind third-placed Luigi Musso. An outstanding achievement.

Ten months later the King of the Road was dead.

# Bira, B

WHEN YOU'RE WEIGHED DOWN with a name like Prince Birabongse Bhanutej Bhanubandh you've got to do something about it if you want to go motor racing, so this Siamese tongue twister became 'B Bira.' That was the pseudonym under which a small, doll-like grandson of King Mongkut of Siam (Thailand) – played by Yul Brynner in the 1950s hit film *The King and I* – made his name in motor sport.

Bira was sent to Britain from Siam in 1927, when he was 13 years old, to be educated at Eton and Cambridge University, but at 21 he talked his wealthy cousin Prince Chula, who was also living in England, into financing his motor racing. They started out in local events in 1935, but became more serious about their sport a year later. The two formed the White Mouse Stable and established their base in Hammersmith, London, bought two ERA B Types and lured the car constructor's chief mechanic away from the factory to work for them. Bira, who had never raced before, became one of the marque's most successful drivers. He won the Coup Prince Rainier for voiturettes at Monte Carlo in April 1936 from established stars like Raymond Mays and Luigi Villoresi, an event considered the world's most important small car race.

He and Chula also bought Whitney Straight's 2.9-litre Maserati 8CM, in which the remarkable little Siamese prince came sixth in the Donington Grand Prix, famously won by Dick Seaman and Hans Ruesch in their Alfa Romeo 8C-35. And Bira won at Albi in one of the ERAs, by which time the British press was calling him the Caracciola of voiturette motor racing. Such was his talent that the works BMW team invited him to drive one of its cars in the 1936 Tourist Trophy, but he had starter motor trouble and the entire field charged off without him. He eventually got the car going and came seventh – breaking Tazio Nuvolari's

2-litre class lap record three times as he did so! By the end of the year, this naturally talented novice had won the coveted British Racing Drivers' Club Gold Star.

In 1937 the cousins made a big mistake. They bought two second-hand Delages, one of them from Dick Seaman, who wouldn't need his any more as he was about to become a Mercedes-Benz Grand Prix driver, but the cars were a total disaster. Each was slower than the princes' one remaining ERA, which they took to the Isle of Man for the RAC International Light Car Race, the year's top 1500cc event in Britain. The factory ERAs were also entered for the race, but it was Prince Bira who got away first in the pouring rain, leaving the works cars driven by Raymond Mays and Pat Fairfield in his wake: and he won. Two days after his 23rd birthday Bira won the London Grand Prix at Crystal Palace, and then the 12 Hours of Donington sports car race in the White Mouse Delahaye, partnered by HG Dobbs. All of which secured him his second BRDC Gold Star.

War was looming by 1938, so Princes Bira and Chula decided to compete in fewer races, only two of which would be outside Britain. They sold the Delahaye, as sports car events were not in their programme, and bought a faster ERA C Type. The season started well, with Bira taking two second places at Brooklands, one in the C Type and the other in the Maserati 8CM. He won the Crystal Palace Coronation Trophy in the ERA, as he did the Brooklands Easter meeting, where he beat Dobson's ERA and the Maseratis of Gigi Villoresi and Toulo de Graffenried.

By this time Bira had built up such an outstanding record that he took Pat Fairfield's place in the factory ERA team after the likeable South African had crashed at the 1937 24 Hours of Le Mans and died from his injuries. Soon afterwards the Siamese prince won the 1500cc voiturette race in Cork, beating his own team leader Raymond Mays, Gigi Villoresi and Gianfranco Comotti. Bira was on course for a record third successive BRDC Gold Star, with 48 points to second-placed Arthur Dobson's 18, but then things started to go wrong. Bira retired on the first lap at the Bremgarten circuit in Switzerland, led from the start of the JCC 200 Mile race at Brooklands but dropped to second after a muffed pit stop, and then his Maserati was hit in the back by another car during the Dunlop 50th Jubilee race at Brooklands, and he was taken to hospital with head injuries. But he eventually turned the situation around and came second at Crystal Palace and, ironically, won the Siam Trophy, put up by Prince Chula, at Brooklands, which secured him his record third Gold Star.

With the 1939 season in the offing, ERA had all but ceased to exist due to lack of finance and Prince Bira decided to cut his programme to 12 races. Meanwhile, the tenacious prince had had his old Maserati painted in Siam's national colours of blue and yellow, and he won his first race of the season, the JCC International Trophy at Brooklands, in this car, then the Sydenham Trophy at the Palace and the Nuffield Trophy at Donington in his Zoller-supercharged ERA, which was his final victory before the outbreak of war on 3 September.

After the Second World War Prince Bira drove Enrico Plate's Maserati 4CLT/48 and came a creditable second to Louis Chiron's Lago-Talbot in the 1949 Grand Prix of France, then third in the car in the Italian GP at Monza. In the early 1950s Bira also drove HWMs, OSCAs, a Simca-Gordini and a Connaught A-Lea Francis before buying his own Maserati A6GCS, into which he slipped a 2.5-litre engine. He won the 1954 Grand Prix de Frontiéres in Belgium in the A6 before becoming the first private entrant to take delivery of a 250F. Prince Bira came sixth in the Grand Prix of Belgium and fourth in the French driving the 250F and won the non-championship 1955 New Zealand Grand Prix at Ardmore, beating the Ferrari 500s and a youngster by the name of Jack Brabham, who came fourth in a Cooper-Bristol. After that Prince Bira retired from racing and went to live in Thailand.

A man of many talents, Bira was an outstanding sculptor, whose work was exhibited in some of the world's most prominent art galleries and academies and who accepted commissions. One of his early projects was a memorial to the late ERA star Pat Fairfield, which was unveiled at the Silverstone circuit by Britain's racing nobleman Earl Howe.

Bira piloted his own glider and aircraft for many years and was also a model railway enthusiast. His 'train set' literally filled one of the large rooms in his sumptuous house in Cornwall. He later became deeply involved in Thailand's international sporting aspirations and had a chequered career as a businessman, basing himself first on a yacht moored in Nice harbour and then in a villa in Geneva.

Prince Bira was on one of his regular business trips to London when he had a heart attack, collapsed and died on a platform of Baron's Court underground railway station on 23 December 1985. He was 71.

# Birkin, Sir Henry ('Tim')

IN THE 1920S AND 1930s, British schoolboys devoured every word they could find about their favourite comic book heroes like Biggles and Dick Barton Special Agent. But in Sir Henry Birkin Bt they had a real live, walking, talking hero, and they idolised him all the more. He was a passably handsome heir to a wealthy family, drove a series of dramatic racing cars, won big deal races and was one of the Bentley Boys. What chance did Biggles or Dick Barton have against that?

Birkin himself was a kind of 'son of comic book,' because his schoolmates christened the super-energetic Sir Henry 'Tim' after the Julius Stafford Baker comic book character 'Tiger Tim.' And it stuck. So Birkin was Tim to all his adoring fans. And they were legion.

Sir Tim, whose family money came from the tranquil business of making and selling Nottingham lace, was born on 26 July 1896, and at the outbreak of the First World War, when he was 18, he first served as a private in the 7th Sherwood Foresters – also jokingly known as 'The Robin Hoods' – before being commissioned into the British Army's Royal Flying Corps. He went to Palestine with the Corps as a young Lieutenant and that's where he caught malaria, which would dog him for the rest of his short life.

He dabbled in motor racing in 1921, but was soon pushed into retiring from the sport by his family, as their lace business, they said, needed him. That lasted six years until Sir Tim entered a 3-litre Bentley in a Brooklands Six Hour race. Scorned by his family for his self-indulgence, he bought a 4½-litre Bentley in 1928, liked it, scored some reasonable results with it and decided he would race for a living. He eventually graduated to the works Bentley team to become one of the famous Bentley Boys and led the first 20 laps of that year's 24 Hours of Le Mans until he was slowed by a jammed wheel – but still managed to finish fifth.

Birkin was convinced that the big, heavy 4½-litre Bentleys would go a lot faster if they were supercharged, but WO Bentley, its manufacturer, would have none of it. He said a blower would 'pervert the design and corrupt the performance' of his cars. So Sir Tim called in the technical assistance of Clive Gallop, supercharger specialist at Amherst Villiers, and got the fabulously wealthy Hon Dorothy Paget to finance the undertaking, as he had spent all the money his family would allow him. In his private engineering works in Welwyn Garden City, Hertfordshire, Birkin added his precious Roots-type supercharger, driven from the crankshaft, to the front of his Bentley's radiator, which looked rather unusual to say the least. He had created the world's first Blower Bentley, which put out a massive (for the period) 242hp.

The car made its debut at Brooklands at the end of June 1929. But it was unreliable. Even so, Wolf Barnato, who ended up owning Bentley, convinced WO to build 50 Blowers for homologation, as Le Mans was in their sights again. But it wasn't an easy task. The cars were not ready for the 1929 Le Mans, so Birkin shared a Bentley Speed Six with Barnato – and they won.

It was still a struggle, but at least two Blower Bentleys were at Le Mans the following year, entered privately by Birkin. And that's when the baronet really earned his spurs, not because he won – he didn't – but because of the ruthless hounding he gave Rudolf Caracciola's Mercedes-Benz SSK in an incredibly gutsy, fearless pursuit that really was the stuff of schoolboy heroes, before both cars were forced to retire.

Then Birkin put in possibly his most remarkable performance to take second place from some of the cream of motor racing, because when you boil it down, Sir Tim's Blower Bentley was really an ultra-fast, stripped down road car that was not meant for racing at all. After his fearsome performance at Le Mans, Birkin entered his supercharged car for the French Automobile Club du Midi's race on the Morlaas road circuit. This was originally billed as a Grand Prix, but there were not many entries, so the organisers turned it into a Formule Libre race and that attracted a grid of 51 cars. The gaggle of Bugattis was driven by the likes of Louis Chiron, French-Algerian ace Marcel Lehoux, Philippe Etancelin, William Grover-Williams and newcomer Jean-Pierre Wimille. And then there was Sir Tim Birkin in his Blower Bentley, minus any amount of road-going gear like headlights and mudguards for lightness. The circuit was a series of long straights, which suited the big, powerful Blower Bentley and not so much the agile little Bugattis, which were more at home on the tortuous goat tracks of the Targa Florio.

Chiron led for much of the race, but waning oil pressure forced him to let Etancelin slip past. Then Birkin passed Chiron, blowing his horn furiously to make the Monegasque move over – and that has to be a first for motor racing – before the 2.5-ton flame-belching Bentley, now universally known as the Brooklands Battleship, could get past! By this time, Etancelin was well over two minutes ahead of the rest of the field and won, with Birkin and his massive road car taking a dramatic second.

But the bottom fell out of Sir Tim's world at the end of 1930, when Bentley Motors withdrew from racing, and its new owner, Woolf Barnato, sold the business to Rolls Royce a year later, even though they did not activate the brand for a number of years. Then Dorothy Paget withdrew her financial support, so Birkin took on Mike Couper as his new partner. They did everything to keep the little tuner company's head above water, even producing a rich kids' miniature version of Brooklands with small electric cars that ran on rails. But Couper packed it in two years later and the small factory closed.

Birkin still wouldn't give up racing to go and make lace in Nottingham, and who can blame him? Instead, he won the 1931 24 Hours of Le Mans with Earl Howe in an Alfa Romeo 8C 2300 and received a telegram from Fascist leader Benito Mussolini, who claimed the win for Italy, conveniently forgetting his country's car was driven by a couple of blue-blooded Englishmen.

On 24 March 1932 Sir Tim set a new record of 137.96mph on the Brooklands Outer Circuit in his Blower Bentley. And on 7 May 1933 he drove Bernard Rubin's Maserati 8C into third place in the Tripoli Grand Prix, preceded only by Achille Varzi and Tazio Nuvolari. But during a pit stop he burned his arm on a searingly hot exhaust pipe and the wound turned septic. The result of that, mingled with another bout of malaria, is said to have caused the death of this gallant and courageous racer in a London nursing home on 22 June 1933.

Sir Tim is buried in Blakeney churchyard under a gravestone declaring he was 'A Racing Motorist of International Fame.'

And a superhero to a generation of British schoolboys.

# Boillot, André

A TARGA FLORIO HAD been staged every year from 1906 until the 1914–18 war, so Vincenzo Florio was determined to get it going again before the end of 1919. But it wasn't until May that the wealthy Sicilian began to tour Europe to drum up entries, so the race had to be scheduled for the end of the year. Given that most vehicle manufacturers were busy converting to peacetime production and had not built a single racing car for at least four years, he did well to cobble together an entry of 21 cars.

One of them was *La Belle Hélène*, named by some romantic after the operetta by Jacques Offenbach. It was a small, light, 2.5-litre Peugeot L25 powered by a four-cylinder, twin overhead camshaft engine with four valves per cylinder. And it was to be driven by 28-year-old André Boillot, brother of Grand Prix winner Georges, who was shot down and killed over the trenches in 1916.

Incredibly, *La Belle Hélène* had almost 125,000 miles on the clock before she even got to Sicily, where the race, usually held in the balmy Sicilian spring, was to be run on 23 November. The car was originally built for André to race in the 1914 Coupe de l'Auto on the Auvergne circuit in France, but that was overtaken by events. During the war *La Belle Hélène* was first used to ferry senior officers about the battlefields and afterwards as Peugeot top executive transport. In early 1919 the car was shipped to the United States for André to drive in the year's Indianapolis 500, where it blew a tyre and crashed when lying third with five laps to go.

The 1919 Targa was to be over four laps of the medium-sized Madonie Mountain circuit for a total of almost 270 miles. That may not seem much, but two previous days of pouring rain had turned the route – a series of narrow earthen roads and goat tracks – into a quagmire. And on race day a violent thunderstorm worsened an already bad situation as lightning ripped through the dark sky, gale force winds howled along the valleys and snowdrifts started to build up on the high ground.

The nightmare weather apart, André's biggest problem was René Thomas, whose straight-eight, 32-valve twin overhead camshaft Ballot had twice the power of his Peugeot, although that was not always a trump card in the convoluted Targa Florio. Boillot decided that, bad weather or not, his only chance was to drive at ten-tenths throughout the entire race in a do-or-die effort to counter the brute force of Thomas' mount.

Car after car rumbled and slithered away from the Cerda start line in the pouring rain on their way to the first 67 miles of mud and snow, at the end of which Thomas was in the lead. Boillot was true to his word and drove right on the edge, but it sapped his strength and smothered him with mud that choked and blinded him. The visibility was terrible and *La Belle Hélène* slid off the 'road' six times on the first lap. That meant André and his riding mechanic had to climb down into the mud with each off-road excursion and manhandle their car back on to the road in the rain and cold. Gradually, though, the storm faded away and shafts of sunlight began the seemingly impossible task of drying out the flooded route. The agile little Peugeot soldiered on and, incredibly, by the end of the third lap and almost six hours of exceptionally difficult racing, Boillot was eight minutes ahead of Thomas.

René blanched during his final pit stop when he was told André had overtaken him. For his last lap, Boillot bravely opted for dry weather tyres, as several hours of sunshine had made the going easier. Then he accelerated away like a mad thing, sliding through the corners and bends of the narrow little roads with practised agility. Thomas was nowhere to be seen, so André put two and two together and got five: he thought his rival had used his car's power to pull away from him in the better weather and was well in the lead. Tired beyond belief, Boillot still kept up his pace.

What he could not have known was that René had pushed his Ballot a little too hard: his car had spun off the road and crashed as he tried to hustle the big straight-eight round one of the mountain hairpins. He was out of the race.

With every muscle in his body pleading for rest, his mind an exhausted blank, Boillot willed his car along the seaside straight for the fourth and last time. He turned up towards the Cerda finish line but, in a bout of brain fade, managed to put *La Belle Hélène* into a skid. The car spun and crashed into the grandstand wall just yards from the finish line, sending the exhausted Boillot and his mechanic sprawling in the gooey mud. Slowly, a crowd of spectators gently lifted the dazed but uninjured men back into the Peugeot; André ground the gears into reverse and crossed the finish line – backwards!

It was Thomas' team owner, Ernest Ballot, who rushed to the pair and convinced them they should go back up the track and cross the line facing the right way. André's backwards victory was probably legal, but it would still be wide open to protest. So Boillot did as he was told and drove the car to where he hit the stand, turned and crossed the finish line nose first. Then he collapsed from total exhaustion. He had strong-armed the little Peugeot over the worst possible 'roads' and through about 6000 hairpins and bends at speed for 7hr 51min 1sec and had nothing left to give. But he had won at an average speed of 34.2mph and, to confirm just how convincingly, second-placed Antonio Moriondo didn't turn up for another half an hour!

André continued to race for another 13 years after that and did reasonably well. He came fourth in the 1921 Grand Prix of France driving a Sunbeam and second in the 1929 event in a Peugeot 174S, both on the 24 Hours of Le Mans circuit. He had another two disappointing outings in the Indy 500, but won the Targa's twin, the Coppa Florio, in 1922 in a Peugeot 174/S3.8 and in 1925 driving a four-litre Peugeot, on the Medio Circuito delle Madonie. The following year he won the 24 Hours of Spa-Francorchamps with Louis Rigal in a sleeve-valve Peugeot, and in 1927 the Coupe de la Commission Sportive at Montlhéry in a single-seater by the French manufacturer.

On 1–2 June 1932 Boillot broke the 24-hour Class F speed record at Miramas near Avignon in a 1.5-litre, four-cylinder Peugeot 301C, covering 1646.98 miles (2650km) at an average speed of 68.657mph (110.47kph) before leaving for a hillclimb at La Charte. He was to compete in a Bugatti-engined Peugeot 201, which skidded off the road, crashed into a tree and caught fire during practice. Boillot was rushed to Chateauroux, where he died of head injuries a week later.

*Postscript*

Enzo Ferraro also competed in the 1919 Targa Florio, his second race, in a CMN 15/20, but he finished over the limit, having taken slightly more than ten hours to complete the distance.

# Boillot, Georges

A FREAK SHOT BY a German Fokker pilot 8000ft above the First World War battlefield of Verdun put a bullet right through the heart of Georges Boillot and deprived the world of one of the greatest racing drivers of the 20th century. The 31-year-old Frenchman crumpled in his cockpit and was soon thrown out of his biplane as it corkscrewed lazily to the ground and crashed. Boillot's body was found and he was buried the following day at Vadelaincourt, not far from Verdun, but toward the end of the funeral service German artillery shells began to pepper the area, bringing a swift end to the proceedings.

The swashbuckling, moustachioed Boillot was a larger-than-life character who started racing in 1908. He startled the more conservative Parisians with his gung-ho antics, which included handbrake turns in the city centre so that he could park his car right outside his favourite bar. Boillot never did settle down to a more mature way of life, as he was naturally ebullient and felt he was projecting the right kind of image for a racing driver. But he and his countrymen were being drawn into the inevitability of the First World War as political tensions started to rise and eventually reached breaking point on the Old Continent.

Georges, though, had a lot of racing to do before he joined up. His two main rivals were the great Jules Goux and Victor Rigal, both of whom raced Peugeots, the cars in which Boillot competed throughout his brief but mercurial career.

He was born in Valentigney, Doubs, on 3 August 1884, the town in which Peugeot was first established. So it was inevitable that Georges became a mechanic, but in 1908 not so inevitable that he started motor racing. At Peugeot's invitation, he joined Paul Zuccarelli and Jules Goux in setting up the French manufacturer's first foray into motor sport. After the 1909 Coupe de l'Auto at Rambouillet, Boillot's next event was the 1910 Targa Florio, in which he won the Voiturette Cup in a 2-litre Peugeot. In fact, Peugeot swept the board, with Giosuè Giuppone coming second in a similar car and Jules Goux taking third in another Peugeot 2.0. All before a meagre group of 100 or so spectators in the stands and a few curious shepherds casting an eye over this newfangled lunacy called motor car racing from the surrounding hills.

Georges' flamboyant driving style cost him races during the early days, but he eventually realised he had to become more mature if he was going to win, and that calmer approach to his trade eventually paid off. He won the 1912 Grand Prix of France at Dieppe in a compact little Peugeot L76 at an average speed of 68.502mph, beating men of the calibre of Louis Wagner, Victor Regal (one of his Peugeot rivals down, Jules Goux to go) and Dario Resta, although he did not put in the fastest lap: David Bruce-Brown did that in a Fiat S74, covering the 47.840-mile circuit in 36min 32sec.

But the 1913 French Grand Prix was a sad affair indeed. It was won by Georges Boillot driving a Peugeot EX3, all right, when he finally picked off his other archrival, teammate and friend Jules Goux, who was at the wheel of another EX3. But all that was preceded by death. One of the founders of the Italian car manufacturer Itala, chemical engineer and erstwhile racing driver Guido Bigio, was killed testing one of his company's cars for the event. In a completely different incident, Paul Zuccarelli died after crashing his Peugeot EX3. And a spectator was killed when member of the Irish brewing family Kenelm Lee Guinness' Sunbeam hit him before it plunged into a river.

A year later Boillot completely dominated America's Indianapolis 500, at which he got the ball rolling by putting up the fastest qualifying time – even though the starting order was decided by ballot. He seemed well on his way to victory until the last lap, when niggling tyre problems suddenly became big tyre problems and torpedoed his brave attempt to win at the Brickyard. Georges had no choice but to retire, which let René Thomas and his Delage through for the win. But before he did so, Boillot set a lap record of 99.85mph, which was not broken for another five years until Thomas clocked 104.70mph qualifying for the 1919 Indy in an eight-cylinder, 5-litre Ballot.

In the 1914 French Grand Prix at Lyon, Boillot took on no fewer than five 4.5-litre Mercedes-Benzes. Things were looking bleak indeed as Max

Sailer went straight into the lead in a Mercedes GP and stayed there for the first five of the 23.38-mile laps. But the German car was ailing, and Sailer eventually went out with engine trouble, although not before setting the fastest lap, which was never bettered that day, of 20min 6sec. Georges took the lead after that, until Christian Lautenschlager's Mercedes went ahead on elapsed time on the 17th of the Grand Prix's 20 laps. Boillot still did not give up, though, and kept his loud pedal hard down until his Peugeot EX5 seemed like it was coming apart at the seams. But even the determined Frenchman had to call it a day when his engine finally gave up the ghost on the last lap to let Lautenschlager through to win. In fact, it was a Mercedes Grand Slam, with Louis Wagner second and Otto Satzer third.

Do or die to the last, Georges Boillot said, after being called up for First World War service, that he would win either a military cross or a wooden one. He got both.

At first he was seconded by General Joseph Joffre to be the officer's driver at a time when communications were by people on bikes or in cars rather than radios and telephones. With Boillot driving his staff car like a mad thing, the general often zoomed along the rudimentary French roads from his headquarters on the Marne, midway between Paris and Nancy, at 70–80mph to visit his commanders. But chauffeuring the general around was not Boillot's idea of fighting a war, so having gained his pilot's licence in 1911, he volunteered for the French Air Force and by early 1916 was flying a spotter plane over Verdun. He graduated to fighters in April of that year and got into a dogfight with a larger twin-engined German plane, which he shot down. But he had to crash-land his own aircraft, which was riddled with bullets and no longer serviceable. Georges was awarded the Legion d'Honneur for his bravery.

About a month later, Boillot was patrolling the skies over Verdun in the early morning when he was jumped by four Fokkers, and the German pilot of one got lucky and shot and killed the great French hero.

Boillot's last race win was at Boulogne in late 1913 and when the event resumed after the war the organisers instituted the Boillot Cup in honour of the great French driver. Then Jules Goux formed a post-war committee and set up a fund to receive contributions towards a memorial to his friend Georges, which was built near the circuit. Sadly, the memorial did not survive the Second World War, when it was destroyed by the occupying Germans.

# Bonnier, Joakim ('Jo')

FLUENT IN SIX LANGUAGES, tall, with regular features set off by an immaculately clipped goatee beard and moustache, Jo Bonnier crammed a lot into his 42 years. He was an accomplished Formula 1 and sports car racer, president of the Grand Prix Drivers' Association, and ran his own art gallery. But he never quite hit the big time, although winning the Targa Florio twice plus a Grand Prix wasn't far off the mark.

Born on 31 January 1930 into a wealthy family with its own publishing business (called Bonnier Aktiebolag), in Stockholm, Sweden, Jo was educated in the Swedish capital, Paris and Oxford, but rejected the business life. He yearned to break loose and race. So he started with an old Harley Davidson motorcycle when he was 17, then went rallying and ice racing. Before settling for a motor racing career, he became an officer in the Swedish navy and saw service in destroyers.

After that, Bonnier graduated to sports cars and first competed in an Alfa Romeo Disco Volante, before his debut Formula 1 race in the 1956 Italian Grand Prix at Monza. He shared a rather tired Maserati 250F with 47-year-old Gigi Villoresi, but the car expired after seven laps. Jo continued in 1957 with a Scuderia Centro Sud 250F and came a reasonable seventh in the Argentine GP, followed by a handful of retirements. He ran his own 250F for most of 1958 and drove that into second places at both Syracuse and Caen – performances that caught the eye of BRM, who were struggling to make its engines competitive on the newly stipulated aviation fuel, and he was given a two-year contract. Jo showed the team it was on the right road when he took fourth in the last GP of the season at the Ain Diab circuit near Casablanca, Morocco. This was no walkover, as he was up against the GP cream, including winner Stirling Moss and, thanks to Stirling's sense of fair play, new World Champion Mike Hawthorn.

The BRM P52s had brake problems at Monaco, so the team went off to Zandvoort with Moss to do some extensive testing a week before the 1959 Grand Prix of Holland on 31 May. Gradually, the great Englishman honed the brakes and car into a contender on the Dutch circuit, then went back to his usual Rob Walker Cooper Climax, while Bonnier and Harry Schell took their BRMs back. Blustery weather conditions on the Dutch coast meant lap times were down, but come Saturday evening who should be sitting on pole but Joakim Bonnier. He led from the outset, but was overtaken by hard-charging Masten Gregory's Cooper-Climax, and that began a nose-to-tail pursuit by the Swede until the American's car began to jump out of gear; so Jo overtook him on lap 12 and led the race comfortably for a while. But Stirling and Jack Brabham were making up ground in their Cooper-Climaxes and alternated in the lead. Then Brabham's gearbox started producing the same erratic performance and Bonnier overtook him. Moss caught Brabham on lap 46 and by the 60th Stirling was right on Jo's tail. He slipped past the Swede and it seemed it was all over – until Stirling came dawdling into the pits three laps later with an equally uncooperative gearbox, and stayed there. Bonnier led for the remaining 12 laps to cross the finish line to take his one and only Grand Prix win at an average speed of 93.48mph.

Jo did best in sports racers, though. He signed for Porsche for 1959 and immediately started to bring in the results, like third in the 12 Hours of Sebring, the year's first round of the World Sports Car Championship, and second in the last counter, the RAC Tourist Trophy at Goodwood, in a 718 RSK shared in both races with Wolfgang von Trips. A year later he scored the first of his Targa Florio wins with Hans Herrmann in a 718 RS60: he was the fastest in practice and put in the quickest lap of the race with a mighty 42min and 46sec over the 44.739-mile circuit. He took another second in the ADAC 1000 Kilometres at the Nürburgring a couple of weeks later, this time with Belgian Olivier Gendebien in an RS60, and helped Porsche into second place behind Ferrari in the championship.

Porsche 718 RSKs were also converted into Formula 2 single-seaters and, redesignated 787, they pulled off an astonishing 1-2-3 at Britain's Aintree circuit driven by Moss, Bonnier and Graham Hill respectively. And amid the squalls and glowering black clouds of the Eifel mountains, Jo scored a courageous win for Porsche in the German Grand Prix, which had been downgraded by the locals to a Formula 2 event and run on the south loop of the Nürburgring.

There was more of the same in 1961, when Jo and Dan Gurney came second in the Targa driving a Porsche 718 RS61, and Bonnier got 1962 off to a good start with victory in the 12 Hours of Sebring driving a Ferrari 250TR with Lucien Bianchi, then a convincing third in the 1962 Sicilian event with local star Nino Vaccarella driving a 718 GTR. Better was to come in 1963, when Jo won his second Targa Florio with Carlo Maria Abate in a Porsche 718 GTR, the car's agility a major advantage in the wet, slippery conditions that did almost as much to defeat the challenging Ferraris as the German cars.

Bonnier also came close to winning the 1964 24 Hours of Le Mans with his old pal Graham Hill in a Ferrari 330P, which they took to a fine second place. The two did win the year's 12 Hours of Reims together in a Ferrari 250 LM, and in early October they scored again with a win in the 1000 Kilometres of Paris at the Montlhéry circuit in a Ferrari 330P.

After a dismal 1965 driving Brabham-Climaxes, Jo ran his own Cooper-Maserati for a couple of seasons from 1964, then competed in a string of other cars including a McLaren-BRM, Honda, Lotus 63 and a McLaren-BRM M5A, without much to show for his efforts. So the M5A literally ended up hanging on a wall in Bonnier's home as a little interior decoration.

Jo became more interested in other activities, like his art gallery in Lausanne, and was the first GP driver to take up residence in Switzerland for fiscal reasons. Together with Jackie Stewart, Bonnier was also a major driving force behind the Grand Prix Drivers' Association (GPDA), which was formed in 1961: he became its first vice-president and then president, fighting for greater safety in motor racing.

Meanwhile, Bonnier came second with Herbert Müller of Switzerland in the Austrian GP for sports cars driving a Lola T70-Chevrolet, and won the 1970 European 2-Litre Sports Car Championship in a Lola T210-Ford. The following year he won the 1000 Kilometres of Barcelona with fellow Swede Ronnie Peterson in a T212 and took third once more in the Targa Florio in the same car, co-driven by Dickie Attwood.

But it all ended at about 8:00am one foggy Sunday morning during the 1972 24 Hours of Le Mans. Bonnier was overtaking a slower Ferrari but clipped the Italian car. The Lola flew off the track, threw Jo to his death and exploded on impact with the ground.

# Bordino, Pietro

ONE CAN ONLY GUESS at what Pietro Bordino could have done with a straight-eight Miller in the United States in the early 1920s. As it was, he was lumbered with big red Fiats, which did well in Europe but were woefully unsuited to the banked boards of American motor racing. But, like Tazio Nuvolari and Gilles Villeneuve after him, *Il Diavolo Rosso* or 'The Red Devil' – as Bordino was known in Italy – was a blisteringly fast and unflinching driver who was able to make the cumbersome Fiats do things for which they were never designed.

Bordino was born in Turin on 22 November 1887, the son of a Fiat factory watchman. He became one of the company's apprentice mechanics until he was spotted by the great racing driver Vincenzo Lancia. The small, lightly built lad was just the right size to be Lancia's riding mechanic, so he recruited the boy and the two competed regularly together. After that Pietro moved on to another great champion, Felice Nazzaro, before making his way to Savannah in 1908 with the rest of the Fiat team. Big prize money, a high quality track and reliable crowd control were too tempting for some of the European teams to turn down, so major races at the Georgia circuit were a preferred destination for some of the Old World's movers and shakers, including Fiat. Bordino was to have ridden with Lancia once more in the year's Automobile Club of America Grand Prize at Savannah, but the drive was switched to 25-year-old Ralph DePalma. The Italo-American recorded the race's fastest lap before mechanical trouble dropped him and his equally youthful riding mechanic to ninth.

Back in Europe, Pietro, now 23, graduated to driving in 1911 and won the year's six-mile Chateau Thierry hillclimb for Fiat with an astonishingly accomplished performance. And he was introduced to the 'Best of Turin,' alias the Fiat S76, a massive 28,353cc giant of a car built especially to set land speed records. He did precisely that at Brooklands, where he coerced the huge 290hp beast to a record 120.30mph over a mile. He continued to compete in cars and on motorcycles right up to the outbreak of the First World War.

The big 3-litre Fiat 802 was, to say the least, a handful: it was even claimed that no human being could exploit its power to the full, a bit of PR spin doctoring that Bordino proved was just that during the 1921 Grand Prix of Italy, on the town circuit of Montichieri in the province of Brescia. He manipulated the awesome power of the mighty Fiat with great skill and courage but didn't win: a Ballot 3L driven by Jules Goux did that. But Pietro did put in the fastest lap of the day at 6min 54.2sec for the 10.750-mile circuit before he retired with magneto trouble. Bordino was to record fastest laps in his next three Grands Prix. He did so in a six-cylinder Fiat 804 in the 1922 Grand Prix of France on the 8.3-mile Strasbourg circuit, where his time was 5min 43sec, but he retired on lap 58 of 60. He was lying second to team leader Felice Nazzaro and tried to close up on the veteran to make his performance look that bit more convincing, but his engine failed and he was out, although he was classified fourth. Pietro's moment came a few months later driving the 804 in the Italian Grand Prix at brand new Monza Autodrome, where he not only set the fastest lap again but also won. That signalled a brief changing of the guard, as Bordino beat his Fiat teammate and old mentor Felice Nazzaro, with whom he was once a riding mechanic. After that, *Il Diavolo Rosso* was hailed as the fastest driver in Europe.

Fiat was victim of its own success in the early 1920s, when head-hunters sucked it almost dry of its talented racing car designers and steered the technicians to teams with bigger bank rolls. That meant the Turin monolith quickly lost competitive ground to the likes of Alfa Romeo, Delage and Sunbeam, so Fiat took Europe's fastest driver with it and went looking for pastures new and, it hoped, a bottomless new market in the United States. But it got it wrong, completely misjudging the progress made by Duesenberg and Miller. That was confirmed in the 250-mile Los Angeles Speedway race at the 1.25-mile wooden board track, on part of the site of which the Beverly Wiltshire Hotel now stands. Bordino's Fiat eventually gave up the ghost on lap 139, but Pietro did win a short 25-miler on the same circuit at an average 114.8mph, although he did not do so well at Fresno where he came fifth. Another sprint over 50 miles fell to the Red Devil at Cotati near Santa

Rosa, but he could only make ninth in a 100-mile race there. After an eighth place at Culver City in December and a sixth in the same town the following March, Bordino qualified eighth for the 1925 Indianapolis 500, in which he finished a disappointing tenth.

The Italian couldn't believe how the tables had been turned. He had arrived in America as Europe's fastest, but could only win small-fry events and fail miserably at Indy, a set of circumstances that could more readily have been laid at the door of superior American racecar design and his clumsy Fiat than with him losing his touch.

The Red Devil went back to Europe determined to show he was still competitive, at least among his own kind. Fiat entered him and one of its new-wave 1.5-litre twin-sixes for the 1927 Milan Grand Prix, one of two events at Monza on 4 September. The first was the GP of Italy, won by Robert Benoist in a Delage 15S8. The Frenchman had also qualified for the second race, but he sent word that he was tired after his victory and would not compete.

In heavy rain, Bordino drove an explosive race full of his old fire with a combination of almost unthinkable speed in such conditions and long, lurid slides through the corners. Inevitably, Pietro was back to setting fastest laps, and recorded one of 96.49mph that day at Monza, winning the race with a breakneck average speed of 94.57mph by 41 seconds from an Alfa P2 driven by Giuseppe Campari.

Pietro was taken on by Bugatti in 1928, who entered three supercharged 2300s for that year's Mille Miglia, one to be driven by Pietro Bordino, who many considered the best road racer of his time. But Bordino's car developed brake problems in the Apennines and he had to stop to change brake shoes. All that time lost and a car not up to scratch meant that the great Red Devil, toast of Europe and America, could only manage seventh in his class.

Pietro was now 41 years old and, as the passing of time would have it, Tazio Nuvolari was the coming man. Still, the Red Devil led the Circuito di Pozzo in a T35B until he retired with engine trouble and Nuvolari took the win. In April, Bordino was practising for the Circuito di Alessandria in a T35B when his steering jammed; the car went out of control, rolled and slithered into a ravine. The mortally injured Red Devil died before the medics could get to him.

# Borzacchini,
# Mario Umberto (Baconin)

IT'S WRONG TO CALL Baconin Borzacchini the 'eternal second,' as some motor sport historians do. Sure, he came second in quite a number of races, but that's very much to his credit, not his detriment. And he also won a lot during his short life.

In fact, of the 109 races he competed in before his untimely death at 34 on 10 September 1933, he won 10 of them outright, took 31 class wins – driving cars with little or no chance of overall victory – and came second in 21 of them. Not exactly the results of an also-ran.

Funny name, though. His father Remo was a communist who admired Russian anarchist Mikhail Bakunin. So when Remo's wife Maria presented him with a fine baby boy on 29 September 1898 the kid got lumbered with an Italian approximation of the name. The baby was called Baconin Francesco Domenico Borzacchini and he carried that handle throughout most of his life. As he became more successful, though, Italy's ruling Fascists took an increasingly dim view of one of its motor racing heroes calling himself by a communist agitator's name. So Borzacchini changed it to Mario Umberto.

But that was long after he started racing an Ansaldo 4CS in 1923 and won his class in the Coppa Della Mengara. He later switched to a French Salmson, which had a primitive clutch system and no differential, so it kept wanting to fly off the road as it went into corners. That, plus equally primitive suspension front and rear, meant the car couldn't absorb undulations. The brakes weren't much good either, but Borzacchini's ability overcame all those problems to win three races outright and take 10 class wins out of a total of 15 races.

That led to an offer from an upcoming young Italian company called Maserati, and Borzacchini won them five races outright, three class victories, and in 1929 broke the flying 10km world land speed record at Cremona by averaging 152.90mph in a 16-cylinder Maserati V4.

Baconin won his class and came second overall in the 260-mile 1929 Grand Prix of Tripoli driving a Maserati 1700 Tipo Monza, but it was a different story at the 1930 race. Borzacchini's ultra-powerful 12-cylinder Maserati beat stars like Gastone Brilli Peri and Clemente Biondetti in Talbots and Luigi Arcangeli in a Maserati 2000 to run away with the win at an average of 91.07mph, and set a fastest lap of 93.34mph.

Baconin's success at Maserati was enough for Alfa Romeo to come calling. His first event for them was in its 6C 1750 GS at the 1930 Pontedecimo-Giovi hillclimb, in which he beat Tazio Nuvolari, Giuseppe Campari and Achille Varzi to win outright at a record average of 50.98mph.

The following year was Borzacchini's first attempt at the Mille Miglia. All the big-name Italian drivers were there, most in Alfa Romeos, bracing themselves for the onslaught of German wunderkind Rudolf Caracciola in his enormous, highly potent Mercedes-Benz SSKL. The Alfas kept throwing their treads, for which Borzacchini had to change 11 tyres. He was leading at 18 minutes up on the German through the twiddly bits between Rome and the Adriatic, but he had dropped to fourth as the race hit the fast, flat roads of the Padana Plain for the run to Brescia, and that's where Caracciola made the SSKL's power count. By then Borzacchini had lost his brakes and had no more tyres, and he crashed within sight of the finish. Rudy won and Campari saved Alfa's face in second.

In 1931 Borzacchini also scored a class win in the Targa Florio, seconds in the Italian, French and Belgian Grands Prix in Alfa 8C Monzas, and won the Circuito Principe Piemonte at Avalleno driving an Alfa 2000.

There was no last gasp retirement in the 1932 Mille Miglia. Baconin shadowed first Caracciola until his demise, then new leader Campari – until Giuseppe's co-driver Carlo Sozzi crashed their Alfa into a wall. Borzacchini-Bignami won the race in their works 8C 2300 with 15 minutes over nearest rivals Scarfiotti-D'Ippolito.

The 1933 Tripoli GP was at the new Mellaha circuit. Benito Mussolini and his Fascist henchmen decided to make a big PR exercise out of the event, so the Italian-run Auto Club of Tripoli staged a lottery on who would win. The cash prizes totalled a huge 5,400,000 lire, or $362,416 at the 1933 exchange rate, so Nuvolari, Varzi and Borzacchini did a deal with their three lottery ticket holders that one of them would win. First across the line was Varzi, second Nuvolari, and Borzacchini retired. But the six split the $362,416 prize and each became $60,402 the richer.

On 10 September 1933 Monza had a double whammy in store for the race fans: the Grand Prix of Italy, which had been postponed, plus the Grand Prix of Monza. Two races, two different formulae.

That morning the Italian GP took place over 40 laps of the old 10km circuit, and the afternoon GP of Monza was on the 4.5km high-speed oval track. The Italian GP turned out to be an exciting battle between Tazio Nuvolari's 3-litre Maserati 8CM and the Alfa Romeo P3s of Luigi Fagioli – the winner – and Louis Chiron, and went off without a hitch.

The Grand Prix of Monza was another matter altogether, as three of Europe's top racing drivers crashed and died within a few hours of each other at more or less the same spot on the circuit. They were Giuseppe Campari, the great Italian Champion in his farewell race; Mario Umberto Borzacchini, the rising star; and Count Stanislas Czaykowski, winner of the year's British Empire Trophy.

The Monza GP was split into three heats of 14 laps each on the banked circuit and a final of 22 laps. During the first heat, Trossi's Duesenberg had piston trouble, broke its sump and belched oil over the south curve. A service car with a broom sticking out of one of its passenger windows chased off to the spot, which was doused with sand and swept.

The second heat was flagged away at 3:00pm, with Campari and his works Alfa Romeo P3 in the lead and Borzacchini right on his tail in the very Maserati 8CM that Giuseppe had driven to victory in the French GP three months earlier. Campari went hard into the right side of the south curve at around 110mph, but suddenly swerved to the left up near the top of the banking, tried to correct but juddered along the rim of the retaining wall, rolled over the top, and down the embankment. Campari was crushed to death as the P3 thumped down on top of him.

Borzacchini was too close to Campari's Alfa to do anything other than fly over the retaining wall himself. He was thrown from his tumbling car, his body slammed into a tree, and he died of his injuries at Monza hospital soon afterwards.

Yet despite the deaths of two great Italian heroes, the heat continued. Marcel Lehoux won in a Bugatti T51.

Then came the final, which Count Stanislas Czaykowski led in his Bugatti until the eighth lap, when a column of black smoke suddenly billowed into the sky. The count's car had crashed about 50 yards from where Campari and Borzacchini had come to grief.

The race was stopped after 14 of its 22 laps and Lehoux was declared the winner.

# Brabham, Jack

WHEN JACK BRABHAM WAS demobbed from the Royal Australian Air Force in 1947, even he didn't realise he was about to establish an Australian motor racing dynasty. But that is exactly what he did. Jack would win no fewer than three Formula 1 World Championships, the last in 1966 in the most pleasing way of all – driving a car of his own construction – and paved the way for at least three generations of his family to go motor racing.

His eldest son Geoff was the 1979 SCCA Super Vee Champion, won the 1981 Can-Am Championship and, remarkably, won the IMSA GTP title for four consecutive years in 1988–91; second son Gary was the 1989 British Formula 3000 Champion; and third son David won the 1987 Formula Pacific Championship, was the 1989 British F3 Champion, won the 1996 Japanese GT title with John Nielson and became the 1998 IMSA GT Champion with Andy Wallace. Geoff's own son Matthew began in karts and by 2010 he had stepped up to the Victorian Formula Ford Championship.

Jack's grandfather was a Londoner who emigrated to Australia in 1885. The future triple Formula 1 World Champion was born in the Huntsville suburb of Sydney on 2 April 1926. Like so many of his predecessors, he was fascinated by all things mechanical and learnt to drive when he was 12 years old. He eventually started a small mechanical engineering business in 1947 and began racing midget cars in 1948, winning events in both Australia and New Zealand.

Brabham senior soon became an extremely competitive driver and broke new ground in 1954 by forging a sponsorship deal for his Cooper-Bristol with Redex of round-Australia marathon fame. This, by the way, was 14 years before Colin Chapman's landmark Gold Leaf Team Lotus livery, so the people who ran motor racing Down Under at the time made Brabham take the Redex promotional material off his car.

In 1955 Jack decided to try his luck in Britain and eventually made his way to Charles and John Cooper's garage in Surbiton, where he brought all his practical mechanical genius and driving prowess to bear on their pioneering mid-engined Formula 1 cars. He made his debut in the 1955 British Grand Prix at Aintree driving a Cooper T40-Bristol, which he qualified 25th but retired from the race with engine trouble. It was much the same with a Maserati 250F at the British circuit the following year, but things started to improve in 1957, when he placed sixth in a Cooper T43-Climax in the Grand Prix of Monaco.

After a season of even better placings in 1958, Brabham won his first Grand Prix at Monaco in 1959 driving a Cooper T51-Climax, and then won the year's British GP for good measure. Strong performances by Stirling Moss (Cooper T51-Climax) and Tony Brooks (Ferrari Dino 246) meant that the '59 World Championship would be fought out between all three of them in the season's United States finale at Sebring. But Moss and Brooks both retired early, leaving Jack a clear run to the championship, although he did it the hard way by running out of fuel towards the end. He managed to push his car over the line to claim fourth place in a race won by his New Zealand teammate Bruce McLaren who, at 22, became the youngest driver to win a GP.

The 1960 was really Jack's season, and by that time he had earned himself the nickname 'Black Jack' because of his no-nonsense way of motor racing. Driving a Cooper T53-Climax, he won in Holland, Belgium, France, Britain and Portugal to become World Champion for the second successive year. His young friend Bruce was the runner-up in the other Cooper.

Surrounded by big, front-engined monsters, Jack even shocked fans at the 1961 Indianapolis 500 by taking ninth place in his little rear-engined Cooper Climax T54.

Brabham had long been thinking of building his own racing cars and left Cooper at the end of 1961 to do just that. He joined forces with his old Aussie mate and designer Ron Tauranac and they quickly built their first car, which made its debut in the Grand Prix of Germany at the Nürburgring on 5 August 1962. Jack qualified the BT3-Climax 24th but was involved in an accident and retired. But at the end of the season Brabham, car and driver, took a couple of useful fourth places in the United States and South African GPs.

Dan Gurney joined the team from Porsche for 1963 and he managed two seconds and a third in the BT7-Climax. A year later the tall American gave Brabham its first F1 victory, in the French Grand Prix at Rouen, and followed that up with another win in Mexico; but after that the team wouldn't win again for the remainder of the 1.5-litre F1 formula.

The 3-litre formula proved to be quite another matter. Although a number of teams were late in coming up with their new, more powerful cars for 1966, Brabham most certainly was not one of them. Jack had been to see Repco, the Australian spare parts manufacturer, which had produced a 2.5-litre V8 on an Oldsmobile block for the Tasman series. He convinced the company to develop a 3-litre Holden-based F1 unit for his cars, and he was about to score big.

Jack became the first man to win a modern Grand Prix in a car with his own name on its nose: the place was Reims and the car the Brabham BT19-Repco. He and his New Zealand teammate, Denny Hulme, made it a Brabham 1-2 at the British GP at Brands Hatch. And then came the Grand Prix of Holland. For some time Brabham, who was 40, had been taking flack from the press, as writers were saying he was too old for F1. So he 'hobbled' out on to the Zandvoort track wearing a fake white beard and 'supported' by a walking stick – then promptly won the race! He twisted the knife a little more by winning the German GP a couple of weeks later, and gave it an almighty wrench at the end of the 1966 season by becoming the first man to win the World Championship in his own car.

The show was not over yet, not by a long chalk. It was Denny's turn next. Hulme won in Monaco and Germany and scored a string of high placings to become the 1967 F1 World Champion in a Brabham BT24-Repco.

Denny moved to McLaren for 1968 and Jochen Rindt came from Cooper-Maserati to take over the New Zealander's seat. Jack put his money on the new Repco 860 V8 unit that year, but the engine was troublesome – so much so that the Austrian, who had managed to put the BT26-Repco on pole in France and Canada, ended up with a mere eight championship points and Jack just two. Jochen moved to Lotus for 1969, while Brabham parted company with Repco and switched to Ford DFV power. Jackie Ickx was the next man in the second car and won the 1969 German and Canadian Grands Prix in the Brabham BT26-Ford. He came second in the World Drivers' Championship and the team second in the constructors' table.

Brabham was 44 when he won his last F1 race in South Africa driving a Brabham BT33-Ford, and he decided to stop racing at the end of the season to pursue his many business interests. By then he had done it all, won it all. It was time for the next generation to take over.

Jack was awarded an OBE in 1967 and became the first modern driver to be knighted for his services to motor racing in 1979.

# Bracco, Giovanni

'AMONG MY DRIVERS GIOVANNI Bracco was, perhaps, the one who scored the most spectacular success,' Enzo Ferrari once said about the fun-loving, booze-loving winner of the 1952 Mille Miglia. Bracco won other races, but he will always be remembered for his climb from nowhere to victory, chain smoking and swigging red wine as he went, to win one of the most exciting Brescia–Rome–Brescia marathons in the 30-year history of the famous Italian road race.

This lively industrialist from Biella was one of Italy's truly great road racers. He made his point big time in a Lancia Aurelia B20 GT co-driven by a lad from his home town named Umberto Maglioli in the 1951 Mille Miglia on 28 April 1951. Nobody gave tuppence for the Lancia's chances against a vast field of 26 Ferraris entered for the event, and they certainly didn't expect him to be breathing down the neck of eventual winner Luigi Villoresi in his much more powerful works 4101cc V12 Ferrari Tipo 340 Vignale. But, like many bolts out of the blue, Bracco-Maglioli and their Lancia made jaws drop, hundreds of thousands of spectators cheered themselves hoarse, and radio listeners ears tingled, as their 1750cc saloon – which had, admittedly, been more than breathed on by the great Vittorio Jano – climbed its way up the field and held station two minutes from Villoresi's exhaust pipes towards the end. As was often the case, the closing stages on the Padana Plain with its long, long straights made all the difference to a high-powered car and Villoresi eventually won the race with a 20-minute lead over Bracco. But what a Jack and the Giant Killer affair it had been.

Ironically, Villoresi was recovering from injuries and couldn't compete in the 1952 Mille Miglia, so Bracco took his place – but at his own expense. He had to buy his own Vignale-bodied Ferrari 250S Berlinetta powered by a Gioacchino Colombo-designed experimental 12-cylinder, 4100cc engine and pay his own expenses in the race. His was one of 27 Ferraris in the one-day 978-mile marathon: two of the three racing Marzotto boys were there, both Vittorio and Paolo in their brace of Ferrari Tipo 225Ss. But the serious opposition would come from Alfred Neubauer and his entourage, which included veteran Rudolf Caracciola, new boy Karl Kling and 1939 European Championship winner – the equivalent of today's Formula 1 World Championship – Hermann Lang, all of whom had been practising the route for weeks before the race in their Mercedes road cars and, occasionally, their 300 SL coupés.

After Lang crashed in the early stages of the race, it was Bracco who led at the Ravenna control, nearly five minutes ahead of Kling and Vittorio Marzotto, who were just 12 seconds apart after 186 miles of foot-to-the-floor racing. But Bracco was losing time, as his tyres were wearing faster than expected, so he just made the Pescara control and service area in the lead with the carcasses of his cross plies there for all to see! The rears were replaced but there had been a mix-up and the service crew had the wrong-size fronts, so Bracco was forced to continue with the worn ones, watching his step and reducing his speed as he tiptoed down to Rome. That meant the lead in the Italian capital was firmly in Kling's hands, with Taruffi second in a Formula 1-engined Ferrari Tipo 340S and Bracco down at a galling third, thanks to a tyre mix-up that was no fault of his own.

Feeling at home in more ways than one Piero Taruffi, who came from Rome, began his bid for the lead along the undulating, ancient Via Cassia and eventually took command, only to see his chance of winning the famous race for the first time disappear before his very eyes as another in a long line of transmission problems struck and put him out in a trice. Disaster also hit Paolo Marzotto's 225S, which stuttered to a halt with a broken piston; and Biondetti's dreams of a fifth victory literally went up in smoke as his Ferrari was accidentally set on fire and burnt out at a refuelling stop at Siena.

Meanwhile, Bracco chased Kling for all he was worth, the inevitable cigarette drooping from his lips as he went. He was further fortified by a bottle of Chianti that he kept close at hand. His spectacular driving brought him to within four minutes of Kaiser Karl as Giovanni's favourite playgrounds, the Futa and Raticosa Passes, loomed. He relished the hairpins of the winding roads going up the passes and down the other side, because that is where he almost beat Villoresi the previous year; so lighting another cigarette and knocking back another slug of Chianti to warm his belly, he was ready for the twisting, turning ballet once more.

Racing genius that he was, Bracco ignored the lack of roadside barriers as he masterfully clipped the edges of the narrow mountain roads in thick fog, so that at Bologna around 60 miles on he had overtaken Kling and pulled two minutes ahead of the German. In war, he would have been awarded the Victoria Cross for acts of courage beyond the call of duty on the Futa and Raticosa. But at the end of the 1952 Mille Miglia he would be content with the race's elegant winner's cup if he got across the finish line first.

Now, Bracco was ready to turn the tables. He was not struggling with a 1750cc Lancia any more, but was ready to turn loose the full fury of that big Colombo experimental V12 and launch himself at Brescia 150 miles away. Giovanni got his 'VC.' He was the first across the finish line at Brescia to win the 1952 Mille Miglia from Kling by 12min 42sec at an average speed of 80.4mph.

Inevitably, Bracco was the hero of the moment. Radio listeners all over Italy ran out into the streets and burst into an orgy of cheering and beering, exhausted but delighted by the industrialist's victory. And once across the line at Brescia, Giovanni was immediately dragged from his Ferrari by his adoring fans and carried shoulder-high in triumph.

A year later, at the dinner preceding the 1953 Mille Miglia, tradition demanded that Bracco was awarded his 'VC,' a handsome gold-encrusted solid silver cup, able to hold a good five bottles of his favourite red wine in one go. It was one of the many trophies he received that night, and he nonchalantly rested his right forearm on it, his hand holding the eternal cigarette, as he made his highly charged acceptance speech. Then Bracco went into a no-holds-barred celebration: rivers of booze, including Chianti he swigged from a bottle – some found its way down the front of his expensive double breasted jacket – as a normally unruffled Bruno Boni, Mayor of Brescia, looked on in sheer amazement.

Bracco and Paolo Marzotto won the 12 Hours of Pescara that year – in 1948 Giovanni won the same race in a Ferrari 166C – driving the Ferrari 250S. He raced a Maserati 200S in 1955 but never again with the success he achieved with such panache in those heroic 1951 and 1952 Mille Miglias.

Giovanni Bracco died in 1968 at the age of 60, some say due to too much good living.

# Brivio, Antonio

MARQUIS ANTONIO BRIVIO WAS one of the great pre-war Italian drivers, a gentleman racer every bit as professional as the big names of his day, Tazio Nuvolari and Achille Varzi. He belonged to a small elite who had that little bit extra: sensitive, courageous, a tough and daring fighter who would never give up.

Those were the qualities that helped Brivio win the 1933 and 1935 Targa Florios and catapulted him headlong into motor racing's eternal hall of fame by helping him win the 1936 Mille Miglia for Alfa Romeo. From that moment on, Brivio became one of a select band of superstars – Nuvolari, Varzi, Brivio, Villoresi, Biondetti, Taruffi and Moss – who are the only drivers to have won both of the sport's most famous road races. As well as a whole string of other important Italian national races, the marquis also won the 24 Hours of Spa and the Swedish and Turin Grands Prix.

Antonio competed in the 1930s, when the sport was largely confined to the wealthy, an exclusive club of intrepid racers who were as big on courage as the money they spent on their fine cars. Brivio and his contemporaries also knew how to have fun before and after a race, but the consequences of such revelry were never allowed to detract from their on-track performance.

'The 1936 Mille Miglia was a race in which I competed by sheer fluke,' said Brivio. 'Ferrari wanted Nuvolari and I shielded from all risks, because the following weekend we were to drive for him in the Monaco GP. In that Mille Miglia, the 2900 Alfa Romeo powered by the P3 engine was due to make its debut with Mario Tadini at the wheel, but he was suddenly taken ill and Ferrari offered me the drive. I accepted with enthusiasm and practised for two days before the start, together with the other team members, Carlo Pintacuda and Giuseppe Farina.

'My co-driver was Carlo Ongaro, a very good Ferrari mechanic but he never drove.

'It was a nail-biting Mille Miglia: after losing the lights of my car nine times and nearly 1000 miles, my winning margin was just 32 seconds.'

Brivio thought that was his last Mille Miglia, and so it was for 16 years, until in 1952 he competed in the Brescia–Rome–Brescia classic once more, but again purely by chance and not in the way he would have wished.

'I took part as an amateur,' he emphasised, 'not as a professional driver. Once I stopped racing, I became the president of CSAI [the Italian motor sport sanctioning body] and was vice-president of the ACI [the Automobile Club of Italy] for 16 years. Wearing those hats, I went to see Ferrari to resolve one of the problems that always seemed to crop up when he was around. After we had sorted it out, he told me he had a free 2-litre car for the forthcoming Mille Miglia. He offered it to me, suggesting I race together with a journalist. That seemed interesting, so I accepted. Ferrari himself telephoned my wife to respectfully ask for her permission.

'In the race, the car's gears turned out to be incredibly stiff. At Florence, I decided to pack it in, all because of those gears. I did the uphill Futa Pass panting like an amateur. Then, going down the other side, I found my rhythm again; later, I discovered I was ninth overall and leading the 2000cc Sport class. And I hadn't raced since 1937. We eventually came ninth overall and won our class.'

Brivio said the Targa Florio and the Mille Miglia were two very different events.

'The Targa Florio was the tougher race – 72km to be repeated seven times, a total of 504km, always cornering, only one straight, and awful surfaces.'

He talked almost casually of such legendary races and his victories in them, even though he beat men like Giuseppe Campari, Tazio Nuvolari, Achille Varzi, Giuseppe Farina, Clemente Biondetti and Louis Chiron – the top talent of the day. Yet it rankled that people regarded him as a gentleman driver.

'In the beginning, I might have approached the whole thing as a gentleman driver, but in the end I was just as professional as Nuvolari and Varzi.'

Enzo Ferrari featured strongly in Antonio Brivio's memories of motor racing. He said, 'Knowing my love of racing, Ferrari would pay me small retainers and the smallest amounts of prize money. I complained to him about this. After all, I was runner-up to Nuvolari five times. Unfortunately Tazio was always there; it was madness to think that I could beat him. So I asked Ferrari for an increase in pay to equal the amount he paid the other great drivers, but he wouldn't agree. That's why I went over to Bugatti in 1934. The Bugatti, by the way, was a car that always broke down. At Spa that year, I was only just able to finish the Belgian GP, but I did come second to Dreyfus, setting the lap record and beating Nuvolari's own time. Dreyfus only beat me because I had to change plugs three times.

'Ferrari was a tough one,' Brivio continued. 'I often argued with him. Once, when he was very angry, he opened the drawer of his desk and showed me his gun. Obviously, he only wanted to frighten me.

'But he had his soft side too; for example, he adored Nuvolari, unfortunately for me. He agreed to Nuvolari's every wish, letting him race anywhere he wanted. The whole team was run with Tazio in mind until they fell out for the usual reason: money. So Nuvolari went off to race for Maserati and Bugatti. Later, they made up: it was always on the cards.'

Marquis Antonio married in February 1937, but not before he reached a special agreement with his future wife. 'I told her I would marry her as long as I could continue racing: she agreed. But I stopped racing in 1938 and later became an air force pilot in the Second World War.'

Three of the great pre-war racing drivers came from Biella, the textile capital of Italy: Brivio, Carlo Felice Trossi and Giovanni Bracco. Was there a common thread that ran through the lives of all three, some unifying accident of birth, or was their ability to drive a racecar fast simply a question of individual talent?

Brivio thought it was just coincidence, and continued: 'Trossi was rich because his father had died in a car accident and Carlo inherited a big textile factory, which was very profitable. He had a huge amount of money. He even bought a castle together with my grandfather, who was also from Biella. Grandfather had a large textile factory too, which I later ran for many years.

'When I left racing, I became president of Federtessili, the textile manufacturers' association of Italy. I have done many things. For 16 years I was on the Italian Olympic Committee.

'But cars have given me a great deal. When I am a little sad my mind goes back to my racing days and I feel better,' Brivio concluded.

Marquis Antonio Brivio died on 29 January 1995.

*Note*

This material was translated from Italian into English and augmented by Robert Newman. Brivio quotes are by kind permission of Mille Miglia Editrice, Brescia, Italy.

# Brooks, Tony

QUIET, THOUGHTFUL, MODEST: TONY Brooks was all of those things, which is probably why his name isn't exactly on the tip of everyone's tongue when reminiscing about post-war motor racing heroes. But this unpretentious young man was the strong, determined driver who lit up fast circuits like Spa and Monza in works Vanwalls and Ferraris and twice came close to winning the world title.

Born in Dunkinfield, Cheshire, on 25 February 1932, Charles Anthony Stanford Brooks, alias Tony, was a 20-year-old dental student at Manchester University when he started club motor racing in his spare time, driving first a Healey and later a Frazer-Nash. He graduated to the works Aston Martin team in 1955 and surprised the pundits when he and Peter Collins came third in the Goodwood 9 Hours driving a DB3S. After some lower formula single-seater placings, Brooks was invited to drive a Connaught in the Syracuse Grand Prix in Sicily. That was a bit of a shock, but, rather absent-mindedly, he accepted, swotting for his dentistry finals on the journey to the Mediterranean island.

The opposition wasn't quite what Connaught expected, because the Ferraris didn't compete. But there was stiff opposition from Gigi Villoresi, Luigi Musso and Harry Schell in Maserati 250Fs, which their drivers said handled like a dream but were underpowered. Although Tony had never even sat in a Formula 1 car before, he ended up lapping the Sicilian circuit in the Alta-engined Connaught B in competitive times. So competitive that he won the non-championship Formula 1 race by two minutes from Musso, and even set the fastest lap of 104.23mph. Not bad for a 23-year-old dental student and ex-clubbie.

His couple of outings in a BRM in 1956 were a bit of a damp squib, so in 1957 Brooks joined Vanwall, where he was about to do great things. He was number two to Stirling Moss, with Stuart Lewis-Evans in the number three spot. Brooks did well from the outset by qualifying his Vanwall VW7 fourth for the Monaco Grand Prix in May and coming second to winner Juan Manuel Fangio in the race. But in June he crashed his works Aston Martin DBR1/300 on lap 141 of the 24 Hours of Le Mans and, although he broke no bones, he was just out of hospital and still feeling pretty sore by the time the British Grand Prix at Aintree came round in July. It was an uncomfortable ride and Tony had dropped down to ninth place when he was called in on lap 28 so that Moss, whose Vanwall VW4 was giving trouble, could take over Brooks' VW4 and win the race. A joint victory and Tony's first F1 win.

The Vanwalls weren't really competitive for the rest of 1957, but 1958 was a knives drawn season-long battle between the much-improved Britishers and the Ferraris, with the green team late consolidating its performance capability. It wasn't until May and the third race of the season in Holland that Stirling won in a VW10. Then came Spa-Francorchamps, which pleased Tony no end as he loved the circuit and had won there in Astons twice to prove it.

The circuit had been somewhat sorted, with a few corners smoothed out and a total distance 14.10km instead of the previous 14.12. Race day was warm and sunny. Moss shot away in the lead with Brooks close at hand in second, but going into Stavelot Stirling uncharacteristically missed a gear and sent his Vanwall's engine revs through the roof, which put him out. So Tony inherited the lead and then set about earning it. He was hounded for much of the race by Mike Hawthorn in his Ferrari Dino 246, but by lap 14 Tony had pulled out 40 seconds on Mike, who later closed up again. Brooks experienced the stuff of heart attacks going into La Source, where his gearbox seized and he was only just able to crawl to the chequered flag and victory, with Hawthorn crossing the line in second 20 seconds later.

Mike Hawthorn and Peter Collins won the French and British Grands Prix respectively in their Ferraris, but come the German GP Vanwall were running extremely low on engines, so much so that they only entered Moss and Brooks and left Lewis-Evans to spectate. Both the British cars were on the front line of the Nürburgring grid for the start, in between Hawthorn on pole and Collins with the fourth fastest time. Stirling got away first with Tony following him, but as Moss widened the gap magneto trouble started to plague his car and eventually put him out on lap four, while the two

Ferraris passed Brooks and eventually left him 30 seconds down on them both. Come lap nine, Brooks had overtaken Hawthorn, but on lap 11 the two ended up side by side as they went into the South Curve until Brooks pulled ahead again and then took Collins, who crashed at Pflanzgarten, was thrown out of his Ferrari and hit a tree. He died in hospital soon afterwards.

Hawthorn retired with mechanical problems while Brooks was still in the lead and Tony ended up winning the race by three minutes from Roy Salvadori's Cooper.

Brooks won the Italian Grand Prix even though he had to make an unscheduled pit stop to stem an oil leak: that made it three GP victories to Stirling's four. Hawthorn only had one, but he still became the 1958 Formula 1 World Champion by amassing just enough points – 42, compared to Stirling's 41 and Tony's 24. But to placate ruffled feathers somewhat, Vanwall won the constructors' world title.

In 1959 Tony was invited to join Scuderia Ferrari and got down to work straight away by coming second to Jack Brabham at Monaco in a Dino 246. It didn't take him long to snatch his first Ferrari victory two months later at Reims. As they were flagged away, Tony in the works Dino out-accelerated Jack Brabham's Cooper T51-Climax to take the lead, which he never lost.

He won the German GP on the Avus part-banked circuit near Berlin that year, leading Dan Gurney and Phil Hill across the line in a Ferrari 1-2-3 to finish even closer to the top of the table in second place with 27 points to new World Champion Jack Brabham's 31. And that was his last F1 victory.

Tony had more or less had his fill of F1 by the end of 1959 and was looking beyond the sport for other rewarding things to do with his life. He bought a garage at Weybridge, Surrey, left Ferrari and joined Yeoman Credit Cooper in 1960 to drive its hardly competitive T51-Climax. Not that it did him much good, except for a fourth at Monaco and a fifth in the GP of Portugal. The following year he moved to BRM but its P48/57 Climax wasn't up to much either, so he retired at the end of that season to pursue his business interests.

Although he was a qualified dentist, he decided not to practise that profession, but invested his time in building up his Weybridge garage Lancia dealership near the historic old Brooklands circuit. Now over 80 and retired from the business, Tony still takes part in media events, especially the Goodwood Festival of Speed.

# Bruce-Brown, David

ASK ANYONE WHO WAS the first American to win a Grand Prix and chances are they will say Phil Hill or Dan Gurney, heroes of the '50s and '60s. But it was much earlier than that. The first was David Loney Bruce-Brown, a strikingly handsome young New Yorker and son of a fabulously wealthy family, who won the 1910 American Grand Prize – same thing, different language – on 12 November 1910, so over a century ago. He was 23 years old at the time and had proved himself to be a towering natural talent with a glittering career in front of him. Yet he hardly had a career at all, because it was cut pitifully short on 1 October 1912 when he crashed and was fatally injured during practice for that year's Grand Prize at Milwaukee.

At 18 the lantern-jawed David loved anything to do with the relatively new sport of motor racing, and first tried his hand at it in his mother's car, which he crashed and wrote off. Enthusiasm undimmed, Bruce-Brown wangled himself a job as a junior mechanic with the Fiat team at the 1905 Daytona Beach races. After the professionals had had their fun, the amateurs were allowed to compete in a one-mile event, for which Bruce-Brown was loaned one of the racing Fiats – and he won. It was not long before the well-heeled young man bought himself a powerful Benz and proved his worth by winning a string of amateur events in 1909. From there he took the giant leap to Grand Prix racing, where he came up against the world's top drivers.

Even in the early days of the 20th century there was a lot of political infighting in motor racing, a sport in which the Savannah Automobile Club of Georgia was determined to make its mark. But the club was given a swingeing slap in the face when it was told it would not be allowed to stage one of the legendary Vanderbilt Cup events. The Automobile Club of America came to the rescue: it invited the Savannah club to run its 1908 Grand Prize, which another mythical American driver, Ralph DePalma, would have won had it not been for mechanical problems with his big red Fiat. Instead, that race went to Christian Lautenschlager of Germany in a Mercedes. There was no 1909 American GP, so the scene was set for Mr Bruce-Brown to make history a year later.

The 1910 American Grand Prize was to be over 24 laps of the well-surfaced 17.3-mile road circuit through a forest near Savannah. Seven cars from Europe were entered, three of them by Benz for the French veteran Victor Hémery – six days away from his 34th birthday – and Americans Willie Haupt and young David Bruce-Brown. The Fiat team thought it was on to a good thing, as it still employed 1908 Grand Prize winner Louis Wagner and also fielded their ex-test driver and now motor racing ace Felice Nazzaro plus Italo-American Ralph DePalma, who fascinated the team with his Bronx-accented Italian. There were also nine home-grown cars, but they were thought to stand little chance against the 10- and 12-litre foreigners.

The 30 starters were sent on their way at 30-second intervals and, sure enough, Haupt took the lead, but Felice Nazzaro in a Fiat set the fastest lap of 13min 42sec for the 17.3-mile circuit on the seventh time around before spinning, plummeting down a deep ravine and breaking his rear axle. DePalma took over command towards the end with Bruce-Brown lying second until the last lap, when a stone punched a hole in the radiator of Ralph's Fiat, making the car's engine come to the boil. In the end, Hémery crossed the finish line first, but as it was a staggered-start race Bruce-Brown, who was next across the line, won by 1.42 seconds. Bob Burman came third in a Marquette-Buick. Crestfallen, the men from Fiat tried unsuccessfully to console themselves, as both their top cars had dropped out of the fight due to accidental damage.

Despite family pressure to stop racing – his mother was horrified at the mere thought of it – the dashing David continued to compete and had clearly shown he was well on the way to becoming a star of major proportions. So Fiat entered him for the first Indianapolis 500, which took place on 30 May 1911, and he excelled in that too. Bruce-Brown started 25th, but 13 laps later he was leading the race: unfortunately, though, he was slowed by engine trouble with the end in sight and that let Ray Harroun and his Marmon through to take the win. As David struggled, Ralph Mulford also passed him in his Detroit-built Lozier, but that was it: Bruce-Brown finished third, an outstanding achievement by the young amateur.

In late November the American motor racing fraternity made for Savannah for two major events that would take place within three days of each other. The first was the Vanderbilt Cup, in which David Bruce-Brown's Fiat broke a wheel and he retired. The race, on the same 17.3-mile Savannah road circuit as the 1910 Grand Prize, was won by American Ralph Mulford, who had beaten the big names from the US and Europe in his Lozier. Seventy-two hours later the 1911 Grand Prize took place on the same circuit, and David drove the outlandishly powerful 14-litre, 75hp Fiat S74 – a long way from being one of the Italian team's junior mechanics at Daytona just few years earlier. He was in the lead by lap 20 of 24, although he was being pressed by fellow Americans Ralph Mulford in that Lozier again, and Ralph DePalma's Benz. All three stopped for fuel on lap 22 and bedlam broke out as the massive crowd cheered its favourite driver. With just over 34 miles to go, the first out of the pits was Mulford, but he crashed almost immediately. David won, Eddie Hearne came second in a Benz and Ralph DePalma third – an all-American driver top three finish.

Bruce-Brown was entered by Fiat, together with DePalma and Wagner, for his first European escapade, the 1912 Automobile Club of France Grand Prix at Dieppe at the end of June. The big bangers were up against three new, shaft-driven Peugeot L76s, which were smaller, lighter and powered by a four-cylinder twin overhead camshaft engine with four valves per cylinder. David took the lead on the first 47.84-mile lap and was still there at the end of day one of the two-day affair after 478.4 miles. It rained on the second day, and Bruce-Brown had his work cut out trying to hold on to his lead in the cumbersome S74 as Georges Boillot's nimble little Peugeot came after him. The chase lasted well over 100 miles before the Fiat's fuel pipe broke. David was able to repair the errant tube, but he had to take on extra fuel to get back to the pits and that was against the regulations, so he was disqualified. But there was no escaping the fact that the race's fastest lap of 36min 32sec was his.

Just over three months later, Bruce-Brown and his mechanic were killed when a tyre on their S74 gave out and the big Fiat overturned. America's first Grand Prix winner was no more.

# Campari, Giuseppe

NO OTHER GRAND PRIX winner has ever sung Puccini, Verdi and Leoncavallo on stage or been able to cook like a master chef. Only Giuseppe Campari: he could do all of those things, as well as win top-flight motor races.

In 1912 Campari shut his modest suburban repair shop in Milan and went to work for the new ALFA company as a mechanic. There he began to find out what he really was: a uniquely talented individual, rather than just one more bit of rather overweight factory fodder. Giuseppe blossomed into a great ace, a heroic capturer of headlines in a career that spanned 20 years. Just before he died so tragically at Monza at the age of 41, Campari announced he would soon stop racing cars and begin a new profession as an opera singer.

Some sneered and gave Campari a hard time about his love of opera. They ridiculed him when he took to the stage of a provincial opera house and turned in a more than competent rendition of Ruggiero Leoncavallo's emotional *Vesti la Giuba* from *I Pagliaci*. But none poked fun at him as they ate one of his gourmet dinners at his home on a cold winter's night!

Campari won more than 30 Grands Prix and classics like the Mille Miglia for Alfa Romeo and Maserati, and the 1928 and 1931 Italian Championships, and he was a member of the four-man works Alfa Romeo team that won the 1925 World Grand Prix Championship.

Giuseppe Campari was born on 8 June 1892 in Lodi, 20 miles south-east of Milan, but he and his family moved to the big city soon afterwards. He opened a small, one-man workshop on the outskirts of Milan, but was soon invited to join the new ALFA company as a mechanic, yet after just a few months he had become an ALFA test driver. And that was one step away from motor racing, which he began to instinctively feel was his destiny.

It didn't take long for Campari to get into racing; the 1913 Parma-Poggio di Berceto hillclimb was his first event and he came second in an Alfa 40/60HP.

Oddly, Giuseppe, although just 22, was not called up during the First World War but remained at Alfa throughout, returning to racing two years after the armistice. In 1920 he became the first driver to win at the Circuit of Mugello in an Alfa Romeo 40/60 HP and did it all over again in 1921. At the end of 1923 he was asked to test Vittorio Jano's new 8-cylinder in-line P2, and the car designer was so impressed that he invited Giuseppe to join the Alfa Romeo racing team. A year later Campari won the Grand Prix of France, to give Jano's mould-breaking supercharged 2-litre its first-ever victory.

The following year, Antonio Ascari – Campari's teammate and close friend – was killed when his P2 overturned in the French GP as the team competed for the first Grand Prix World Championship. Nevertheless, Alfa Romeo still won the world title in September 1925 with Count Gastone Brilli Peri's victory in the Grand Prix of Italy, the last round in the championship.

By this time Giuseppe Campari had become famous, a hero, yet he remained the simple and unassuming man he had always been. The 32-year-old was well-off and had bought himself a house, where he lived with his wife, soprano Lina Cavalleri. By that time he had even sung the lead role of Alfredo in Verdi's *La Traviata* at the Donizetti Opera House in Bergamo, a city about 40 miles east of Milan.

Alfa Romeo returned to motor racing in 1927 after a two-year sabbatical, and Campari won the Coppa Acerbo by a lap in a P2 on the ultra-fast Pescara circuit.

But, setting his contribution to Alfa's 1925 world title to one side, 1928 was Giuseppe's really big year. He started by winning the Mille Miglia with Giulio Ramponi in the supercharged Alfa 1500 Gran Turismo and won the 1928 Italian Championship for the first time.

Campari and Ramponi won the Mille Miglia again in 1929 when giving the new Alfa 6C-1750 its debut, but after that, nothing; 1930 was no different and also saw the retirement of the P2 after a remarkably long and distinguished career. Vittorio Jano's 8C 2300 Tipo B P3, which many believe was one of the greatest racing cars of all time, was waiting in the wings.

Scuderia Ferrari entered two of the new Alfa 8C-2300s camouflaged with Zagato bodies for the 1931 Mille Miglia, while Alfa themselves fielded a pair of 1750 Supersports, in one of which Campari came second overall. With Nuvolari he won the Grand Prix of Italy in the same car that year, and ended his season by pocketing the 1931 Italian Championship.

But in 1932 Campari was increasingly – but unjustifiably – relegated to number three driver, behind Tazio Nuvolari and Baconin Borzacchini, who had joined from Maserati. Alfa handed its material over to Scuderia Ferrari at the end of 1932 and that didn't please the great Campari, so he left the Scuderia and stopped racing until the Maserati brothers invited him to drive for them.

Campari's first Maserati outing was in the 1933 Grand Prix of Tripoli and he led the race from lap 5 to lap 15 in his works 2800 before it broke and he retired.

The 1933 Grand Prix of France at Montlhéry on 11 June was a straight fight between Maserati and Alfa Romeo. Giuseppe Campari had the old but still quick 8C 2800 again, but was up against a massive field of no fewer than 12 Alfas. Still, the ageing Maserati was remarkably quick and Giuseppe went from a 30-second deficit on local star Philippe Etancelin and his blue Alfa Monza, to just three seconds. Then Etancelin started losing his clutch before coming to a complete stop at the side of the track. Campari shot past the stricken Frenchman to win his last Grand Prix.

By 3:00pm on 10 September 1933 Giuseppe was back in an Alfa again and was first away in his P3 in the second heat of the Grand Prix of Monza, with Borzacchini's Maserati stuck to his tail. As the two went into the circuit's banked south bend they were said to have come upon a pool of oil, which had supposedly spewed from Count Carlo Felice Trossi's troubled Duesenberg. Others said there was no patch of oil and that the two simply got it wrong. Whatever the cause, Campari dived to the right and into the banked corner, but slithered to the left again. He tried to bring his Alfa back in check, but it charged wildly along the retaining wall for 100m before cannoning off the elevation and overturning in a ditch. Borzacchini had been on the left trying to overtake Campari as all this was happening and tried desperately to avoid Campari's crazed Alfa, but lost control of his own car, flew off the track into the trackside vegetation, torpedoed through a fence of wire netting, was thrown out and slammed against a tree.

Campari was killed instantly. Borzacchini's injuries were massive: he died 20 minutes after reaching Monza hospital.

In a singular display of poor judgement, the organisers allowed the race final to take place after that. Count Stanislas Czaykowski rolled his Bugatti on the self-same south bend: his car caught fire as it disappeared over the edge of the banking where he, too, died.

# Caracciola, Rudolf

SO CALM AND COLLECTED was Rudolf Caracciola that they called him the man without a nervous system. He exerted cool, unruffled control as he dominated the 650hp Mercedes-Benz titans of his day.

When Caracciola raced a car it seemed as if gravity had been temporarily switched off, or at least it did until 20 April 1933. Rudi crashed heavily that day in an Alfa Romeo P3. His right leg was hideously shattered and a constant source of pain for the rest of his life. Yet he pulled off most of his greatest triumphs *after* the Monaco accident, winning 15 Grands Prix and three European titles – but gravity did not seem to get switched off so much any more. Rudi was reduced to being the greatest driver of his day and one of the greatest of all time instead of a miracle worker.

Otto Wilhelm Rudolf Caracciola was born in Remagen, Germany, on 30 January 1901. During his distinguished career he won the European Championships of 1935, 1937 and 1938, 137 races, scored six victories at the notorious Nürburgring and became the first foreigner to win the Mille Miglia.

Always crazy about motor racing, Caracciola joined Dresden manufacturer Fanfir and drove one of its cars in his first race, at Avus on 1 June 1922, when he came fourth. Later he was invited to an interview at the Mercedes-Benz headquarters in Stuttgart, after which he was told he had got the job, but as a car salesman!

Eventually Rudi was permitted to race one of M-B's cars – and that is how it all began. He only competed in hillclimbs and other provincial events in 1923, but he won 13 of them. He continued like that for another two seasons and scored 37 victories in a blown 1500cc Mercedes.

Caracciola made the big time in 1926, when he competed in the first German Grand Prix – for sports cars – at Avus in a 2-litre, eight-cylinder

Mercedes. His was an unofficial entry, with no works support or servicing, but he still won. Meanwhile, he had met and fallen in love with a beautiful girl named Charlotte Liemann, a Berlin restaurateur's daughter, and they soon married.

By that time Rudolf was becoming famous, and in 1927 he won a sports car event at the Nürburgring in a 7-litre S-Model Mercedes, underlining his ability the following year by winning the German Grand Prix again. Winning the Tourist Trophy in 1929 in pouring rain reinforced his reputation as *Der Regenmeister*.

Rudi decided to recce the Mille Miglia in 1930 and entered an enormous Mercedes-Benz SSK for the purpose. Even without knowing the roads and more intent on a look-see than seriously competing, he and co-driver Christian Werner still managed sixth place. The following year Caracciola became the first non-Italian to win the classic, driving his own big six-cylinder 300hp SSKL.

With Mercedes temporarily retired, Rudolf signed for Alfa Romeo for 1932, but the regular drivers – Nuvolari, Campari and Borzacchini – rebelled. They tried to make Caracciola's life difficult, even forcing Alfa to paint Rudi's 8C Monza German white rather than Italian red. But the truth was that they knew Caracciola could beat them all.

After an unpleasant but not unsuccessful year – Rudi won the German and Monza Grands Prix and became European Mountain Champion – Alfa took a sabbatical, so Caracciola was out of a job again.

Rudi and Charlotte had become great friends with Louis Chiron and his companion, Alice 'Baby' Hoffmann. After problems with Bugatti, Chiron was fired and suggested he and Rudolf form their own team. Baby, the estranged wife of Hoffmann-La Roche pharmaceuticals millionaire Alfred Hoffmann, was wealthy, so she bought the new Scuderia CC's (Chiron-Caracciola) three Alfa Romeos and two Bugattis to compete in all of 1933's Grands Prix plus the 24 Hours of Le Mans.

Unfortunately, the new venture failed almost immediately, because in April Rudi was severely injured when he crashed his Alfa Romeo Monza practising for the 1933 Monaco Grand Prix. It took a year for his right leg to heal; towards the end of those 12 painful months Rudolf took another harsh body blow. Charly was killed in an avalanche while skiing.

Rudolf tried out his mended leg testing a Silver Arrow during a private session at Avus in May 1934. He did well, although everyone could see he was in great pain. He eventually made his comeback at Montlhéry, but his Mercedes' engine broke and his pal Chiron won in an Alfa.

Meanwhile, Rudi became caught up in the speed records craze and shot back into the limelight by setting eight between 1934 and 1939, reaching speeds of up to 269.924mph on sealed-off German autobahns.

Soon Caracciola's racing career was booming again. He won the 1935 Tripoli, Eifel, French, Belgian and Swiss Grands Prix in the eight-cylinder 462hp Mercedes, and those victories brought him the first of his three European Championships.

Rudolf began the 1936 season with a win at Monaco in a more powerful 494hp M-B and followed that up with another at Tunis a month later. But Mercedes decided its cars were not sufficiently competitive, so the company pulled out of racing before season's end and used the time to design a better car for 1937.

The result was the 5.6-litre Mercedes-Benz W125, which swept almost all before it as Rudolf sprinted towards another European Championship by winning the Grands Prix of Germany, Switzerland, Italy and Czechoslovakia. He married Baby the same year.

*Der Regenmeister*'s uncanny car control in the wet was never more in evidence than in the 1938 Grand Prix of Switzerland at Bremgarten. The race took place in a non-stop deluge, and although Britain's Dick Seaman took the lead he was unable to keep Caracciola bottled up for long. Rudi's wet weather car control amazed spectators, but his car was overheating, so he could only make third – still good enough to win him the 1938 European Championship.

The following year was not so positive for Caracciola. Hermann Lang, the flat-capped racing mechanic turned driver, was the faster man. At 40 Rudi's phenomenal skills were fading, but not completely: he won his sixth German Grand Prix at the Nürburgring in 1939. But that, more or less, was it. Lang carried off the 1939 European Championship, after which – war.

In 1945 Caracciola went to Indianapolis to compete in the 500, but crashed his Thorne Engineering Special into the wall in unexplained circumstances during a flying lap. He was thrown out of the car and sustained severe head injuries, which even two years later still left him hobbling along with a stick, anchored to Baby's arm and falling over his words. But with his eventual return to health came his determination to race again at 51 years old, in the right kind of race.

That was the 1952 Mille Miglia. Mercedes entered him in a 300 SL and he did well: he came fourth in the race he had won 21 years earlier.

Rudi's last hurrah was the 1952 sports car race at Bern, Switzerland. The 300 SL's brakes locked up on the 13th lap and the car cannoned into a tree. This time Rudi's left femur was broken. He grudgingly retired, much to Baby's relief, and the couple lived quietly together at their Swiss home until Rudolf died of a liver disorder on 28 September 1959. Baby lived on for another 17 years before being buried next to Rudi in the cemetery at Ruvigliana.

# Chinetti, Luigi

AN ALFA ROMEO CAR mechanic who rose to become one of the greatest endurance drivers of his generation, the man responsible for establishing Ferrari in the United States, and patron of his own highly successful motor racing team. Almost too much to be rolled into one man, but that, in a nutshell, was Luigi Chinetti.

To begin with, Chinetti won the 24 Hours of Le Mans three times, was a double winner of the 24 Hours of Spa and the 12 Hours of Paris, and won the brutal Carrera Americana dash across all of Mexico, partnered by Piero Taruffi. He established the successful Ferrari car sales operation in the USA, formed the North American Racing Team (NART), winners of the classic 24 Hours of Daytona, the 24 Hours of Le Mans, the 1000 Kilometres of Paris et al. And he made sure the cream of 1960s motor racing drove his blue and white cars, people like Mario Andretti, Stirling Moss, Dan Gurney, Richie Ginther, Graham Hill and Umberto Maglioli.

Yet Luigi Chinetti was born in July 1901 in an obscure northern Italian village called Jerago con Orago, which even today has a population of just 5000. He loved all things mechanical, so when he was 16 he joined the Alfa Romeo test department as a trainee mechanic. Fascism began to rear its ugly head in Italy a few years later, so Luigi moved to Paris, where he first worked as an Alfa car salesman and then started his own business tuning and servicing well-heeled clients' sports and racing cars.

Soon he decided to have a go himself and competed in minor events until he joined wealthy industrialist Raymond Sommer in a supercharged Alfa Romeo 8C 2300 LM in the 1932 24 Hours of Le Mans. But Chinetti was taken ill after just four hours at the wheel, the remaining 20 being driven to victory by the Frenchman. Luigi went back to Le Mans again in 1933, determined to make up for his previous year's lack of wheel time. Sommer, partnered by Tazio Nuvolari, won again, but just 9.5 seconds behind him came the Luigi Chinetti/Philippe de Gunsburg Alfa 8C 2300 to take second place. Such was Chinetti's growing stature that he was paired with veteran Louis Chiron to drive an Alfa Romeo 8C 2300 LM in the '33 24 Hours of Spa over 9.3 miles of closed public roads between the towns of Francorchamps, Malmedy and Stavelot. Of the 33 starters, the 17 finishers were led home by the Chinetti/Chiron car at an average speed of 72.66mph.

In 1934 Luigi teamed up with French textile magnate Philippe Etancelin to drive a 2.3-litre supercharged Alfa 8C 2300 at Le Mans. They won at an average of 74.355mph and set a fastest lap of 5min 41sec. So by then Chinetti had entered the French marathon three times, won it twice and come second once.

As the Nazi stranglehold was tightening on Europe, Chinetti was asked by wealthy Paris-based Lucy O'Reilly Schell to look after the two bright blue Maserati 8CTFs she had entered for the 1940 500 Miles of Indianapolis, to be driven by René Dreyfus and René Le Brègue. The project started to go haywire when Dreyfus blew his engine and Le Brègue's car began running rough. That's when Chinetti stepped in and sorted the second Maserati in an overnight repair marathon. Le Brègue managed to qualify last at 118.981mph and covered 192 laps of the race to come 10th out of 20 finishers.

Chinetti stayed in the US for the duration, working for Italian car dealer and importer Alfred Momo, and became an American citizen in 1946. Soon afterwards he returned to Italy and visited a friend from their Alfa Romeo days, one Enzo Ferrari, now a constructor in his own right, and convinced the Commendatore to allow him to sell Ferraris in the United States.

Not that Luigi had switched to being a full-time businessman: he still felt the urge to race and was invited by Lord Selsdon to share the Scottish nobleman's Ferrari 166 Inter at the 1948 12 Hours of Paris, which they won. Selsdon then invited Chinetti back to drive a 166 MM in the 1949 24 Hours of Le Mans, the first after the Second World War. This time Luigi did the lion's share of the driving – 23 hours and 30 minutes' worth – and virtually won the race single-handed to become the first man to win Le Mans three times. Soon after that he and Jean Lucas won the 1949 24 Hours of Spa, also in a Ferrari 166 MM.

Luigi continued to race as he established his Ferrari sales operation in the US, and won the 1950 12 Hours of Paris at Montlhéry with Lucas, again in a Ferrari 166 MM.

The Ferrari image was given a major boost at the 1951 Carrera Panamericana, for which Enzo Ferrari – egged on by Chinetti – sent two of his 212 Inter Vignales to join the other 95 starters at Tuxtla Gutiérrez on the border between Mexico and Guatemala. It was the fifth Carrera, which Chinetti/Taruffi won at an average of 88.2mph in a record time of 21hr 57min 52sec over the five days.

In 1958, with the help of wealthy George Arents and Jan de Vroom, Luigi set up his North American Racing Team (NART) to compete in grand tourer races. Cherry-picking some of NART's greatest results from its more than 200 races, close to the top of the list has to be the 1964 24 Hours of Daytona won for Chinetti's team by Phil Hill, Pedro Rodriguez and David Piper.

The oddball event was a 1964 World Championship Grand Prix. To protest against the motor sport governing body failing to homologate his 250 LM sports coupé, Enzo Ferrari jacked in his competitor's licence, but had no intention of giving up hope of winning the Formula 1 World Championship at its penultimate round at Watkins Glen on 4 October. That day the Maranello Ferraris weren't their traditional red; they were in NART's blue and white, entered by the American team for Maranello.

And with a little help from Lorenzo Bandini, John Surtees came second at the Glen to clinch the World Drivers' title and Ferrari the Constructors' Championship.

But NART's crowning glory has to be victory in the 1965 24 Hours of Le Mans with a Ferrari 250 LM – homologated now and in red livery – driven by Jochen Rindt and Masten Gregory. They were up against withering odds in the shape of the fuel-guzzling 7-litre Ford GT40 MkIIs that overheated, the cause of their eventual demise. Rindt was gaining 12 seconds a lap on the leading yellow-painted Belgian Ferrari 250 LM when the front-runner had a blow-out and lost a section of its rear aluminium bodywork, all of which took five laps to put right. Far more than Rindt/Gregory needed to win.

More victories followed in NART's outstandingly successful 1965, and the team continued to race until 1982, its cars driven by some of the greatest names in motor racing history.

To mark the team's outstanding success, in 1967 Maranello produced just ten appropriately named Ferrari 275 GTB/4 NART Spyder drophead road cars.

After all that excitement, Luigi Chinetti continued to sell Ferraris and held the record for selling more of Maranello's dream cars than anyone else in the world. He died at the age of 93 on 17 August 1994.

# Chiron, Louis

LOUIS ALEXANDRE CHIRON WAS, and still is, Monaco's very own hero. He was born in the principality's capital in 1899, when his father was maître d' at the city's Hotel De Paris. Louis won the Monaco Grand Prix twice and even drove a Lancia Aurelia GT to victory in the 1954 Monte Carlo Rally. When he retired from motor sport he became one of the GP's organisers and clerk of the course. Although Chiron died at his Monaco home in 1979, he still keeps an eye on his hometown race – a bust of him overlooks a section of the Grand Prix circuit.

Chiron had been crazy about cars and motor racing since childhood and learnt to drive when he was barely a teenager. He joined a French Army regiment during the First World War, but was seconded from that when he was 18 to chauffeur first Field Marshal Foch and then Marshal Petain.

In the early '20s Louis worked at the Hotel de Paris as a professional dancing partner, earning his daily bread tripping the light fantastic with well-heeled middle-aged ladies. One of his wealthy female admirers even bought him a Bugatti Brescia, in which he did well in local races. The following year, Alfred and Alice 'Baby' Hoffmann – he was the heir to the Hoffmann-La Roche pharmaceutical fortune – were holidaying in Monte Carlo and became enthralled by the young blade's amateur motor racing exploits. As Herr Hoffmann also owned the Nerka spark plug company, with whose products Bugatti raced, he decided it would be good publicity for his firm if he bought the charming young Monegasque a Bugatti T35C to race, entered by the company and with Baby doing his lap charts. Chiron was so successful that he caught the eye of Meo Costantini, and the Bugatti team boss invited him to join the factory squad for 1928.

Chiron's promise turned to solid gold on 25 July, when he won the Grand Prix of San Sebastián on the 11-mile Lasarte public road circuit in a T35C.

That was the start of a phenomenal run of success for Louis, who went on to win the 1928 Grand Prix of Spain – at Lasarte again – and the Italian GP.

William Grover-Williams won the inaugural Monaco Grand Prix and the French in a Bugatti T35B, but Chiron bagged the German in a T35C and the Spanish driving a T35B and set the fastest lap in each of them.

In 1930 Louis had another go at his hometown Grand Prix, but he came second to René Dreyfus' T35B. All Chiron had to show for his considerable efforts that year was victory in the Grand Prix of Belgium.

Sixteen of the 23 cars on the grid for the 1931 Grand Prix of Monaco were Bugattis, the rest Maserati 26Ms and Peugeots plus the massive Mercedes-Benz SSKL with which Rudolf Caracciola struggled through the narrow, twisting city course. Although he was slow to get away, Chiron chased the leaders in his works Bugatti T51 and, after an almighty battle with Dreyfus in one of the Maseratis, won his home Grand Prix for the first time. A couple of months later the Monegasque hero shared the win in the French GP with Achille Varzi in a T51 and closed the season with a victory in Czechoslovakia's Masaryk Grand Prix.

It wasn't Chiron's fault that he was only able to win once – the Masaryk again – in 1932. The Bugattis were losing their competitive edge to the Alfa Romeo Monzas and P3s. But Louis, who was now one of motor racing's established stars, was becoming a prima donna and ignoring Costantini's team orders, so the Italian fired him.

Meanwhile Baby was becoming more than Chiron's timekeeper, and divorced Alfred so that she could live with Louis. The rich, stunningly beautiful Alice and her Monegasque beau saw a lot of Rudolf Caracciola and his wife Charly in 1932, and eventually the two men agreed to form their own team for 1933 and call it Scuderia CC, expenses and winnings shared 50:50. With Baby's financial help they bought three Alfa Romeo 8C Monzas and entered the Monaco Grand Prix, the Caracciola car in white with a blue stripe and Chiron's blue with a white stripe. But during practice Caracciola lost his brakes, crashed his Alfa at Tabac and sustained multiple fractures of the thigh, which would leave him with one leg slightly shorter than the other. So that was the end of Scuderia CC.

In August 1933 Chiron accepted an invitation to join Scuderia Ferrari and was soon basking in the warm glow of victory again. In what was left of 1933 he won the Grands Prix of Marseilles, Czechoslovakia and Spain in

Alfa Romeo Tipo B P3s, and, partnered by Enzo Ferrari's old sidekick Luigi Chinetti, also won the year's 24 Hours of Spa-Francorchamps in an Alfa 2300 Monza.

Louis had two more years with the Scuderia and won the 1934 Grand Prix of France at Montlhéry for them, where he charged through from third row on the grid in the Alfa Romeo Tipo B P3 to take the lead, which, except for refuelling and tyre changes, he kept right through to the end and victory.

After that, Mercedes-Benz and Auto Union got a grip on Grand Prix racing and wouldn't let go, winning 57 of the 70 Grands Prix between the first in 1934 and the outbreak of the Second World War.

Scuderia Ferrari was still battling on with its now obsolete P3 and later the uncompetitive Tipo C 8C-35, but with the exception of Tazio Nuvolari's amazing win in the 1935 German GP little came of it. So Chiron left for Mercedes-Benz, where his old friend Caracciola had persuaded team boss Alfred Neubauer to take him on; but Louis was strangely unsuccessful, only coming sixth in the Spanish and Eifel GPs. To be fair, the 750 formula Mercedes was well below par, although Caracciola did win the Monaco and Tunisian GPs with the W25C.

By now Caracciola was a widower, having lost Charly in a skiing accident. He fell for Baby Hoffmann – she was fed up with Chiron continually refusing to marry her – so she married Rudy instead. They lived in Lugano, Switzerland, where the German ace had a fine house and agreed to store the factory Mercedes until the armistice. Chiron was furious at losing Baby at first, but during the Second World War he spent months at a time as a guest of the Caracciolas and eventually married a Swiss girl.

The war over, Chiron signed for Lago Talbot and won the 1947 French Grand Prix in a Talbot T26C. He took second at Monaco in the same car a year later, then won the 1949 French GP in it. He scored a fine third for Maserati in the 1950 Monaco GP and sixth in the Grand Prix of France. After his surprise win in a Lancia Aurelia in the 1954 Monte Carlo Rally, Chiron ended his career in a D50, which he drove to sixth place in the 1955 Grand Prix of Monaco.

In 1968, 69-year-old Louis Chiron handed the Monaco Grand Prix clerk of the course baton to Paul Frère, but he continued to turn up at each subsequent event, dressed like a prosperous stockbroker. He died in his Monte Carlo home in June 1979.

# Clark, Jim

IT'S THE SAME WITH the assassination of President John F Kennedy and the horrors of 9/11. I know exactly where I was and what I was doing on 7 April 1968, when Jim Clark, who we all thought to be invulnerable, was killed in a Lotus 48 in a minor F2 race at Hockenheim.

I was enjoying a late lunch with friends at our home in Folkestone, England. When the news came through, I – like the rest of the world – was stunned. My appetite evaporated. Our happy lunch party turned into numbed silence. There was no point in continuing, so, with a few sombre farewells, our friends drove back to London. Our day, our lives, had been momentarily shattered by the loss of this unassuming, quietly spoken, hyper-talented Scot. A man who had won the 1963 and 1965 Formula 1 World Championships, proved unbeatable in 25 championship Grands Prix, won another 19 non-title GPs, the Indianapolis 500 and three Tasman Cups.

Jim made his mark with his usual style Down Under, when he and his F1 mates used to escape the snow and ice of Europe's winter to do the Tasman Cup series. He won the series, organised jointly by the Australian and New Zealand motor sport authorities, in 1965, 1967 and 1968, a record never bettered, although it was equalled in the 1970s by New Zealander Graham McRae.

Clark won Levin, Wigram, Teretonga Park and Warwick Farm for Colin Chapman in 1965 at the wheel of a Lotus 32B-Climax, though he could only manage the Australian Grand Prix at Warwick Farm in 1966. But he was king of the series again in 1967 with wins at Levin, Wigram and Teretonga Park again, plus Lakeside. Another four victories snared Clark his third Tasman Cup in 1968, just over a month before his tragic death, with fine victories in the legendary Lotus 49 T-Ford Cosworth DFV at Wigram, Surfers Paradise, Warwick Farm and the Australian GP at Sandown.

These were a long way from the club rallies and driving tests in which this Scottish farmer from Chirnside near Duns drove his 1956 Sunbeam Talbot 90 saloon. Through his friend Ian Scott-Watson, in 1958 Jim had moved up to a Porsche 356, a D-Type Jaguar and then a Lotus Elite. He entered the car for the Boxing Day sports fest at Brands Hatch and that is where Jim Clark the farmer started to turn into Jim Clark the racing driver and farmer. At Brands he fought his way to the front of a pack that included Lotus owner Colin Chapman, who was no slouch at the wheel. But the ultra-fast Scot hit a back marker and dropped out of the race, which Chapman won. Colin could not get the quick, quiet Scot out of his mind and invited Jim to join the 1960 Lotus Formula Junior team, which offered the newcomer little resistance and a lot of fun. Clark did so well that Chapman then asked him to have a go at the year's Dutch Grand Prix at Zandvoort in a Lotus 18, from which he retired with a seized engine while lying fourth.

After feeling his way in motor racing's top formula in 1961, Jim hit the 1962 Grand Prix season in the V8-engined Lotus 24 like a whirlwind and won the GPs of Belgium, Great Britain and the United States at Watkins Glen to end up second to new World Champion Graham Hill. It could even have been Jim's title and not Graham's if Clark's car had not sprung an engine oil leak during the South African GP. The Scot was forced out after leading for 61 of the 82 laps, having taken pole position and set the race's fastest lap of 1min 30sec.

Seven Grands Prix fell to Clark and his Lotus 25-Climax in 1963: the Belgian, Dutch, French, British, Italian, Mexican and this time the South African too, in a triumphant season. Jim just about doubled the points of his nearest rivals Richie Ginther and Graham Hill, who came equal second, to take the World Championship with panache. But in 1964 Chapman's golden touch was not so golden. Clark began the season in fighting form with wins in Holland, Belgium and Britain. The Spa win was bizarre to say the least: Clark ran out of fuel as soon as he crossed the finish line, not knowing that his rivals Graham Hill in a BRM P261 and Dan Gurney driving a Brabham BT11-Climax had run dry too, and were lucky to scrape in at fifth and sixth. However, Jim's Lotus 25-Climax came unstuck during the second half of the year as it was hampered by reliability problems. Men like Graham Hill, Dan Gurney, John Surtees and Lorenzo Bandini were stealing his thunder – and his title. John Surtees became 1964 F1 World Champion in the Ferrari Dino

156, the only man to win world titles on two wheels and four. Jim had to be content with third place in the title chase.

Clark's other World Championship year was 1965, when he blazed a path through the opposition to win the Grands Prix of South Africa, Belgium, France, Britain, Holland and Germany in the Lotus 33, after which Coventry Climax withdrew from F1 as 1966 ushered in the 3-litre formula. That left Lotus – and a number of other teams – scratching around for new engines. Chapman soldiered on with the Climax at first, but then he did a deal with BRM to use its hugely complicated H16 3-litre motor, which was really two 1.5-litre V8s put together. Amazing talent that he was, Jim coerced the BRM-engined Lotus 34 to the top of the pile to win the USGP at Watkins Glen, trailed home by three Cooper Maseratis in second, third and fourth places, driven by Jochen Rindt, John Surtees and Jo Siffert.

Ford famously came to Lotus' rescue for 1967. The two signed an exclusive deal to use Cosworth's new Ford-financed DFV engine, which was to become the most successful F1 power unit ever. Clark just blew away the opposition when he gave the DFV motor its debut in the fabled Lotus 49 at the 1967 Grand Prix of Holland, which he won from reigning World Champion Jack Brabham. The Clark-Lotus-Ford Cosworth DFV combination would go on to win the British, US and Mexican GPs, but that only got Jim to third place in the championship, which was won by Denny Hulme in one of his boss' BT24-Repcos, with 'Black Jack' Brabham second.

Jim gave notice that he was spoiling for another fight for the F1 world title on New Year's Day 1968, when he won the South African Grand Prix to bring his total World Championship GP score to 25 and break Juan Manuel Fangio's record of 24 world title race victories. But the '68 championship would never be his. He was down to compete in the BOAC 1000 race at Britain's Brand Hatch on that fateful 7 April, but he chose to do an unimportant F2 event in Germany instead. The event was the Deutschland Trophae European F2 Championship race at Hockenheim, where it was raining, but not heavily so. Yet on lap five, Clark's Lotus flew off the track into a clump of trees at 150mph and he was killed.

# Collins, Peter

ENZO FERRARI TELEPHONED HIS driver Peter Collins before the 1956 Grand Prix of Italy for one of 'those' conversations. The Great Man said he wouldn't ask Peter to give up his chance of winning the year's Formula 1 World Championship in favour of Juan Manuel Fangio, but he wanted to know the younger man's opinion on the matter. Collins came back to his boss like a shot, saying he never thought a 25-year-old like him could take on the considerable responsibilities of being World Champion. He had plenty of time ahead of him and Fangio, who was 45 by then, deserved to win it. Peter concluded by saying he would always be ready to hand over his car to the Argentine if doing so would help the older driver win the title.

To some, those could have seemed empty words, but not to a well brought-up young Briton in the mid-1950s. Things were different then. The British were even more obsessed with fair play and doing the right thing. Like his contemporaries, Peter had had such principles drummed into him from childhood.

Born in Kidderminster on 6 November 1931, Peter Collins carried his well-developed sense of sportsmanship to the absolute limit at Monza on 2 September 1956, the last round in the World Championship. He just threw away his chance of winning the year's F1 title.

It went something like this. Fangio just had to finish the Italian Grand Prix in the points to become the 1956 World Champion, but the steering arm broke on his Lancia-Ferrari D50 on the tenth lap and he was forced to retire. Peter had to win the GP in his D50 to take the World Championship. The Englishman was holding a strong second place and was closing in on race leader Stirling Moss in a Maserati 250F. But with 13 laps to go, Collins came into the pits for new tyres, saw Fangio was out of the race and immediately gave his car to the disappointed Argentine.

Juan Manuel said later, 'Collins saw me standing around and, without anyone asking him to do so, immediately offered me his car. It was a fantastic gesture. I got in and finished second, so I won the World Championship again thanks to Collins and his English sense of sportsmanship.'

It turned out that Peter didn't have plenty of time ahead of him at all. His Ferrari Dino 246 crashed at the Nürburgring's Pflanzgarten on 3 August 1958 while he was leading the Grand Prix of Germany. He was thrown out of the gyrating car but hit a tree and died of severe head injuries in a Bonn hospital the same day.

Like Stirling Moss and Mike Hawthorn, Peter was a product of the cut and thrust of post-war British 500cc and 1000cc Formula 3 racing. In 1952 he and Stirling were teammates for a bit in John Heath's hand-to-mouth HWM enterprise, until Moss departed to drive ERAs and Connaughts. Peter's best placing was sixth in the HWM 52-Alta at the Grand Prix of France, but he won the BARC 9 Hours saloon car event at Goodwood in a DB3 for Aston Martin. HWM was even less competitive in 1953, so Collins signed to race sports cars for Aston that year and won the Tourist Trophy at Dundrod with Pat Griffiths in a DB3S. A handful of outings in Vanwalls in 1954 yielded little on the Formula 1 front, and the best he could do for Aston was third with Griffith in the 1000 Kilometres of Buenos Aires.

In 1955 he came second driving a DB3S with Paul Frère in the 24 Hours of Le Mans and won the non-championship International Trophy race at Silverstone in a Maserati 250F. That same year he partnered Moss in a Mercedes-Benz 300 SLR to a spectacular win in the Targa Florio, a victory that almost never happened. Stirling had a major moment after which the car ended up on a rock in a sunken field, with all four wheels off the ground. Spectators helped him to get the battered car back into the race. Then, towards the end, Peter had a dramatic moment when he misjudged a corner and went off. But they won the Targa – the last 1955 World Sports Car Championship event – to earn the title for Mercedes.

It was a drive that did much to interest Enzo Ferrari, who signed Peter for 1956. The young Briton was now in the heady company of three-times Formula 1 World Champion Juan Manuel Fangio and young chargers Eugenio Castellotti, Luigi Musso and Alfonso de Portago, and he did well. Peter and Fangio came second in a Lancia-Ferrari D50 at the Grand Prix of Monaco, the first time he handed over his car to the Argentine. It all started when JMF was leading and went into St Devote too fast on the second lap; his car spun wildly and slithered back down the slope into the path of the rest of the field. Collins slipped by to climb up to second place, but then let a battling Fangio pass him. On lap 54 Peter was called into the pits as he was closing in on leader Moss and handed his car over to Fangio, who came second.

After that Peter won two Grands Prix in succession at Spa-Francorchamps and on his home patch at Silverstone. So victory in the last Grand Prix of the season at Monza would have made Collins the 1956 Formula 1 World Champion. But he gave his car and his title to Fangio.

By the time the 1956 Mille Miglia was due to take place Peter had already won the Giro di Sicilia for Ferrari. His co-driver for the rainswept race in a 3431cc Ferrari 860 Monza was his friend and ace photographer Louis Klemantaski. At Pescara, on the way to Rome, they were fourth behind Castellotti's leading works Ferrari, Wolfgang von Trips in a tiny OSCA and Fritz Riess in a Mercedes-Benz. By Rome, Collins had moved up to second, and that's how it stayed all the way back to the Brescia finish. Klemantaski co-drove again in the 1957 Mille Miglia and spent much of his time taking a brilliant series of photographs from the cockpit. It looked like they had the race in the bag, as Collins led most of it until the Ferrari's transmission wilted, worsened and went, forcing him to retire.

That was the year Peter and American actress Louise King were married and set up home on a five-berth cruiser in Monte Carlo harbour, much to the annoyance of Enzo Ferrari, who liked his drivers to be closer to Maranello than that.

Mike Hawthorn joined Collins at Ferrari in 1958 and the two were extremely close, an all-British island in the middle of an Italian sea. They called each other 'Mon Ami Mate' after a character in a comic strip of the period and used to take turns leading races for the devilment of it. Peter did well, coming third at Monaco in a Dino 246 and winning the British Grand Prix at Silverstone in the same car before his fatal accident in Germany 13 days later.

Hawthorn was completely shattered by Peter's death but summoned up enough grit to win the 1958 Formula 1 World Championship, after which he retired from the sport, only to be killed in a road accident in Britain the following year.

# Costantini, Meo

ONE DAY IN 1923, Ettore Bugatti met Bartolomeo 'Meo' Costantini, an encounter that would change both their lives. The suave Costantini, who was one of Italy's highest decorated First World War fighter pilots with six enemy kills to his credit, had returned to motor racing after the hostilities. And Ettore Bugatti was the diviner of those beautiful blue road cars that he delighted in putting to the ultimate test: in motor racing.

Soon after they met Bugatti offered Meo a job, and so began a relationship lasting more than a decade in which Costantini started as a company test driver, became one of its works racers and eventually moved on to become its motor sport director. He was an intimate member of motor racing's Camelot, with its manor house, a private hotel at which Bugatti guests stayed and the factory, all at Molsheim, France. He was one of its most accomplished technical experts and gifted talent-spotters, close to Ettore and his son Jean.

Bartolomeo was an aristocrat who was born in Vittorio Veneto, a small town in north-east Italy, in 1889. He didn't complete his studies at the Turin Polytechnic, but took an officer cadet course in 1909, later to be commissioned as a second lieutenant in the Italian military reserve before taking his pilot's licence. He was also a works driver for Aquila Italiana, a manufacturer that went out of business after the First World War, and even drove one of its cars to a class win in the much-vaunted Parma-Poggio di Berceto hillclimb. But on the outbreak of war he was called up in 1914, promoted to full lieutenant and joined the Italian Air Force. Soon afterwards he was sent to the elite Baracca Squadron – its mascot the black prancing horse on a yellow background that was later given to Enzo Ferrari by the late Francesco Baracca's parents – scored his six kills, was promoted to captain, then major and was decorated three times for bravery.

After the war the young ace acquired a Bugatti T13, which he and a friend modified with shorter, lighter pistons and a new lubrication system. Meo even enjoyed some minor successes with it, not least by taking second place overall in the Circuit of Garda. Then Costantini joined the Bianchi factory team for 1922, but was not mightily successful.

Soon after winning his class in the Alpine Cup driving an Amilcar 1100, Meo met Ettore Bugatti, the world's only car constructor who raced his road cars rather than track specials like Fiat's 805, Alfa Romeo's P2 and Delage's 2LCV. That was what attracted Costantini to the Bugatti job, as well as there being a continuous cross-flow of information between Bugatti's test results from motor racing and its application to improving road car performance. What he raced he sold, what he sold he raced.

The first inkling of Bugatti Grand Prix success came in 1922, when T30s driven by Spaniard Pierre de Vizcaya, Frenchmen Pierre Marco and Jacques Mones-Maury came second, third and fifth in the French Grand Prix. Then de Vizcaya took another third in the Italian GP. Parisian Ernst Friedrich drove the T30 into third place in the GP of France again in 1923, and in 1924 T35s took fifth and sixth in the San Sebastian Grand Prix at Lasarte.

But the Bugattis started to win under Meo's management, starting with his own victory in a 2-litre T35 in the 1925 Targa Florio, a five-lap 540km (335.6-mile) endurance race on the island of Sicily over dusty 'roads' and goat tracks. He demolished the early lead of the Louis Wagner and André Boillot Peugeots by putting in a fastest fifth and last lap of 1hr 28min 37sec at an average speed of 73.123kph (45.44mph). That left the other two trailing by up to eight minutes. Pierre de Vizcaya brought home the only other works T35 in fourth place.

Meo's 1925 win would be the first of Bugatti's five consecutive victories in the Targa under his management. In July of that year he took a 1500cc supercharged T39 to Montlhéry to win the Touring Car Grand Prix, and won a similar race at Monza two months later. Then he rounded off the year by taking third in the GP of Italy in a Bugatti 1500 – a good build-up to even better things in 1926, because the Delages, Alfa Romeos and Mercedes were beginning to feel the hard-charging Bugattis breathing down their necks.

Costantini's management and driving talent at Bugatti peaked in '26, when the cars from Molsheim won the AIACR's World Championship of

Grand Prix Racing. Their year began with a double victory in the Targa and Coppa Florio, two trophies for one event run over the same 108km (67.12-mile) medium Madonie circuit. The 2.3-litre Bugattis came first, second and third, with Meo scoring his second consecutive win, Italian driver Ferdinando Minoia second, Frenchmen Jules Goux third, André Dubonnet fifth in a 2-litre T35, with Italians Pasquale Croce ninth and Antonio Caliri tenth in 1.5-litre Bugattis, an unprecedented show of strength. The Coppa Florio, again awarded to the winner of the Targa, also went to Meo Costantini.

The first Grand Prix of the season was a strange happening indeed. The AIACR had previously cancelled the old 2-litre formula and dictated its Grands Prix would be run to 1500cc rules; but none of the constructors' new cars was ready by 27 June, the day of the first Grand Prix of the season at Miramas, near Marseilles, France – except the Bugattis. Meo entered three supercharged 1500cc 39As, so the rather glum spectators stood for over four hours watching the three Molsheim cars racing against each other. All went swimmingly for 45 laps, after which Pierre de Vizcaya dropped out with engine trouble. That left just two Bugattis to fight it out, but Costantini faded from view after 85 laps, leaving Jules Goux to total the 100 laps in complete isolation and win the season's first GP.

The works Bugattis didn't compete in the rain-soaked 1926 German Grand Prix, so next on their fixture list was the European GP around Lasarte, Spain. There the Delage 15SBs made their debut, but they nearly fried their drivers, as the cars' exhausts ran under the cockpit. Edmund Bourlier and Robert Sénéchal stuck it out to come second in one of the 15SBs, but Jules Goux in a Bugatti T39A won the race, his boss Meo Costantini came third and Minoia in another Molsheim car fifth.

Due to the Sitges track's financial difficulties, the 11-mile Lasarte road circuit played host to the 1926 Grand Prix of Spain and it was another Bugatti benefit, with victory going to Costantini, second place to Goux – who crossed the finish line 17 *minutes* later – and fourth to Minoia, 22 minutes down on the winner. The Bugattis delivered the *coup de grâce* at the Italian Grand Prix at Monza on 5 September, when Sabipa, alias Louis Charaval, won the race and Costantini came third to win the World Championship.

Meo decided to stop competing after winning the Grand Prix of Milan on 12 September 1926, partly due to the death of his good friend Count

Giulio Masetti in that year's Targa Florio and partly because he was 37 years old and wanted to concentrate on the team's management. He continued in that role until Ettore's son Jean took over in 1935.

Costantini fell ill and died on 19 July 1941.

# De Filippis, Maria Teresa

A WOMAN COMPETING IN Formula 1 was unheard of in the '40s and '50s. If any went motor racing at all, they generally decorated the pits in their tight sweaters and three-quarter trousers, scarves about their locks, collecting admiring glances from an exclusively male-populated sport. The more adventurous of them did lap charts for their boyfriends, who were out on the circuit putting their lives on the line – because that is how it was in top-class motor racing in those days – trying to win a race. Until 22-year-old Countess Maria Teresa de Filippis showed up in 1948, a pretty, petite, persevering brunette from Naples, Italy. Fifty years ago she became the first woman ever to compete in a Formula 1 World Championship race, mixing it with the likes of Fangio, Ascari, Hawthorn, Farina, Moss, Brooks and company.

Since then four other women have driven in Formula 1 races. Italy's Lella Lombardi competed in a March in 1975, Davina Galica drove a Surtees in 1976 and a Hesketh in 1978, South African Desirée Wilson did so in 1980 at the wheel of a Williams, and in 1992 Giovanna Amati drove a Brabham. But the little Italian countess was the first.

Maria Teresa, the daughter of a wealthy Neapolitan industrialist, was little more than 16 years old when her father made her drive from Rome to Naples while he had a business meeting in the back of his car with a colleague. She had no driving licence; the trip was her first taste of what was to become a passion that turned into a profession.

She certainly caused a sensation, especially in her early career, goaded as she was by two of her brothers, who weren't very complementary about her ability to drive fast. But they didn't have so much to say on the subject after Maria Teresa won her first race over the 10km between Salerno and Cava de' Tirreni in a Fiat 500; and especially when she began to make it in sports car racing.

Few could conceive of a young woman driving a racing car at 150mph and competing against the top male drivers of the day. Her colleagues called her the *pilotino* or little racing driver when she became part of an elite group that used to spend their off-duty hours enjoying life together. Sometimes four of them would share a car to drive to the track, laughing and joking as they went. During the day they practised, and in the evening they dined, wined and went dancing together. Make no mistake, though – Maria Teresa learnt to be a tough little lady, and would take crap from nobody. It's just that in her day all the drivers were friends and wanted to hang out with each other, an atmosphere completely different from today's Formula 1, in which the drivers stay in their own pits or their team's motorhome and are often at knives-drawn with their 'teammates.'

She did fall in love with one of her colleagues, the dashing, handsome Luigi Musso. They spent two happy years together until his compulsive gambling led to their break-up.

The little countess was courted in a friendly sort of way by many of her driver colleagues, but not Juan Manuel Fangio. He regarded her more as a daughter due to the difference in their ages, he 47 she 31. He was worried by her courage and did all he could to help, advising her and teaching her the tricks of the trade.

And it paid off. Maria Teresa competed in over 100 races between the summer of 1948 and August 1959. She scored over a dozen outright victories and class wins up against the top male competition of the period and branches of the sport – and has a wall full of trophies to prove it. At the start of her career, at 22 years old, she took an honourable eighth in class in the 1948 Coppa d'Oro delle Dolomiti – known as the Mille Miglia of the mountains – driving a Urania-BMW 750, and received her award from the hands of the great Tazio Nuvolari. She made her F1 debut driving a Maserati 250F in a non-World Championship race at the Syracuse track in Sicily, where she came fifth; and she did four world title GPs, her best placing tenth in the 1958 Grand Prix of Belgium at the daunting Spa-Francorchamps circuit.

One of her record winning times that stood for years was in the 1955 'hill' climb from Catania, Sicily, up the side of the Mount Etna volcano; she and her Maserati 2000 covered the 23.62 miles in 21min 24.4sec. And at 29 she came a remarkable ninth overall and fourth in class in a 2-litre Maserati A6GCS at the celebrated 1955 Targa Florio, in which winners Stirling Moss and Peter Collins made sure of the World Sports Car Championship for Mercedes-Benz.

But between 1957 and 1959 Maria Teresa lost some of her greatest friends in fatal accidents. Friends like Eugenio Castellotti, who crashed and died while testing a Lancia-Ferrari D50 at Modena; Alfonso de Portago, who fatally crashed a works Ferrari, which stopped the Mille Miglia for ever; Musso himself died while trying to catch Mike Hawthorn for the lead in the 1958 Grand Prix of France at Reims and the F1 world title; Peter Collins, who crashed his Ferrari at the same year's Grand Prix of Germany, was thrown out and killed; and Hawthorn, who died in a road accident just months after winning the 1958 F1 World Championship. But according to the *pilotino* they never thought about death itself, simply the sadness of seeing so many of their friends die.

They also never thought of safety. The countess and her colleagues raced without seat belts, often even without helmets, just a pair of goggles. It was Stirling Moss who gave her the first Johnson helmet, which she then wore habitually.

The *pilotino* tried unsuccessfully to qualify a Behra-Porsche for the 1959 Grand Prix of Monaco and she was down to drive one of the cars in the Avus, Germany, race on 1 August 1959. But her team owner Jean Behra decided to take the drive himself and flew over the top of the banking to his death. The very next day, sickened by the deaths of so many of her racing friends, Maria Teresa stormed away from motor racing and didn't let it back into her life for another 20 years. No other woman would drive a Formula 1 car in anger again until 1974, when Lella Lombardi attempted to campaign an old, privately owned Brabham BT42-Cosworth in the Grand Prix of Great Britain, for which she was unable to qualify.

Today the countess is a distinguished, white-haired and extremely energetic octogenarian who drives a 400hp Maserati Quattroporte with brio. The manufacturer gave a party to celebrate her 80th birthday, and the winner of that 1958 Belgian Grand Prix, Tony Brooks, travelled from the UK to pay his tribute to her at the celebrations.

Now the *pilotino* has two university student grandchildren and is a lively vice-president of the Club International des Anciens Pilotes, of which she once said, 'We are very close, perhaps because we feel we are the survivors.'

# DePalma, Ralph

ONE OF THE GREATEST, and nice with it, that was Ralph DePalma. He won well over 2500 of his 3000 or so races and other speed events and was a superstar who was much liked for his sunny disposition and sportsmanship.

That was never more clearly the case than when he led the 1912 Indianapolis 500 in his Mercedes Grey Ghost for an incredible 197 laps. But on the 198th a con rod went, so the car coughed and spluttered on three of its four cylinders as it gradually ground to a halt. Meanwhile, Joe Dawson and Don Herr, the eventual winners in their American-built National, snatched the lead from DePalma, whose car shuddered and stopped before it could complete the lap.

So the Italian – DePalma didn't become an American citizen until 1920 – and his riding mechanic, Australian Rupert Jeffkins, got out and pushed, Ralph with one hand on the big car's steering wheel the other on the bulkhead and Jeffkins pushing with all his might at the back. They crossed the line dripping with sweat to complete 198 laps, but Indy rules stated that the car had to compete under its own steam, and so they were relegated to a Did Not Finish.

Sweat pouring down his face and dog-tired after pushing his heavy car that last quarter of a lap, DePalma still went over to Dawson, shook the American's hand and warmly congratulated him as an 80,000 strong crowd cheered themselves hoarse.

Our hero was born Raffaele DePalma, one of four brothers, in the village of Biccari, near the heel of Italy, on 19 December 1882. Ten years later he and his family emigrated to the United States and, like 22 million others from all over the world, they had to suffer the humiliations of Ellis Island before being allowed to make their way to New York. At the time, by the way, New York was dubbed – somewhat tongue in cheek – the 'fourth Italian city' because so many Italians lived there: the ranking by population was Naples, Rome, Milan, New York.

The DePalmas settled in Brooklyn, where Raffaele soon became Ralph and did odd jobs in his father's barber shop. The youngster first tried his hand at bicycle racing, but he thought that was a bit tame, so he moved on to motorcycles and then dirt track car racing, which was much more to his liking. He went on to win the American Automobile Association's national dirt track championships of 1908, 1909, 1910 and 1911, when he also won the first-ever Milwaukee Mile Championship Car Race.

The year of his big Indy disappointment, 1912, he won the US National Driving Championship, but he also crashed and almost died while trying to overtake winner Caleb Bragg's Fiat S74 in the 1912 American Grand Prize, the seventh and last race in the 1912 GP season, held near Milwaukee on 5 October. That put him in hospital for almost three months.

Ralph came out pretty well as good as new and eager to race. So he was made captain of the Mercer team. Its cars broke too easily at first, but by early 1914 they had been licked into shape; then Ralph's employers went and hired Barney Oldfield to drive for them without letting on to DePalma, who was furious, resigned immediately – and was without a drive. One of Ralph's old pals, Jay Schroeder, came to the rescue by taking the Mercedes Grey Ghost out of mothballs and getting it to Santa Monica, California, in short order so that Ralph could drive it in the 1914 Vanderbilt Cup. Who should also be there practising for the event but Oldfield in a Mercer, although any thought of revenge in Ralph's mind was seriously out of order, as he and the Grey Ghost were over 40 seconds a lap down on Barney and the Mercer.

During the early part of the race DePalma was a back marker, but persistence, driving skill and some smart strategy took him up to fifth. Then the top four disintegrated. The lead car crashed, Oldfield pitted for oil and tyres, and the third-placed car broke its prop shaft, so with that lot out of the reckoning Ralph inherited the lead. But on lap 25 of 35 the more powerful Mercer began to catch the Grey Ghost and Oldfield overtook him, though DePalma still managed to stay in his cigar-chewing adversary's slipstream. But Barney's car was getting through its tyres at a rapid rate so he had to pit again, only to see the Grey Ghost take the lead once more and this time stay there. Oldfield was never quite able to catch the Mercedes, so Ralph beat the Mercer to win the 1914 Vanderbilt Cup, which must have been a sweet victory indeed.

DePalma competed in a couple of French Grands Prix including the 1914 race, the last to be held before the outbreak of the First World War, in which he drove a Vauxhall for seven of the race's 20 laps before retiring with a broken gearbox. He made a detour on his way back to the States and bought one of the 4.5-litre, 115hp works Mercedes Grand Prix cars, which he then took back to America, had it painted cream and entered it for the 1915 Indianapolis 500. That turned out to be a battle royal between DePalma and fellow Italian Dario Resta in a Peugeot, in which DePalma led for 132 of the race's 200 laps. Three from the end the Mercedes broke a con rod while in the lead, but although the big cream car slowed DePalma was still able to keep it going fast enough to cross the finish line to win, with oil belching from the engine. That was Ralph's one and only Indy win out of ten tries.

After serving as a pilot in the US air force during the First World War, Ralph joined Packard and developed the 15-litre V12 Liberty engine for them, and to prove it worked he broke the measured mile record on Daytona Beach in a Packard powered by the big unit, setting a new fastest speed of 149.87mph. A year later he joined the under-financed French Ballot team and took second place driving one of its 3Ls in the 1921 Grand Prix of France at Le Mans, which was won by fellow American Jimmy Murphy in a Duesenberg. The Ballot-DePalma relationship was not to last long, though, as the company and DePalma begged to differ over a gear change system Ralph had invented, so he left.

Ralph won the 1929 Canadian National Championship and continued stock car racing, during much of which time he continued to race and break speed records in an assortment of Duesenbergs, Packards, Millers and Chryslers until he retired in 1936. He was an honorary referee at the Indianapolis 500, a duty he performed for the last time at the age of 72 in 1954. He was appointed a consultant engineer to the Mobil Oil Company and worked for them until he died of cancer in 1956.

# Dreyfus, René

THE ASHTRAYS WERE A collector's delight, shaped like Bugatti radiators and advertising the Le Chanteclair Restaurant and Bar at 18 East 49th Street, New York City – a gourmet's heaven, with a very French menu of specialities that included coquille Chanteclair, Feuillet au Roquefort and, on Fridays, filets de sole Cardinal, with wines to match.

Opened in 1953, with a menu and wine cellar like that Le Chanteclair built up a healthy business clientele. Many of its diners knew nothing of the place's motor racing heritage, although the bar was home to a host of motor sport memorabilia and autographed photographs of famous drivers. Others knew, though, and many of them made the pilgrimage from the far side of the world to pay homage, to relive old times and races. Because Le Chanteclair was owned by René Dreyfus, motor racing hero of France, and his brother Maurice.

In the 1930s René was a privateer who took on the factory teams and beat them. Maurice was his manager and business partner throughout that illustrious career and on into Le Chanteclair.

On the circuits, René was always the underdog because his cars were not the latest specification – the manufacturer saw to that. A factory team being beaten by a privateer in a car identical to the works racers? Do me a favour. Even so, Dreyfus won the 1930 Grand Prix of Monaco in his own Bugatti T35B, soundly beating Monte Carlo-born Bugatti factory star Louis Chiron. His other big win was in the 1934 Grand Prix of Belgium in a Bugatti T59, heading the likes of Antonio Brivio, Raymond Sommer and Robert Benoist.

Born in Nice on 6 May 1905, at nine years old René was able to drive his father's Clement-Bayard, and at 18 the Dreyfus brothers bought a 6hp Mathis, which René drove to a class win in the 1923 Circuit des Gattires. By 1929 the youngster had won three French Riviera Championships. That was the year of the first Monaco Grand Prix, won by the legendary William Grover-Williams in a Bugatti T35B, but René came an honourable fifth and won his class driving his T37A in the same race.

After his 1930 GP of Monaco win there was still no works drive for René, so he started to mull over how he could compete against the factory teams on equal terms. Eventually he came up with an idea that, like most good ones, flew in the face of convention. He decided he would not refuel. He had extra tanks welded into his Bug so that he could race non-stop from start to finish. The establishment pooh-poohed the move, but René charged on unmolested to win the 1930 Grand Prix d'Esterel Plage and the Marne GP, the 1931 Grand Prix de Brignoles, the 1933 GP of Nancy, the 1934 Belgian GP at Spa-Francorchamps, all in Bugattis; the 1935 GPs of Marne and Dieppe in Scuderia Ferrari Alfa Romeo P3s, the 1937 Grand Prix of Florence in a Maserati 6CM, the 1938 GP of Cork in a Delahaye; took second in the 1935 Monaco GP in a Ferrari P3 and the Italian GP, sharing the driving with Tazio Nuvolari in an Alfa Romeo Tipo 8C Tipo 35; came third in the 1932 Monaco and Belgian GPs in a T51 and the 1934 Monaco GP in a T59 – the best Nuvolari could do in that race was fifth in a similar car – third in the 1934 GP of Switzerland in the 59, and scored a mass of top five finishes.

From mid-1934, Mercedes-Benz and Auto Union dominated Grand Prix motor racing supported by government money, so the French administration and the Automobile Club of France invited its manufacturers to develop new cars to compete in the Million Franc Race, with that huge amount of money – almost $1 million at today's rates – going to the winner. The event was to be a time trial held at the Montlhéry circuit, on which competitors were to try and exceed an average speed of 146.508kph over 200km, a record set by an Alfa Romeo P3 in 1934.

Dreyfus was taken on to test Delahaye's new V12, 4496cc T145, and drive it for them in the Prix du Million at Montlhéry, where he blew the competition away with a scorching average of 146.654kph over 200km of the partially banked circuit. That left Jean-Pierre Wimille to make his run in the factory Bugatti T59, but the Bug went out with piston trouble and Dreyfus won the million for Delahaye.

The Delahaye T145 was built with American heiress Lucy O'Reilly Schell's money and was raced by Dreyfus under her Ecurie Bleue colours. Dreyfus beat all comers, including the great Rudolf Caracciola in a works

480hp Mercedes-Benz W154, driving the Delahaye in the 1938 Grand Prix of Pau on 10 April – a rare humbling of the 1935, 1937 and soon to be 1938 European Champion. Two weeks later Dreyfus did it again, this time winning the Cork GP in Corrigrohane, Ireland, with Prince Bira of Siam second in a Maserati 8CM.

But the Second World War was creeping up on motor racing and Dreyfus was commissioned into the French army, but was given special permission to drive Lucy O'Reilly Schell's Maserati 8CTF in the 1940 Indianapolis 500. Lucy sent two cars, the other for René Le Brègue; but Dreyfus blew his Maserati's engine and had to share Le Brègue's rough-sounding Ecurie Bleue entry. None other than Luigi Chinetti helped cure the O'R-Schell Spl's ills and eventually it qualified on the last row of the grid. Le Brègue drove the first half of the race and, as arranged, Dreyfus took over midway. Despite a misunderstanding of the rules, he finished a creditable tenth eight laps behind winner Wilbur Shaw in the Boyle Special Maserati 8CTF.

By that time Germany had invaded France, so there was no way René, who was Jewish, could return home. When the US entered the war he became a GI and served in the Italian campaign. He took out American citizenship in 1945 and a year later he and Maurice made their first foray into the restaurant business by opening the all-French cuisine Le Gourmet on the West Side of Manhattan. But that eventually became too small, so the Dreyfus brothers sold up and put their money into Le Chanteclair, which became hugely popular.

René raced on and off well into the 1950s, the last time being the 1955 12 Hours of Sebring in an Arnholt-Bristol Bolide, in which he came a disappointing 29th.

Twenty-five years later, at 75 years old, he was invited back to the Grand Prix of Monaco to commemorate the 50th anniversary of his 1930 win. Just before the GP he drove a lap of honour in a Bugatti T35B at jaw-dropping race speeds, to the applause of thousands of spectators. On stage at the event's gala dinner that evening were two cars: the Williams FW07B-Ford, in which Carlos Reutemann had won that afternoon, and the 1930 Bugatti T35B. Master of ceremonies Jackie Stewart asked GP winner Reutemann to sit in his Williams and René to climb aboard the Bugatti to an inevitable standing ovation. Then René returned to his Le Chanteclair.

# Etancelin, Philippe

IF YOU EVER SEE a photograph of Philippe Etancelin in action, chances are you will never forget him. Because he's the one who raced cars wearing his cap back to front.

'Phi Phi,' as Etancelin was nicknamed, was one of those moneyed gentleman drivers, a wool merchant who loved to race. But unlike some of his kind he was skilful and fiercely competitive. He won 16 Grands Prix, some of them, admittedly, lesser events, but others were absolute top liners, such as the Grand Prix of France and the 24 Hours of Le Mans. Philippe could muster all the skill and aggression of a top professional when it was called for, as confirmed by his nine-lap, wheel-to-wheel battle in an Alfa Monza with the hyper-tenacious Tazio Nuvolari's Maserati 8CM during the 1933 Grand Prix of Nice. But Philippe's list of victories is less crowded than it might have been, because he took his business commitments seriously and even stopped racing for a year to fulfil them.

Born in Rouen, France, in 1896 to a wealthy family that had made its fortune in the wool industry, Phi Phi began racing a Bugatti T35B in minor events when he was 20 years old.

He had his first big success in 1927, when he won the Grand Prix de la Marne and established himself as one of France's fastest racing drivers. He bought a T35C in 1929 and literally cleaned up in the Marne again, the Reims, Comminges and La Baule GPs. He scored one of his two most important victories in 1930, when he won the Grand Prix of France at Pau, beating drivers of the calibre of William Grover-Williams and Sir 'Tim' Birkin. Louis Chiron, at the time Guy Bouriat's reserve driver, took an early lead in a Bugatti T35C, but had to pit with a puncture on lap 12, which let Etancelin slip through into the lead, where he stayed, untroubled by anyone. He won from second-placed Birkin's howling Blower Bentley by

3min 26sec. He also won the Grands Prix of Grenoble and St Raphael that year.

When Alfa Romeo decided it was ready to sell its Monzas to private entrants Philippe was the first in line, and had his new 8C painted an uncharacteristic French racing blue. He campaigned the car to good effect, winning the Grands Prix of Grenoble and Comminges again, the Dieppe and the Circuit du Dauphine. Then the Alfa P3 exploded on to the scene and just about no racecar was safe from its speed and agility, including the Monzas, although Etancelin did manage to win with his car once more, at Peronne.

In 1933 Phi Phi ran his Monza for the third successive year to win at the Grands Prix of Reims and Peronne, plus the GPs de Picardie and de la Marne; and he nearly turned motor racing on its ear during the season's Grand Prix of France at Montlhéry, where he was about to win the race from Italian ace Giuseppe Campari and the opera-singing gourmet's rather outdated Maserati 8C 3000. But with Philippe firmly in the lead on the 39th of 40 laps the Monza's clutch started playing up, which slowed the blue Alfa sufficiently to allow Campari to pass him and take the win. Even so, Phi Phi still hung on and managed to finish second, ahead of distinguished racers like Raymond Sommer and Algerian tearaway Guy Moll.

Etancelin was quite a problem for Scuderia Ferrari in 1934, as Maranello had decided not to compete against the all-conquering Mercedes-Benzes and Auto Unions at each European Championship Grand Prix, but to pick up easier money in lesser events. Because Philippe had acquired a Maserati 8CM he was the one who gave the Scuderia some stiff opposition that season; consequently those smaller events were not as easy as Ferrari had hoped, and the Frenchman scored a string of high placings and even beat the Scuderia's P3s to win the Grand Prix of Dieppe, knocking the Scuderia's Marcel Lehoux and his Alfa Romeo Tipo B P3 firmly into second place.

But Etancelin didn't cut his ties with Alfa completely. He was another talented driver who joined forces with Scuderia Ferrari's long-distance specialist Luigi Chinetti – Louis Chiron did so in 1933 and won the 24 Hours of Spa with the Italian – to win the 1934 24 Hours of Le Mans. The '34 Le Mans was a nerve-racking event for its eventual winners, who were seven laps in front by the seventh hour with only the Rileys holding a distant candle to their Alfa Romeo 8C 2300. Nerve-racking because the Alfa had a slow fuel leak, so with a huge lead in hand Etancelin and Chinetti decided to take it a little easier. Even so, their 8C 2300 was so much quicker than the competition that they won by 13 laps from the Jean Sébilleau-Georges Delaroche Riley 6/12 Racing, and Philippe recorded the fastest lap on the 13.492-mile Sarthe circuit of 5min 41sec, an average of 88.53mph.

A year later Phi Phi raced two different Maseratis, both of which were outclassed. One was a 6C-34 belonging to Carlo Felice Trossi's Scuderia Subalpina, in which Etancelin could only manage a fourth at Monaco. The other was his own new Maserati V8R1, which he drove into third place and on to the podium of the Grand Prix of Tunis, a counter towards the European Championship. His only win of the year was in the V8R1 at the Grand Prix of Pau.

Etancelin did not race at all in 1937, but devoted himself to his wool business. He did compete in a 4.5-litre Lago-Talbot in 1938/9, but was unceremoniously elbowed aside by the German juggernaut. The best he and the Talbot could manage was to take third place in the Grand Prix of Pau, behind the Mercedes-Benz of winner Hermann Lang and second-placed Manfred von Brauchitsch.

After the Second World War, Philippe became the first driver to race an Alfa Romeo when he bought an old Monza with which to compete in the symbolic 1945 Bois de Boulogne races, French motor racing's way of saluting peace.

There were some undistinguished outings in a Maserati and a Delage until 1948, when Phi Phi acquired one of the new Lago Talbot 26Cs and campaigned that for the next four years. At well over 50 years old he was still able to put up a fight: he scored some creditable placings and actually won the 1949 Grand Prix of Paris at Montlhéry. But his finest hour that year came in the Grand Prix of Italy at Monza, where he gave Alberto Ascari and his Ferrari 125 a really hard time in an effort to snatch the lead from the Italian. In the end Phi Phi had to settle for second, ahead of Prince Bira, Tullo de Graffenried and Raymond Sommer.

In 1953, when he was 56 years old, Philippe retired from motor racing and was awarded the Légion d'Honneur. He became a regular at the meetings of the Anciens Pilotes retired racing drivers' club until his death aged 84 at his home in the exclusive Neuilly-sur-Seine near Paris on 13 October 1981.

# Fagioli, Luigi

FAGIOLI WAS TOUGH. BUILT like a heavyweight boxer, his attitude could be as hard as his appearance. He was an explosive cocktail of hard-nosed single-mindedness, ruthlessness and driving talent that gave no quarter and expected none.

Yet he was a truly great racing driver, often beating superstars like Tazio Nuvolari and Rudolf Caracciola. He won a total of ten Grands Prix and has held the record for being the oldest driver to win a World Championship GP since 1951.

Born in Osimo, near Ancona, Italy, in 1898, Fagioli was a qualified accountant and helped to run the family pasta business. At 27 he bought a Salmson 1100 and won 24 minor events in it; and he came fifth in his first Grand Prix driving a Maserati 26M at Monza. Maserati offered him a supercharged 4.5-litre 16-cylinder car for the 1931 GP of Monza, which he won brilliantly, trouncing the Alfa Romeos of Tazio Nuvolari and Baconin Borzacchini.

Fagioli's greatest moments in 1932 were his two epic battles with Nuvolari at Monza. One was in June in the town's own Grand Prix and the other in September, during the GP of Italy; both races won the hard way by Tazio with the Fagioli coming a close second each time.

Luigi replaced Nuvolari at Scuderia Ferrari in 1933 and won the Italian GP at Monza – especially pleasing because he beat Nuvolari. And he became champion of Italy for the first time at the end of the season.

The AIACR thought limiting Grand Prix cars' weight to 750kg meant engine power would be reduced. But Daimler Benz and Auto Union managed to squeeze engines of up to six litres into its cars and still meet the weight limit. So they were the acts to beat from 1934 on.

At Mercedes, Alfred Neubauer was short of good drivers. Rudolf

Caracciola was recovering slowly from a horrendous accident practising for the 1933 Monaco GP, while Manfred von Brauchitsch and Ernst Henne had no experience of circuits outside Germany; so Neubauer engaged Fagioli, but didn't know all hell was about to break loose.

Two Mercedes-Benz W25s were entered for the 1934 Eifel GP at the Nürburgring, for von Brauchitsch and Fagioli. The German shot into the lead but Fagioli soon overtook him, much to Neubauer's displeasure. So the Mercedes team boss ordered Fagioli to let von Brauchitsch pass, which he did. But he took his W25A right up to the rear of the Brauchitsch car and stayed there, harassing the wild, twitchy German as if he were about to overtake.

When Luigi made his first pit stop he was fuming and bellowed his annoyance in an avalanche of Italian that Neubauer did not understand. The mighty team boss boomed orders back in German, which Luigi did not understand. Fagioli roared off in a cloud of blue tyre smoke and stubbornly glued himself to the tail of von Brauchitsch's Mercedes again. After 13 farcical laps another pit stop, but this time Fagioli climbed out of his perfectly healthy Mercedes-Benz W25A and left the track. If he couldn't drive to win, he wouldn't drive at all.

The Italian won the Coppa Acerbo, but Mercedes were almost wiped out in the Grand Prix of Switzerland at Bern, after which Luigi won the Grands Prix of Italy and Spain.

The Spanish GP was a race of Italian duplicity. Caracciola led, followed by an aggressive Fagioli. To save the cars – and his friend Caracciola – Neubauer ordered Rudi to ease off, as he had a good lead. But the Italian eventually passed Caracciola, to the fury of Alfred Neubauer.

All of which left Fagioli to mull over a fairly satisfactory first season, and a rather ruffled Mercedes to ponder his insurrection.

Luigi signed for Mercedes-Benz again for 1935, as Stuttgart still needed the Italian's race-winning capability. And he won Monaco, becoming the first driver to lead the GP from start to finish.

Next up was the French. Caracciola slowed as he was firmly in the lead at Montlhéry. Fagioli saw what was going on, speeded up and slipped past the German to snatch the lead. But Rudi pulled level with Fagioli in front of the stands and the two started a blazing row at over 80mph. The gentlemanly British magazine *The Motor* caustically reported them as 'apparently exchanging light after-luncheon conversation.' Then Fagioli's W25B retired with plug trouble, leaving Caracciola to cruise to victory.

Luigi swore he would win the Grand Prix of Peñya Rhin, so that meant another violent Fagioli-Caracciola clash. Rudi took the lead and relegated Fagioli to second. Alfred Neubauer astutely chose that moment to signal 'maintain your positions,' but Luigi still eased his Mercedes past Caracciola to take command and victory.

Weeks later at the Belgian GP at Spa Caracciola led from the start, so Luigi pressured him, setting one fastest lap after another. Rudolf kept the quicker Italian bottled up behind him and, predictably, Fagioli was fuming. So Luigi repeatedly drew level with Rudi at La Source, Stavelot and down the hill past the pits, hurling abuse at the German. Neubauer signalled Fagioli to come into the pits, where Luigi and his boss had yet another slanging match, after which the Italian just stomped off and Caracciola won.

Rudi won the 1935 finale in Spain, giving him six victories to Fagioli's three, and on top of that Caracciola won the first of his three European Championships. That made Luigi an unhappy man.

Before the 1936 season began Alfred Neubauer thought of dropping Fagioli, but he needed Luigi's skill, if not his rebelliousness, and reneged. Caracciola won Monaco and Tunis, but all the Italian managed was modest placings. So the Stuttgart team withdrew before season's end. They needed a better car and that was the W125, which made Mercedes competitive again in 1937.

Fagioli had had enough and decided it was time to go. But where? He was 38 and his rheumatism was becoming a real problem. Still, he signed for Auto Union for 1937, but it was a year to forget. At Tunis, Luigi and his Auto Union were mixing it with Caracciola and his Mercedes. The Italian was certain Rudi had purposely blocked him and he was furious. After the race Fagioli picked up a heavy tyre hammer, stalked over to the Mercedes-Benz pits and threw the tool at his rival. It missed, so Luigi grabbed a knife and was about to stick it into Caracciola when Alfred Neubauer and a mechanic stopped him.

Due to his chronic rheumatism, Fagioli only competed in three of the 16 races, after which war broke out.

In 1951, aged 52, Luigi signed for Alfa Romeo F1, where his teammates were Juan Manuel Fangio and Giuseppe Farina. The trio won all the season's

Grands Prix. Luigi shared an Alfa 159 with Fangio in the GP of France and won, setting a record as the oldest man ever to win a GP – rheumatism and all – that still stands today.

The Italian drove a works Lancia Aurelia B20 to third overall in the 1952 Mille Miglia and he and the car were entered for the Monte Carlo Prize, a Grand Prix of Monaco support race. Practising on 31 May, Luigi's Aurelia charged erratically out of the principality's famous tunnel, smashed into a stone balustrade and threw the Italian out. He was rushed to hospital with head injuries, a broken arm and a broken leg but died there three weeks later.

A turbulent life was over.

# Fangio, Juan Manuel

ONE OF THE REMARKABLE things about Juan Manuel Fangio is that he only competed in 51 Grands Prix, yet he won five Formula 1 World Championships. Another is that he won 24 of those 51 GPs, almost half of them from pole position – a success rate of 47%.

People still say Fangio didn't like sports car racing, a popular belief that was really caused by mechanical breakdowns and bad luck. He was leading the 1953 Mille Miglia when his Alfa Romeo's steering arm broke and he was left with only one to guide the car, but he still finished second. He came second again in the 1955 Mille Miglia, because his Mercedes-Benz 300 SLR would only fire on seven cylinders. And he lost ten minutes in the '55 Targa Florio while the Mercedes mechanics tried to free a jammed fuel filler cap, but he still finished second.

Years later Juan Manuel said he would have loved to win the Mille Miglia, but it was not to be. His destiny was to win in Grand Prix cars.

In many ways Fangio was a simple man who reflected his humble origins, yet there was something instinctively special about him. The son of an Italian immigrant, he was born in the potato-farming town of Balcarce, about 400km south of Buenos Aires, on 24 June 1911. He started work in a local garage at ten years old and became a mechanic. Not exactly the makings of a man who would later ooze class and radiate an almost royal presence.

Fangio was one of the great South American long-distance *carrettera* racing drivers for ten years. Between 1938 and 1947 he won 14 such events, which ran for thousands of miles, in cars like a Chevrolet TC and a Ford T-Chevrolet. In the summer of 1948, at the already advanced age of 37, he travelled to Europe to see how they raced in the Old World. While in France he was invited by Amédée Gordini to take over a 1.4-litre Simca-Gordini from an injured Maurice Trintignant and was lying sixth in the F2 Coupe des Petites Cylindrées at Reims when he retired.

A year later Juan Manuel led his country's automobile club team, Equipo Argentino, to Europe, where they campaigned Maserati 4CLT/48s. Fangio reeled off three straight victories driving one of the blue and yellow cars in the Grands Prix of San Remo (Italy), Pau and Roussillon (France). He followed them with another win in the Marseilles GP in a more agile Simca-Gordini, before winning the Monza Autodrome Grand Prix in a Ferrari 166 F2 and then the GP of Albi (France) in the Maserati. That, understandably, made the Argentine the sensation of the season and spurred Alfa Romeo on to signing him for 1950, the first year of the Formula 1 World Championship.

Fangio played it really cool in the 1950 Grand Prix of Monaco. There had been a mass pile-up at Tabac: Farina's Alfa skidded on seawater that had slopped over the harbour wall and then his 158 hit some stone steps. Nine other cars happened on the scene and collided or simply stopped. It was chaos. But Fangio, who was leading the race and on his second lap, noticed the spectators were not watching him. Suspecting trouble up ahead, he slowed down enough to be able to pick his way through the mayhem and win his first World Championship Grand Prix. Although he won the Belgian and French title counters too – plus another seven non-championship GPs – the first world title went to his teammate Giuseppe Farina. Juan Manuel 'only' won another three GPs in 1951, but this time he became World Champion, with 31 points to Alberto Ascari's 25.

Then, disaster. Fangio missed a lift from Dundrod – where he retired his disastrous BRM V16 Mk1 from the 1952 Ulster Trophy – to Milan in Prince Bira's private plane, as he was to compete in the Grand Prix of Monza. He managed to catch a flight to Paris, but bad weather grounded all aircraft. So Fangio borrowed a car and drove to Monza, where he was to make his Maserati debut driving an A6GCM in an F2 race. He was exhausted, crashed his Maserati and damaged a vertebra in his neck. He said later that he got to Monza at 2:00pm, was racing at 2:30 pm and in hospital at 3:00pm. The injury kept Juan Manuel out of motor sport for the rest of the season. He took revenge in 1953, though, because one of his five victories included the Grand Prix of Italy at Monza. And he also won the Carrera Panamericana driving a Lancia D24.

Mercedes-Benz signed Juan Manuel for 1954, but its magnificent W196s were not ready until the French GP in July, so the Stuttgart firm allowed him to drive for Maserati in the meantime. He won the Argentine and Belgian Grands Prix in the 250F and took a stack of points to Mercedes, for whom he won at Reims in the delicious W196 Streamliner's debut. He also won the German, Swiss and Italian GPs with the open-wheel W196, and that secured his second world title. The 1955 season proved to be a similar story: Fangio, who was teamed with Stirling Moss that year, won in Argentina, Belgium, Holland and Italy with Moss right on his tail: in fact, they raced so closely together that fans called them 'The Train.' Regardless, that gave Juan Manuel title number three.

Mercedes-Benz retired from motor racing at the end of 1955, so Fangio moved to Ferrari for 1956. His mount was the Lancia-Ferrari D50, with which he won in Argentina, Britain and Germany. He only needed to finish in the points in the Italian GP at Monza, but a steering arm broke and he was forced to retire his car. Fangio's teammate Peter Collins famously handed over his D50 to Juan Manuel, who finished second in the borrowed car to win the 1956 World Championship. Title number four.

Fangio won his fifth title in 1957, when he joined Maserati once more and won the Grands Prix of Argentina, Monaco, France and Germany, where he drove the race of his life. He was leading at the Nürburgring when he pitted for more rear tyres and fuel after lap 12. It was a messy pit stop in which the fumbling mechanics lost him his 30-second lead plus another 48 seconds. So Fangio rejoined the epic race in third place. He went into every corner in a higher gear than usual in a hair-raising attempt to catch the leading Ferraris of Collins, who was lying second, and leader Mike Hawthorn. Juan Manuel had ten of the 'Ring's 14.167-mile laps in which to overtake the D50s and he broke his own lap record on each one of them. He won the race and his fifth World Championship.

He started to race a works Maserati 250F again in 1958, but found he had lost his appetite for competing and announced his retirement at the French Grand Prix at Reims on 6 July. He was 47 years old.

Afterwards Juan Manuel became president of Mercedes-Benz in Argentina, and continued to travel the world well into his 80s as motor racing's elder statesman. He died in a Buenos Aires clinic at 4:10 am on 17 July 1995.

# Farina, Giuseppe

A GRADUATE IN MECHANICAL engineering, they called Giuseppe Farina *Il dottore*, the doctor. An austere, intolerant man, in 1950 Emilio Giuseppe ('Nino') Farina became the first driver to win the modern Formula 1 World Championship. He was also famous for his laid-back (literally), straight-arm driving style, which many of the young blades of the day tried to emulate, not least Stirling Moss. But Nino was an irascible man, who had little regard, at times even contempt, for his fellow competitors.

Born in Turin on 30 June 1906, Giuseppe was the nephew of Italian body-stylist Pinin Farina. He graduated from the Turin Polytechnic in mechanical engineering and began his racing career by crashing his Alfa Romeo 6C 1500cc during the 1932 Aosta-Grand St Bernard mountain climb, which gave him a broken shoulder and a badly cut face. After convalescence, in 1934 he drove a Scuderia Subalpina Alfa Romeo Monza, very much 'yesterday's' car. As the old Monza was not exactly cutting edge, he bought a Maserati 4CM at the end of the year and successfully took on the fading Alfa Romeo Tipo B P3s of Scuderia Ferrari, collecting his first significant victory in the voiturette curtain-raiser to the Grand Prix of Czechoslovakia at Brno.

Enzo Ferrari took him on as a promising youngster in 1936 and, after finding his feet, Nino won the Princess of Piedmont Cup the following year in an Alfa Romeo 12C 36 and continued to win voiturette races, becoming the 1937 Italian Drivers' Champion. In early 1938 Scuderia Ferrari became part of Alfa Corse: Giuseppe was kept on by the new masters and competed in Grands Prix in 308s and 312s – not exactly state-of-the-art racing cars – without much success. But he did retain his Italian Drivers' Championship that year, as he did in 1939, when he became Alfa's team leader. That was when he got his hands on the gorgeous 158, which would canonise him. He won the 1939 Ciano Cup and the Prixe Berne, but he took his biggest 'pre-war' win in the 1940 Grand Prix of Tripoli, when the rest of Europe had already been at war for months.

It was the Second World War that sabotaged Farina's motor racing career just as his abilities were coming to the boil. Back in the saddle, so to speak, in 1946, Nino pulled off his first post-war win driving an Alfa Romeo 158 in the 1946 Grand Prix of Nations in Geneva, but little else. Farina was not selected to drive for Alfa in 1947, so he campaigned an independent 32-valve Maserati 3-litre, in which he won first the 1948 Grand Prix of Mar del Plata in Argentina and then amazed the world by taking pole position in the '48 Grand Prix of Monaco, passing early leader Jean-Pierre Wimille in the 1430cc Simca-Gordini, winning the race and setting the fastest lap of 1min 53.9sec as he went. Full house.

*Il dottore* made his Alfa Romeo comeback in 1950. The war had cheated him of his best years, but he was still about to make motor racing history at the ripe old age of 44. Mind you, his teammate Luigi Fagioli was an even riper 52. But 'young' Juan Manuel Fangio was a mere 38.

The first race of the new Formula 1 World Championship was the Grand Prix of Great Britain at the ex-wartime airfield of Silverstone. The event was also given the title Grand Prix of Europe, and most of the British royal family turned out to add a little more gloss to the occasion. King George VI, Queen Elizabeth, Princess Margaret and Countess Mountbatten worked their way along the line of drivers, clearly fascinated by these supermen who were about to play out a different kind of Battle of Britain before them. In fact, it wasn't so much a battle as spectacle, gladiators on wheels. Ferrari did not enter, but there were four Alfa 158s for the 'Three Fs,' as Farina, Fangio and Fagioli were called, and an extra one for Reg Parnell.

The front row of the grid told the story of the race. All four Alfa 158s were there, gleaming in the feeble British sunshine. And all four sprinted away from the rest of the field, so that by Copse the order was Farina, Fagioli, Fangio, Parnell. And that is pretty much how it stayed, with the exception of Fangio dropping out on lap 62 of 70 with a broken oil pipe. Farina won, Fagioli came second and Parnell third.

But Monaco was Fangio's. He took pole position with a scorching 1min 50.2sec. Nino was also on the front row next to the Argentine at 2.6 seconds slower, but the surprise of the day was José Froilán Gonzalez, who coerced his Maserati 4CLT/48 into joining them up front. Farina got away first, but Fangio took command halfway around. Then, disaster. Farina hit a mass of water that had slopped over the sea wall and on to the circuit at Tabac, skidded, belted a set of concrete steps and stopped, and ten other cars piled up in his wake. Fangio got an inkling that something was wrong as he charged along on his second lap: he slowed drastically, picked his way through the carnage and won.

But the Argentine was not so lucky at the next race at Bremgarten, Switzerland, where he dropped a valve on lap 33 of 42 and retired, enabling Nino to redress the balance. A little revenge with victory at the Grand Prix of Belgium put JMF back in the running for the title, with a mere fourth place for Giuseppe Farina. Same again in the French GP, which Fangio won: Farina lost seven minutes in the pits with fuel starvation problems, which dropped him to an eventual seventh place.

The showdown between the two was at the Grand Prix of Italy, where Nino ruled the roost with a dashing display of aggressive driving to win the first Formula 1 World Championship, while Fangio just faded away with engine trouble less than halfway through the race. Needless to say, the Italian crowd went ballistic, mostly because their countryman had won the title but also because Alfa drivers took the top three places in the championship: Farina with 30 points, Fangio 27 and Fagioli on 24.

After that high, Nino's career wound down. He stayed with Alfa for 1951 and won at Spa in a 159. Next he joined Ferrari as a second stringer to Alberto Ascari and won the 1953 German GP in a F2 500. He also won the WSCC 24 Hours of Spa in a 340 MM shared with Mike Hawthorn and the 1954 1000 Kilometres of Buenos Aires with Umberto Maglioli in a Ferrari 375 MM, but was severely burnt in an accident at Monza. His last Grand Prix drive was at Spa, where he came third in a not very Supersqualo. Farina retired after a couple of half-hearted mid-'50s stabs at the Indianapolis 500.

Ironically, the haughty Italian was killed in a banal road accident in 1966, when his Lotus Cortina skidded on ice and crashed at Chambery en route to the Grand Prix of France.

# Fittipaldi, Emerson

LIKE MARIO ANDRETTI AND Nigel Mansell, Emerson Fittipaldi is one of the elite. A driver who has won the Formula 1 World Championship (twice) and the CART title, with a record in both that reads like any self-respecting Walter Mitty's wish list. He won 14 Grands Prix – not to mention non-title 'oddments' like the Race of Champions (Brands Hatch), the International Trophy (Silverstone), the Italian Republic GP (Vallelunga) and the President Medici GP (Brazil) – and 23 CART races, including two Indianapolis 500s, in his long and extremely distinguished career.

On top of that, he set a record in 1972 at 25 years old by becoming the youngest driver ever to win the F1 world title – a record that stood for 33 years, until 24-year-old Fernando Alonso came along in 2005 and broke it.

Emerson was a genius behind the wheel, overflowing with natural talent spiked with a keen strategic mind, with which only a handful of drivers have graced the motor racing circuits of the world – Varzi, Fangio, Senna, Schumacher, some of the sport's greatest, to which Fittipaldi's name can be added without fear of contradiction.

Emerson was born into a racing family in São Paolo, Brazil, as his father Wilson Senior and his mother Juzy both raced production cars after the Second World War. And dad was a much-respected Brazilian motor racing journalist, who later guided his youngest son's career for some time.

Like Argentine Juan Manuel Fangio before him, young Emerson worked as a mechanic. He flirted with motorcycle racing when he was 14 and moved on to hydrofoils two years later, but reasoned that they were too risky, so he turned to karts and then cars. That led first to him winning the Brazilian kart title, two years after which he switched to a Volkswagen-engined Formula Vee car built by his brother Wilson Jr, in which he also won his country's national championship.

Emerson made his way to Europe in 1969 and quickly attracted attention with his victorious march through the lesser formulae. So much so that he was signed by Colin Chapman for a full European Formula 2 Championship, in which he came a steady points-scoring third, the title going to Clay Regazzoni.

Frank Williams tried his damnedest to sign Fittipaldi to drive his de Tomaso after Piers Courage was killed at Zandvoort, but it did not happen. Wily old Chapman had the Brazilian locked up in a contract from which not even Harry Houdini could have escaped. By way of encouragement, the Lotus boss gave Emerson his first Formula 1 outing in a 49C at the 1970 British Grand Prix, and the youngster came eighth; two weeks later he scored his first F1 points with a fourth in Germany. Then disaster struck: number one driver Jochen Rindt was killed practising for the Italian GP at Monza in September, and his teammate, John Miles, was becoming disenchanted with Formula 1. So that pitched Fittipaldi right into the thick of it as, effectively, the Lotus number one at the tender age of 23. The young man showed he could handle the job a fortnight later by winning the US Grand Prix at Watkins Glen in a Lotus 72 against quality opposition like Chris Amon, Derek Bell and Pedro Rodriguez.

Fittipaldi went off the boil in 1971, a year in which Lotus competed the entire season without a win for the first time since 1959. But 1972 was a completely different story: Fittipaldi became World Champion. He dominated the European Formula 1 scene with victories in Spain, Belgium, Britain, Austria and Italy to take the title away from 1971 champion Jackie Stewart with 61 points to the Scot's 45.

After a rather uncomfortable 1973 with his new, exceptionally competitive teammate Ronnie Peterson – Fittipaldi won three GPs to the Swede's four – Emerson surprised everyone by signing with McLaren for big money and became the 1974 World Champion with wins at home in Brazil, Belgium and Canada, beating his old sparring partner Clay Regazzoni to the title by 55 points to the Swiss driver's 52. Niki Lauda proved all but unstoppable in the Ferrari 312T in 1975, although Emerson did manage to win in Argentina and Britain to come second in the championship in the slower Cosworth-engined McLaren M23.

Then, at the height of his F1 career, he amazed everyone by announcing he was leaving Woking to join his brother's new Fittipaldi Automotive F1 team, which had risen from the ashes of Walter Wolf Racing. But out of 103 starts the best the Copersucar (Brazilian sugar) sponsored squad could achieve was Emerson's second place in the 1978 Brazilian GP. After another four less than mediocre seasons, Emmo decided to leave Formula 1 at the comparatively young age of 33. Back then he cited the deaths of some of his motor racing friends as the reason, but later said he had become too involved in trying to make the team work, to the detriment of his personal life: sponsorship dried up and the team faded away at the end of 1982.

But Emerson was still very much a talent and, like many other F1 refugees, he set sail for the USA, where he started in IMSA before gravitating to CART in 1984 and the beginning of the second phase of his stunning career. He took his time finding his feet in North American single-seater racing and drove for two small teams before injury opened up a spot in Patrick Racing, with whom he scored his first victory after 15 months in a March 85C-Cosworth in the Michigan 500. That was it, until his win at Elkhart Lake in October 1986, after which 1987 brought two more CART victories in the Cleveland Grand Prix and the Molson Indy at Toronto.

Fittipaldi left Patrick Racing for Penske in 1989, and that's where he astonished everyone. He won the year's CART championship with five victories – one was the Indianapolis 500 – and three subsequent races in succession in the Penske PC18-Chevrolet. The Indy win was spectacular because Emerson led for 158 of the race's 200 laps and became the first winner at the Brickyard to earn over $1 million in prize money.

Despite the best efforts of talents like Michael Andretti, Al Unser Jr and Bobby Rahal, a year never went by between 1987 and 1995 without Emerson earning his ride to Victory Lane. It was a period in which he won 21 races including the 1993 Indy, a victory he famously celebrated by drinking orange juice instead of the traditional milk to help promote the Brazilian citrus industry.

Seven months off his 50th birthday Emerson was still competing in Champ Car when he was seriously injured in an accident at the Michigan International Speedway, and that brought his phenomenal career to an end. Worse still, while recovering from the accident he was flying his private plane over his orange grove estate near São Paolo in September 1997 when the aircraft lost power and fell 300ft to the ground, causing him serious back injuries.

Emerson returned to Champcars as a team owner in 2003. He also made a surprise comeback behind the wheel in the Grand Prix Masters race at Kyalami, South Africa, in 2005. There he came second to Nigel Mansell, the man he narrowly beat to take his second Indy win, and gave us all a stylish reminder of one of the most outstanding careers in motor racing history.

# Gendebien, Olivier

WEALTHY BELGIAN ARISTOCRAT OLIVIER Gendebien has the unique distinction of being Ferrari's most successful GT and sports car racer. He won 24 top endurance classics, including the 24 Hours of Le Mans four years out of five, the Targa Florio, 12 Hours of Sebring, the 12 Hours of Reims twice, the Tour de France Automobile three times and the 1000 Kilometres of the Nürburgring between 1958 and 1962.

But he never won the race he loved most, the Mille Miglia. He once said, 'The atmosphere, the incredible spectators and an exciting route made it the greatest race in the world.' Olivier did, however, win the GT class of the legendary one-day marathon in 1956 and 1957, but only managed a respective fifth and third overall. The victory of which he was most proud was a race within a race – the Tazio Nuvolari Grand Prix over the Cremona–Mantua–Brescia section of the last Mille Miglia. Driving a 3-litre factory Ferrari 250 GT, he was faster along that flat, more or less arrow-straight road than either the event's winner Piero Taruffi or second-placed Wolfgang von Trips, who both drove more powerful 3.7-litre Ferraris. Olivier set a record average speed of 123.92mph over the home straight to win the coveted gold tortoise, awarded in memory of the great Italian ace.

Born in Brussels on 12 January 1924, Gendebien was heir to the family's Solvay industrial holdings that controls one of the world's leading pharmaceutical groups. Like Robert Benoist, William Grover-Williams and Jean-Pierre Wimille, Gendebien was a Second World War resistance fighter, and acted as a liaison officer between British agents parachuted into Belgium. He studied agriculture after the war and then spent four years in the Belgian Congo clearing forestry land for the construction of a residential area of what is now the city of Kisangani, once called Stanleyville. During that time he had his first taste of motor sport as a rally co-driver to his friend

Charles Fraikin. When they got back to Belgium the two competed together and won the hairy 1955 Liège–Rome–Liège Rally and the Coppa d'Oro delle Dolomiti – considered by many to be the alpine version of the Mille Miglia – in Olivier's own Mercedes-Benz 300 SL. Gendebien also came fifth in the year's 24 Hours of Le Mans with Wolfgang Seidel in a Porsche 550 Spyder.

Those exploits attracted Enzo Ferrari's attention and he signed Gendebien to campaign Maranello's sports racing cars in 1956, although neither had an inkling of just how successful their partnership was going to be. The majority of Olivier's victories were achieved at the wheel of some of the most mouth-watering Ferraris ever built, not least the 250 Testa Rossa. He won a total of 20 races for the Prancing Horse, 10 of which contributed to Maranello winning the World Sports Car Championship in 1957, '58, '60, '61 and '62, as did his many strong podium placings.

'Olivier Gendebien knew how to transfer the nobility of his origins to a car with elegant and judicious vehemence,' Enzo Ferrari once said rather poetically of his endurance star. The Belgian was fast and consistent, not only on the smoother circuits of the world but also on the convoluted goat tracks of the Targa Florio.

Gendebien's remarkable cascade of victories was all achieved during a short, five-year motor racing career. He did not compete for long, because his wife pushed him into retiring at 38 years old due to the danger of a sport in which almost 30 of his fellow racing drivers were killed. After winning his fourth 24 Hours of Le Mans, Olivier called it a day and announced his retirement.

Only Carroll Shelby and Roy Salvadori in their legendary Aston Martin DBR1 stopped Gendebien from winning the 1959 24 Hours of Le Mans, otherwise he would have won at Le Sarthe during each one of those five years. The Belgian superstar won the great French endurance race in a Ferrari 250 Testa Rossa with Phil Hill in 1958 and then scored a hat-trick by winning the race in a similar car with French journalist Paul Frère in 1960, with Phil Hill again in a Testa Rossa in 1961 and in a 330 LM in 1962.

Sebring was another hat-trick. Olivier won the Florida classic for the first time in 1959 with Americans Dan Gurney, Phil Hill and Chuck Daigh in a Testa Rossa, with Hans Herrmann driving a Porsche 718 RS60 in 1960 – one of the few WSCC counters in which he did not compete in a Ferrari – and in 1961 with Phil Hill in a Ferrari 250 TR. The Belgian and the Californian were successfully paired again in 1962 for the 1000 Kilometres of Nürburgring, Gendebien's penultimate victory in his remarkable career.

The Sicilian Targa Florio was the oddball round in the WSCC. It was usually run over ten or more laps of the Piccolo Circuito delle Madonie, covering anywhere between 448 and 672 miles. No smooth race tracks here, the Targa's route was made up of narrow public roads, which were supposed to be closed but were infested with wandering spectators, their cars often parked on the circuit itself or dangerously close to it. The rough road surfaces of the event played havoc with tyres and suspensions and the 3000 or more hairpins and corners called for masterful car control. Yet Olivier was a three-time winner of that wild and woolly race too. He triumphed in the Targa for the first time in 1958 driving a Testa Rossa with Luigi Musso, then with German aristocrat Wolfgang von Trips in a 2.4-litre Ferrari Dino 246 SP in 1961 and in a similar car in 1962 in company with Willy Mairesse and baby-faced Ricardo Rodriguez.

Paul Frère shared Ferrari 250 GTs with Gendebien when he won the 12 Hours of Reims in 1957 and 1958 – the years he also won the Giro di Sicilia – but Olivier drove the Ferrari to victory on his own at Montlhéry to win the 1960 1000 Kilometres of Paris.

Gendebien's Formula 1 record is far more modest, not because he was no good in a single-seater Grand Prix car, but because only 15 such drives came his way. It was almost as if Enzo Ferrari held out F1 rides to Olivier like a carrot to a donkey, as a completely unnecessary encouragement to do well in sports cars. Whatever the reason, the Belgian rarely competed in Grands Prix. His first F1 outing was in one of Maranello's Lancia-Ferrari D50s, which he drove into a solid fifth place in the Grand Prix of Argentina. He did better in a Cooper-TR51 Climax in 1960, taking third before his home crowd at Spa-Francorchamps – he beat the Ferrari Dino 246s of fifth-placed Wolfgang von Trips and Richie Ginther in sixth, which must have been satisfying – and an outstanding second two weeks later in the Grand Prix of France at Reims, his old stomping ground.

After retirement from racing Gendebien spent the rest of his working life as a businessman and got his kicks from skiing, tennis and equestrian events, at all of which he did extraordinarily well.

In 1998, the year of his death, Olivier was awarded the Belgian Order of the Crown by his country's monarch, King Albert II.

# Ginther, Richie

'ALL.' THAT WAS THE single word on the pit signal Romolo Tavoni held out to Ferrari's tester and number three driver Richie Ginther as the American shot past the pits in works Ferrari Dino 156 number 36, during the closing stages of the 1961 Grand Prix of Monaco. First Wolfgang von Trips and then Phil Hill had tirelessly chased Stirling Moss, who was leading in his more agile Lotus 18 Climax, but they were wilting. 'All' simply meant it was Ginther's turn to pull out all the stops and do everything possible to win the race. And that set Richie off on just about the finest drive of his career.

Ginther had already got himself on the front row of the grid with a second-fastest qualifying time of 1min 39.3sec to pole-winner Moss' 1min 39.1sec. On race day Richie went straight into the lead and held it for 13 laps: he had even opened up a seven-second lead on Stirling by lap five. But Moss increased his pace, so that four laps later the Briton was right on Ginther's tail, and as lap 14 began he slipped past the Californian. On lap 24 Ferrari team leader Phil Hill passed Richie to hound Stirling and, showing great determination, the two Ferraris had whittled Moss' lead down to eight seconds: by lap 60 they were within three seconds of the English ace. The three-car duel mesmerised the crowd as the trio pulled away from the rest of the field, the Ferraris trying everything to nail Moss. At the three-quarter mark Ginther overtook team leader Hill to move into second place, hence Tavoni's pit signal. Richie started to pull away from Hill and set a new fastest lap time of 1min 36.3sec nine laps later, his speed and persistence reducing Stirling's lead to just over three seconds. No matter what Moss did, Ginther was always there, waiting for the moment to pounce – but it never came: instead, Moss restated his determination by equalling Ginther's fastest lap time. And that was it. Moss won and Ginther came second 3.6 seconds later.

Back in the Ferrari pits, Tavoni shook a dazed Richie by the hand and congratulated him on his outstanding drive. Franco Gozzi, Enzo Ferrari's lieutenant, embraced the exhausted American and said afterwards, 'He was shattered, all in. He really had given everything.' Later, Stirling Moss said of Ginther, 'He kept the pressure on, and I know because I was trying damned hard.'

In one of his less charming moments, Enzo Ferrari once referred to Richie as 'a little bag of bones,' because the American was short and painfully thin. But the Californian was big enough to duel successfully with the giants of his day in both Formula 1 and top-notch endurance racing. He came second to Jim Clark in the 1963 Formula 1 World Championship and his driving record includes 67 F1 starts, 52 of them in world title events, a win for Honda in Mexico, 9 second places, 16 top-three finishes and 14 front-row starts.

Freckle-faced Richie was born in Granada Hills, California, on 5 August 1930 and initially worked in the tool and die department of nearby Douglas Aircraft. In his spare time he helped future F1 World Champion Phil Hill maintain his collection of vintage road cars. He broke into motor racing driving an MG TC in the Pebble Beach Handicap and came third and, after national service in Korea, competed in 195 SCCA and other US races between 1953 and 1959, winning 27 of them. Richie hit the big time with his friend Phil Hill when they drove a 4.1-litre Ferrari 340 Mexico in the 1953 Carrera Panamericana, but they came to grief when the car shot over a cliff, although they escaped unhurt.

Richie first tried his hand at the European big time in the 1957 24 Hours of Le Mans, from which he retired the Equipo Los Amigos Ferrari 500TRC with mechanical trouble after 129 laps when lying 30th. Three years later he became a Ferrari test driver and was first asked to race for Maranello in the 1960 Grand Prix of Monaco, where he drove a Dino 246P into an impressive debut sixth place, and did so again in Holland.

There is not much the Italian *tifosi* like more than a Ferrari 1-2 at Monza, and the team's two Californians gave them just that after commandeering the grid, Phil Hill on pole, Richie Ginther next to him. The duo dominated the race, Ginther leading for 24 and Hill 26 of the race's 50 laps. After his outstanding second to Moss at Monaco in 1961, Ginther drove the legendary Dino 156 to fifth in Holland, third in Belgium and Britain to end up fifth in the World Championship, ahead of Jim Clark, Bruce McLaren, Tony Brooks and John Surtees.

Richie's three-year sojourn at BRM was even more successful and took him to second behind Jim Clark in the 1963 World Championship with three second places (Monaco again, Italy, Watkins Glen) and a couple of thirds (Germany and Mexico).

The American may not have had the killer instinct of a habitual winner, but he was incredibly skilful, reliable and consistent, and those are the qualities he took to Honda in 1965. After a year of trial and error, the team got to the Mexico City track three days before the GP to acclimatise its cars to a circuit 6000ft above sea level – and it paid off. When the flag fell on race day, Ginther leapt into the lead and stayed there for the full 65 laps, despite a persistent challenge from Dan Gurney's Brabham Climax. Richie controlled the race beautifully and won from Dan by 2.89 seconds. It was Honda's first Formula 1 World Championship victory.

F1 cars doubled their cubic capacity to 3-litres for 1966, but many of them – including the new Honda – were not ready, so Ginther drove a couple of races for Cooper-Maserati: nothing spectacular there, and the bulky 3-litre Honda turned out to be unprepossessing. A tyre on the car threw its tread during the Italian GP at Monza, catapulting the 12-cylinder RA273 into a clump of trees. A month later, though, Richie and the Honda were back in business at the USGP at Watkins Glen and were third on the opening lap, but gearbox trouble slowed the car and Ginther finished the race 27 laps down on winner Jim Clark. After that, Richie and the Honda came fourth in Mexico City, and he even set the race's fastest lap, on the 3.107-mile circuit, of 1min 53.75sec.

Ginther signed with his friend Dan Gurney's brand new Anglo-American Racers team for 1967, a commitment that included Indy. And it was there that Richie decided to pack it all in: he had had enough. He dabbled in Californian motor racing for a while and then dropped out of sight. He did attend a couple of motor racing events, one being in 1977 to witness Niki Lauda win Goodyear's 100th GP. The other was at Donington for BRM's 40th anniversary. Weak and ill, Richie still did a few laps before bringing the 1.5-litre BRM into the pits, exhausted. While holidaying near Bordeaux, France, Ginther suffered a heart attack and died on 20 September 1989. He was 59.

# González,
# José Froilán

NOW, HERE'S A GIANT killer. A man who beat the hell out of Mercedes-Benz at least twice and won Ferrari's first-ever World Championship Grand Prix by beating the most successful racing car of all time.

González only competed in 26 World Championship Grands Prix in his turbulent career, but winning that first Ferrari world title event meant he made a far greater impact on the sport than that handful of races would suggest.

Born in Arrecifes, Argentina, in October 1922, González was a tubby baby who grew up to be a tubby man with an XXL head. His countrymen called him *El Cabazon*, or 'Fat Head,' the British the more conservative 'Pampas Bull.' He was a flailing windmill of a driver, whose style was the complete opposite of his fellow countryman and friend Juan Manuel Fangio, the master of seemingly effortless speed and precision. Even so, José Froilán was one of the few drivers to beat the five-times World Champion.

'I confess I have never understood why this man tired himself out and worried so much,' Enzo Ferrari once said of González. 'But I must say, however, that he was a courageous, strong-willed yet generous driver.'

The son of a Chevrolet dealer, González was a talented sportsman whose skill at cycling and road racing belied his tubby appearance. By 1948 he was ready to delve into motor racing in Europe and toured the Continent with Fangio. He returned to Europe in 1950, when he raced a Maserati 48/CLT without causing much of a stir. But things changed in early 1951 when Mercedes-Benz, anxious to get back into racing, wanted to see how competitive its pre-war two-stage supercharged 163s still were; so they sent three of them to Argentina early in the year to compete in two Formule Libre races. They needn't have bothered, because González beat them in both the General Perón and Eva Perón Grands Prix in a Ferrari 166C. That gave him the key to the door of Maranello and he became one of the team's works drivers.

Up until then Ferrari had never won a World Championship Grand Prix. They came pretty close with Piero Taruffi driving a 375 into second place in the 1951 Grand Prix of Switzerland at Bremgarten, and Alberto Ascari and Gigi Villoresi taking second and third respectively in the Belgian GP at Spa-Francorchamps that same year. But *El Cabazon* was about to break the ice for the famous Scuderia. Ferrari had been mercilessly hounding Alfa Romeo, whose 158/159 had been winning consistently since 1938, without success. But one warm, sunny day at Silverstone – a contradiction in terms to many British people – González, in scintillating form, threw down the gauntlet by taking pole position with a remarkable time of 1min 43.4sec, a full second quicker than Alfa's Juan Manuel Fangio.

The Pampas Bull didn't make as good a use of his pole as he might have done. It was Felice Bonetto's factory Alfa Romeo 158 that burst through from the second row of the grid and shot into the lead, where he stayed for the first lap. González was second, all flailing arms and over the limit as he sent straw bales and marker barrels flying: but he drove the race of his life. Fangio was working away with economical precision further down the order and eventually overtook Farina, Ascari and *El Cabazon* to move into the lead on lap 10. José Froilán managed to stay with Fangio, by which time the two Argentines had pulled out 25 seconds on the rest of the field. On the 38th of the 90 laps the crowd roared their approval as underdog González overtook a hard-working Fangio to take over command of the race. But the Alfas, which were doing only a kilometre to every litre of fuel, stopped to tank up, and that enabled the Pampas Bull to increase his lead to 72 seconds. He stopped to refuel in turn and rejoined the fray in just 23 seconds, still almost a minute ahead of Juan Manuel. With such a huge lead, González eased off a little for the rest of the race, but still crossed the finish line with 51 seconds in hand to win Ferrari's first World Championship Grand Prix. The Scuderia fans were ecstatic, but that was nothing to virtually the whole of Argentina, where fans had lived every second of the race on the radio with not one but two of their countrymen battling it out for honours. The whole country went berserk as the Argentines celebrated the famous victory with rivers of booze.

González didn't win again that year, but took second places in the

French and Italian GPs and a third in Germany that rocketed him to third in the World Championship, one point behind second-placed Alberto Ascari and seven from Fangio, the new World Champion.

In 1952 González moved to the Maserati factory team in time for the Italian Grand Prix at Monza, where he led for 38 of its 80 laps but eventually came second, although he did set a fastest lap of 2min 6sec on the 3.91-mile circuit. He stayed with Maserati for 1953 and drove first an A6GCM then an A6SSG, but without scoring another win.

So it was back to Ferrari for 1954, and that yielded another victory, ironically at the scene of his former triumph at Silverstone in a 625 (555), a giant-killing win for which he led from start to finish, beat his teammate Mike Hawthorn into second place and trounced the (almost) all-conquering Mercedes-Benz W196s. A third at home in Argentina and another in Italy gave him second place in the World Championship, which was won yet again by his opponent and friend Juan Manuel Fangio. Being back at Ferrari also gave *El Cabazon* the chance to race sports cars, which he did masterfully with Maurice Trintignant when they won the 1954 24 Hours of Le Mans in a 375 Plus.

González was seriously injured when he crashed his Ferrari in the 1954 Tourist Trophy at Dundrod in September, and that more or less brought his motor racing career to an end. He did take pole and come second with Giuseppe Farina and Maurice Trintignant driving a Ferrari 625 (555) at home in the 1955 Grand Prix of Argentina, and guested in a Vanwall in the British GP at Silverstone, where his driveshaft broke on the start line. His last GP was his home event in a Ferrari Dino 246, where he came a disappointing tenth.

José often visited Maranello and enjoyed high jinks with his friend Franco Gozzi, Enzo Ferrari's self-confessed lieutenant. On one of his European trips he attended the 2011 British Grand Prix, at which he was honoured by Ferrari and FIA to mark the 60th anniversary of his winning Ferrari's first-ever Formula 1 World Championship Grand Prix. As a particular tribute to the Pampas Bull, for four laps before the race Fernando Alonso drove the very Ferrari 375 F1 in which González gave the Prancing Horse that first win. The cherry on the cake was Alonso winning the 2011 GPGB that day before the massive British crowd and an emotional José Froilán González.

# Goux, Jules

JULES GOUX WAS BORN in Valentigney, France, on 6 April 1885, and he died there on 6 March 1965. In between those two dates, he fitted in one hell of a racing career and had a hand in developing the Peugeot Straight-4 which, with its twin overhead camshafts and four valves per cylinder, is still the preferred layout for performance petrol engines today.

The young Jules was weaned on the French heroes who won the Gordon Bennett and city-to-city races, like Marcel Renault, Fernand Charron, Leonce Giradot and Leon Théry. He began racing himself when he was barely into his 20s, scoring his first big victory at 23 years old driving a brutishly ugly Lion-Peugeot in the 1908 Catalan Cup road race around Sitges, near Barcelona, forerunner of the Spanish Grand Prix. Then he went back with the same car in 1909 and won the race all over again, later adding the '09 Sicilian Cup race win to his tally.

All that success attracted the attention of company founder Robert Peugeot, who initially hired Goux as his chauffeur, then offered him the chance to join his company's engineering staff and racing team. There, Jules' teammate was glamour boy 'Gorgeous' Georges Boillot. Both Boillot and Goux had been sentenced to driving uncompetitive Fiats until that time. Soon after joining Peugeot, Jules worked with Paul Zuccarelli and Ernest Henry on the development of the famous Straight-4 engine, with its DOHC and four valves per cylinder. And he won the 1912 Sarthe Cup at Le Mans in a Peugeot L76 powered by an engine of the new layout, one of the first cars to adopt the new format.

Before leaving for the United States to try his luck in the Indianapolis 500, Jules tried out the speed of his Peugeot L76 at Britain's Brooklands, where he covered 160 miles and 307 yards in 60 minutes, further proof of the car's speed capability.

Then the big one. Goux became the first European-born racing driver and the first rookie to win the Indianapolis 500. The Peugeot L76 was fuelled by petrol and did about ten miles to the gallon, but Jules and his riding mechanic Emil Begin were fuelled by champagne and they did the 500 miles on six bottles of the stuff. They guzzled the bubbly during pit stops – although some minimised the story a bit by saying they only got through four bottles! Said Goux after the race, 'Without fine wine, I wouldn't have won.' There is no record of Peugeot or Goux being sponsored by a major champagne producer, but apparently they drank some of the bubbly, washed their mouths with the rest and then spat it out. Or so the story goes. Regardless, the result was a major feather in Peugeot's cap, as the company had set out to prove L76's speed capability and they did that all right. The car averaged 78.719mph, faster than the previous two winners. Jules finished over eight minutes ahead of second-placed Spencer Wishart in a Mercer and was giving an impromptu press conference as Wishart and Charlie Metz's Stutz were still fighting it out for second.

In fact, Goux did rather well out of Indy, where he competed five times between 1913 and 1922, because he finished in the top four for three years running, and married local Indianapolis girl Ruth Davis during his final year there.

Just before the outbreak of the First World War, Jules came fourth in the 1914 Grand Prix of France driving a Peugeot EX3, then – war.

Motor racing resumed after the horror of the trenches, but it took the Auto Club of France until three years after the conflict to revive its Grand Prix in 1921, although the ACF was in for a major culture shock: the Le Mans race was won by an American, Jimmy Murphy, in a Duesenberg. But Goux sort of salvaged some national honour by coming third in a Ballot 2LS. He did better than that a few weeks later. He won the first-ever Italian Grand Prix in a Ballot 3L on a road circuit at Montichiari near Brescia, with his teammate Jean Chassagne second. But the 'Mad Mullah,' as they called Pietro Bordino, put up the fastest lap before his Fiat 802's generator went, recording an average of 93.45mph, just under 4mph faster than the winner's average.

The next three years were rocky for Goux. He plugged away in Ballots in 1922, but crashed out of the French Grand Prix and didn't even show up for the Italian at the brand new Monza circuit. He switched to Rolland-Pilain for 1923, but didn't appear for the French GP either. The 1924 Grand Prix of Italy was a slightly different story, as Jules not only turned up but also persuaded his Rolland-Pilain Schmidt into fifth place, unlike to the results he had been used to.

Then he found Bugatti and things started to look up, even if it was with a fifth place in the 1925 French GP in a T35. But he knew the potential was there.

The 1926 Grand Prix of France was an oddball race indeed. The AIACR had dispensed with the old 3-litre formula and brought in the new 1500cc maximum, but most of the teams had struggled unsuccessfully to develop their new cars in time – all except Bugatti. The Talbots, SIMA-Violets and Delages entered for drivers of the calibre of Henry Segrave, Robert Benoist and Albert Divo didn't show up. So that left the Bugatti 39As of Meo Costantini, Pierre de Vizcaya and Jules to compete against each other in complete isolation, which didn't exactly endear the Association to some pretty disappointed spectators.

De Vizcaya dropped out with engine trouble after 45 laps, Costantini managed 85 laps but was not classified, so that left Jules Goux to save the day and complete the full 100 to win in 4hr 38min 43.8sec. It was a triumph for the Frenchman, but sheer boredom for the spectators watching a single car lap the Miramas circuit near Marseilles on its own for the last 15 'tours.'

At least Delage had got its act together for the Grand Prix of Europe at Lasarte near San Sebastian, Spain, and they did well. Jules Goux won the race over the 496-mile road circuit in 6hr 51min 52sec, but Edmond Bourlier and Robert Sénéchal came second in a Delage 155B, with Louis Wagner setting a fastest lap of 8min 53.5sec in another 155B.

After that Goux said goodbye to motor racing and worked at the Peugeot factory at Sochaux. He died in the town of his birth of a crab allergy, which had plagued him all his life, on 6 March 1965.

# Gregory, Masten

TAZIO NUVOLARI ALWAYS USED to say that if your car burst into flames, jump out and save yourself before it crashes – a similar philosophy to that of the bespectacled Masten Gregory, who often shocked fellow competitors and spectators alike by standing up and leaping from his troubled cars, once or twice when he was doing more than 100mph, according to Stirling Moss! A technique that still didn't save him from seven major accidents during his 20-year career.

But for all that, Gregory, nicknamed 'the Kansas City Flash,' still won the 1957 1000km Ciudad De Buenos Aires in a factory Ferrari 290 MM shared with Luigi Musso and Eugenio Castellotti, the ADAC Nürburgring 1000 Kilometres with Lucky Casner in an agile little Maserati Birdcage, plus the 1962 non-championship Formula 1 races at Karlskoga, Sweden, and Mosport Park, Canada, for Lotus. But his biggest win was in the 1965 24 Hours of Le Mans with Jochen Rindt in a NART-entered Ferrari 250 LM.

Gregory was born into a wealthy Kansas City family on 29 February 1932 and inherited a substantial amount of money 21 years later. He had already tasted the excitement of motor racing by the time he came into his fortune, and that windfall was his ticket to bigger and better things, starting with his first car – a Mercury-engined Allard in which he scored his first win at Stillwater, Oklahoma.

His approach to big-time European racing was rather unusual. If he was beaten in a race, he simply bought the winner's car. For instance, his Jaguar broke down in the 1954 1000 Kilometres of Buenos Aires, so he just upped and bought the winning Giuseppe Farina-Umberto Maglioli works Ferrari 375 MM, in which Nino had also set the day's fastest lap. The car was transported to Europe and the deep-voiced Missouri driver set about earning his spurs. His driving was, to say the least, rough around the edges early in his career – 'hairy' is how Stirling described it – but the great British Champion would be the first to agree that Masten eventually turned himself into a professional.

He even won the racing drivers' busman's holiday in the Bahamas, where races in the warmth of the island paradise at the end of the year attracted racing refugees from snowy, icy Europe for some non-stop racing, parties and good times. The Kansas City Flash won the 1954 210-mile Nassau Trophy outright in the Ferrari 375 MM.

Masten got his first taste of the 24 Hours of Le Mans during the fateful 1955, in which the privately entered Ferrari 750 Monza he was co-driving with Mike Sparken retired after 23 laps with engine trouble. At the end of lap 35 Pierre Levegh's works Mercedes-Benz 300 SLR crashed, sliced through the packed spectator area beneath the main stand and killed 83 people and injured another 120.

In 1957 Gregory crewed Temple Buell's Ferrari 290 MM with Eugenio Castellotti and Luigi Musso to win the 1000 Kilometres of Buenos Aires, a performance that caught the eye of the generous Mimmo Dei, president of Scuderia Centro Sud, a team that was created to give new talent a chance. The squad ran year-old Maserati 250Fs, in one of which Masten made a brilliant debut by coming third in the '57 Grand Prix of Monaco – the first American to take an F1 World Championship podium place – beaten only by Juan Manuel Fangio in a state-of-the-art 250F and Tony Brooks in a Vanwall VW7. Masten followed that up with a fourth at Pescara and another in the Grand Prix of Italy at Monza. Those three performances won him equal sixth place in the 1957 Formula 1 World Championship, which he shared with fellow American Harry Schell – a resounding start in big-time motor racing.

Injury helped keep Gregory out of the firing line in early 1958, but when he was fit again he did manage fourth in the Italian GP and sixth in the Moroccan, driving Temple Buell's less than competitive Maserati 250F.

As the bizarre kidnapping of Juan Manuel Fangio by Fidel Castro's guerrillas was taking place in Havana on 24 February 1958, 24 sports cars roared away in what was to be the 90-lap Cuban Grand Prix. Stirling Moss took the lead in a 4.1-litre Ferrari, with Masten second in a Ferrari 410S, but Stirling shrewdly let the American take the lead so that he would be the first to find any oil patches that might be lying around. Instead, the man who found an oil patch was local hopeful Garcia Cifuentes in a 2-litre Ferrari: the Cuban lost control of his car and ploughed into a mass of spectators at speed, killing six and injuring 30. As the marshals wildly waved their red flags, the approaching Gregory stood on his brakes and slowed right down. But Stirling knew that the regulations said the flag was invalid unless the clerk of the course himself waved it about; so he slipped his Ferrari into a lower gear and accelerated past the meandering Gregory to win the race and its mountain of prize money. Masten was furious at losing the lead to Moss' superior knowledge of the rulebook, but in characteristic fair-minded fashion Stirling offered to split his winnings with him in exchange for half of Masten's second-place prize money. That made the two even and placated the fuming American.

Masten's prospects brightened no end in 1959 when he joined Cooper, but then he had one of his 'jump out' accidents in a sports car race early in the season and injuries subdued his performance. He did lead the Grand Prix of Holland in a works Cooper T51-Climax for nine laps and eventually took a fine third place. He even got himself on the front row of the grid for the start of the Portuguese GP, in which he came second. But there was a lot of dissent in the Cooper camp as far as Gregory was concerned, and he was replaced for the remainder of the season by rising star Bruce McLaren. The points Masten had scored during his abbreviated season still took him to equal eighth in the F1 World Championship, which he shared with another American, Dan Gurney. Gregory's abrupt departure from Cooper before the end of the 1959 season clearly had a negative influence on other Formula 1 team bosses: he would never get another competitive F1 drive. He did manage to squeeze a Lotus 24-BRM into sixth place on home territory at the 1962 US Grand Prix at Watkins Glen, but that was the last time he scored F1 points.

Then came Gregory's finest hour. He had been taken on by Luigi Chinetti to crew a North American Racing Team 12-cylinder, 3286cc Ferrari 250 LM in the 1965 24 Hours of Le Mans with Austrian meteor Jochen Rindt. Their car came from nowhere to win the race by completing 347 laps of the Sarthe circuit at an average of over 121mph.

Gregory continued to compete in motor racing until his friend Joachim Bonnier was killed at Le Mans in 1972: after that, the American retired from the sport. Masten had always liked Europe, so he based his post-racing life in Amsterdam and became a successful diamond merchant. He particularly liked some areas of Italy and had an apartment in Porto Ercole, where he died in his sleep of a heart attack on 8 November 1985.

# Gurney, Dan

DAN GURNEY'S MOTOR RACING career as a driver, car constructor and team owner is just about as star-spangled as his country's flag. To begin with, he became one of the most successful Americans in Formula 1. He is also the first US driver to have won in NASCAR and Indy Car. And as a constructor, his Eagle-Toyotas won 17 *consecutive* IMSA GTP races, plus back-to-back drivers' and manufacturers' titles.

Dan was born in Port Jefferson on Long Island on 13 April 1931. His father John was a prominent singer with New York's Metropolitan Opera, who retired in 1947 and moved his family to Riverside, California, where Dan soon got into hot-rodding. He was only 19 when he built and ran a car that did 138mph at the Bonneville Salt Flats, but he soon graduated to dragsters and sports cars before serving in the US Army in Korea in the early 1950s.

Back in the States, in 1957 he was asked to test a fast 4.9-litre Ferrari that even top-liners like Carroll Shelby found it hard to tame. He drove it in the first Riverside Grand Prix and came second, which caught Luigi Chinetti's eye. Ferrari's North American importer set up a works drive for the 27-year-old in a Ferrari 250 TR at the 1958 24 Hours of Le Mans, partnered by Californian Bruce Kessler. Dan had worked the car up to fifth when he handed over to Kessler, who became involved in a fiery accident with it, and the Testa Rossa was retired. But that drive opened Maranello's door to the 6ft 3in young American, who was given a works test-drive that matured into Scuderia membership in 1959. That year he took second in the German GP at Avus and third in the GP of Portugal driving Dino 246s, and won the 12 Hours of Sebring with Chuck Daigh, Phil Hill and Olivier Gendebien in a factory Ferrari 250 TR. But the management style of Maranello was not for Gurney, who switched teams and drove an ill-prepared BRM P48 to six retirements in seven races in 1960.

With the change to the 1.5-litre F1 formula, Porsche beckoned in 1961, when Dan joined Jo Bonnier to campaign the Stuttgart firm's 718, which he worked up into second in the French GP at Reims. Gurney picked off another two second places in the Italian and US Grands Prix in the Porsche to give him a season's total of three podium places. Gurney won the 1962 Grand Prix of France at Rouen in the 8-cylinder 804 to give Porsche its only GP win. And a week later the normally impassive German crowd went berserk when Dan won the non-championship Solitude GP right on Porsche's doorstep in Stuttgart. But F1 turned out to be too expensive for Porsche, so the company didn't compete in GP racing in 1962, when Gurney became the first driver Jack Brabham ever hired. Dan gave the Brabham Racing Organisation its first World Championship win in a BT7-Climax in the 1964 French GP at Rouen, and won the year's Mexican GP, firmly putting the Ferraris of John Surtees and Lorenzo Bandini in second and third places. There was no victory for Gurney in 1965, but he did score five consecutive podium places in the Brabham BT11-Climax. Throughout his Brabham period, Dan was one of the few who could rival the great stars of the day, Jim Clark's and Colin Chapman's Lotuses.

Gurney and Carroll Shelby had long wanted to build American racing cars that would give the European constructors a run for their money, so in 1965, with the aid of Goodyear, All-American Racers was set up with its headquarters in Santa Ana, California. The company first focused on the Indianapolis 500, but Gurney wanted to win the Formula 1 World Championship. So, with the new 3-litre regulations just around the corner, he formed an alliance with Westlake, a British engine builder, and called that operation Anglo American Racers. The Westlake power unit was not ready for the 1966 season, so Dan used an obsolete 2.7-litre Coventry Climax engine, but that produced poor results.

The Eagle AAR 104-Westlake was quite another story. The car blew everyone's mind when it won the non-championship 1967 Race of Champions at Britain's Brands Hatch circuit; but then it failed to finish its first three 1967 Grands Prix at Kyalami, Monte Carlo and Zandvoort. However, change was on the way.

Meanwhile, two rivals came together. Dan Gurney was entered for the 1967 24 Hours of Le Mans on 10–11 June with his big on-track rival AJ Foyt, a pairing that some critics said would never work because they would break their Ford GT40 Mk4 in an effort to outdo each other. But the two won the race, roundly beating the works Ferraris. And Dan Gurney established a tradition that has lasted to this day: he sprayed his adoring public with the victors' champagne!

Just one week later, on 18 June 1967, the Eagle AAR 104-Westlake came good when Dan won the Belgian GP at Spa-Francorchamps in the car he built.

But all was not well at Anglo American Racers. On the practical front, the Westlake engine was giving problems, and a universal joint broke when Dan was leading the 1967 Grand Prix of Germany by 42 seconds. The best he could do the rest of the season was third in the Canadian GP at Mosport Park. The team was severely underfinanced, so he had to continue with the Eagle AAR 104-Westlake in 1968, although with little to show for it.

With personal problems calling for his attention, as well as the stress of running both Formula 1 and Indycar programmes, Gurney wound up the Eagle operation and went to drive for McLaren. But the deaths of Jim Clark late in 1968 and of Bruce McLaren in 1970 dimmed Dan's enthusiasm for the sport. His last F1 race was the 1970 British GP for McLaren, from which he retired. He returned to the USA.

In 1962–70 Gurney competed in the Indianapolis 500 nine times. He came second driving an Eagle 68-Ford/Westlake in 1968, did the same again a year later in his Eagle 69 and came third in his Eagle 70-Offenhauser in 1970. He raced USAC Champ Car too, in which he won seven times, and Cam-Am, where he won the second-ever race at Bridgehampton in a Lola T70-Ford and the first two 1970 races at Mosport Park and St Jovite driving McLaren M8D-Chevrolets.

NASCAR also attracted Gurney, who competed in the closed wheel series for the first time in 1962 and from his 16 starts scored five wins. He also made a number of appearances in NASCAR Grand American, a pony car division run from 1968 to 1971.

When Gurney returned from Europe in 1970 he became chairman, CEO and sole owner of All-American Racers, a team that has won 78 times including the Indianapolis 500, 24 Hours of Daytona and the 12 Hours of Sebring plus eight championships. His clients won three Indy 500s and three titles.

Gurney went on to great success with Toyota in the IMSA GTP series, in which the Eagle MkIII Toyotas won an incredible 17 successive races in 1992–93 including the 24 Hours of Daytona and the 12 Hours of Sebring in both years.

After withdrawing from CART in 1986 the team returned as the Toyota works operation, but exited again at the end of the 1999 season, when Goodyear dropped out and the AAR-Toyota relationship came to an end.

# Häkkinen, Mika

DAD WAS A PART-TIME taxi driver and mum was a secretary, and five-year-old Mika plagued the life out of them to let him race a kart. They hired one for him, but he crashed it on the first lap of his first race, so kart racing was a no-no in the Häkkinen family for a while. But Mika kept chipping away at his parents until dad eventually bought him a second-hand kart.

And that started Mika Häkkinen's incredible race to the top. By the time he was 17 he had won five Scandinavian kart championships. That made 1982 F1 World Champion Keke Rosberg take notice. He negotiated a sponsorship deal that took the youngster from Vantaa, Finland, into open-wheel racing, and the lad won three Scandinavian series before progressing to the 1988 European GM-Lotus Championship: he won that too. The next step was F3, and Mika won the 1990 British Formula 3 Championship in a Ralt-Mugen Honda, but the year's Macau Grand Prix just slipped from his grasp in a dramatic last lap accident involving Michael Schumacher. It was the first of many more Schumacher-Häkkinen encounters to come.

By 1991, few were surprised when Mika marched straight into Formula 1. He joined Lotus, which was running John Judd's engines. The young Finn even managed to coax the 102B into fifth place in only his third F1 race, the Grand Prix of San Marino, having clawed his way up from 25th on the grid. Häkkinen stayed with Lotus, now armed with Ford engines, and was joined by new teammate Johnny Herbert. They did well, too, with Mika doing most of the points-scoring, which meant that the once glorious Lotus-Ford at least managed fifth place in the 1992 Constructors' Championship.

McLaren caused quite a stir when they signed Mario's son Michael Andretti for the 1993 F1 season. But Andretti Jr struggled and eventually handed his ride back after a year's best of third at Monza. His replacement in the McLaren MP4/8-Ford was the team's test driver, Mika Häkkinen, who in his first GP at Estoril out-qualified the great Ayrton Senna to start from third place, with Ayrton next to him in fourth. But Mika tried too hard, ran wide and crashed, but still ended his year with a mighty bang by coming third in the Japanese GP, won by his teammate Senna.

Ayrton then left for Williams, which meant Mika became the team's number one driver in 1994, backed by new acquisition Martin Brundle. McLaren had switched to Peugeot engines, but these turned out to be underpowered and unreliable, although Häkkinen still managed six podium places that included a fine second at Spa. McLaren soon divested itself of the Peugeots and began a long-standing relationship with Mercedes-Benz; its engines powered Mika to second places at Monza and Suzuka and a total of nine podium spots.

The Finn was practising for the 1995 Grand Prix of Australia when a tyre blew on his McLaren MP4/10B-Mercedes; he crashed hard into a wall and was almost killed. His life was saved by an emergency tracheotomy performed out on the circuit.

But he was quick to recover, and in 1997 went off in search of that elusive first Grand Prix win. He nearly made it a couple of times, only to see victory slip from his grasp as old rival Michael Schumacher and Damon Hill cleaned up. Then came the Grand Prix of Europe at Jerez, the last GP of the season, which Mika won ahead of second-placed teammate David Coulthard. After that there was no stopping him.

McLaren had recruited design genius Adrian Newey, and from that first coming together emerged the MP4/13-Mercedes-Benz, which Mika loved. To prove it, he won the first race of the season in Australia, and repeated that brilliant performance at the next GP in Brazil. Schumacher won the next round in Hungary, Hill the Belgian, and Schumacher again in Italy; then Häkkinen broke back to take the win at the Nürburgring and topped that off with another victory in the season's last race in Japan. The Finn ended up the 1998 Formula 1 World Champion with 100 points, compared to his second-placed arch-rival Schumacher's 86.

The following year was not an easy one for Mika or McLaren. The cars were surprisingly unreliable, but the Finn kept at it until the season looked like a head-to-head battle with Schumacher and his Ferrari F399. Häkkinen won the second round in Brazil, Michael the third at Imola and the fourth at Monaco, then Mika took Spain and Canada before Schumacher crashed at Silverstone and broke his leg. That resulted in two moves: Ferrari pushed number two driver Eddie Irvine to win the title; and they hired Mika Salo for the rest of the season to back the Irishman.

Eddie won the next race in Austria and Salo earned his wages by leading the German GP and then handing over a certain win to Irvine to boost his championship hopes. Häkkinen won in Hungary in mid-August and came second to Coulthard at Spa. But then McLaren's ever-cool Finn made a mistake at Monza, spun, and that put him out of the race. He got out of his car and just lost it, bursting into tears and hiding from the TV cameras.

A fifth at the 'Ring and a third in Malaysia put Mika right back in contention. Meanwhile, Schumacher limped back into F1 and gave Irvine a helping hand towards winning the title. That made for a fraught Grand Prix of Malaysia, for which Michael took pole and the lead, although he slowed twice so that Irvine could overtake him. It didn't help, because both Ferraris were eventually disqualified due to a technical infringement. So the championship was Häkkinen's by default. But Mika was not having that. The last race of the season was the Japanese GP, and he won it, unwilling to allow some technical discrepancy to earn him his second successive title.

Even so, the Häkkinen-Schumacher battle showed no sign of winding down. The two were at it again in 2000. Mika wanted his third world title on the trot and Michael was anxious to bring the championship back to Maranello. Schumacher reeled off victories in Australia, Brazil and Imola, but Mika won in Spain, Austria, Hungary and Belgium. But the title eventually went to Michael, who said his championship battle with Häkkinen was the most satisfying of his career to date.

The Finn was still in fighting form in 2001, although it seemed he was not quite as sharp as during his championship-winning years. He nevertheless drove brilliantly to win the British and United States Grands Prix in the McLaren MP4/16-Mercedes-Benz.

Mika retired from racing at the end of the 2001 season, but in 2004 toyed with the idea of making an F1 comeback. It all came to nothing, but he did sign with Mercedes-Benz to compete for the Deutsche Tourenwagen Masters in 2005, and he did well, winning at Spa. That deal continued in 2006, but victory eluded him.

There was talk of Häkkinen returning to F1 with McLaren in 2007, but that, too, came to nothing. The vacant spot in the British team went to Lewis Hamilton, who became the 2008 Formula 1 World Champion.

So ended a distinguished career in which Mika won two consecutive F1 titles, 20 Grands Prix in the process, took 26 pole positions, climbed on to the podium 51 times and put in 25 fastest laps.

# Hawthorn, Mike

JOHN MICHAEL HAWTHORN WAS a Yorkshire lad of 24 with hardly any top-level motor racing experience when he drove the race of his life and beat the 1950, 1951 and 1952 Formula 1 World Champions, Giuseppe Farina, Juan Manuel Fangio and Alberto Ascari, at the 1953 Grand Prix of France.

Just 11 months earlier, Mike, his father Leslie and their mechanic Hughie Sewell were in Holland for the Dutch GP and were staying at the same hotel as Ferrari's chief designer, Aurelio Lampredi, and team manager Nello Ugolini. They all had a few drinks together, but Mike had to race his Cooper T20-Bristol at Zandvoort the next day, so he went to bed early and left the others to drink on well into the night. During that rather alcoholic tête-à-tête the two Italians said Mike had impressed them, and they would have a word with Enzo Ferrari when they got back to Maranello. By this time Hawthorn had already come third in the British Grand Prix and fourth in the Belgian driving the Cooper-Bristol. Sure enough, after the Italian GP at Monza three weeks later he was invited to the Modena Aerautodromo to sample a Ferrari 500 F2, which, not to put too fine a point on it, he liked a lot.

Enzo Ferrari asked Hawthorn to sign for the team there and then, but the Briton said he wanted a couple of weeks to think about it. In reality, he was hoping for a competitive British ride, but that never materialised. Two weeks on, a letter from the Commendatore – signed in that violet ink of his – invited Hawthorn to become a Ferrari works driver for 1953. And so this startlingly blond young man, who always raced in a polka dot bow tie and a zip-front blouson, joined a team of giants: Ascari, Farina and Gigi Villoresi. Daunting company.

Hawthorn did well from the word go. He took fourths for Ferrari in Argentina and Holland and a sixth in Belgium, all races won by Alberto

Ascari. Then came the Grand Prix of France, and that was when the Englishman shook the world.

3 July 1953 was a hot day at Reims, with temperatures nudging 100°F. All four Maranello drivers were there with Ferrari 500 F2s, and they were mainly up against the Maserati A6SSGs of Fangio, José Froilán González, Felice Bonetto, Tullo de Graffenried and Onofre Marimon. The rest of the field was made up of an assortment of HWMs, Connaughts, Cooper-Bristols, Gordinis and OSCAs.

From the moment the race started, positions changed at a fast and furious rate, González in the lead on half tanks. At one stage spectators could only gape in disbelief as they watched the Ferraris screaming down the Muizon-Thillois straight three abreast at 160mph! Maranello's cars were so evenly matched that its drivers could only overtake by the stealthy use of slipstreaming. Hawthorn, Ascari, Villoresi, Farina and Fangio's Maserati were all bunched together, each looking for a gap and an extra squirt of speed as they stamped on their accelerators coming out of Thillois.

González led for the first 29 laps, after which he had to pit for more fuel. That left Fangio at the head of the pack with young Mike glued to his tail. The two started to pull away from the rest as the 42-year-old Argentine tried to outfox the blindingly fast young Briton. They drove like men possessed – occasionally grinning at each other as they relished the moment. Fangio led for 17 of the remaining laps to Hawthorn's 14.

The first time he overtook Juan Manuel the Englishman couldn't believe it. He thought his teammates were allowing him to keep Fangio busy, waiting for their moment to pounce – but pounce they did not. Fangio dropped back a few hundred yards as if he had missed a gear, but as Mike came out of a fast right-hander Jean Behra's slower Gordini baulked him. Fangio was soon sitting on the Briton's tail again. To squeeze the last morsel of power from Lampredi's engine, Hawthorn took it over the permitted 7000 rpm to 7600!

Fangio and Hawthorn roared down the straight side-by-side, grinning like schoolboys. Then Juan Manuel braked harder at Thillois than Mike expected and the Ferrari dinged the Maserati's rear end. As their blaring battle bellowed on, Fangio closed the door rather sharply while Mike was trying to nose his way through on the right. Then, as the two were just inches apart at 160mph on the straight, they came up to a slower car.

Mike pulled over on to the grass so that they could pass the back marker, fortunately managed to keep going without lurid grassy skids and slithers, then back they went, wheel-to-wheel again!

Hawthorn quickly decided on his strategy. Initially he thought of coming out of Thillois first with Fangio slipstreaming him, but the 1951 World Champion would simply find a little more speed and beat him to the finish line; and he decided that Fangio was far too sharp a cookie to let Mike slipstream him and then catapult past the Maserati at the critical moment. Hawthorn's only hope was to plunge into Thillois first, fast enough to keep Fangio out of his slipstream, and then open his throttle as wide as it could possibly go.

They went into the last lap and charged down the RN31 like mad things. Then Mike realised Fangio had not dropped into first for Thillois. He knew everything would depend on the perfect timing of his last change into first gear for that last corner. They braked, still inches apart; Hawthorn snicked the Ferrari into first, cut around the apex as closely as he could and straightened his wheels as he stomped on his accelerator. The engine shrieked at well over peak revs, the tyres bit, Mike edged into the lead and won from Fangio by one second.

After the race, one journalist wrote: 'The crowd was yelling, the commentators were screaming. Nobody paid much attention to the rest of the drivers and even they slowed to watch this staggering display.'

Hawthorn continued the season with reasonable placings in the remaining Grands Prix, including third in Germany, to finish his first F1 season fourth in the championship, which was won by his teammate Ascari. It was more of the same in the 1954 season until the Grand Prix of Spain, the last of the year, which turned into another high-speed scrap between Mike and Fangio. Juan Manuel was preparing to move into the lead when his Maserati 250F started to lose oil and speed. Hawthorn's teammate Luigi Musso slipped into the second spot and began to nibble away at Mike's lead, but the Briton kept it all the way to the end and won.

Mike, who only won those three World Championship Grands Prix during his entire career, became the first Briton to win the title. He also won the utterly tragic 1955 24 Hours of Le Mans, as well as the 1953 24 Hours of Spa, the 1954 Tourist and the 1955 12 Hours of Sebring, plus non-title races at Crystal Palace, Goodwood, Silverstone and Pescara.

But nothing quite matched that amazing battle with Fangio at Reims on 3 July 1953.

Just months after winning the world title Mike was involved in a road accident on the A3 Guildford Bypass in his much modified 3.4-litre Jaguar MkI, and was killed. He was just 29 years old.

# Herrmann, Hans

IT WAS 11 IN the morning. A 25-year-old German pastry cook was sleeping after a hard night's baking. Until the phone squealed. He decided to ignore it, turn over and go back to sleep. But it was no good; the phone just rang and rang. So he answered it. At the other end, the gruff voice of Alfred Neubauer invited him to a Mercedes-Benz test session at the Nürburgring. The baker was completely awake after that.

He didn't know it then, but he was on his way to the big time. To winning the Grand Prix of Austria, the 12 Hours of Sebring, the Targa Florio, the Daytona 24 Hours, the 24 Hours of Le Mans.

Stuttgart-born Hans Herrmann had enjoyed a fairly meteoric, if varied, rise to warrant Neubauer's call that day in 1953. He had started out in motor sport two years earlier driving a 1.3-litre Porsche part-funded by his mother, and won his class with it in the Deutschland Rally. After that he graduated to a 1.5-litre Porsche and the Nürburgring, where he won the 1952 Rheinland event against several of Germany's established stars. A fifth in the 1953 Lyon–Charbonnières Rally led him to the 1954 Mille Miglia, where he really made his mark by coming and incredible sixth overall and winning the 1500cc class in a Porsche 550 Spyder, but not before a hair-raising brush with death. The gates of a level crossing were lowered seconds before an express train to Rome was due to thunder by. Hans saw the train coming fast as he also bore down on the crossing, its single-pole barrier already down, forbidding cars to cross the railway line. Herrmann decided it was too late to brake, so he quickly tapped co-driver Herbert Linge's helmet, both ducked and they j-u-u-u-st managed to squeeze under the barrier *and* miss the Rome express before they flashed across the line to Brescia and success.

Then Neubauer's phone call. The *Rennleiter* had invited Paul Frère,

Hans Klenk, Fritz Riess and Günther Bechem to the test session as well as Herrmann. The prize was a place in the 1954 Mercedes-Benz Formula 1 team as fourth driver and teammate to 1951 F1 World Champion Juan Manuel Fangio, wunderkind Stirling Moss and German stalwart Karl Kling.

The invitees each had a Mercedes-Benz 300 SL with which to make their play, although they were told that no times would be taken on the first day. That didn't stop Neubauer secretly timing each man, only to find Belgian Frère was the fastest. But on the second day it was Herrmann who put in the fastest lap, and he repeated that spectacular performance on day three. So just 30 months after his first-ever motor race, Hans was chosen to drive with the gods, Fangio, Moss and Kling – in M-B's post-war return to Formula 1, no less.

That relationship lasted the best part of two years rather than two full seasons, as the open-wheel and streamliner W196s were late arriving. When they did, they made everything else look prehistoric. With special Mercedes dispensation, Fangio drove for Maserati during the first part of the season and won the Argentine and Belgian GPs in a works 250F, which counted towards his 1954 Formula 1 World Championship, which he followed up by winning the 1955 title too. But it was a dream that came to an end late in 1955, when M-B retired from motor racing after one of its 300 SLRs, driven by Pierre Levegh, collided with another car during the 1955 24 Hours of Le Mans, flew off the Sarthe circuit and into the crowd, killing over 80 spectators. Hans went from Neubauer protégé and potential F1 World Champion to occasional outings for Cooper, Maserati and BRM, in which he had a serious accident. His BRM P25 lost its brakes at Berlin's Avus circuit during the German Grand Prix. The car flipped and rolled violently, disintegrating as it went, and threw Herrmann out as it continued its crazed rampage. That put Hans out of racing for many months.

When he returned he started working with Porsche, who were trying to get its 718 right. He won the 1960 12 Hours of Sebring with Olivier Gendebien in the 160hp 718 RS 60, and the Targa Florio in a similar car co-driven by Jo Bonnier. The following year the car was turned into an F1 challenger, but it could not do much challenging, so Herrmann's return to F1 after his Mercedes-Cooper-Maserati-BRM escapades was less than sparkling.

He moved on to what he thought were greener pastures in 1962 when he joined Abarth, but its involvement in racing was small beer compared to what he was used to. Minor races and hillclimbs in the middle of nowhere. But he put up with it until 1965, and learned a lot about development testing.

Abarth was not for him, though, so it was back to Porsche and a return to the World Sports Car Championship, trying to bring the 906, 907 and 908 models up to scratch. And he did well, winning the 1966 Grand Prix of Austria for sports cars at Zeltweg in a 906 co-driven by Gerhard Mitter and scoring podium places in the rather gutless 2-litre 906. Then the Porsche 907 came good, in which Herrmann won the 1968 24 Hours of Daytona with Vic Elford, Jochen Neerpasch, Rolf Stommelen and Jo Siffert. He and Siffert went on to dominate that year's 12 Hours of Sebring, where Hans also took pole position, taking the Stuttgart firm to third in the World Sports Car Championship.

The one that got away was the 1000 Kilometres of the Nürburgring. Herrmann never won it, although he had competed in it each year since 1953. But he did come second three years in succession – which must be some kind of record – with Rolf Stommelen in 1968 in a Porsche 908 and in 1969 in a 908/2.

The 1970 season looked promising from mid-April, when Hans and Dickie Attwood took their Porsche 917K to third in the BOAC 1000 Kilometres, a round in the International Championship of Makes. Then they came second in the ADAC 1000 Kilometres of the Nürburgring driving a 903/8, all limbering up for the big one. Herrmann and Attwood gave Porsche its first-ever win in the 24 Hours of Le Mans in the fabled 917K, which was actually entered by Porsche of Salzburg and backed by the Porsche founder's family. And Porsche won the title once called the World Sports Car Championship.

And that was it. Tongue in cheek, Herrmann had promised his wife he would retire from motor racing if he won at the Sarthe in 1970, but now he was as good as his word and hung up his helmet. Sort of. He continued to demonstrate the sports racecars of his past at special commemorative events for many years after setting up a highly successful car accessory firm in his home town of Maichingen, Germany. The only two trophies he keeps in his office are the ones for winning the 24 Hours of Daytona and the 24 Hours of Lea Mans. The rest are in the cellar of his home a few hundred metres up the road.

# Hill, Damon

DAMON GRAHAM DEVEREUX HILL is the only son of a Formula 1 World Champion to have also won the title. His father Graham won the 1962 and 1968 championships and Damon the 1996.

But never has a World Champion's biography been more aptly entitled than Damon's *From Zero to Hero*. After Graham's death in a 1975 flying accident, the Hill family were left in a difficult financial situation, so when Damon started work it wasn't amid the glamour of the motor racing business but as a builder's labourer and, later, a motorcycle courier, to pay his way through school.

Born in 1960, the young Hill first competed on motorbikes and showed promise, but his mother Bette was worried about him racing on two wheels so she convinced Damon to take a racing car course in 1983, when the future World Champion showed 'above average aptitude,' according to his tutors. He didn't compete much in 1984 but set out along the time-honoured beginners' route of the British Formula Ford Championship in 1985, when he won no fewer than six races in a Manadient Racing Van Diemen.

After an on-off disappointment with West Surrey Racing in the 1986 British Formula 3 Championship, Hill decided to go it alone and finance his own motor sport. He borrowed £100,000 and eventually got a ride with Murray Taylor Racing, for which he put in a solid series of performances. He won once in both 1987 and 1988 for Intersport, to finish third in the championship. Various stabs at Formula 3000 followed, with victories in 1989 for Footwork in a Mooncraft-Mugen Honda, Middlebridge Racing in its Lola T90/50-Ford Cosworth in 1990, and Jordan in its Lola T91/50-Ford Cosworth in 1991; and in 1989 Damon had his first go at the 24 Hours of Le Mans in a Richard Lloyd Racing Porsche 935 3.0L Turbo Flat 6, which dropped out with engine trouble after 228 laps.

In 1991 Hill became Frank Williams' test driver while still plugging away at F3000. Then came his first real F1 chance with precariously financed Brabham, which had seen much better days. Italy's Giovanna Amati's sponsorship dried up, so three races into the 1992 F1 championship Damon took over her seat and, unlike the Italian, was able to qualify the Brabham for the British GP. It must have rankled when a Williams, for whom Hill continued as test driver, won the race driven by Nigel Mansell, while Damon came in last in the Brabham BT60-Judd. He also qualified the car for the GP of Hungary, in which he finished 11th. After that the Brabham team imploded.

Damon's big break came when reigning World Champion Nigel Mansell set sail for the USA to compete in the country's CART Championship, which he won at his first attempt, and Riccardo Patrese left for Benetton. Frank Williams suddenly promoted Damon to the number two car, with Alain Prost – back from his F1 sabbatical – as the team's number one. And that is when Hill first clashed with Michael Schumacher, then a Benetton driver.

After years of financial deprivation, scratching around for sponsorship and doing his best to make threadbare teams work, 33-year-old Damon became a Grand Prix winner. He didn't just win one GP, but three of them in succession – the Hungarian, Belgian and Italian – between 15 August and 12 September, to make a major contribution to Williams-Renault winning the world constructors' title. And those first remarkable victories helped take him to third in the championship table behind winner Prost, no less, and runner-up Senna.

Prost retired from driving at the end of 1993 and Ayrton Senna was brought in as the Williams-Renault team leader, with Damon in the second car once more. But tragedy struck on 1 May 1994 when the Brazilian crashed and died at Imola in the Grand Prix of San Marino; and that dumped Hill firmly into the hot seat as Williams-Renault's number one. Schumacher won the first four races of the season – including the San Marino – but Hill took the Spanish Grand Prix, then the British, which his father Graham never did. Michael tried to overtake Hill in the race's parade lap and ignored the black flag, for which he was excluded from the results; the German was also handed a two-race ban, just when he was leading the World Championship. Damon won the Belgian, Italian and Portuguese GPs on the trot.

Then came the Australian. By this time Michael had accused Damon of not being a world-class driver, and that brought their rivalry to the boil in Adelaide. Schumi ran off the track and hit a wall with the right side of his car while leading, but kept going; Hill came up to pass the Benetton and the two cars 'collided,' forcing both drivers to retire. After that, the man the German said was not a world-class driver won the Japanese GP. But Michael won the world title with 92 points to Hill's 91. Amid all that turmoil, Williams-Renault still became the World Champion constructors again, thanks mainly to Damon. Years later, Hill explicitly accused the German of deliberately causing the Adelaide 'accident.'

The 1995 season was a carve-up, with Schumacher accusing Hill of 'brake testing' him in the pack at the French GP, the two crashing into each other at the British, Belgian and Italian Grands Prix. Even Bernie Ecclestone had to weigh in with a firm bollocking for the pair of them. It was the brawl of a season, with Michael winning the championship for a second time in his Benetton B195-Renault with victories in Brazil, France, at Hockenheim, in Belgium, at the Nürburgring, in the Pacific at Aida and Japan, while Hill was runner-up again with wins in the Argentine, San Marino, Hungarian and Australian Grands Prix.

The 1996 season was dynamite for Hill, who won eight GPs that year and the World Championship, 28 years after his father's world title. Damon never qualified off the front row of the grid, and also set four fastest laps. Yet amazingly, the World Champion was dropped from the Williams line-up for 1997. Hill had offers from McLaren and Ferrari, but their money was not up to the reigning World Champion's expectations, so he joined Arrows for what turned out to be an almost embarrassingly disappointing season: Hill came 12th in the title table driving the A18-Yamaha. He left Jackie Oliver and moved to Jordan for 1998, when his number two was Ralf Schumacher, Michael's younger brother. Predictably, sparks flew again, with Ralf accusing Damon of dangerous driving at the Canadian Grand Prix and Hill saying the young Schumacher purposely took Heinz-Harald Frentzen's Williams out of the race. With all that tension eating away at the pair of them, Damon was still able to win a wet Belgian Grand Prix, a rare victory for underdog Jordan.

Damon only managed seven points in the championship driving the Jordan 199-Mugen in 1999, at the end of which he retired. He had won the

1996 Formula 1 World Championship, of course, plus 22 Grands Prix, took 42 podium places, 20 pole positions and set 19 fastest laps.

As well as various business interests, Hill succeeded Sir Jackie Stewart as president of the British Racing Drivers' Club, owners of Silverstone. He makes occasional appearances at prestige events like the Goodwood Festival of Speed and the BRM 50th anniversary bash, and is a fine guitarist. He formed his own band, The Conrods, with which he played from 1999 until 2003.

# Hill, Graham

SOME SAID GRAHAM HILL wasn't a natural: he had to work hard at his motor racing. Many would say, so what? Few work so well at anything that they equal Hill's outstanding record of winning the 1962 and 1968 Formula 1 World Championships, 14 Championship Grands Prix, the 1966 Indianapolis 500 and the 1974 24 Hours of Le Mans.

Graham was a true Brit, as English as they come. He was so British that, when he asked Enzo Ferrari if there would ever be a place for him at Maranello, the Commendatore said, 'No, you're too English.'

Graham's dry humour, broad grin and carefully trimmed Cark Gable moustache captivated legions of fans. And his victories made him a people's hero, a status earned by his opportunism, determination and sheer hard work. He was also a natural communicator, as cool on television as he was giving one of his hilarious after-dinner speeches.

Londoner Graham Hill, a straight talker with a delightful if sometimes barbed sense of humour, couldn't even drive a car in 1952, when he completed his National Service at the age of 23. So he bought a 1934 Morris Eight and taught himself to drive. He joined the London Rowing Club as an oarsman and helped its first eight to win the 1953 Grand Challenge at Henley. His relationship with the club was one that would last his entire life: his helmet was always in the club's Oxford blue, with eight white oar-like vertical stripes, a tradition perpetuated by his son Damon years later.

In 1953 Graham spotted a magazine advertisement offering a drive in a 500cc Formula 3 racing car at Brands Hatch for five shillings a lap; he enjoyed the experience so much that he gave up his apprenticeship with Smiths Industries to devote all his time to breaking into motor racing. He would later say, with a twinkle in his eye, that he liked sports you could sit down at best.

His first race was in a Cooper-JAP at Brands Hatch in 1964, when he came second in his heat and fourth in the final. He was hooked on motor racing after that and started using his ability as a mechanic and his persuasive tongue to get himself drives. Graham's big chance arrived in August '54, when he talked his way into the fledgling Team Lotus for the day. But after helping Colin Chapman and Mike Costin at Brands Hatch, he didn't even have the price of the fare back to London, so he hitched a ride with the team. During the trip back, Hill persuaded the young Chapman to take him on as a mechanic. The deal was £1 for each day he worked.

Meanwhile, Graham beavered away at landing drives for himself, and then moved to the London tuner Speedwell Conversions, still turning in increasingly impressive performances in other people's cars. His big break came when Chapman asked him to drive a factory Lotus 16-Climax in the 1958 Monaco Grand Prix. Hill worked the car up to fourth before retiring with mechanical ills.

After a string of also-ran efforts with the emergent Lotus, in 1960 Graham joined hard-up BRM, which was being kept afloat by cash injections from the Owen Organisation. His placings became progressively better over the next two seasons, but Sir Alfred Owen had become exasperated with the team and said if BRM didn't win at least two Grands Prix in 1962 he would pull the plug. Not only did Graham win his first Grand Prix at Zandvoort, Holland, in a BRM P57, he also won the year's German, Italian and South African GPs and the Formula 1 World Championship.

The Grands Prix of Monaco and the USA at Watkins Glen turned out to be Hill's forte. He won five times in Monte Carlo in 1963/4/5/8/9 and pulled off another hat trick at the Glen in 1963–65.

To some, Hill was a finicky driver who seemed to mess about with his car for the sake of it. But those who worked with him knew better: he was a genius at setting up the car. And he was an unrelenting worker at the wheel, as his 1965 win at Monaco confirmed. He and his BRM P261 were well in the lead by lap 24 until he was wrong-footed by the faltering Brabham of Bob Anderson and was forced to take the escape road. Hill got back into the race in fifth, 32 seconds down on his new teammate Jackie Stewart. Many would have found the task too daunting, but the determined Graham got down to business and climbed back up the field to win, passing John Surtees in the Ferrari 158, Stewart's BRM, Jack Brabham and his BT7-

Climax and Lorenzo Bandini driving another 158 along the way. That was the talented, hard-grafting Graham Hill at his best.

In many ways, Hill's victory in the 1966 Indianapolis 500 was a controversial one. For instance, AJ Foyt blamed the Briton for the 11-car pile-up that erupted during the first lap, meaning the race had to be restarted. Some say a timekeeper's error favoured Hill in the Lola T90-Ford at the expense of Jim Clark in a Lotus 38-Ford. The fact remains that Graham came up from behind to win at the Brickyard on 30 May 1966, to become one of only a handful of winners of both the Formula 1 World Championship and the Indy 500.

Hill won his second World Championship in 1968 – the year his friend and teammate Jim Clark was killed at Hockenheim – with victories in the Lotus 48-Ford in Spain, Monaco and Mexico. But by 1969 Graham was 40 and no longer at his best. His racing career came to a temporary end in a frightening accident at Watkins Glen, after the 49's driveshaft broke. His car rolled and convulsed violently many times and threw Graham out, causing him serious leg injuries. But when the pain had receded a little, he still quipped, 'Tell Bette I won't be dancing for a while.'

Graham didn't want to retire from a hospital ward so he left Chapman and, after a brief spell driving Rob Walker's private Lotus, switched to Brabham for 1971. He amazed everyone on 12 April with a fine win in a BT36 in the European F2 Championship race at Thruxton and on 8 May in the non-championship F1 International Trophy at Silverstone in a BT34. He crowned his career by winning the 1972 24 Hours of Le Mans with Henri Pescarolo in a Matra-Simca MS670. That made Graham the only driver of his day to have hit motor racing's Grand Slam by winning the F1 world title, Indy and Le Mans.

Less in demand in 1973, Hill set up his own F1 team with a Shadow DN1 sponsored by Embassy cigarettes. He drove the car himself at first, but those two seasons were tough going for such an old hand. Even so, by 1975 Graham Hill Racing was making headway, even though Hill was now 46 and was unable to qualify for the Monaco GP. So he recruited 23-year-old Tony Brise and retired from driving to concentrate on running the team. Then on 20 November 1977 Graham's Piper Aztec aeroplane, which he was piloting, flew into dense fog while returning from the Paul Ricard Circuit. Hill and five members of his team, including Tony Brise, were tragically killed when the plane crashed on a golf course at Arkley, Hertfordshire.

# Hill, Phil

IT'S A LONG, LONG way from being a dropout to becoming the first American to win the Formula 1 World Championship. But that's the journey Philip Toll Hill Jr embarked on when he left his studies at the University of Southern California after a couple of years and became a mechanic; then an amateur racing driver; then a Ferrari works driver; then an outstanding sports car racer; and then the 1961 F1 World Champion.

Hill was born in Miami, Florida, on 20 April 1927 and soon became fascinated by cars. He drove one for the first time when he was nine, and was obsessed by them during his school days. Phil soon fell in love with motor racing and devoured all the motor sport magazines he could afford. He moved to California and went to university there in 1945 to study business administration, but that only lasted until 1947, when he went to work as a mechanic for an amateur racer in Los Angeles.

He competed in an MG TC in 1948 and in 1949, and then travelled to the UK to become an SU Carburettor and Jaguar trainee. He returned to the US with a new XK120, in which he won the Pebble Beach road race near Monterey and became an SCCA regular. He competed in the Carrera Panamericana in 1952 driving a Ferrari 212 Export and came sixth; he entered the 1953 Carrera with his friend Richie Ginther as his riding mechanic, but they had a huge accident in their Ferrari 340 America and were lucky to escape alive.

Phil came second with Carroll Shelby in the 1955 12 Hours of Sebring in a 750 Monza, which prompted Ferrari importer Luigi Chinetti to invite him to drive that year's tragic 24 Hours of Le Mans with Umberto Maglioli in a 4.4-litre North American Racing Team Ferrari 118 LM. The two only lasted seven hours before their cooling system gave out, but in recompense Phil became the year's SCCA champion.

A year later, Hill joined the Ferrari works team and scored his first victory in the Swedish Grand Prix, co-driving a 290 MM with Maurice Trintignant; he followed that up a year later by winning the Venezuela Grand Prix in a 335S with Peter Collins.

By this time the American had established his prowess as an endurance racer, which is why it took him some time to make Formula 1. He and Collins took a 250 TR to victory in the 1000 Kilometres of Buenos Aires, first round of the 1958 World Sports Car Championship, and they also won the 12 Hours of Sebring. That was the year Phil won the 24 Hours of Le Mans with Olivier Gendebien in a 250 TR to become the first American to win the race.

The Californian won his second successive Sebring in a Testa Rossa in 1959, aided and abetted by Chuck Daigh, Dan Gurney and Olivier Gendebien, and in 1960 he took the 1000 Kilometres of Buenos Aires once more, this time with Cliff Allison in a TR. His third 12 Hours of Sebring win happened in 1961 with Gendebien in a 250 TR, and he also won his second successive Le Mans with Olivier that year in a Test Rossa.

But Phil was getting so frustrated with his lack of Formula 1 wheel-time that he drove his first F1 World Championship race not in a Ferrari, but in Jo Bonnier's private Maserati 250F in the 1958 French GP, and came seventh. Then the death of Luigi Musso at Reims meant Enzo Ferrari had to make up his Grand Prix driver numbers and chose Phil to compete in the lesser Formula 2 segment of the German GP, where he came fifth. Hill was promoted to the F1 team proper for the Italian Grand Prix, with instructions to watch Mike Hawthorn's back as the Englishman continued his bid for the world title. Phil drove a fine race, set the fastest lap and came third. More of the same in the Moroccan Grand Prix saw Hawthorn clinch the championship and the American come third again.

Hill made yet more history by becoming the first American to win a Grand Prix for 39 years, since Jimmy Murphy beat all comers in the 1921 GP of France in one of Augie Duesenberg's cars. The British teams weren't there, but that didn't detract from Phil's phenomenal performance in the front-engined V6 Ferrari Dino 246 to take pole in the 1960 Italian Grand Prix, win the race and set the fastest lap while doing so.

In March 1961 Hill won his third 12 Hours of Sebring with Gendebien in a Ferrari 250 TR, and three months later won his second 24 Hours of Le Mans in a similar car, which helped Ferrari walk away with the WSCC with 24 points to Maserati's 14. The F1 music changed that year with the introduction of the 1.5-litre formula. Ferrari fielded its powerful rear-engined Dino 156 shark nose, which was up against the Lotus 21s, one of them driven by a young Scot named Jim Clark. Hill won at Spa and scored four podium places so that the world title came down to an in-house battle at Monza during the 1961 Italian Grand Prix between Wolfgang von Trips, who led the championship with 33 points, and Phil Hill, who was second with 29.

Phil led the race from the start, but on lap two von Trips' shark nose and Clark's Lotus appeared to collide at 160mph. The Ferrari flew into the crowd like a mad thing, killing 15 spectators and its driver. Officials kept the race going for fear of panic if they didn't, so Hill roared on to win the race to become the first American to win the Formula 1 World Championship.

Phil continued his success in sports racers in 1962, when he and Gendebien won the Nürburgring 1000 Kilometres in a Dino 246 SP and then their third Le Mans victory, this time driving a 330 LM. But 1962 F1 was another matter altogether for Hill and Ferrari. The reigning World Champion did not win a single Grand Prix as the British teams' technology marched forward unrelentingly and Ferrari's almost stood still.

So Hill left Ferrari at season's end to join the ill-fated ATS, run by sacked Ferrari technical boss Carlo Chiti. The ATS 100 got nowhere and the move continued a steady decline in Phil's Formula 1 fortunes. He joined Cooper in 1964, but neither the T73 nor the T76 Climax did it for him, and the best he was able to do was to take sixth place in the British GP.

Hill's tremendous sports car racing talent was still intact and he won Daytona with Pedro Rodriguez in a Ferrari 250 GTO. But he had become fascinated by Texan Jim Hall's radical Chaparral 2D-Chevrolet and shared one with Jo Bonnier to win the 1965 Nürburgring 1000 Kilometres. Then Phil won the 1966 Laguna Seca round of the year's Can-Am Championship in a Chaparral 2E. The following year he was back in Europe with the winged 2F and won the BOAC Six Hours at Kent's Brands Hatch circuit with Mike Spence.

And that was it. After a distinguished, highly successful motor racing career, Hill retired to run his classic car restoration firm Hill and Vaughn, did TV commentary for ABC and became an insightful contributor to *Road and Track* magazine.

# Hulme, Denny

DENNY HULME WAS ONE of the most reserved men in motor racing. He seldom showed his emotions, which he camouflaged with a likeable but sometimes gruff personality. He never regarded himself as a star, even if that were the case, and often went unrecognised in the most public of places, not least at the Monaco Grand Prix not long before his death in 1992.

Yet Denny was the 1961 New Zealand Gold Star Champion, won the 1967 Formula 1 World Championship and was the 1968 and 1970 Canadian-American Challenge Cup winner. He scored eight championship Grands Prix victories and 33 podium places from 112 starts between 1967 and 1974, and won no fewer than 22 Can-Am races between 1968 and 1972.

Denis Clive Hulme, son of a Victoria Cross winner, was born at Te Puke on New Zealand's South Island on 18 June 1936, and was brought up on a tobacco farm at Motueka. He worked as a mechanic and saved enough to buy an MG TF and later an MGA, both of which he drove in local hillclimbs in 1957/8 before moving on to a single-seater 2000cc Cooper-Climax in 1959. He was selected for the New Zealand Driver to Europe programme and competed on the Continent in F2 the following year, taking a win at Pescara, Italy, in 1960. The following year he had his first taste of top-flight European endurance racing, when he and Angus Hyslop drove a works Abarth 850 S into 14th place and covered 263 laps of the 24 Hours of Le Mans.

In 1963 Denny went to work as a mechanic for Jack Brabham at the Australian's Chessington premises, where the 1959 and 1960 Formula 1 World Champion had just set up his own business with fellow Aussie Ron Tauranac to build F1 cars. Denny was soon given a chance to have a go at Formula 1 himself at Karlskoga, Sweden, in August 1963, where he surprised most people by coming fourth behind some heady talent: the winner was

Jim Clark and second came Trevor Taylor, both in Lotus 25-Climaxes, while third was his guv'nor, Jack Brabham.

The New Zealander competed in his first championship Grand Prix in Monaco in 1965, when he qualified the team's BT7-Climax eighth and finished a creditable eighth. Dan Gurney left Brabham at the end of the '65 season to set up on his own and, having shown such promise, Denny slipped into the number two seat for 1966. Some teams were late developing their new 3-litre engines, but not Brabham. They had exclusive use of a new Holden/Repco power unit, and Hulme did well in the reliable Brabham BT20-Repco by taking third place in the French GP, second in the British and another third in the Mexican, to finish fourth in the championship with 18 points. His boss, of course, won the title and became the first man to do so driving a car of his own construction.

Hulme's big year was 1967. He drove the Brabham BT20-Repco to victory in the Monaco Grand Prix, in which Lorenzo Bandini crashed his Ferrari and later died in hospital, while Denny's boss Jack Brabham dropped out on the first lap with engine trouble. But it was a Brabham 1-2 in the German GP at the Nürburgring, the win going to Hulme to equal Jack's score of two GP victories. But with seconds in France, Britain and Canada and thirds in Holland, the United States and Mexico, Denny won the year's Formula 1 World Championship with 51 points to Jack's 46. Black Jack's consolation prize – if you can talk of a world title in such terms – was the world Constructors' Championship, which Brabham-Repco won with 63 points, 19 points ahead of second-placed Lotus.

The New Zealander also competed in Cam-Am driving Bruce McLaren's M6A-Chevrolet and, astonishingly, won the first three 1967 races at Elkhart Lake, Bridgehampton and Mosport Park, but Bruce won the series with Denny runner-up.

Hulme joined McLaren's Formula 1 team for 1968, and after the South African Grand Prix at Kyalami he must have wondered why: he had to work hard to coerce the old McLaren M5A chassis, powered by an even older BRM V12 engine, into fifth place. But his prayers were answered at the next GP in Spain, where he drove a brand new McLaren M7A with Ford Cosworth power on to the front row of the grid next to Jack Brabham on pole, and into second place in the Grand Prix. The reigning World Champion won the Grands Prix of Italy and Canada in the M7A, but scored nowhere near enough points to retain his title and ended up third in the standings. But all was not lost, because Hulme won the Can-Am Challenge Cup that year with yet another three fine victories in the McLaren M6A-Chevrolet at Elkhart Lake once more, Edmonton and Las Vegas. He even took two fourth places driving Eagle-Fords in the 1967 and 1968 Indianapolis 500s.

The best Denny could do in 1969 in F1 was to win the Mexican finale in a revised but troublesome McLaren M7A to end up sixth in the championship.

Denny may have been a reserved individual who seldom showed his feelings, but he was devastated by Bruce McLaren's death when testing the new M8D-Chevrolet Can-Am car at Goodwood on 2 June 1970. Hulme soldiered on in F1 with reasonable success, consistently placing well in the McLaren M14A to finish fourth in the year's championship ahead of the likes of Brabham, '69 World Champion Jackie Stewart and his fellow countryman Chris Amon. And, driving the M8D-Chevrolet that Bruce died testing, Denny won six of the ten 1970 Can-Am races to take his second North American title.

The 1971 F1 Championship was disappointing: Denny finished equal ninth with four other drivers. Victory in the 1972 South African Grand Prix – McLaren's only win of the season – two seconds and four thirds took Hulme to third in the year's F1 title chase. In 1973 he added another win to his tally when Ronnie Peterson's Lotus 72D punctured in front of his home crowd at Anderstorp in the Grand Prix of Sweden. Denny had been playing his usual waiting game in the McLaren M23 and shot past the tall, blond Swede's slowing Lotus on the last lap to take the win.

Hulme would win one more Grand Prix, in Buenos Aires in 1974 before he retired. As was often the case, he carefully stayed in contention, administering his car and tyres in the Grand Prix of Argentina, which was being led by up-and-coming local boy Carlos Reutemann in a Brabham BT44 until he ran out of fuel two laps from the end. Once more, Denny slipped through to win the last GP of his distinguished career.

The New Zealander still enjoyed motor sport after retiring from the big league, racing touring cars and even trucks. But on 4 October 1992 he suffered a fatal heart attack in Australia's famous Bathurst 1000 while hammering down the Conrod Straight in a BMW M3 on the New South Wales circuit. His car hit the straight's left wall, and although Denny managed to bring the car to a desperate halt, when the marshals reached the stricken BMW he was already dead.

Hulme was inducted into the American Motorsports Hall of Fame in 1998.

# Hunt, James

'SEX – THE BREAKFAST of Champions' was the legend on the T-shirt James Hunt often wore under his driving suit. Ex-public schoolboy irreverence that only partially sums up this deceptively talented, sophisticated and intelligent man. He personified that much-overworked term charisma, but he was also an instinctively brilliant, hard-charging driver who won the 1976 Formula 1 World Championship, 10 Grands Prix, scored 23 podium places and took 14 pole positions.

Despite all that success, James never really took himself or the establishment too seriously, preferring to turn up to sponsors' parties in a T-shirt, jeans and bare feet or, when he was in a good mood, a dinner jacket and tennis shoes. After he retired from F1, he became one of the two BBC TV Grand Prix commentators, partnering national icon Murray Walker. But it was James who almost singlehandedly brought the disappearing millions back to their televisions to watch Grand Prix motor racing and hear his startling blend of upmarket charm and pithy straight talking. 'Bullshit' is a term that sometimes slipped out of James and on to the BBC airwaves if he didn't agree with some driver's antics or remarks.

James Simon Wallis Hunt was born on 29 August 1947, the son of a London stockbroker. Educated at Wellington, he began by racing a Mini, moved into Formula Ford in the late 1960s, then F3. But there he got stuck with uncompetitive machinery.

His lucky break came in the summer of 1972, when the enthusiastic Lord Alexander Hesketh and his partner 'Bubbles' Horsley took James into F2 to drive a second-hand March 712M, and he did well. On the surface the Hesketh team was like a mobile Disneyland: bright, fun-loving, full of cultured accents and not adverse to a glass of champagne. But underneath all that froth was a deadly serious team of professionals with precise objectives and the engineers to achieve them. Lord Alexander wanted to do a full European F2 season in 1973, but soon discovered F1 didn't cost that much more; so he bought a Surtees TS9B, in which James came an amazing third in his first Grand Prix, a non-championship event at Brands Hatch.

Next, Hesketh ran a Harvey Postlethwaite-designed 450hp March 731-Cosworth DFV that Hunt drove for the first time at the 1973 Monaco GP – a race described by Nelson Piquet as like riding a bicycle through the corridors of your apartment – but James retired with engine trouble. The rest of the season was a different story, though, with Hunt scoring his first F1 point in the French GP, fourth place in the British, stepping on to the podium for the first time with a third at Zandvoort and taking an outstanding second in the USGP at Watkins Glen. That lot took him to eighth in the World Championship.

Postlethwaite joined his lordship's team for 1974 and there he designed the Hesketh 308, but he spent much of the year sorting out its niggling problems, although Hunt did make third in Sweden, Austria and at Watkins Glen. In 1975 the car and James really came good and he won his first GP by beating Niki Lauda's Ferrari, no less, in Holland. However, the cost of Formula 1 began to weigh heavily on the Hesketh purse, so, with no multi-million dollar sponsors breaking his door down, Lord Alexander withdrew from the sport.

Just weeks later Emerson Fittipaldi left McLaren to join his brother Wilson's Copersucar team, and Hunt was contacted by the team's Teddy Meyer, but the Briton steadfastly refused to sign any contract that stipulated he should wear suits at sponsors' events – a run-in that was settled in James' favour. He immediately showed he meant business and took pole in his first race for McLaren in Brazil.

Of course, 1976 was James' big year, one in which he was a constant threat to Ferrari. He ended a run of five consecutive Maranello victories with his win in the McLaren M23-Ford at the Spanish GP, Lauda repaired the damage somewhat by winning Belgium and Monaco, then James won in France. But then Niki had his near-fatal crash on the second lap of the Nürburgring during the Grand Prix of Germany. The Austrian hovered between life and death before starting to recover, while James was piling up the points with wins at the self-same German GP and then in Holland. The next race was the Grand Prix of Italy, and that was the scene of one of the most courageous returns to the circuit in the entire history of the sport. With his wounds still bleeding beneath his helmet, Lauda made a painful but successful comeback – just 43 days after he was so badly burnt in the blazing 312T2 – to take fourth place at Monza and earn enough points to stay at the top of the championship table. Hunt retired.

The Briton got back into the game by reeling off another couple of wins in Canada and the USGP and was within three points of championship leader Lauda by the time the circus descended on a sombre, rain-soaked Fuji track for the Grand Prix of Japan.

The race was run in appallingly wet and dangerous conditions, meaning drivers could hardly see anything in front of them as the cars threw huge plumes of impenetrable spray high into the air. Niki couldn't blink because his eyelids had been burnt off, and he retired, as he believed his life was more important than a second World Championship. Hunt was also having a hard time in the deluge. One of his tyres punctured, then he had an over-long pit stop and couldn't make out his team's signals, but he did come third – enough to beat Niki to the title with 69 points to Lauda's 68. The race was won by Mario Andretti in a much-improved Lotus 77.

The McLaren M26 wouldn't work properly during the early part of the 1977 season, but it bucked itself up as the year wore on so that James was able to win at Watkins Glen and Fuji. The following year the Lotus 77 bit a big chunk out of the season in which Mario Andretti became World Champion, while Hunt could only muster a mere eight points That was the year when Ronnie Peterson's Lotus crashed at the first corner in the Italian GP and burst into flames. James, Patrick Depailler and Clay Regazzoni dragged Ronnie from the blazing car, but he died in hospital the next day. James was deeply distressed by the loss of his close friend and remained so for years afterwards.

He moved to Walter Wolf Racing for 1979 but its ground-effect car was uncompetitive, so he left motor racing after the Monaco GP.

James retired to Marbella, where he was seldom without a beautiful girl on his arm as he gobbled up the carefree life of discos, nightclubs and the seaside. And he indulged his talents playing squash, tennis, cricket and football, and was a great trumpet and piano player.

Hunt's wife Suzy left him for Welsh actor Richard Burton, after which his second wife Sarah gave him two sons. Later he became a leading budgerigar and parrot breeder, of all things, and used to cart them around in an old Austin A35 van. He died of a heart attack at the ridiculously young age of 45 on 15 June 1993, not long after he had proposed marriage to his partner, Helen.

# Ickx, Jacky

JACKY ICKX'S MOTOR RACING CV is enough to make your head spin. Believe it or not, it all started with a 50cc Puch trials bike his dad gave him to boost his tepid interest in motor sport. It did that all right!

By the time Jacky was 38 he had won the 1967 European F2 Championship, eight F1 Grands Prix – most of them for Ferrari – *six* 24 Hours of Le Mans, the 1979 Can-Am championship and the 1983 Paris Dakar Rally.

He was World Championship material, no doubt about that. But he never really got the breaks when they mattered most. For instance, he came fourth in the drivers' championship in Mauro Forghieri's Ferrari 312 in 1968. A year later, he was second to Jackie Stewart in the Scot's first year as champion. And in 1970 he lost the crown to Jochen Rindt, the only man to win the title posthumously. He came equal fourth with Jo Siffert in '71, fourth again in '72, and nowhere in '73.

After the Puch trials triumphs Jacky progressed to a Lotus Cortina, in which he won the 1965 Belgian Saloon Car Championship. But he started to make his mark in the 1967 German Grand Prix, a race for both Formula 1 and 2 cars. He drove a Tyrrell Matra MS7-Ford with such panache that his F2 car was fighting it out with F1's big names. After four laps he had overtaken 12 F1 cars and moved into fifth place – until his suspension broke. The Belgian went on to win in Zandvoort, Holland, and Vallelunga, Rome, and amassed points at several other races to win the 1967 European Formula 2 Championship with spirited driving that earned him 41 points to runner-up Frank Gardner's 34. Jacky also made his F1 debut that year and scored first time out. He put up a gutsy performance in a Cooper T81B-Maserati to score sixth and a point in the Grand Prix of Italy at the ultra-fast Monza circuit.

Then came the big one. Ickx was invited to join Ferrari for 1968, and put in a brilliant drive to win the French GP at Rouen in a 312. But Jacky switched to Brabham in 1969 with some help from Gulf Oil, who wanted him to drive 4.9-litre V8 Ford GT40s instead of his old team's Ferrari 330 P4, and it worked. Ickx and Jackie Oliver won the 12 Hours of Sebring for them in March and then the 24 Hours of Le Mans in June, driving those big bangers. The early part of Jacky's season with Brabham was not that rewarding, but then Black Jack severely injured his foot in an accident while testing, so the team's whole focus swung over to the Belgian. After lowly placings early on, Ickx came third in the French GP, second in the British and won the German Grand Prix at the old Nürburgring just before they ironed out the bumps, then won the GP of Canada and wound up the year with a second in Mexico – a major contribution to Brabham coming second in the F1 World Championship for constructors.

Ickx went back to Ferrari for 1970, where technical wizard Mauro Forghieri and his team had come up with the outstanding flat-12 312 B. Again Jacky got off to a slowish start, but then he began to come good, with thirds at Zandvoort and Hockenheim before giving Ferrari its first victory since mid-1968 in the Austrian GP; he followed that up with another two wins, in Canada and Mexico. But that wasn't enough to win him the Formula 1 World Championship for drivers either. The title went posthumously to Jochen Rindt, with 45 points to runner-up Jacky's 40.

There was no such success for Ferrari in 1971, but things brightened up in 1972 when Jacky came third in the Argentine GP and second in both Spain and Monaco before taking pole and the win in the Grand Prix of Germany at his favourite Nürburgring; and that was his last F1 win. He left Ferrari to join Ronnie Peterson at Lotus partway through 1973, but his only moment of success there was victory in a sodden non-title Race of Champions at Brand Hatch. He left Chapman's team in mid-1975 and competed for Wolf-Williams in 1976, then Mo Nunn's Ensign and later Ligier.

Jacky continued his remarkable run of success in the 24 Hours of Le Mans, which he won in three consecutive years: 1975 with Derek Bell in a Mirage-GR8; in 1976 with Dutchman Gijs van Lennep driving a Porsche 936; and in 1977 in a 936 again, which he drove with American Hurley Heywood and Jürgen Barth of Germany.

North America beckoned in 1979, when Jacky agreed to drive a Lola T333CS-Chevrolet for Carl Haas Racing in the much-vaunted Cam-Am Challenge. That year, Ickx won races at Charlotte, Mosport, Elkhart Lake, Brainerd and the closing event at Riverside, to become the year's Can-Am Champion.

After that Jacky made it a total of six Le Mans victories, with wins in 1981 and 1982 – both with Derek Bell in Porsche 956s – and he took two successive World Endurance Championships, in 1982 and 1986.

His endurance prowess meant he became known as 'Monsieur Le Mans.' To cement his association with the town and race, he was made an honorary citizen of Le Mans at a special reception in the circuit's Georges Durand grandstand on Friday 16 June 2000, in recognition of his remarkable tally of six victories.

Of all his Le Mans wins, Jacky's favourite is the 1977 race, in which the works Porsche 936/77 he shared with Henri Pescarolo retired after only 45 laps. Ickx was wisely switched to the Jürgen Barth/Hurley Haywood car, which was lying 42nd at the time. In an incredible display of absolute driving talent, Jacky sliced his way through back markers, slapped down a weak Renault challenge and took the lead! But then one of the Porsche's cylinders started giving trouble, so an hour before race's end the car pitted and its dud cylinder had its ignition and injection removed. The smoking 936/77 rejoined the race and kept going until the finish to take the win, having covered 342 laps to the second-placed Vern Schuppan/Jean-Pierre Jarier 2-litre V6 Renault turbo's 331.

The Paris Dakar Rally had been running for four years by the time Ickx entered in 1983 with Claude Brasseur to drive a Mercedes-Benz 280 G, the first year the harrowing marathon was run across the Ténéré desert. Unfortunately a sandstorm blew up and 40 competitors lost their way, but Jacky and Brasseur won.

Ickx accepted an offer to become Formula 1 race director at Monaco, which caused a stir. In pouring rain he red-flagged the 1984 race, handing the win to Alain Prost in a McLaren MP4/3-Porsche, just as the Frenchman was being reeled in by acknowledged wet weather master and newcomer Ayrton Senna in a much-improved Toleman TG184-Hart. Stopping the race caused a controversial outcry, and only half-points were assigned to the top six drivers. As luck would have it, Prost lost the year's F1 World

Championship for drivers by half a point, scoring 71.5 points to new World Champion Niki Lauda's 72.

At the time of writing, Jacky was still Monaco's F1 race director.

# Ireland, Innes

NOW HERE IS A man of his word – and it cost him dearly. In 1961 Innes agreed to drive for Formula 1 team UDT-Laystall, run by Ken Gregory and Alfred Moss, respectively Stirling's manager and father. Literally a day later Ireland was asked to become Graham Hill's teammate at BRM, but he declined, saying he had given his word to Gregory and Moss and couldn't break it.

Ironically, in 1962 the UDT-Laystall V8 Climax-engined Lotus 24 was a massive flop. Ireland had to retire it from every championship race in which he competed; but the BRMs were a huge success. Hill went on to win the year's Formula 1 World Championship for drivers and a lot more besides as long as the 1.5-litre formula remained in force.

The gossips said Ireland the hell-raiser was incompatible with Sir Alfred Owen, BRM's owner and a strict Methodist, and that was the real reason why he didn't join that team. But if that were the case, why would Owen invite a man to drive for him one day and kick him out the next?

Ireland was a driver of tremendous talent and courage who could have become World Champion with the right material. Instead, he was fated to drive cars that hardly ever measured up to his speed capability, determination and downright fearlessness. So he ended up with one World Championship Grand Prix victory to his name, plus a handful of others that didn't count towards the title.

Certainly, Innes loved life. A well-known F1 team manager once said he lived without sense, without an analyst, and provoked astonishment and affection in everyone. Sure enough, he liked his whisky, cigarettes and women, and lived the kind of life people popularly expected drivers of the Golden Era of motor racing to enjoy. But he was also a gentleman and great company.

I went to Stirling Moss' 60th birthday party, where Innes was the main speaker. He had everyone in stitches for a full 30 minutes as he sipped his whisky, before bread rolls thrown at him by his appreciative audience suggested he had outstayed his welcome. He sat down to a standing ovation for his fun speech.

Born in Mytholmroyd in West Yorkshire on 12 June 1930, Robert McGregor Innes Ireland was the son of a Scottish veterinary surgeon. The family moved back to Kirkcudbright, Scotland, when Innes was still a boy. He had no love for school, but later trained as an engineering apprentice with Rolls Royce, first in Glasgow and then in London. He was called up for national service in the early '50s and earned a commission as a second lieutenant in the King's Own Scottish Borderers before being seconded to the Parachute Regiment, with whom he served in the Suez Canal zone in 1953/4.

After army service, Ireland set up and ran a small engineering company in Surrey, specialising in maintaining Rolls Royces and Bentleys. He also bought himself a second-hand Riley Brooklands Nine, in which he raced occasionally and won the National Goodwood Handicap in both 1955 and 1956. But he didn't get serious about his motor sport until 1957. He did well in sports car events, and managed fifth place in the 1958 RAC Tourist Trophy at Goodwood with Masten Gregory in a Jaguar D-Type before taking the big step into Formula 1 with Colin Chapman's Team Lotus in 1959, when he managed fourth in the Dutch Grand Prix at Zandvoort and fifth in the USGP at Sebring driving Lotus 16-Climaxes.

The following year he won non-championship GPs at Goodwood and Snetterton in a Lotus 18-Climax, in both of which he beat Stirling Moss in his Rob Walker Racing Cooper. Ireland came fourth in the 1960 Formula 1 World Championship for drivers and gave his team a distinct leg-up to finish second to World Champions Cooper in the constructors' table with an outstanding second place to winner Jack Brabham in Holland and another to Stirling Moss in the USGP at Riverside. For all of those considerable feats he was awarded the British Racing Drivers' Club (BRDC) International Trophy, and made an acceptance speech that brought the house down.

It looked like curtains for Ireland's F1 career after he crashed badly at the 1961 Grand Prix of Monaco, but he bounced back later that season to win Germany's Solitude GP at Stuttgart and the Grand Prix of Austria at Zeltweg in a Lotus 21-Climax. His big day, though, was on 8 October '61, which almost did not happen. Practising for the USGP a couple of days before the race at its new Watkins Glen venue in New York State, the steering broke on his Lotus 18 and the car flew off the circuit, but this time Innes came out of it uninjured.

Ireland was back in the fourth row of the grid for the Sunday's USGP but by the end of the first lap he had worked his way up to third, tailed by Graham Hill, Dan Gurney, Masten Gregory, Jo Bonnier and Tony Brooks, although he spun on lap three and that dropped him back to 11th. Innes fought back fearlessly, so that five laps later he was back up to sixth and eventually moved into second behind Stirling Moss until the Briton's engine broke on lap 59 and Ireland took the lead. He was hotly pursued by Graham Hill in the BRM until the latter pitted with a magneto problem. Then Dan Gurney took over pursuit in the Porsche 718 and he hounded Ireland until the finish, when Innes scored his one and only World Championship victory, with the American second and Brooks third in another BRM.

Soon afterwards Colin Chapman abruptly fired Innes for having handed over his works 4-cylinder Lotus 18/21 to rival Rob Walker Racing team driver Stirling Moss, who was unhappy with the 8-cylinder car he had been testing during qualifying for the 1961 Grand Prix of Italy. That upset Chapman and his sponsors, hence the sacking, which left Ireland with a bitterness that affected him for the rest of his life. The Scot never forgave Chapman for his perfunctory sacking and believed – wrongly – that Jim Clark was behind it. To Ireland's eternal regret, he and Clark never patched things up before the double World Champion was killed in that insignificant F2 race at Hockenheim in 1968.

Ireland competed in seven 24 Hours of Le Mans races between 1958 and 1966, driving for Lotus before his bust up with Colin Chapman, then the legendary Ecurie Ecosse, UDT-Laystall, Aston Martin, Maranello Concessionaires, Alan Mann Racing and Comstock Racing. His best finish was sixth in 1964 with Tony Maggs of South Africa in a Ferrari 250 GTO.

His last major race was the 1967 Daytona 500 in which he completed 126 laps driving the Ray Fox 1966 Dodge before retiring with engine trouble.

Innes wrote well, as confirmed by his brilliant autobiography *All Arms and Elbows*. He eventually turned to journalism in the late '60s as sports editor of the British motoring magazine *Autocar* and later the well-respected American magazine *Road and Track*.

In 1992 Innes was elected president of the BRDC, an appointment he held until his death from cancer on 22 October 1993.

# Jones, Alan

WITH A DAD LIKE Stan Jones it was hardly surprising that Alan became a motor racing nut when he was still a kid. Stan won the 1954 New Zealand International Grand Prix, four 1955 Victorian Trophies at Fisherman's Bend, Melbourne, became the 1958 Australian Gold Star Champion and won the 1959 Grand Prix of Australia, all in Maseratis and Coopers – and Alan was usually there to see him do it. His father's success soon nurtured an ambition in young Alan to become World Champion one day, and his tough, uncompromising character helped make sure he did just that.

It was a struggle, though, because Alan didn't have an easy time working his way through a six-year period in British junior formulae. Wealthy Australian Harry Stiller financed him in Formula Atlantic in 1974, driving a March 74B, and he almost won the title, ending the season as runner-up with 41 points, just two away from champion Jim Crawford with 43. Stiller stuck with him for a while and helped Alan into Formula 1 by buying one of Lord Alexander Hesketh's leftover 308s after his lordship stepped out of F1. Jones qualified the old car 20th making his F1 debut in the 1975 Grand Prix of Spain, but retired after a lap three collision. It was much the same story in the Monaco, Belgian and Swedish GPs, after which Stiller dropped out and AJ moved to Graham Hill's Embassy cigarettes sponsored team. The Hill GH1-Ford worked better than the Hesketh, and Jones scored his first World Championship points in one by coming fifth in the Grand Prix of Germany at the tricky Nürburgring to end up 17th in the drivers' title table.

Jones went to work for John Surtees in 1976 and did a little better by taking fifths in the British and Belgian Grands Prix in the Durex contraceptive sponsored TS19-Ford before coming fourth in Japan.

Shadow's gifted Tom Pryce was killed in an accident at the 1977 South African Grand Prix at Kyalami after his DN8A hit a marshal, who was crossing the track to extinguish an electrical fire in Renzo Zorzi's abandoned sister car, so Alan was recruited to take Tom's place from the next race at Long Beach. It was a hard grind in the Ford-powered Shadow at first, with retirements in California and Spain, but Alan came sixth in Monte Carlo and fifth in Belgium, only to fall back into low-finish retirement mode in Sweden, France, Britain and Germany. Jones eventually broke out of the slump to win the Grand Prix of Austria in the DN8A at the Österreichring on 14 August, relegating 1975 World Champion Niki Lauda and his Ferrari to second place before Niki's home crowd. A third in Italy and fourths in Canada and Japan took the Australian to seventh place in the World Championship table.

The 1978 season was somewhat of a milestone for AJ, as he was signed by Frank Williams. Alan persevered with the FW06-Ford, but from the Grand Prix of Argentina on 15 January until Monza on 11 September there was little to show for his determination other than low finishes and a lot of retirements – although he did get a much-needed morale boost from his second place behind winner Carlos Reutemann's Ferrari 312T3 in the US Grand Prix at Watkins Glen. But while F1 proved generally frustrating, the American Can-Am series was pure joy. Jones won Road Atlanta, Mid-Ohio, Elkhart Lake, Mosport Park and Riverside in the big Group 7 Lola T33CS-Chevrolet road-racer entered by Carl Haas, and was crowned champion.

It looked like it was going to be more of the same in 1979, as AJ slogged away in the Williams without a win during the first half of the year, although he did come third at Long Beach in April. After that there was another drought until the Grand Prix of Great Britain at Silverstone on 14 July, when the Australian took pole position with a time of 1min 11.88sec for the 2.932-mile circuit and his teammate Clay Regazzoni gave the British team its first Grand Prix win. Despite Alan's flurry of victories in the German, Austrian, Dutch and Canadian Grands Prix things came good a little too late for him to have any serious chance of winning the World Championship, which went to Ferrari's Jody Scheckter, with Alan third.

Patrick Head produced a B-version of the FW07 for 1980 and Carlos Reutemann made the move from Lotus to take over from Regazzoni, which was just as well. Williams needed all the help it could get to stave off a determined challenge from Bernie Ecclestone's Brabham. Jones got back into the groove right away by taking pole, setting the fastest lap and winning the Grand Prix of Argentina from an ever-menacing second-placed Nelson Piquet in the Ford-powered BT49. Reutemann won Monaco, but Alan came back strongly to win the French and British Grands Prix. Piquet was just as determined and chased Jones hard, winning in Holland and Italy. But Alan won at Montreal and Watkins Glen to achieve that childhood dream. He became the 1980 Formula 1 World Champion and Frank Williams' first world title winner, with a lead of 13 points over the hard-charging Piquet.

Reutemann was another strong challenger in 1980, when his consistency took him to third in the title chase. He and Jones helped Williams win the World Constructors' Championship by earning a thumping 120 points, which put the British team a massive 54 ahead of second placed Ligier.

The previous season's 'old guard' fought it out for the titles again in 1981, with the younger generation's Alain Prost in the new Renault RE30 and Gilles Villeneuve in a Ferrari 126CK keeping them on their toes. Jones, so often blighted by minor mechanical failures, won the first and last Grands Prix of the season in Buenos Aires and Las Vegas. But sandwiched between those two were three victories each by Piquet and Prost, two each by AJ's teammate Reutemann and Gilles, all of which took vital points away from Alan's efforts to become champion for the second successive year. The drivers' title went to Nelson, but AJ and Reutemann made sure Williams retained the Constructors' Championship, with second-placed Brabham trailing by just five points.

Jones took a year off to put time in on his farm in 1982, but he kept his hand in by competing in Porsche sports racers for the Australian National Championship. He came back to F1 in an Arrows A6 at Long Beach in 1983 but retired from the race and left it at that. He accepted Carl Haas' lucrative offer to make a comeback in 1985 in the American's Beatrice Foods sponsored Lola THL1-Hart at the Grand Prix of Italy, but he suffered a series of discouraging retirements and scored no points. Jones stayed on with Hass for 1986, but it was more of the same so he called it a day.

The following year AJ raced for TOM's Team Toyota in Japan, touring cars in Australia and became a TV commentator for the country's Channel Nine. In 2005 He became the head of the Australian A1 Grand Prix team.

# Junek, Elisabeth

NO WAY DID ELISABETH Junek look like a racing driver. She was, well, a woman to begin with, and there were not many of them hefting potent racing cars around in the 1920s. And she was petite, her fair hair framing a kind, gently smiling face. Even when she raced she always wore skirts, topped by a white blouson. But at the wheel of one of her Bugattis she was dynamite. Out came no-nonsense determination and courage, which she applied to her racing with a fast, shrewd mind to beat some of the greats of her day, among them Tazio Nuvolari, Achille Varzi, Luigi Fagioli and René Dreyfus.

The men fancied her like crazy, of course. She was a favourite of Vincenzo Florio, the inventor and patron of the Targa Florio. Even the dour Varzi, who was a bit of a ladies' man, was known to wink in her direction and hold her small hand far too long after he had shaken it. But Elisabeth took all this flirting in good spirit and was courteous to them all – until she raced against them. Then her claws came out and she gave no quarter, as good at the cut and thrust of motor racing as any of them, at times better.

She won in her native Czechoslovakia and even twice at the daunting Nürburgring, but she will be best remembered for her prowess in the rough and tumble of that series of goat tracks and unsurfaced 'roads' called the Targa Florio. It is there that she made motor sport history.

Her real name was Alžběta Pospíšilová and she was born on 6 November 1900, the sixth of eight children, to a blacksmith and his wife in Olomouc, Moravia, in an obscure part of the Austro-Hungarian Empire. By the time she was 16 she spoke fluent German and reasonable French, which helped her get a job in the Olomouc branch of a mortgage bank. There she met her future husband Vincenc Junek, who had been invalided out of the army during the First World War after being shot in the hand.

Vincenc was quickly promoted to senior bank positions in Brno and Prague and made sure his diminutive assistant Elisabeth followed him in each case. Then they separated. Elisabeth headed for Paris to improve her French and Vincenc became an increasingly successful banker. He was wealthy by the time he arrived in the French capital to visit 'his' Elisabeth and he proposed to her. Not under the smile of the Mona Lisa or on the romantic banks of the Seine, but in a Bugatti showroom. He liked fast cars and wanted to race them.

Years later Elisabeth remembered herself thinking, 'If he is going to be the love of my life, I'd better learn to love these damned cars.' So when the couple returned to Prague, she took driving lessons and passed her test. Meanwhile, Vincenc had started racing and had won the 1922 Zbraslav-Jiloviste hillclimb, believed to be the oldest in Europe.

It was not long before the Juneks began competing in national races as a husband and wife team, Elisabeth the riding mechanic. But Vincenc's wartime hand injury meant it was painful to change gear, so Elisabeth took over the driver's seat and her husband became the mechanic.

The Juneks' relationship with the Targa Florio was like that of a moth to a flame. In 1927 the couple took their Bugatti 35 B/2.3 to the island, where little Elisabeth's performance was electrifying. She was fourth and fighting it out with the likes of Emilio Materassi – who eventually won the race in his Bugatti 35 C/2000 – 1927 Mille Miglia winner Ferdinando Minoia, 1919 Targa winner André Boillot and Ernesto Maserati, before she had to retire with a broken main gear in her car's steering box.

Elisabeth wanted more. She and Vincenc were back in Sicily for the 1928 Targa Florio and this time they really meant business. The couple arrived on the island two months before the race, which was scheduled for 6 May 1928. They had brought three cars with them: an eight-cylinder supercharged 2300 Bugatti racecar, an identical spare plus a road car in which to practise. She drove the circuit constantly, marking rocks, trees, walls and the like to help her recognise sections of the 108km route. Then she and Vincenc went out and drove the circuit fast, over and over again, in their spare Bugatti until Elisabeth had the route firmly fixed in her mind.

The start of the 1928 Targa Florio was charged with excitement. Louis Chiron took the lead in his Bugatti 35 C/2.0, hotly pursued by Giuseppe

Campari's Alfa Romeo 6C 1500 MMS, Albert Divo in a Bugatti 35 B/2.3 and right behind the trio was Elisabeth. After the first 108km she was fourth, 29 seconds behind Chiron, 20 from Campari and 18 from Divo.

Elisabeth moved up even closer to Divo, who was decidedly miffed at being challenged by a *woman*. So much so that he lost concentration and made an inevitable mistake, skidded and ended up in a field of turnips. Chiron came to a sudden halt with a flat tyre and two minutes went up in smoke while he changed a wheel. So now Campari was in the lead. Chiron got going again, but not before Elisabeth overtook him to take third. Then she started stalking the irritated Divo again. Amazingly, she passed Divo and hared off after leader Campari. She overtook him too, and was the new leader. She had become the only woman ever to lead the Targa Florio.

A stunned silence fell over the spectators as the commentator told them a small, slim woman was ahead of *all* their heroes. Elisabeth pressed on and opened up a 21-second lead on Campari and was 40 seconds ahead of Divo.

But the Alfa Romeo pits signalled Campari that Elisabeth was running away with the race, after which he drove much harder to gradually chip away at the deficit and overtake her. Meanwhile, Elisabeth – who had been in the lead for well over two hours – was feeling the strain; her stamina was ebbing away. She skidded; her Bugatti slowed slightly, and though she kept it on the road that error let Divo through to second. But worse was to come. A puncture. Vincenc quickly changed the wheel, but that cost two minutes, which allowed Caberto Conelli and Louis Chiron through in their Bugattis.

After 7hr 49sec of strength-sapping high-speed roulette, Elisabeth Junek and her riding mechanic husband came fifth. She had beaten men like Minoia, Luigi Fagioli, René Dreyfus and Ernesto Maserati. Her drive would be remembered as part of motor sport history.

The spectators stood and cheered her performance for all they were worth. Vincenzo Florio took her hand and said he believed the moral victory in his race was hers. Divo, who had won, smiled half-heartedly and said he agreed.

In July 1928 Elisabeth and Vincenc competed in the Grand Prix of Germany at the Nürburgring in their Bugatti 35 B. She did the first stint and handed over to her husband only to see him and the car fly off the track, killing Vincenc outright.

A distraught Elisabeth sold all her racing cars and never competed again. But she was never forgotten. In 1989, at the age of 89, she was suitably fêted when she attended a Bugatti reunion in the United States. She died five years later.

# Kling, Karl

A MAN BORN TOO late to join Rudolf Caracciola, Manfred Von Brauchitsch and Hermann Lang in their rampage through Grand Prix motor racing in the 1930s, and too early to give Juan Manuel Fangio, Stirling Moss and Hans Herrmann any real competition in the W196 of 1954 and 1955, Karl Kling can, nevertheless, not be dismissed lightly, because he was still a major influence on Mercedes-Benz in motor racing as both a driver and, after Alfred Neubauer, as its team manager.

Karl was not exactly on friendly terms with the Mille Miglia, although he always performed well in the Italian classic before coming to grief in one way or another. For instance, he was leading the 1952 race out of Rome by eight minutes, but then was delayed at a Siena tyre-change when a wheel jammed. The mechanics freed it, but Kling had lost his lead and had to fight fading brakes to gingerly edge back up to second by the Brescia finish line. Mercedes loaned him to Alfa Romeo for a number of 1953 races, including the Mille Miglia. He led the race in a Disco Volante until the car's transmission broke on the Radicofani Pass. And he was lying fourth driving an Alfa Romeo 6C 3000 CM in the 1955 Mille Miglia when he went off, crashed into two trees and ended up in a ditch with a broken leg.

Kling was born on 16 September 1910 at Giessen, the German university town, and served his Mercedes-Benz apprenticeship at concessionaire Neils & Kraft. He joined Mercedes in Stuttgart as a customer service engineer and soon made it known that he liked motor racing. He eventually got himself into the works cross country trials team – a motor sport rather like today's special stage rallying – driving either a four-cylinder 2-litre or six-cylinder 2.6-litre Merc, and became so successful at it that he was invited to Monza in 1939 to show what he could do in the M-B Grand Prix cars being developed for the following season. Cue the Second World War, which put a stop to all that; Kling spent much of the war servicing Luftwaffe Messerschmitt ME109s, not driving racing cars.

After the war Karl returned to Mercedes-Benz, for whom he and his brother Hans got the shattered Stuttgart plant's first production line working. He also befriended former motorcycle ace Ernst Loof, who dreamt of building sports and racing cars in Germany, and helped him acquire the materials from which to construct them: they were called Veritas RS. Kling then became Loof's racing driver and won the 1948 and 1949 German Sports Car Championships in Veritas RS BMWs. Ernst moved on to single-seaters with his Formula 2 Meteor, but the car was notoriously unreliable, even though Karl did manage to win at Solitude and the Grenzlandring, where he pushed the Veritas up to an average of 126.16mph, Germany's fastest race of 1950. Meanwhile, Kling was a major influence on M-B returning to motor racing in the early 1950s.

Karl's racing skills were not lost on Alfred Neubauer, the mighty Mercedes motor racing boss. He chose Kling and Hermann Lang to join up with a middle-aged South American named Juan Manuel Fangio to see how its suitably revised pre-war V12 supercharged W163s, would stack up against more recent machinery in a couple of 1951 Argentine Grands Prix. Badly, was the answer. José Froilán Gonzáles won them both in a more modern Ferrari 166C, although Karl was the highest-placed of the Mercedes drivers, coming second in the Premio Ciudad Eva Maria Duarte Perón at the Circuito Costanera Norte.

Kling scored Mercedes-Benz's first post-war win in the new, Rudolf Uhlenhaut-developed 300 SL in the Bern Grand Prix at Bremgarten, but retired his 3.0 L16 with electrical problems in the year's 24 Hours of Le Mans while in the lead, making way for eventual winner Hermann Lang-Fritz Riess in a sister car.

But it was a different story at that year's Carrera Panamericana. A *very* different story. Would you believe a 45in wingspan vulture smashed into the Mercedes 300 SL's windscreen at 120mph and knocked out Kling's co-driver/ navigator Hans Klenk, who was covered in cuts from shattered glass and streaming with blood? But when he came to, Klenk insisted Kling carried on at full-speed to a tyre service area about 40 miles up the road, where eight vertical iron bars – vulture bars – were welded on to the body in front of the windscreen. The two went on to win the race by 25 minutes.

It was a great victory that canonised Karl Kling in the eyes of his country so that, not surprisingly, he was voted 1952 Sportsman of the Year by the German sports press.

After his Alfa Romeo stint, in which he crashed and was seriously injured at the Nürburgring, 44-year-old Kling went back to Mercedes-Benz. He was the first to test the car that would become the W196 on the track in the Stuttgart factory's grounds. After that he covered hundreds of miles in the car at Solitude and Hockenheim, before first Fangio and then Moss were recruited to drive the Silver Arrow and its sport racer derivative, the 300 SLR.

The W196's first outing was in Streamliner form – quite the most beautiful racing car I have *ever* seen – in the 1954 Grand Prix of France at Reims. The two cars dominated the race – sending oil drums flying, as the drivers could not see over those beautifully sculpted wings – and came first driven by Fangio, with Kling inches away from him in second place. The German was narrowly beaten by Fangio at Silverstone, led at the Nürburgring until an overlong pit stop cost him the race, and then won the Grand Prix of Berlin at Avus in one of the W196s, beating Fangio and Hans Herrmann.

Neubauer added 25-year-old Stirling Moss to his driver line-up for 1955, which effectively knocked Karl back to number three. While Stirling won the Mille Miglia in a record time that still stands today, Kling crashed in the same race and was out until the year's Monaco GP, by which time Moss was the established number two to reigning World Champion Fangio. Karl faded further and further into the background while Fangio-Moss – people called them 'The Train,' because Stirling was always inches away from the back of Fangio's car – dominated the season. But not before he won the Grand Prix of Sweden in a 300 SL.

At the end of 1955 Mercedes announced its retirement from motor racing but didn't want Kling to drive for another car maker, so his driving career was all but over, hemmed in as it had been by two great eras. So when Neubauer retired from team management in 1958 Kling was named his successor, looking after Mercedes-Benz privateers. But the company did have a rally programme on the go and Kling ran it; he decided to compete himself, too, and won the punishing 1959 Algiers-Cape Rally in a Mercedes 190 *diesel*, and two years later the Algiers-Central Africa Rally.

Karl Kling retired in 1968 but remained available to Mercedes as an adviser until 1975.

He died on 18 March 2003 at the age of 92.

# Lang, Hermann

HERMANN LANG SO NEARLY didn't get a shot at the European Championship, motor racing's premier title before the Second World War. Family pressures, Alfred Neubauer's initial rejection, the Depression and a strong dose of in-house class distinction nearly saw to that. But Lang shrugged it all off and battled on to win the championship, awarded to him by the German motor racing authorities rather than the governing body of European motor sport, the AIACR.

'Hermännle,' as he was nicknamed, started out as a motorcycle mechanic for Standard of Stuttgart and in 1927 bought his own racing bike, on which he won his first race at the Solitude circuit near his home town. He mostly competed in sidecar events for the next few years and, at 22 years old, won the 1931 German Hillclimb Sidecar Championship. By that time his brothers Albert and Karl had been killed in the sport, but, despite opposition from his mother and future wife Lydia, he pressed on until he was seriously injured himself in a race pile-up that killed two other riders. He recovered just as the Depression set in, only to lose his job at Standard.

It took time, but Hermann found work as a diesel locomotive driver whose route took him past the Daimler-Benz factory each day, so he applied for a job there. Because of his motorcycle racing background, his application didn't go the usual route to personnel but was sent to Daimler's motor sport director Alfred Neubauer, who replied saying he didn't need any racing drivers.

But Lang kept at it and eventually got himself in as a Daimler-Benz experimental department mechanic, which just happened to be developing the W25 for the firm's 1934 return to Grand Prix motor racing. On a long train journey back to Stuttgart from testing W25s at Monza that spring, Lang chatted with his boss Ludwig Krauss about his motorcycle racing successes and thought nothing more of it – until Krauss told him a month later that he was putting the 25-year-old's name forward as a Mercedes-Benz reserve driver.

Time dragged on for a year before he was asked to test-drive the supercharged W25 being prepared for Italian star Luigi Fagioli, but positive news though that was it produced no dramatic invitation to join the team. Then Lang was asked to a test session at Monza in 1935 with two other hopefuls, motorcycle racer Karl Soenius and sports car driver Bobby Kohlrausch. Hermann proved to be the best all-rounder and particularly impressed Neubauer with his start and cornering techniques.

At 26 Hermännle got his first big break by competing in the 1936 Eifelrennen at the Nürburgring, driving a rather long-in-the-tooth Mercedes-Benz W25A, when the team's elite – Rudolf Caracciola, Manfred von Brauchitsch and Luigi Fagioli – wielded W25Bs. He was lying third in pouring rain when he went into a giddying spin at Pflanzgarten and slithered into a ditch. He got going again and took a well-deserved fifth, but that began his lifetime hatred for wet tracks.

But Lang wasn't palmed off with an old car again for the 1936 Grand Prix of Germany. He had the same material as his 'teammates,' driving the best his employers had to offer, a W25K that put him fourth on the grid, ahead of all three of them! He even took the lead until he broke the little finger of his right hand making an extra-fast gearchange, but he continued to race, even though he was in excruciating pain. It wasn't long before Neubauer guessed something was up, called Lang in and gave his car to Caracciola, who had retired earlier, while Lang's finger was splinted. Then the *Rennleiter* gave him von Brauchitsch's car, which he drove to seventh place, his heroism earning him rapturous cheers and applause from the 400,000 or so at the 'Ring.

That led to a contract as a Mercedes-Benz senior driver in 1937, when the first race in the championship was the Grand Prix of Tripoli at the Mellaha circuit. Lang beat all-comers by stealth and sheer speed. Lying fourth in a new W125, he kept the in-fighting Caracciola, von Brauchitsch and Hans Stuck's Auto Union in his sights until their tyres gradually started to go off, and then pounced. He won the fastest Grand Prix ever run up to that time and covered the 40-lap race distance at a mind-blowing average of 134mph.

Back in Europe, Hermännle won the Avus Grand Prix driving a

streamlined Mercedes-Benz W125 that produced a shattering top speed of 236.17mph. But his 1937 winning streak came to an abrupt end in the Czech Grand Prix at the Masaryk circuit near Brno. His Mercedes went into a lurid skid on sand thrown up by a car in front, hit a huge rock, took flight, somersaulted over a kind of ditch packed with spectators, two of whom were killed, and juddered to a halt. Hermann was only slightly injured, but a court case was brought against him, from which he was acquitted.

By the time 1938 came around, Lang had proved himself a skilful and successful racing driver who could mix it with the world's best and win. But his moneyed, upper class 'teammates' still begrudged this poorly educated, working-class ex-mechanic his rightful place in the team. Once more, though, he beat them all by winning the Tripoli Grand Prix again that year, when the best von Brauchitsch could do was to come second behind 'the mechanic,' while Caracciola came third. Hermann turned the screw a little more at Livorno, where he won the prestigious Coppa Ciano to become a rightful challenger to the prowess of his teammates.

And he won that challenge in 1939 with straight victories in the Grands Prix of Pau, Tripoli – for the third consecutive year in a purpose-built W165 – the Eifel, Belgian and Swiss, before the Second World War stepped in and put a stop to motor racing. So, with the war going on, the German motor racing authorities declared Lang the 1939 European Champion. That season he had won five out of eight Grands Prix, set the fastest practice lap seven times and the fastest race lap four.

The war cost Hermann Lang the best years of his motor sport career, because by the time he was able to get back to racing in 1946 he was pushing 37. First, he used his savings to buy a Veritas Meteor to compete in Formula 2, but that proved unreliable. Meanwhile, Mercedes were anxious to get back into motor racing, so its first move was to update the pre-war supercharged W163, which Lang drove into second place in the 1951 Buenos Aires Grand Prix. But the W163's potential was no longer there, so the company decided to develop an all-new car.

Meanwhile, Hermännle went sports car racing and won the 1952 24 Hours of Le Mans with Fritz Riess, then, driving solo, the 1000 Kilometres of the Nürburgring in works Mercedes-Benz 300 SLs. He and co-driver Erwin Grupp also came second to Karl Kling and Hans Klenk in that year's Carrera Panamericana. Then Hermann tried Grand Prix racing again, first in a factory Maserati A6 GCM in 1953 and then a Mercedes-Benz W196 a year later, but he could only muster two points during those two seasons. The magic had gone.

Ever a realist, Hermann knew he had had his day and returned to the Mercedes-Benz factory, where he worked as a customer service inspector until he retired. He died on 19 October 1987.

# Lauda, Niki

'THE VICTORY TO PETERSON, the Glory to Lauda,' screamed the headline in *L'Equipe*, the top French sports newspaper, on 13 September 1976. And then it told the story of how Andreas-Nikolaus 'Niki' Lauda had come back from the brink of death – he had been given the last rites – just 43 days after his horrific accident at the Nürburgring, to set the second-fastest lap and take fourth place in the Grand Prix of Italy at Monza the previous day. It was a truly heroic performance in the works Ferrari 312T2 by a man whose head was still swathed in rather bloody bandages, but whose sheer guts, technical prowess and determination were to win him three F1 world titles and 25 championship Grands Prix.

It was a struggle to get going, though. Niki was born into a wealthy Viennese family on 22 February 1949, but his father wouldn't hear of him taking up a motor racing career – this after he had raced a Mini, a Formula Vee and moved up to more powerful sports racers like Porsche and Chevron. So Lauda decided to go it alone in 1972 and negotiated a large loan from an Austrian bank to buy himself the second seat in the works March Formula 1 team. It turned out that its Ford-powered cars were uncompetitive and the team came only sixth in the Constructors' World Championship with a measly 15 points to winner Lotus' 61.

Always the pragmatist, Lauda reasoned that the only way out of debt was to press on. He was invited to test drive a BRM at the Paul Ricard circuit in France and managed to go faster than team driver Vern Schuppan. The Austrian told BRM he could deliver sponsorship, but in reality he paid the team with the proceeds of yet another bank loan. None other than team owner Louis Stanley eventually lifted the gloom from Niki's financial horizon. After Lauda's fine performance in the 1973 Monaco Grand Prix before his gearbox broke, the BRM boss said he would forget Niki's sponsorship prospects and give him a salaried place in the team if he signed a three-year contract: Lauda didn't have to think twice about that one. His best performance in the uncompetitive BRM P160E was fifth at the Belgian GP. Meanwhile, the team's other driver, Clay Regazzoni, told Enzo Ferrari of Niki's promise during one of the Swiss driver's visits to Maranello, so Lauda was invited to test a *Rossa* at Fiorano, where he proved Regazzoni right.

After a heated argument with Louis Stanley, who wanted Lauda to stay, money changed hands and 'The Little Austrian,' as Enzo Ferrari called Niki, became a Maranello works driver. He immediately showed what he could do by taking second in the 312B3 at the season's first Grand Prix in Argentina, and went on to win in Spain and Holland to finish fourth in the World Championship. The following year he won the title, with victories in Monaco, Belgium, Sweden, France and the United States (Watkins Glen) to give Ferrari its first World Championship in 11 years.

The Little Austrian had won the 1976 Brazilian, South African, Belgian, Monaco and British GPs by the time he had his horrific 150mph accident on the first lap of the Grand Prix of Germany at the 'Ring. Lauda sat slumped and unconscious in his battered, blazing Ferrari 312T2 as four other heroes – drivers Guy Edwards, Arturo Merzario, Brett Lunger and Harald Ertl – tried to rescue him: it was Merzario who literally plunged into the flames with complete disregard for his own life and unfastened Niki's safety harness so that he could be extracted from the wreckage. Severely burned about the face and head, Lauda hovered between life and death for four days: his lungs had been scorched and toxic fumes from the Ferrari's burning body had poisoned him. That is when Maranello motor sport director Marco Piccinini called in a priest and had him give Niki the last rites. As they were being administered, Lauda said later that he couldn't speak or move, but his mind was lucid. He was amazed to see the priest and Piccinini praying and thought: 'What the f**k are you doing? I won't die.'

Lauda fought back in time to take fourth at Monza in the Ferrari 312T2 with an amazingly courageous performance. A third at Watkins Glen meant he had a three-point championship lead by the time the Circus got to the Fuji circuit in Japan for the season's finale. The track had been flooded for hours by torrential rain, and the after-effects of the Nürburgring crash left Niki with no physical or mental reserves with which to compete in such dangerous conditions, so he retired and effectively handed the title to McLaren's James Hunt. The Italian press savaged him for it: some journalists even accused him of being yellow. They were lambasting a man who had already won the World Championship in a Ferrari and made a superhuman effort at Monza so soon after his accident: a heinous, not to say foolish, stance. But Lauda had the last laugh in 1977. Driving the Mauro Forghieri-designed Ferrari 312T2, he won the South African, German and Dutch Grands Prix, retook the World Championship in the Ferrari 312T2 with 72 points to runner-up Wolf's Jody Scheckter with 55, and was instrumental in Maranello also winning the constructors' world title. So much for being yellow.

After that Niki moved to Brabham-Alfa Romeo for two years. There he drove Gordon Murray's BT46B 'vacuum cleaner,' an F1 car with a huge fan at the back that generated massive downforce, in which he won the Swedish GP. Laughingly, the team said the fan was for cooling purposes, but FISA said it was to increase downforce and banned the car. Lauda still won the Grand Prix of Italy in a fanless BT46, but only came fourth in the championship table, 20 points behind winner Mario Andretti.

In 1980/1 Niki took a two-year sabbatical from Formula 1 to concentrate on setting up his own airline: he hardly appeared at the Grand Prix circuits. But McLaren's Ron Dennis dangled an extraordinarily large bag of gold at him, which was his if he would return to Formula 1 – and that did the trick. Lauda won the Grands Prix of Long Beach and Britain in the Ford-powered McLaren MP4-1B, but that was only enough to net him fifth place in the Drivers' World Championship with 30 points to new champion Keke Rosberg's 44. He didn't win a race in 1983.

The 1984 season was an explosive one for McLaren; Niki and his teammate Alain Prost won 12 of the year's 16 Grands Prix in the fabulous McLaren MP4/2-TAG Porsche. Five of them went to Lauda – South Africa, France, Britain, Austria and Italy – and seven to Prost. Niki only qualified 11th for the last race of the season at Estoril in Portugal, but worked his way up to second behind winner Alain Prost. As only half-points were awarded at the year's Monaco Grand Prix, Niki became the 1984 Formula 1 World Champion with 72 points to Alain's 71½.

The Little Austrian did score one more Grand Prix victory at Zandvoort in the McLaren MP4/2B-TAG Porsche, but that was it. He retired from racing for the second and last time and set about turning LaudaAir into a successful long-haul operator, based in Vienna and flying the Far East and Australian routes.

# Maglioli, Umberto

UMBERTO MAGLIOLI WAS A man who clearly knew where he was coming from. He once said he was good at driving extremely powerful cars, and explained that if he and nine other top drivers each competed in 100hp racers, he would probably come ninth or tenth; if the same ten raced against each other in 250hp cars he would cross the finish line fifth or sixth; but if they each had 500hp mounts he would win, especially if none of the other competitors knew the route, because he could interpret roads instinctively.

That special gift helped him to win the tortuous Targa Florio three times, a record that was never broken. But he is probably best remembered for winning Mexico's last Carrera Panamericana in 1954 in a massively powerful 5-litre Ferrari 375 Plus. Umberto adored speed, an addiction that earned him the nickname 'the Mad Italian.'

Born in Bioglio in the Italian region of Biella on 5 June 1928, Umberto got his first intoxicating taste of real motor racing by co-driving a Lancia Aprilia with Giovanni Bracco in the 1948 Mille Miglia. He once said of Bracco, who also came from Biella and would go on to win the Brescia–Rome–Brescia marathon in 1952, 'He was my mentor. He helped me to refine certain aspects of my driving. Without wanting to, though, he also taught me what I shouldn't do, like exceed maximum revs, brake with brutal force and be rough with the gearbox. But I consider the car a living thing and I always had a mental block when it came to ill-treating a vehicle. I believe that, if I had a choice between winning a race by over revving an engine and coming second without doing so, I'd choose the latter.'

The pair came 17th in the 1948 Mille Miglia, tried again to no avail in a Ferrari 166 S in 1949, and then scored an up to 2000cc class win in 1950 in the same car. They were the heroes of the 1951 event in their Lancia Aurelia, fighting a running battle with eventual winner Gigi Villoresi before coming second and winning the up to 2000cc category again. The following year Bracco was given a factory Ferrari 250 S and Maglioli struck out on his own in a Lancia Aurelia: they both did well, Bracco extraordinarily so as he won the event outright, while Maglioli won the up to 1500cc class. It was Umberto's turn to be given a works drive in the 1953 race, but he was forced to retire the factory 2900cc Lancia Aurelia with mechanical trouble. Not so in the year's Targa Florio, which Maglioli won in a 3-litre D20, narrowly beating Emilio Giletti and Juan Manuel Fangio in Maserati A6GCSs. Umberto also co-drove a 4.5-litre Ferrari 340 MM to victory with Mike Hawthorn in the 1953 12 Hours of Pescara.

At the end of the '53 season Maglioli was also given his first crack at Formula 1, and he did well to work the uncompetitive Ferrari 553 Squalo (shark) up to eighth in the Grand Prix of Italy at Monza. His occasional F1 career would stagger on in much the same way with Ferrari and Maserati until the end of the 1957 season, by which time he had taken a couple of thirds in the GPs of Italy and Argentina.

Road racing was another story altogether, never more so than in 1954, when Maglioli certainly did his share of helping Ferrari to win the World Sports Car Championship for the second consecutive year. He and Giuseppe Farina came first in the Buenos Aires 1000 Kilometres in a 375 MM, he won the non-championship Shell Gold Cup at Imola driving a 500 Mondial, and the Supercortemaggiore Grand Prix in a 735 S with Mike Hawthorn. But his biggest title contribution was victory in the Carrera Panamericana, a mad dash from one side of Mexico to another, which was stopped because it cost too many lives.

The Mexican marathon was perfect for a lover of powerful racing cars and an instinctive road-reader like Maglioli. It was a 1907.27-mile blind dash across Mexico, from Tuxla Gutierrez on the country's frontier with Guatemala to Ciudad Juarez, just inside the Mexican border near El Paso, Texas. Umberto administered his car carefully, because if he had given his 330hp Ferrari 375 Plus its head on the first leg, with its temptingly straight but highly abrasive road surfaces, he would have knocked out a set of tyres about every 45 miles! The big push had to wait until the last segment, when all the car's power could be unleashed to produce up to 170mph. He covered the race distance on his own in the car in 17hr 40min 26sec at an average speed of 107.64mph and crossed the line over 24 minutes ahead of Phil Hill and Richie Ginther in their 375 MM. But a strange thing happened after his great victory as he left the car briefly to get a Coke. An American, who had bought the Ferrari before the race, simply climbed into the Carrera winner, started it up and drove it away. Maglioli never saw it again!

The 1955 season was a little less eventful for Umberto, although he did manage third in the Mille Miglia driving a Ferrari 118 LM, won the Circuit of Mugello, the Aosta-Gran San Bernardo hillclimb and the Targa di Mugello in 750 Monzas.

Maglioli began his long and successful career with Porsche by coming fourth overall and taking a class win driving a 550 RS in the 1956 Nürburgring 1000 Kilometres, but his big victory of the year was at the wheel of a Porsche 550A RS in the Targa Florio, which was the Stuttgart constructor's first win in the great Sicilian classic. He had been down to share an OSCA with Giulio Cabianca, until Huschke von Hanstein – Porsche's motor sport director – invited him to switch to one of the German cars. Umberto's co-driver was to be the Porsche team boss, who had won the 1940 Mille Miglia for BMW, but von Hanstein withdrew and Umberto did the entire race on his own. Vincenzo Florio, who admired Maglioli greatly, said, as he presented the Biella driver with the impressive plaque, or *targa*, that winning this race for a second time meant that he could not hope to win it for a third. How wrong the old *patron* was!

Motor racing took a back seat to Umberto's business interests after that, as he had a company in Lugano, Switzerland, that made precision watches. But he did win the 1964 12 Hours of Sebring with Mike Parkes in a Ferrari 275 P.

Umberto also proved Vincenzo Florio wrong some time after the old man's death and gave Porsche another Targa victory in 1968, when he shared a 907 with Britain's Vic Elford. The pair took 6hr 28min 47sec to cover the ten 44.739km laps of the Piccolo Madonie circuit, taking pole position and setting a fastest lap of 36min 2.3sec as they went.

After that Umberto concentrated on business until his death on 7 February 1999, four months before his 71st birthday.

# Mairesse, Willy

HE WAS THE KIND of fighter Enzo Ferrari adored. One who wouldn't rest until he had wrung the absolute maximum out of a car or crashed it in the process. And he often did. Before he was taken on at Maranello in 1960 he had laid to rest the crumpled remains of a Porsche 1500, a Peugeot 203, a Mercedes-Benz 300 SL and three Ferrari Berlinettas.

Born in the small village of Momignies, Belgium, on 1 October 1928, the spotlight first focused on Mairesse in 1955, when he won the 1300cc class of the murderous Liège–Rome–Liège road race in his own Peugeot 203. A year later he rallied and raced his own new Mercedes-Benz 300 SL and this time he won the merciless, non-stop marathon from Liège to Rome and back. That got him noticed by Ferrari's importer for Belgium and Enzo's close ally, Jacques Swaters, who ran Ecurie Nationale Belge. Mairesse drove for the team from 1957–59 but, surprisingly, turned in poor results. But it was Willy's long-running battle with Olivier Gendebien in the '59 Tour de France Automobile that caught the Commendatore's eye, so, with Swaters' backing, in 1960 Mairesse packed his bags for Maranello.

He made his Ferrari Formula 1 debut in the 1960 Grand Prix of Belgium at Spa-Francorchamps in June, when he was into some determined cut and thrust with Chris Bristow and the Briton's Cooper Climax. After continually swapping the lead, the Cooper crept ahead by a whisker, but on the wrong line; Bristow tried to correct, but lost control. The car flew off the circuit, threw its driver out and Bristow was killed. Mairesse was shocked but continued until he had to retire on lap 24 with transmission problems.

That same year Willy finally broke Gendebien's steely grip on the Tour de France Automobile, which the suave Belgian had won three times in succession. Mairesse unseated his countryman for the win in 1960 and repeated the process in 1961, all in Ferrari 250 GTs.

Willy's F1 career at Ferrari rumbled on for a total of 13 Grands Prix with the Belgian national team, Ferrari and even Lotus. For Maranello, he won the non-championship GPs of Brussels (156 V6) and Naples (Dino 156), but the rest were peppered with accidents, like the collision with Trevor Taylor's Lotus Climax in Willy's home GP at Spa in '62. The two were dicing for second just inches apart for about 20 of the race's 32 laps before Taylor's Lotus slipped out of gear and the cars touched. Both cannoned off the circuit, the Mairesse Ferrari in a ball of flame, the two drivers thrown from their cars. The Englishman ended up with his pride and body bruised, but Mairesse had more serious injuries, although he was back in time to drive his works Ferrari Dino 156 into fourth place – Maranello's highest-placed car – in the Grand Prix of Italy.

Transmission and engine problems put Willy out of the Monaco and Belgian GPs in 1963. He qualified seventh for the GP of Germany but crashed at Flugplatz on the initial lap, during which an ambulance man was killed and the Belgian came away with severe arm injuries.

But Willy's sports car racing career was altogether better. Maybe he wasn't Ferrari's most prolific winner – that honour went to Gendebien – but he claimed a brace of Targa Florios, the 1000 Kilometres of the Nürburgring plus the 24 Hours of Spa.

The first Sicilian win was in 1962 at the wheel of a Ferrari 246 SP co-driven by Ricardo Rodriguez and Olivier Gendebien. Mairesse leapt into the lead on the first lap, with Dan Gurney trying hard to hold him in a Porsche 718 WRS, but that was not to be. The tattered Stuttgart car eventually dropped out with heavy accident damage, while the Ferrari crew covered the 720km of the 'small' Madonie Circuit at an average speed of 63.468mph, the lap record of 40 minutes dead going to Willy.

High on the Targa win, Mairesse drove a Ferrari 250 GTO with Mike Parkes to take second in the 1962 1000 Kilometres of the Nürburgring, won by his old sparring partner Gendebien and Phil Hill in a 246 SP, both results major contributors to Ferrari winning the World Sports Car Championship for the sixth time. The following year got off to a good start with seconds for Mairesse in both the 12 Hours of Sebring (Ferrari 250 P) and the Targa Florio (Dino 196 SP), and he won the 1000 Kilometres of the 'Ring with Surtees in the 250 P.

Willy's Ferrari career ended in another fiery incident. He was leading the 1963 24 Hours of Le Mans in a 250 P on lap 252 when there was an explosion behind the car's dashboard after petrol vapour had seeped out of the fuel filler cap, and the car burst into flames. A stunned and burnt Mairesse was able to scramble out of the blazing Ferrari and hobble back to the pits, his arms badly scorched, where he kept repeating 'la voiture brûle.'

Those injuries kept Mairesse out of motor racing for most of 1964, although he did join the Equipe Nationale Belge team's trip to Angola, where he took pole position and won the local Grand Prix in a Ferrari 250 LM. The following year he and Frenchman Jean Beurlys took a healthy third and won the GT category of the 24 Hours of Le Mans driving a Ferrari 275 GTB, and did the same again in 1967.

World Championship sports car racing became a battlefield between Ford and Ferrari in the early-mid 1960s and hostilities were at fever pitch after Maranello had refused the Americans' takeover bid. So it was no surprise that ex-works Ferrari driver Mairesse was recruited by Ford for the 1966 1000 Kilometres of Monza, which Surtees-Parkes won for Ferrari, but Willy and his old partner Herbert Müller took third in their GT40. Mairesse slipped back into a Ferrari 250 LM for the 1965 Spa Grand Prix and he won that at an average of 126.359mph.

The second Targa win came the day after heavy rain had left the event's narrow 'roads' flooded and strewn with the remains of landslides. It was meteorological gloom for an event that was celebrating its 60th anniversary and its 50th running. Still, the competitors slithered their way past rogue rocks, through mud and slime to either oblivion or the finish line. Not surprisingly the attrition rate was high, with works Ferraris and Porsches skidding out of contention throughout the entire race. The Mairesse-Müller Porsche 906-6/2.0 had managed to pull out a six-minute lead on the sole surviving Ferrari Dino of Guichet-Baghetti and kept it to win – which was the start of a five-year stranglehold on the race by the Stuttgart company, whose winning car gobbled up the ten 72km laps in 7hr 16min 32sec at an average 61.492mph.

Willy's last race was the 1968 Le Mans, in which he had agreed to drive Belgian Claude Dubois' privately entered Mk1 Ford GT40. But he lost control of the car on the Mulsanne straight and he smashed it into a wall. He was in a coma for two weeks, after which he was disabled, had severe eye problems and lost his fighting spirit. He committed suicide in a dingy apartment in Ostend on 2 September 1969.

# Mansell, Nigel

WHAT CAN YOU SAY about a man who wins the 1992 Formula 1 World Championship, moves to the United States almost immediately afterwards and promptly wins the 1993 CART series? Brilliant? Phenomenal? Sensational? Yes, all of those understatements. But Nigel Mansell's achievements in motor racing are worth more, much more.

Nigel could be a whinger, melodramatic and in need of constant love from his fans. But he was also incredibly brave, determined, aggressive, brimming with natural talent, had remarkable car control and believed in himself unshakably. Anyone who saw him win the 1989 Grand Prix of Hungary for Ferrari would have to agree with that. He even unretired himself in 2005 at 52 years old and embarked on an occasional new career in the Grand Prix Masters series. And he beat the hell out of the rest of the field in the year's Grand Prix of South Africa, then won the 2006 Qatar GP, which included the likes of Emerson Fittipaldi, Alan Jones, Riccardo Patrese and Patrick Tambay.

Everyone knows about Nigel's early years: the struggling young racer trying to break into the big time; the qualified engineer working for Lucas Girling during the week and racing at the weekend, backed by his astute wife Rosanne, who agreed to him selling their apartment to keep going; the crash in a Unipart-backed March 793 in Formula 3 at Oulton Park, where he tangled with a kamikaze-like Andrea De Cesaris. They were at each other's throats when the Italian dived for a hole that wasn't there, clouted Nigel's March and sent it somersaulting off the track. That broke a couple of the Englishman's vertebrae. Two days later Colin Chapman called and invited Mansell to the chance of a lifetime: a Formula 1 test at the Paul Ricard with other aspirants. Nigel accepted, broken vertebrae and all. He knew a testing contract and the second driver's seat were up for grabs at Lotus. He also knew the more experienced Jan Lammers, Eddie Cheever and Elio De Angeles were after the same seat. So he shrewdly aimed for the tester's job. And, with his agonising Oulton back injury dulled by painkillers, he got the 1980 test and development driver deal. De Angeles won the second seat, with Mario Andretti as team leader.

Chapman gave Mansell his F1 break at the 1980 Grand Prix of Austria, and the newcomer qualified the team's oldest Lotus 81-Ford on the last row of the grid. Fuel leaked into the cockpit before the start and continued to trickle in throughout the race, which Nigel found was incredibly painful. He got the car up to 13th but its engine blew on lap 41, and that ended his uncomfortable Grand Prix debut.

Mansell's first podium finish was a third in the 1981 Belgian GP in a Lotus 81, and he racked up a few more points in Spain and Las Vegas, for which Chapman gave him a pay rise. But that didn't sit well with team manager Peter Warr, who once said, 'Mansell won't win a Grand Prix as long as he has a hole in his arse.' How wrong, not to say vulgar, that was.

The brilliant Colin Chapman, the driving force behind Lotus, and Nigel's mentor, died towards the end of 1982. Warr, his hand now strengthened, wanted Mansell out, but British cigarette manufacturer and Lotus sponsor John Player insisted there should be an English driver in the team. That kept Nigel racing in 1983 and 1984, but with very little to show for it, except thirds in the '83 GP of Europe at Brands Hatch, the '84 French at Dijon-Prenois and the Dutch at Zandvoort.

Enzo Ferrari liked Mansell's style and asked his motor sport director Marco Piccinini to talk to the Briton because he reminded the Commendatore of Peter Collins. Nigel was duly contacted and visited Maranello one Sunday, when he signed a note agreeing to collaborate with the team the following year. A couple of days later, though, Mansell sent word that he had spoken to his lawyer and declined the Ferrari offer, saying the signed note was not binding. Ferrari fumed and hissed, suggesting the Briton was using the negotiations to help him obtain a wage increase from Lotus.

Not true. At the end of 1984 Peter Warr whisked Ayrton Senna away from Toleman, so Mansell's days at Lotus were already numbered.

After all that, Nigel signed for Frank Williams to be Keke Rosberg's number two in 1985. The ultra-fast Williams-Honda was the shot in the arm Mansell needed. After more than 70 attempts, he won two World Championship Grands Prix in a row, the European at Brands Hatch and the South African at Kyalami. But at the end of the year Nigel's friend Keke went off to McLaren and the prickly Nelson Piquet joined Williams. For the next couple years the two were at daggers drawn, trying to beat each other to the world title. Mansell won a total of ten Grands Prix in '86 and '87, but it was Piquet who won the 1987 Formula 1 World Championship.

Then the Honda engine supply dried up and Williams was forced to settle for the 3.5-litre V8 Judd for 1988. The team didn't score a single victory that year. Nigel had already had enough by mid-season and signed for Ferrari for 1989.

He won on his Ferrari debut race. It was the 1989 Grand Prix of Brazil and he was in John Barnard's first car for Maranello, the semi-automatic gearbox 640. That was a spirited enough drive, but Nigel redefined himself with his astounding feat at the Hungaroring five months later, performing all sorts of gifted acrobatics with the Ferrari 640 to win on a track not exactly known for overtaking. After that the Italian *tifosi* christened him *Il Leone*, the lion.

But Nigel hated the political infighting so typical of Ferrari and he accepted Frank Williams' offer to drive for the British team again in 1991. The trick was to try to get the avant-garde Williams FW14 Renault to stay together long enough to win a race. Teammate Riccardo Patrese started the ball rolling with victory in Mexico, where Nigel came second. Then Mansell won in France, Britain, Germany, Italy and Spain, but that was still not enough for him to lay his hands on his first World Championship, which went to Ayrton Senna in the McLaren MP47A-Honda. Nigel was runner-up for the third time.

With the Williams-Renault now sorted, Mansell went after the 1992 World Championship with that case-hardened determination of his. He won nine Grands Prix that year, scored a massive 108 points to second-placed Patrese's mere 56 and, at last, became motor racing's king of the world. But Nigel didn't like how the Williams team was shaping up for 1993, with Prost and Senna banging on Williams' door. So he took his World Championship and set sail for the United States, where he won the '93 CART title at first try.

His final tally was one F1 World Championship, 31 Grands Prix victories, the 1993 CART title and five US wins.

Nigel made various motor racing comebacks, one with Williams in 1994 and another with McLaren in 1995. He and his sons Leo and Greg qualified for the 2010 24 Hours of Le Mans, but on lap four one of the 4.5-litre Ginetta Zytek's tyres punctured and the car crashed. Nigel, who was driving, suffered a bump on the head but quickly recovered.

# Marzotto, Giannino, Paolo, Vittorio and Umberto

THE STORY OF THE four Marzotto brothers and their brief but mercurial motor racing careers was mostly about Giannino winning the Mille Miglia twice, in 1950 and 1953, which put him up there with greats like Giuseppe Campari, who won the race in 1928 and 1929, and Tazio Nuvolari, the 1930 and 1933 winner.

That's not to dismiss the successes of Giannino's three brothers, who pulled off some incredible performances during the same period. Like Vittorio winning the 1952 Grand Prix of Monaco, Paolo's double victory in the 1952 and 1953 Coppa d'Oro delle Dolomiti – the alpine 'Mille Miglia' through the 11,000ft Dolomite Mountains in northern Italy – or Umberto winning his class in the same event.

The Marzottos were the epitome of that dying breed, the gentleman driver. Young, fast, wealthy and each one a nobleman with the title of count before his name. But Giannino was the star. He was the one who beat five-times F1 World Champion Juan Manuel Fangio twice in the Mille Miglia. And it is not true to say that was because JMF was not a good road racer. The Argentine first made his name by winning a long list of just such races in South America. As the great man often said, he loved road racing but he was just unlucky at it in Europe. The Mille Miglia is the one trophy missing from the collection in his Balcarce museum, and he always regretted that.

Giannino was a versatile star. He was as successful on the Mille Miglia's 'closed' public roads as he was on the dusty mountain tracks of the Coppa d'Oro, a race he won in 1950 driving a Ferrari 195 S; and on racing circuits like Rouen-Les-Essarts, where he won the 1951 Grand Prix of Europe in a single-seater Ferrari 166 F2.

The brothers, from Valdagno in northern Italy, were all sons of Count Gaetano Marzotto Jr, himself a useful road racer and head of the Marzotto Group at the time. Established almost 200 years ago, the group is now one of the world's leading textile industries and owns a hotel chain.

The brothers formed their own team, Scuderia Marzotto, and mainly raced Ferraris in the early 1950s. They didn't specialise in little country events, but took on the world's best. For instance, in the 1950 and 1953 Mille Miglias Giannino beat not only Fangio but also Gigi Villoresi, Mike Hawthorn and even Clemente Biondetti, the only man to win the race four times. All four brothers competed in that year's Italian classic, Giannino famously wearing an immaculate double-breasted suit, shirt, tie and waistcoat. And he admitted to stowing a hot water bottle under this suave get-up to ease his stomach cramp, but that disappeared after a few kilometres so he threw the bottle away. In the end Giannino won, Vittorio came ninth.

Paolo was not so lucky. He tried to brake for a railway level crossing but the pedal went right down to the floor. So he shouted 'Get down!' to his co-driver Marino Marini as the open-top 166 MM beat a fast approaching train and just made it under both the crossing's barriers before coming to a halt and retiring. Umberto's Ferrari hit a tree and broke in half, so that was his race over too.

A year later, the reigning Mille Miglia winner clashed with Enzo Ferrari. Giannino believed the Commendatore's cars could go faster if they were more aerodynamic. So the Count and his friend Sergio Reggiani came up with their own 'optical intuition' design, a bulbous, rounded body shape that coach-builder Fontana eased on to a Ferrari 212 Export chassis: the car was nicknamed 'The Egg.' But the ugly duckling went well, because Giannino was 11 minutes ahead of eventual winner Gigi Villoresi and his Ferrari 340 America when The Egg dropped out with tyre trouble just beyond Pesaro.

Meanwhile, Vittorio kept the Marzotto colours flying with a resounding win in the 1951 Giro di Sicilia in his Ferrari 212 Export, beating stars of the day like Piero Taruffi, Giovanni Bracco and Clemente Biondetti.

All four did well in the 1952 Coppa d'Oro delle Dolomiti. Paolo won in a Ferrari 225 S with Giannino second driving a Ferrari 340 America, Vittorio came fifth in another Ferrari 225 S and Umberto seventh in a Ferrari 212

Export. And they totally dominated the race's over 1100cc Sport Class, which Paulo won, with Giannino second, Vittorio third and Umberto fourth. A record that was never broken.

In 1952 Paolo added a few more scalps to his belt, including victory in the Giro di Sicilia in a Ferrari 166 MM and the 12 Hours of Pescara driving a 250 S, followed home in second place by Giannino in a 340 America.

At the age of 24 Vittorio beat established stars like Eugenio Castellotti and the up-and-coming Peter Collins to win the 1952 Grand Prix of Monaco – which was for sports cars that year – in a Scuderia Marzotto Ferrari 225 S.

Relations between Enzo Ferrari and the brothers cooled after they set up Scuderia Marzotto and The Egg saga, so in 1953 Giannino went looking for another car in which to try to win his second Mille Miglia. Alfa Romeo had promised him a Disco Volante, but that dried up, and Gianni Lancia said all his cars were spoken for. Meanwhile, Giannino's regular co-driver Marco Crosara had been doing a little fence-mending with Enzo Ferrari. Eventually the two went to Maranello, where the Commendatore showed them to a shed. It housed a rather tired-looking 340 America in which Gigi Villoresi had just won the Giro di Sicilia. That was the only car on offer, so the two youngsters took it, won the 1953 Mille Miglia in it and set a record average speed of 89mph to boot.

Paolo won the Coppa d'Oro for a second successive time in a Ferrari 250 MM in 1953, as well as the race's International Sport Category. Giannino and Paolo even competed in the 1953 24 Hours of Le Mans and drove one of Maranello's 340 MMs into fifth place, the only Scuderia Ferrari car to finish.

Giannino and Paolo also drove works Ferraris in the 1954 Mille Miglia, the 1950 and 1953 victor in a 275 S and his younger brother a 2-litre 500 Mondial. Giannino, co-driven by his sister-in-law Gioia Tortima, got as far as Fano. His car was breaking up, with the body panels being vibrated loose by a rogue auxiliary oil tank, so he retired. But Paolo was having a great race, one of the highlights of which was his no-quarter battle with Luigi Musso in a Maserati A6G CS. In the end Paolo roared across the Brescia finish line just nine seconds ahead of third-placed Musso after 12 hours of close-quarter racing.

Paolo's swansong was the 1955 Mille Miglia in which he drove a works Ferrari 4500, but its tyres couldn't take the car's power output. One of them threw a tread at 175mph, so he slowed gingerly to change the wheel – but then saw that the spare was a different size!

Gradually business interests demanded more of the brothers' time, so their motor racing careers had to be set aside. Giannino, who died in 2012, became managing director of the family textiles business. Paolo is now the chairman of the company that produces the outstanding Santa Margherita wines. Umberto went into the family business, as did Vittorio, who died in February 1999.

# McLaren, Bruce

WE CALLED IT THE 'Bruce and Denny Show' and *it* was total dominance of the Can-Am Championship by McLaren Cars from 1967 to 1971, during which they won 43 of the series' races, *23 of them consecutively.* It was an astounding performance, in which New Zealander Bruce McLaren won the championships of 1967 and 1969, his countryman and teammate Denny Hulme those of 1968 and 1970, and American Peter Revson the 1971, all in McLaren cars.

But Bruce was killed in mid-1970 when he was only 32 years old, testing his new Can-Am car at Britain's Goodwood circuit. He had won four Formula 1 World Championship Grands Prix – which never really reflected his single-seater ability – two Can-Am titles and nine races, the 24 Hours of Le Mans, and was poised to make a full frontal attack on the Indianapolis 500.

Bruce's dad owned a garage in the Auckland suburb of Remuera in New Zealand, where the lad used to hang around the workshop before a run-in with Perthes, a disease that affected his hip and left his left leg shorter than his right. An unpleasant two years in traction was a help, not a cure, because Bruce was left with a noticeable limp. But that didn't stop him from winning the 1958 Driver to Europe scheme run by the New Zealand International Grand Prix Association after scoring good results in his own Cooper F2 car.

McLaren's British F2 performances caught Jack Brabham's eye and that got the youngster a ride alongside Black Jack in the works Cooper team. Bruce made his mark pretty soon and won the '59 USGP at Sebring, the youngest Grand Prix winner at the time, as he was only 20. Jack came fourth in the same race and that was enough to secure him his first world title.

The 1960 season was Bruce's best in F1 as he finished second to Jack in the World Championship, mainly supporting the Australian and placing well. But when Brabham retired from the Grand Prix of Argentina with gearbox trouble McLaren went for it, beating an impressive field of Ferraris, Lotuses, BRMs and Maseratis to win.

With Jack's departure to form his own team at the end of 1961 the young New Zealander took over as Cooper's team leader, but that was the year the little Surbiton company's performance began to wane. There were no F1 championship victories for Bruce and Cooper in 1962, but McLaren did manage to put his works Cooper-Climax on the front row of the grid at the 1962 Monaco GP with Graham Hill (BRM) and Jim Clark (Lotus-Climax). Graham's mastery of the Monte Carlo circuit soon began to show and by lap 56 of a scheduled 100 the Briton was 48 seconds ahead of Bruce; but Hill's oil pressure was dropping and he was forced to let McLaren through on lap 93 to win.

Bruce was unhappy when Charles Cooper refused to build two cars for him to race in the 1963/4 Tasman Cup Championship. So McLaren, who stayed on at Cooper for a total of seven years, built the cars himself and raced them down under as Bruce McLaren Motor Racing entries.

The young New Zealander won the 1964 Tasman Cup Championship with three consecutive victories at Pukekohe, Wigram and Teretonga Park, but his American teammate Tim Mayer crashed and died while practising for the last race in the series at Longford, Tasmania. Qualified lawyer Teddy Mayer, who had been managing his late brother's career, joined forces with Bruce and brought money and more brainpower to the fledgling McLaren team.

McLaren left Cooper at the end of 1965 and rolled out his own F1 team, an all-Kiwi driving affair with Chris Amon as his number two. That didn't last long, because Chris was head-hunted by Ferrari to drive for Maranello. But before he left the two won the 1966 24 Hours of Le Mans in one of the Shelby American Inc Ford GT40s.

McLaren Motor Racing was on the threshold of something really great as Bruce and Chris became two of the earliest competitors in Can-Am in 1966, driving the McLaren M1A and then the M1B. The cars were not exactly earth-shattering performers, so Bruce came back with his Chevrolet-powered M6A in 1967 and Chris' spot was taken over by another New

Zealander, Denny Hulme. And that was when the curtain went up on the Bruce and Denny show.

Hulme won the first three Can-Am races in the McLaren M6A-Chevrolet, but Bruce stepped in and took both the Laguna Seca and Riverside rounds, which, with his better placings, made him the 1967 Can-Am Champion.

By then the fans had well and truly caught the big banger bug and were packing the circuits by 1 September 1968, when the McLaren M6As and M8As took hold of the series and didn't let go of it for two whole years. They won 23 consecutive races, 11 falling to Denny, seven to Bruce, two to Dan Gurney, one to Mark Donohue, another to Canadian John Cannon and a single victory to Peter Gethin before Tony Dean brought a temporary end to all that in a Porsche 908 by winning Road Atlanta on 13 September 1970. It was only a brief respite, though, because the McLarens were back on the warpath at Brainerd on 27 September, when they began another 15-race victory run before Porsche became top dog with the fabled 917.

The McLaren F1 effort continued into 1969 with Bruce and Denny scoring many top six placings but no more victories.

Bruce was down to drive Carroll Shelby's STP turbine car at Indianapolis in 1968, but the American withdrew the jet-powered monster because he considered it too powerful. McLaren still had his sights set on the Brickyard and in mid-1969 got designer Gordon Coppuck to create the turbocharged M15 based on the team's all-conquering Can-Am car. Testing confirmed the car could be competitive, but during a practice session the fuel filler cap snapped open and covered tester Denny Hulme's hands and the car itself with blazing methanol. That put Hulme out of racing and meant that he could not drive one of the three M15s readied for Indy; the remaining two were campaigned by Carl Williams and Peter Revson, who covered 197 and 87 of the 200 laps respectively. And the M15 won Indy's coveted award for engineering excellence.

Then tragedy struck. Bruce was killed testing his new M8D Can-Am contender at Goodwood on 2 June 1970. After the shock and horror of losing its quiet, charismatic, highly successful boss, the team decided the best tribute they could pay him was to continue, which they did in spectacular fashion in F1, Can-Am and Indy, where Mark Donohue won the 500 in a McLaren in 1972 and Johnny Rutherford in 1974 and 1976.

Bruce's achievements were staggering. He was a Grand Prix winner four times over, his cars had become the dominant force in Can-Am and stayed that way for five mind-blowing years, and he was about to take Indianapolis by storm. Some said he was thinking of retiring from racing before he died. His business was certainly a success and a road-going version of his M6 Can-Am racer was on the cards: prototypes had already been built.

But the McLaren team went on to become one of the greatest in the history of Formula 1, a fitting tribute to its founder.

# Moll, Guy

ENZO FERRARI WAS ALWAYS a sucker for fighters who would never give up, like Tazio Nuvolari, Guy Moll and Gilles Villeneuve. In fact, he thought Moll could become the anti-Nuvolari, so talented was the little Algerian. But Guy's brief yet spectacular career came to a sudden halt on 15 August 1934 in the Coppa Acerbo race at Pescara, Italy.

Described by some as the greatest natural talent ever, Guillaume Laurent (Guy) Moll was born on 28 May 1910 to a Spanish mother and a French father, who had emigrated to Algeria. After completing his schooling, he first competed in a local race driving a Lorraine-Dietrich loaned to him for the occasion by wealthy Algerian garage-owner and gentleman driver Marcel Lehoux. The young man's benefactor also put Moll down for the Grand Prix of Oran in northern Algeria and this time loaned his protégé a Bugatti T35C, in which Moll immediately took the lead but had to retire with mechanical problems.

It was only a matter of time before Guy made his mark in motor racing. His first important European event was the 1932 Grand Prix of Marseilles, in which he and the T35C gave Nuvolari and the French gentleman racer Raymond Sommer a run for their money, but eventually came third after a daggers-drawn tussle won by Tazio with Sommer second.

The son of wealthy parents, Guy bought himself an Alfa Romeo 8C Monza, which he campaigned throughout 1933. He started by coming fifth in his new acquisition at the Grand Prix of France at Montlhéry, then took third in the car in the Grands Prix of Nîmes, Nice, Comminges and Marseilles again, ending his season with two fine second places in the GPs of Pau and Monza, the latter won by his moneyed mentor Marcel Lehoux.

The youngster was going places, because his fighting, never-give-up style impressed Enzo Ferrari, who signed him for Scuderia Ferrari at the end of

1933. Guy made his big-time debut in one of the Scuderia's Alfa Romeo Tipo B P3s. And that was when he shook the racing world rigid by winning the most prestigious Grand Prix of them all at Monaco, the season's first major event. He beat the likes of second-placed Louis Chiron, who was competing in his home town, Rene Dreyfus (third), Lehoux (fourth), Tazio Nuvolari (fifth) and Achille Varzi (sixth). Heady stuff! And he was only 23.

Just over a month later a truly international cast turned out at the brand new Mellaha circuit in Libya for the Grand Prix of Tripoli, organised by one of the founders of the Mille Miglia, Renzo Castagneto. They included Frenchmen Jean-Pierre Wimille and René Dreyfus, Italians Achille Varzi, Piero Taruffi, Carlo Felice Trossi and Felice Bonetto, Americans Peter de Paolo and Whitney Straight, Englishmen George Eyston and Hugh Hamilton, Monegasque Louis Chiron and Algerian Guy Moll. They were to perform in their various Alfa Romeos, Maseratis, Millers and Bugattis before a massive crowd of almost 100,000 spectators. And did those spectators get their money's worth!

Taruffi shot into the lead in his Maserati 5000, chased by Varzi's Alfa Romeo Tipo B P3, followed by Chiron and Trossi in similar cars. But Taruffi was only able to hold on to command for five laps, after which Chiron passed him. The Monegasque was still leading by the 15th lap, hounded by his teammate Varzi, Hamilton in another Maserati 3000 and Moll's P3, in which he had sliced his way through the pack from the third row of the grid. With the waltz of the pit stops for more fuel and tyres, Moll slipped into third place behind leader Chiron, with Philippe Etancelin's Maserati 3000 in second. Then, towards the end of the race, Chiron lost it and spun, which cost him time and let 23-year-old Moll through into the second spot to turn on one of the most dramatic racecar chases of all time.

Moll's quarry was Varzi, and the young Algerian drove like a demon to catch the Italian in an electrifying display of courage and car control that had the crowds cheering themselves hoarse. Guy edged his Alfa right up to within millimetres of Achille's exhaust pipe and was still gaining on the great Italian as they crossed the finish line, with Varzi just a wheel ahead of the young pretender.

Carlo Felice Trossi and Moll shared a P3 for the Grand Prix of France at Montlhéry, where they came third. In fact, Guy scored a series of podium finishes that year before winning the Avusrennen in pouring rain on the converted autobahn circuit near Berlin in a weird, cumbersome-looking streamlined version of a 3.2-litre P3 designed for Scuderia Ferrari by Giuseppe Pallavicino, an engineer with Italy's Aeronautica Breda.

A full turnout of the new Auto Union Type As and Mercedes-Benz W25s travelled to Pescara for the Coppa Acerbo, run over the famous 16-mile road circuit in mid-August. They made the Italian cars seem obsolete, and the Scuderia Ferrari drivers had to bust a gut to keep up with the Silver Arrows. Things started to look decidedly bleak in practice, during which Achille Varzi blew two of the Scuderia's 2.9-litre P3 engines trying to hold back the German tide. Chiron's P3 literally went up in smoke.

Pit-stop poker once again reshuffled the field so that Mercedes' new acquisition Luigi Fagioli was in the lead with none other than Guy Moll lying second, 37 seconds behind him. In his mad dash to overcome the Silver Arrows, Guy set the race's fastest lap of 10min 51sec at an average speed of 89.1mph, and by lap 16 Moll had chopped Fagioli's lead to 29 seconds: the young Algerian stood a good chance of winning if he could just maintain that kind of progress.

But on lap 17 Moll went into a lurid skid and stalled his P3's engine, giving away time he could ill afford. He soon got his car going again, and as he charged through the village of Capelle he could see German racing motorcyclist and record-breaker Ernst Henne plodding along in his factory Mercedes. Guy floored the accelerator and pulled out to lap the dawdling Henne on the Montesilvano straight. But suddenly his Alfa went into a frightening skid for no apparent reason, upended, rolled over wildly several times and crashed. Guy, just 24 years old, was fatally injured and died soon afterwards.

There were the usual know-all remarks about Moll's youth and, therefore, his supposed inexperience. But wiser motor racing enthusiasts knew different. They acknowledged that the real problem was probably a technological one. By 1934 engine power was so far ahead of chassis and brake design that the real challenge was not pushing the cars through corners, but keeping them on the road when all that power was unleashed. The cross-ply form of tyre construction was also less advanced than the engines that drove them, so they often threw a tread or blew out in motor racing of that period. Any one of these factors could have prominently figured in the accident in which Guy Moll, one of the greatest natural talents of his era, was killed.

In 1935 the Municipality of Montesilvano named a square after the dead Algerian driver and placed a commemorative plaque on the wall of Villa Carmine, near the site of his fatal accident.

# Moss, Stirling

AN IRASCIBLE MOTORCYCLE COP in a 1970s British TV advertisement for Renault pulled up next to the car he had been chasing and asked the driver gruffly, 'Who do you think you are, Stirling Moss?' The man at the wheel just turned to the policeman and grinned. Because he *was* Stirling Moss! And that just shows the unprecedented popularity that this hyper-energetic, extraordinarily efficient human being, and one of the greatest racing drivers of the 20th century, has enjoyed since the early 1950s. Even well into his 80s he was still a major celebrity. Just seeing him walk into a London restaurant the diners would start nudging each other and whispering, 'That's Stirling Moss!' Such is the impact he has had on British society and motor racing fans for more than six decades.

Britain was not the only nation that wrung its hands in anguish as its battered hero lay unconscious in hospital for a month after his horrific accident at St Mary's corner, Goodwood, on 23 April 1962. The whole world heaved a huge sigh of relief when Moss eventually pulled out of it and began charging around the hospital's corridors in a suspiciously fast wheelchair.

Stirling is a highly articulate man with a roguish twinkle in his eye, a love of life and a sense of fun that seems to know no bounds. He is also a man only the churlish would deny a place in their list of the five greatest racing drivers of all time.

His success rate was phenomenal in a sport that was not as kind to him as it might have been. I am sure Stirling is sick to death of reading about him being a king without a crown, the driver who was runner-up to four Formula 1 World Champions, and does not need this author to say he long ago came to terms with this weird quirk of fate. But he did.

Anyway, one only has to look up his entry in any motor racing Who's Who to be reminded of his stunning achievements.

Alfred Moss, Stirling's father, was not only a successful dentist but was also a gifted amateur racing driver, who competed in the Indianapolis 500 in the 1920s: and our hero's mother Aileen was an enthusiastic rally and trials competitor. As children, Stirling and his late sister Pat were outstanding show-jumpers before both graduated to cars, in which Pat became the world's top woman rally driver of her day.

Stirling started by racing a BMW 328 in 1947 and the following year broke into 500cc F3 racing to become its undisputed star, battling with courage and inspiration against other rising stars of his day like Peter Collins, Stuart Lewis-Evans and one Bernie Ecclestone. Between 1950–52 he also raced for the under-financed and under-developed British HWM F2 outfit and was invited by Enzo Ferrari to drive one of his cars in the Bari Grand Prix down there on the heel of Italy. But after struggling across post-war Europe and down the length of Italy to claim his drive, Moss was told the car had been reassigned to Piero Taruffi without so much as a by-your-leave. A slap in the face if ever there was one that embittered Stirling towards Enzo Ferrari for years to come.

In 1953 Mercedes-Benz had let slip that they would be coming back to Grand Prix racing in a year's time. American writer Ken Gregory, Stirling's manager at the time, and Alfred Moss campaigned for a place in the German team for him, but wily old Alfred Neubauer was not so sure. He wanted to see Moss Jr compete in a full-blown F1 car before he would say yes or no. He got his proof. Stirling was pulling away from Juan Manuel Fangio's state-of-the-art Mercedes W196 in the 1954 Grand Prix of Italy until waning oil pressure meant his private Maserati 250F finished tenth, nine laps down on the Argentine. But Neubauer had got the message and invited Moss to join the M-B team for 1955.

And what a year that was. Moss won his homeland's Grand Prix at Aintree in the Mercedes-Benz W196 and the '55 Mille Miglia navigated by the late Denis Jenkinson in a 300 SLR, in which he set an unbeaten record average speed of 98.5mph. He and Juan Manuel Fangio were battling Mike Hawthorn's Jaguar for the lead in the 1955 24 Hours of Le Mans before Pierre Levegh's disintegrating Mercedes killed over 80 people, injured 120 more and the German team withdrew from the event. And Stirling and Peter Collins drove the 300 SLR to victory in the 1955 Targa Florio to give their Stuttgart employers the World Sports Car Championship. But Mercedes retired from racing at the end of 1955, so Moss moved to Maserati as its team leader and won the 1956 Monaco and Italian Grands Prix for them in the fabled 250F.

Steadfastly patriotic, Stirling achieved a long-held ambition to lead an all-British team into combat when he joined Vanwall in 1957. He won the British Grand Prix at Aintree again that year with Tony Brooks, plus the GP of Pescara, and relished beating the Lancia Ferrari D50s in the Italian GP at Monza to win, a little recompense for the Bari slight. The following year it was more of the same, but this time Moss led Vanwall to the Formula 1 Constructors' World Championship. The British team withdrew at the end of '58 and Moss moved to Rob Walker's private squad to score a string of Grand Prix victories in the gentleman entrant's Coopers and Lotuses.

Stirling still had little time for Ferrari after its shabby treatment of him at Bari, but his mood was mellowing. He was down to drive a Ferrari Dino 156 for Rob Walker in 1962 until the Goodwood accident shattered his career. Imagine what could have been: Stirling driving a privately entered Ferrari and beating the Commendatore's cars!

Hardly a year after Goodwood, Moss tested himself at the wheel of a sports racing car, but decided to retire. He felt he was not at the top of his game any more, but now believes his retirement decision may have been premature.

But what a glittering career he had had. He competed in a total of 529 races and won 212 of them, including 16 World Championship Grands Prix at a time when there were nine or so races to a season and not the 16 and more of today; he was runner-up to the Formula 1 World Champion four times; he won 20 non-title GPs; 12 World Sports Car Championship races, and was a major contributor to Mercedes winning the 1955 WSCC title; 12 other major races, among them four Tourist Trophies, the 1956 Australian GP and the 1956, 1959 and 1962 Grands Prix of New Zealand; and 159 other less exalted but still hotly contested races.

Stirling was knighted in 2000, and said at the time, 'I can't begin to put into words just how much receiving this honour and being able to share it with my wife Susie has meant to me. Motor sport and this country have given me so much. And to know that I am remembered 40 years after my forced retirement has to be the best feeling in the world.'

# Musso, Luigi

A RATHER PRICKLY YOUNG man from Rome, Luigi Musso had many qualities of a great champion but was killed before he could become one. Enzo Ferrari himself likened this Italian diplomat's son to two of the sport's greats, Felice Nazzaro and Achille Varzi.

In fact, Musso was a sports all-rounder, an especially gifted horseman and fencer and a crack shot. He first tried his hand at motor racing in a Patriarca Giannini 750, which he crashed into a statue of the great Italian hero Giuseppe Garibaldi at Trapani on the 1950 Giro D'Italia and retired. In need of a car, Luigi bought his brother Giuseppe's Stanguellini 750S and his performances in that car attracted the attention of Maserati, so he became one of the three up-and-coming youngsters the Modena company offered works drives for 1953, together with Sergio Mantovani and Emilio Giletti. He ended up the year's Italian Sports Prototype Champion.

The Maserati offer saved Musso from the unhappy life of a soft under-bellied gentleman driver at the rather advanced age of 29 at the end of 1953, when he ran a semi-works Maserati A6SSG and came a creditable seventh in the year's Grand Prix of Italy. Luigi really made heads turn in the 1954 Mille Miglia by fighting a race-long running battle in a 2-litre works Maserati A6GCS with the new synchromesh gearbox against Paulo Marzotto's Ferrari Tipo 500 Mondial. Neither would give an inch as they vied for second place over the 1000 miles, which eventually went to Marzotto with nine seconds over Musso, who took a well-deserved, perhaps slightly disappointing, third place. He graduated to a Maserati 250F that year, when he came second in the Grand Prix of Spain, followed in 1955 by third in Holland and fifth in the UK, modest results that were still good enough to earn him an invitation from Enzo Ferrari to join Juan Manuel Fangio, Peter Collins and Eugenio Castellotti at Maranello.

Luigi competed in a Lancia-Ferrari D50 in 1956 and won first time out in a shared drive with Fangio in the Grand Prix of Argentina on 22 January, when the Argentine triple World Champion took over his car while lying fifth to win by over 24 seconds from Jean Behra in a Maserati. But the Italian fractured an arm when he crashed out of the 1000 Kilometres of the Nürburgring in late May, and didn't race again until the Grand Prix of Germany in August, when there were fireworks. Luigi was forced to hand over his D50 to Eugenio Castellotti, whose Lancia-Ferrari had broken down. Never an easy man to work with, losing his car like that didn't sit too well with Musso. So when he was told to hand over his car again – this time to Fangio, who needed to finish in the points in the 1956 Grand Prix of Italy to win his fourth Formula 1 World Championship – Musso refused. He hadn't worked his way up to second for nothing, he said, and insisted on continuing the race, which he rejoined and briefly took the lead before a steering arm gave out. That incident, by the way, led to Peter Collins' incredibly selfless gesture of voluntarily giving his D50 to Fangio, who came second in the Englishman's car and won the title.

As Fangio left for Maserati, Mike Hawthorn arrived at Maranello to take his place and join his friend Collins, Castellotti and Musso, who had had a varied 1956 driving a Maserati 250F, a BRM P25 and a Vanwall VW2, with only four championship points to show for it. Luigi took another January victory in Argentina in 1957, when he won the 1000 Kilometres of Buenos Aires with Eugenio and Masten Gregory in a Ferrari 290 MM. He also came second in the British and French Grands Prix and took fourth in Germany, which was enough to boost him to third in the Formula 1 World Championship.

Musso felt he was homing in on the world title, but the closer he got to it the more risks he took and the more he pushed himself and his car beyond the limit. Even in a minor race at Monza, for instance, he took pole position with a blood-curdling display of motorised athletics, which included full opposite lock slides around the edge of the famous banking and inches of daylight under his Ferrari's tyres.

Victory in the 1958 Grand Prix of Syracuse made Luigi feel he had the measure of the new Ferrari 246, and with half the season gone both Musso and Mike Hawthorn were in the running for the Formula 1 World Championship when they turned up at Reims for the Grand Prix of France.

And, of course, both were determined to squeeze as many points as they could out of the race.

Their new Ferrari Dino 246s had not held the road as well as they should have at the preceding Grand Prix of Belgium, so the cars' suspensions was modified during the three weeks before Reims and that improved their performance no end.

Musso was feeling pretty confident because he had won the non-championship Coupe de Vitesse F1 race at Reims the previous year, having taken Juan Manuel Fangio's advice. The Argentine had told Luigi that, if he kept his foot flat to the floor going through the Muizon hairpin at the end of the main straight, where everyone else lifted, he could gain at least half a second a lap. So Luigi did, and he was sure that this rather hairy technique had helped him to victory. The only problem was that 'Luigino,' as Musso was nicknamed, won in a Lancia-Ferrari D50 in 1957, but the '58 Dino 246 was a more powerful car with completely different handling characteristics. So keeping his foot hard down in the Dino was likely to produce a whole new set of circumstances – fatal, as it turned out.

During practice on 5 July Musso floored the 246's accelerator but, sure enough, he immediately found he was running a bigger risk than in the D50. Even so, he set the second fastest time of 2min 22.4sec on the 5.187-mile road circuit and ended up sitting next to poleman Hawthorn for the start of the race. Yet it was Harry Schell, the third man on the front row, who got away first in his BRM P25; but Mike took the lead from him at the end of the first straight, with Musso, Collins, Brooks, Fangio and Behra following in that order.

Peter Collins' air scoop above the magneto flew off and lodged under his brake pedal on lap five, so he shot up the Muizon escape road to safety. Five laps later, while charging into the Muizon hairpin at over 140mph, Musso's Ferrari skidded out of control and somersaulted over a ditch; Luigi was thrown out of the car and was killed.

Years later, Enzo Ferrari said the truth about Musso's death would probably never be known, and felt that the newspaper reports of the day were unreliable, as they predominantly reflected the fear of the marshals nearest to the accident rather than what actually happened. He said he was certain that Luigino kept his accelerator pressed firmly to the floor in the heat of the moment as he went into the Muizon hairpin for the tenth time.

# Nazzaro, Felice

FELICE NAZZARO HAD BRAINS as well as a heavy right foot and he used them well to work his way up from a factory shop floor to motor racing stardom in a career that spanned three decades. His favourite technique was to hang back and let the leaders burn themselves or their cars out and then pounce.

That's how he won the 1907 world motor racing grand slam, the Targa Florio, Germany's Kaiserpreis and the French Grand Prix, all run under different regulations. Fifteen years, a world war and a great deal of technological progress later he won the GP of France again, an incredible achievement.

This motor racing superstar was born in a small cluster of houses and stables called Monteu da Po, about 30km from Turin, on 29 January 1881. He became an apprentice mechanic at Ceirano, a carmaker bought by Fiat at the turn of the century. When he was 19 years old he joined Fiat's racing team, mixing it with the legendary Vincenzo Lancia and Alessandro Cagno. He was almost 20 when he had his first big win, beating 31 other entrants in a works 3.8-litre Fiat 8 HP to win the 1901 Giro d'Italia, from Milan to Rome and back.

In 1902 he was asked to deliver a new Fiat to Ignazio Florio, a wealthy Sicilian industrialist, who invited Felice to stay on, look after his fleet of new cars and become his chauffeur: Nazzaro remained for four years. During that time, Ignazio's younger brother Vincenzo pumped Felice for racing techniques. The younger Florio began organising and competing in races himself, the most famous being his Targa Florio, which was to become one of the world's top motor sport events. Felice competed in the 1905 Coppa Florio, coming sixth in a Fiat 100 HP 16.3.

Fiat entered a full team for the 1907 Targa Florio, its 28/40 HP 7/4s being driven by the flamboyant Vincenzo Lancia, Felice and Aldo Weillschott to battle it out against 47 other cars. Lancia set a furious pace and put up the race's fastest average speed of 34.01mph to take the lead by the end of the first of three laps that covered a total of 278 miles. Felice hung back, waiting. Coming into lap two strategist Nazzaro began to reel in the erratic Lancia and eventually took him. While Louis Wagner's transmission broke and his Darracq teammate René Hanriot's driveshaft went, Lancia was still goading his flagging Fiat to unexpectedly quick times. Even so, Nazzaro was first across the finish line to win, a full 12 minutes ahead of the flashy Vincenzo.

Kaiser Wilhelm decreed that a German race should take place in his beloved Taunus Mountains and he personally designed the Kaiserpreis trophy for the event, in which 40 cars competed. Attended by the Kaiser, two heats took place on 13 June 1907, from which the top 20 cars were to compete in the 195-mile race itself the following day. Over 100,000 spectators watched as the cars were flagged away at two-minute intervals, including Nazzaro in his customary Fiat 28/40 and an excited 24-year-old Vincenzo Florio, who had chosen a Darraq. Felice set a cracking pace and a lap record of 1hr 23min, while Pöge in a Mercedes dropped out with carburettor problems, Hugo Wilhelm hit a milestone and Gabriel stopped in the mountains with a leaking fuel tank. Nazzaro and his Fiat crossed the line first, so a rather miffed Kaiser had to hand over his personally designed *preis* to an Italian ex-shop floor worker instead of a German.

The 1907 Grand Prix of France was a Formule Libre event with a catch: the winner would have to average better than 9.5mpg. The race was pure Nazzaro. He played it cool in his 16,286cc Fiat as all 38 cars roared off on the 48-mile triangular circuit just outside Dieppe. Louis Wagner's Fiat took the lead, but he retired on lap four, which handed command to Arthur Duray in a Lorraine-Dietrich. The Frenchman really got moving and looked like the winner until he retired with engine problems on lap nine. Felice had been watching and waiting, so with one lap to go he moved into the lead, then won at an average 70.6mph over the 778 miles.

A year later Nazzaro became the first man to break the 200kph barrier in a match race at Brooklands, but although he touched 205kph at one point he eventually turned in an average of 185kph. The challenge was between Frank Newton's Napier Samson L48 and Nazzaro in the famous

Fiat Mephistopheles, a massive 18,146cc monster. The Napier's crankshaft broke, so Felice was declared the winner at 107mph (172.163kph) by the British track's timekeeper 'Ebby' Ebblewhite; but the circuit's new electric timing equipment registered 120mph (193.08kph) – each of which still made Nazzaro the world's fastest man on four wheels.

Nazzaro won the 1908 Coppa Florio at Bologna on 6 September driving a Fiat 100 HP 12.0. He covered the 328.29 miles at an average speed of 74.23mph, a 4hr 25min 21sec slog around the 52.82-mile road circuit outside the city. And he was leading the American Grand Prize at Savannah, Georgia, on the last of 16 laps in a Fiat 100 HP when a tyre burst and he limped home in third place.

In 1912 Felice decided to go into car manufacturing on his own and built a sober-looking 4.4-litre side valve Nazzaro, which he entered for the following year's two-day Targa Florio. Typical of the man, he hung back on the first day of the race and made the overnight stop at Agrigento 30 minutes after the leader. But it was a different story on day two racing back to Palermo, when he drove so fast he made up the 30-minute deficit and won by a massive 85 minutes, covering the 651 miles of at an average of 33.685mph. A year later he and his Nazzaro won the Coppa Florio, which was run in Sicily this time, beating upstarts like Giuseppe Campari, who came fourth in his works Alfa Romeo 40/60 HP. But Felice's attempt at winning the year's French GP with three specially built 16-valve overhead camshaft Nazzaros blew up in his face when they all retired with engine trouble.

The Nazzaro company folded in 1916, but it was revived by a Florentine firm in 1920 and, although the Nazzaros were the same dated old car under the skin, Guido Meregalli did win the 1920 Targa Florio in one. The last Nazzaro was sold in 1922.

Felice went back to Fiat and, incredibly, won the Grand Prix of France at Strasbourg in one of its 2-litre 804/404s, completing the 500-mile race at an average of 79.2mph and setting a fastest lap over the 8.3-mile circuit of 87.75mph. Not bad for a 42-year-old who hadn't competed in such a long-distance race for nine years!

The Monza circuit was opened by Nazzaro and Pietro Bordino in 1922 and a year later Felice came second there for Fiat. He also finished second at Monza in the 1923 European Grand Prix, but was ready to give way to younger drivers.

So Nazzaro became Fiat's competitions manager for a brief spell until the company withdrew from racing in 1929. He died in his home town on 21 March 1940 after a long illness.

# Nice, Hellé

EXOTIC DOESN'T CUT IT when it comes to describing this gutsy, fun-loving, vivacious show-off beauty, who was born to a country postman and his wife on 15 December 1900 in Aunay-sous-Auneau, about 50 miles south-west of Paris. At 16 she broke loose from her provincial shackles and invaded the capital city, where she became a dancer, then a stripper and after that a racing driver. In the 1930s she was a star, by far the most famous woman in France, who eventually competed in over 70 top-class motor races.

Few expected Hélène Delangle to amount to much as she emerged from her dull family home and hit the bright lights of Paris. She was an attractive girl, so the villagers thought malevolently that she would end up on the game. But they were wrong. OK, under the stage name Hellé Nice she danced in the capital's music halls, graduated to a solo act with a sideline of quasi-nude modelling and stripping, but then she became the well-paid partner of homosexual dancer Robert Lizet. They both cavorted bare-breasted in the scantiest of knickers before the cabaret audiences of Europe and were highly successful. Hellé, who was not above indiscreet affairs with noblemen and other rich 'Good Time Charlies,' did so well at it that she was able to buy her own home and a yacht!

In the 1920s and '30s Paris was the centre of French car production, and a Journée Feminine de l'Automobile was held each June at nearby Montlhéry. Hellé fancied her chances and, helped by a friend, persuaded Jules Daubecq that a beautiful young exotic dancer driving one of his cars in the 1929 event might help sales. He agreed and prepared one of his Omega Sixes for her. She won the 30-lap, 150km race having started last on the grid. Then she won the 50km Grand Prix Feminin at the circuit for good measure.

Of course, a beautiful young girl who had become a successful racing driver was irresistible to the French press. Hellé's open face, stunning smile and big blue eyes beamed from just about every national newspaper, magazine and newsreel in France, where she literally became a star overnight. This at a time when you could count the world's female motor racing drivers on the fingers of two hands and probably wouldn't need all the fingers. Hellé had France – and later America – eating out of her dainty little hand.

Naturally, Hellé and her exploits had been duly noted by Ettore Bugatti, always on the lookout for driving talent, and it wouldn't hurt that she was beautiful with it. So he invited her to his personal 'Camelot' – manor house, small hotel for guests and his famous factory – at Molsheim, where he did not hide his distaste for her brash personality. But his son, heir and brilliant designer Jean could not keep his eyes off her. There was talk of an affair between the two, although nothing was ever confirmed.

The visit paid dividends. Bugatti agreed to lend Hellé a T35C and all the support she needed to try to break the Montlhéry speed record. The day was a bitterly cold 18 December 1929, when Hellé covered 10km of the Paris track in the T35C at an average of 123.057mph. She had her record. After that, she lashed out 40,000 francs on a frugally discounted new Bugatti T35C and was invited to compete in the car in the company's annual Bugatti Grand Prix at Le Mans. She came an incredible third.

Meanwhile, the Americans had heard of this beautiful French racing driver and Hellé signed a contract with the Hot News Agency of New York to give speed exhibitions in racing cars on United States board and dust tracks, one of her mounts Ralph DePalma's Miller 91. But the skittish board tracks were dangerous and she sighed deeply with relief as she headed back to France relatively unscathed after weeks of demonstrations across the US.

Back home, Hellé won the women's category of the 7th Championnat Automobile des Artistes in her beloved Bugatti and then went on to compete in five French Grands Prix and the GP of Monza. She didn't win any of them, but quite a few male stars of the day crossed the finish line after she did. All the time, Hellé worked the press and newsreels until she became so famous she was doing a series of product endorsement advertisements for the likes of Esso, Lucky Strike and others, and making a mint.

By 1933 the Bugatti had lost its edge, so one of Hellé's lovers – gifted amateur racer and Algerian garage owner Marcel Lehoux – found her an

Alfa Romeo 2300 Monza, which she campaigned with great zeal. She was invited to compete in the Grand Prix of Monza in September and there, knee-deep amongst the motor racing stars of the day, she came third in heat two and ninth in the final. She just managed to avoid a pool of oil on the banking in her heat, but Giuseppe Campari and Baconin Borzacchini were not so lucky. They both skidded and gyrated, then somersaulted over the treacherous banking to their deaths.

Hellé went on to second place behind the great Hans Stuck in the Mont Ventoux Hillclimb. She drove the Monza into fourth in the Picardy Grand Prix, won the La Turbie Monaco Hillclimb outright, then the Ladies Cup in the 1936 Monte Carlo Rally before heading for Brazil. She was lying second in the Monza at the São Paolo Grand Prix when she crashed into a straw bale at over 100mph and was seriously injured. The Alfa flew off into the crowd, killed four spectators and injured over 30 others. Hellé came out of a coma after three days but spent another two months in hospital, but she was haunted by the accident and was never the same again.

She laid plans to compete in the 1937 Mille Miglia and the Tripoli Grand Prix, but they never came off. She did join Simone des Forest, Odette Siko and Claire Descollas in a highly successful record-breaking attempt at Montlhéry for the Yacco Oil Company. They drove the 3.6-litre V8 Matford – a huge car built in France by Ford and Ettore Bugatti's old sparring partner Emile Mathis – non-stop for ten days at the circuit to set no fewer than 26 world and international Class C records, many of which still stand today. After that came the war.

Hellé entered the first post-war Monte Carlo Rally in 1949 and attended a party to mark the return of motor sport after the insanity of WW2. There, Louis Chiron strode up to her and, in a loud voice, accused her of being a Gestapo agent. Hellé, like the rest of the room, was astounded. She wanted the floor to open up and swallow her. There was no truth in the accusation, except perhaps that years earlier she had rejected Chiron's advances and he had decided on an especially despicable form of revenge. But it ended her racing career and turned much of France against her. She was a star no more and lived out her days in poverty with only her press cuttings and tarnished trophies to attest to a heroine's past.

Hélène Delangle, alias Hellé Nice, died a pauper's death in a bare, unheated rented room in the back streets of Nice on 1 October 1984.

# Nuvolari, Tazio

THE AMIABLE WARMTH OF mid-summer had already eased its way over to Mantua, Italy, by 13 June 1948, when the cream of Italian motor racing assembled there as a mark of respect for Tazio Nuvolari. It was the day of the Coppa Alberto and Giorgio Nuvolari, a race organised by the Automobile Club of Mantua, of which Tazio was president, and was named after his two dead sons.

That day, Nuvolari put his thoughts into words and admitted to himself and his old friend and rival, Achille Varzi, that he was definitely going to retire.

They were all there: Alberto Ascari, Felice Bonetto, Gigi Villoresi, Achille Varzi, Franco Cortese and, of course, the boys' father Tazio Nuvolari, who was slowly dying. The great volumes of exhaust fumes he had inhaled during his 28-year career were destroying his lungs.

It was a career that was distinguished indeed: 124 motorcycle races, 49 victories, 34 class wins, 40 fastest laps; his performance in cars was even more spectacular: 229 races, 92 victories (including 16 Grands Prix, two Mille Miglias, two Targa Florios, two Tourist Trophies and America's Vanderbilt Cup), 38 class wins and 59 fastest laps – statistics that confirm the Flying Mantuan's achievements, but not why a man of just 5ft 5in and slender build was so successful. That was because he always raced on the limit, taking big powerful cars and making them do what he wanted. But it cost him a total of 14 accidents and, eventually, his life.

Nuvolari and Varzi were the Schumacher and Vettel of their day. They met in 1923 and became friends, but later inevitable rivalry developed between them that was much inflated by the press.

They came face to face that summer's day in 1948, looked at each other, neither saying a word until Nuvolari broke the ice.

'I've finished,' he said simply. He meant he was going to retire.

'Me too,' said Varzi.

Nuvolari led for eight laps in his Ferrari 125 S, then dropped out. Felice Bonetto won in a Cisitalia D 46 4C. When it was over, Nuvolari and Varzi said their goodbyes and, after a second's hesitation, they embraced.

Nineteen days later, Varzi crashed and died in a works Alfa 158 practising for the Grand Prix of Switzerland. Nuvolari's torment continued for another five years.

Tazio raced four more times, his body racked by fits of deep coughing. He only finished one of the four, coming fifth overall in a Cisitalia-Abarth 204 A in Sicily's 1950 Palermo-Monte Pelligrini hillclimb.

Tazio Giorgio Nuvolari was born at 9:00am on 16 November 1892 in Castel d'Ario, near Mantua. His first memory of motor racing was seeing Vincenzo Lancia win the nearby Circuito di Brescia in a Fiat. And he fell in love with speed.

After First World War military service as an ambulance driver, Tazio married the beautiful Carolina Perini in 1915 and in 1922 he opened his own car dealership in Castel d'Ario. In 1925 Alfa's racing boss Vittorio Jano invited Tazio to a driver test session at Monza and Nuvolari shocked Jano by setting a fastest time of 3min 36sec in a P2. That even beat star works driver Antonio Ascari's fastest lap. But Nuvolari crashed, so Jano swore it would be a long time before Tazio got his hands on another works Alfa.

And that was for the 1930 Mille Miglia, with Nuvolari and Varzi both driving Alfa 1750 Zagatos. They constantly swapped the lead, so the Alfa bosses ordered them to cool it, otherwise both cars would be written off in an accident. From that was born 'the legend of the switched-off lights' in which Tazio, coming up fast on leader Varzi, is supposed to have switched off his car's lights so that his teammate couldn't see him. The fact is Tazio simply decided to hell with team orders, speeded up and passed Varzi to win.

A stunt that sent Nuvolari's popularity with the public and press skyrocketing happened in 1931 when he raced a Caproni 100 aircraft in his Alfa Romeo 8C 2300 at Lottario, near Rome, and only lost by a few yards.

The following year superstar dramatist Gabriele D'Annunzio gave him a small gold tortoise with the dedication, 'To the fastest man in the world, the slowest animal.' Loving the irony of it, Tazio had his 'TN' initials added to the little animal's back and adopted the tortoise as his trademark.

In 1933 his victories included the 24 Hours of Le Mans with young French industrialist Raymond Sommer, and his second Mille Miglia win with his mechanic and fellow Mantuan Decimo Compagnoni, both times in Scuderia Ferrari Alfas. Then he and Ferrari argued violently because Tazio won the Grand Prix of Belgium in his own Maserati 8CM. Tazio accused Ferrari of providing him with inferior cars and not paying him enough. And he demanded Scuderia Ferrari changed its name to Scuderia Nuvolari, but that suggestion was rejected so he left.

Nuvolari had the most serious accident of his career in 1934, when the Maserati skidded wildly and smashed into a tree. Tazio was thrown out, knocked unconscious and woke up in hospital screaming with pain; the doctors wanted to amputate his shattered left leg, but Carolina persuaded them to save it.

His leg in plaster, a bored Tazio told Compagnoni they were leaving for a race at Avus.

'As spectators?' asked the trusted mechanic.

'To race. Get the Maserati ready,' Nuvolari ordered.

So Compagnoni rigged up a stirrup in the Maserati's cockpit for the injured leg and they left for Germany, where Nuvolari blustered past officialdom and into the race. He came fifth!

Then Tazio and a Maserati 6C 34 won on Ferrari's doorstep at Modena in 1934. Still angry, he sent Ferrari a bale of straw afterwards with a note saying 'For the donkeys in your engines.' However, the two eventually made up and Tazio went back to racing for the Scuderia. He broke Panhard's two international speed records in the amazing twin-engined Alfa Bi-Motori, the standing kilometre record with 199.767mph and the standing mile at 208.981mph. He even beat the high-tech Mercedes-Benz and Auto Unions in an obsolete P3 to win the 1935 German GP.

A year later Tazio won the Vanderbilt Cup race on Long Island in an Alfa Romeo 12C 36, which earned him $32,000 and a huge cup that he sat in for the photographers. In 1938 he accepted Auto Union's offer to replace the late Bernd Rosemeyer, and handled the twitchy rear-engined Auto Union Type D perfectly to win the Grands Prix of Italy and Great Britain. Five days after Britain declared war on Germany, Tazio won the Belgrade GP for AR.

As a result of his exhaust-damaged lungs Nuvolari was coughing blood when he won the first Giorgio and Alberto Nuvolari Cup in a Maserati 4CL in 1947. He almost won the year's Mille Miglia in an open Cisitalia 202 MM, coming second. And he put in a stunning drive in a disintegrating Ferrari 166 S in the 1948 event, but retired with a broken suspension stud after leading for most of the race.

Tazio Nuvolari died at his home in Mantua at 6:30am on 11 August 1953. On his instructions, his body was dressed in his racing gear, complete with gold tortoise, and was laid to rest in the family tomb at Mantua cemetery. Over the entrance to the mausoleum was – and still is – the inscription, in Italian, 'I will race even faster on the roads of Heaven.'

# Peterson, Ronnie

A PLEASANT, MILD-MANNERED MAN out of the cockpit, Ronnie Peterson was explosive in it. He brought his immense instinctive talent to bear on a racing car with spectacular effect to become the fastest Formula 1 driver of the 1970s. In only his second Formula 1 season, this Swedish baker's son was runner-up to 1971 F1 World Champion Jackie Stewart.

Born in the small village of Almby, Sweden, on 14 February 1944, Ronnie cut his teeth on kart racing and won the Swedish Championships of 1963 and 1964. In 1966 he won the European title and during that time became friends with the Sala family, who have built their world-famous Birel karts on the outskirts of Milan, Italy, for three generations. Peterson and the Salas became so close that one of the Italian family's newborn sons was named Ronnie after the Swede. Even when he had become an established Formula 1 star, Peterson always made a point of meeting up with his old Birel friends whenever he competed in Italy.

From karts the tall, courteous Peterson graduated to Formula 3, in which he helped turn the then obscure Italian constructor Tecno into a force to be reckoned with by winning the 1969 European F3 Championship. That spectacular success earned Ronnie a three-year contract with the emergent March in 1970, driving a 701 under Colin Crabbe's Antinique Automobiles banner, before joining the factory team the following year.

He took his promotion to the top echelon of the sport in his stride, and exploded into action in the works March 711-Ford to take no fewer than four second places in the 1971 Grands Prix of Monaco, Britain, Italy and Canada. He scored 33 championship points that year to become World Champion Jackie Stewart's runner-up, ahead of much more experienced drivers like Mario Andretti and Chris Amon. Ronnie's 1971 performance in Formula 2 was even more explosive: he won the European F2 Championship in a March 712M-Ford with four wins in France, Sweden, Austria and Italy.

The 1972 Formula 1 season was a disappointment, however, but not due to any fault of Peterson's. He just couldn't coax any of the three versions of the uncompetitive March 712 into better than third in the Grand Prix of Germany at the Nürburgring.

By this time Ronnie had established himself as a major talent and he was invited to drive for Lotus in 1973, when he scored his first F1 win at the wheel of a Lotus 72D in the Grand Prix of France at the Paul Ricard Circuit. Another three victories at the Österreichring, Monza and Watkins Glen helped shoot him up to third in the year's championship table, which was headed, as in 1971, by Jackie Stewart. Back with Lotus again in 1974, his seat-of-the-pants instinctive genius was the main reason why he was able to win the Monaco, French and Italian Grands Prix in the ageing Lotus 72D. The car was supposed to have been replaced by the 76 in 1974, but the new arrival turned out to be a disaster. So the team brought the 72D out of retirement, improved it and competed with that – until early 1976, when out came the Lotus 77 – then turned it into the 72E from the Monaco Grand Prix. Ronnie won in the Principality with it immediately, setting a fastest lap of 1min 27.9sec for good measure. Always competitive in the warmed over car, Peterson won the French and German GPs in it too, but that kind of comeback couldn't last forever as the competition was improving all the time.

Ronnie wanted to move and had signed for Shadow, but Colin Chapman implored him to stay and said he would speed up the development of the 77 to keep him. So 'SuperSwede,' as the media had labelled him, did the initial Brazilian Grand Prix, quickly fell out of love with the 77 and moved to March, who were delighted to have him back to drive its straightforward 761. That car took him to victory in the Italian GP at Monza, beating the Lauda and Regazzoni Ferraris on their home patch and boosting Peterson's confidence into the bargain.

But another racing disaster loomed when Ronnie was offered a large bag of gold to drive for Ken Tyrrell in 1977. The car was the second, more aerodynamic version of Derek Gardner's six-wheeler, which proved to be a catastrophe. The P34B won nothing that year, although Ronnie did manage to work it up to third place in the Grand Prix of Belgium at Zolder.

So it was back to Lotus for SuperSwede, and this time he got what he wanted: a competitive car. In fact, a legendary one in the Lotus 79, out of which Ronnie squeezed every ounce of performance it could muster as number two to Mario Andretti. The official story was that the two drivers were joint number ones – maybe not every racing driver's dream – but in practice Ronnie slotted into the second spot knowing he was going to get another shot at driving a state-of-the-art Formula 1 car. The arrangement was that Andretti had to win everything he could without Peterson getting in the way as part of the Italo-American's quest for the Formula 1 World Championship.

Ever a gentleman of his word, Ronnie did nothing to challenge Mario all the while his 'number one' was competitive, although he often out-qualified Andretti. Theirs was one of the most effective racing partnerships since the nose-to-tail Fangio-Moss duo, who were nicknamed 'The Train' because they stuck so close together throughout the 1955 season; the Swede likewise stuck to the American's Lotus lap after lap. Peterson did win in South Africa and Austria, when Andretti was plagued with mechanical problems on both counts.

Ronnie's 1978 performance so impressed McLaren that the team offered him its number one drive for 1979, but the Swede didn't live long enough to take them up on it. He was involved in a multi-car pile-up during the start of the 1978 Grand Prix of Italy at Monza, during which his Lotus 79 burst into flames. James Hunt rushed to his friend's blazing car and a lone marshal started squirting the inferno with short, sharp bursts from an extinguisher. The car's steering wheel was ripped off and Ronnie was physically dragged from the burning wreck by Hunt, Clay Regazzoni and Patrick Depailler. They laid him down on the side of the track until he could be taken to hospital, where he fell into a deep coma. A bone marrow embolism entered Ronnie's bloodstream and he died the day after the crash. He had scored enough points to become the posthumous runner-up to Andretti in the 1978 F1 World Championship.

The big blond Swede left a rich legacy of success. He had won ten World Championship Grands Prix, including an Italian hat-trick in 1973, 1974 and 1976, the Six Hours of Watkins Glen with Andrea De Adamich in an Alfa Romeo 33T/3, and then formed a legendary partnership with Tim Schenken. The two were instrumental in Ferrari winning the 1972 World Sports Car Championship with the 312 PB, producing a remarkable series of results that included two victories and four second places. Ferrari scored 160 championship points that year, almost double that of runner-up Alfa Romeo. In addition Ronnie had won four 1971 European Formula 2 Championship races plus the title.

# Piquet, Nelson

IF HIS FATHER HAD had his way, Nelson Souto Maior might have been on the centre court at Wimbledon trading long, powerful baseline shots with Bjorn Borg, who won the British club's singles title five years in succession in 1976–80. The young Brazilian showed distinct promise on the court, so his father bundled him off to California to hone his tennis skills. But Nelson succumbed to the allure of motor sport and adopted the pseudonym Piquet to camouflage his early efforts in kart racing and avoid parental detection.

Happily, the world was not deprived of watching this perceptive, intelligent, sometimes mercurial man make his way from a creditable performance in Brazilian Formula Super Vee to three Formula 1 World Championships and 23 Grands Prix victories.

Born in Rio de Janeiro on 17 August 1952, Nelson didn't take long to break out of the local scene and make his way to Britain and the 1977 European Formula 3 Championship, in which he came third driving a Ralt RT1-Toyota. A few months later he switched to the BP British F3 series in the Ralt and turned more than a few F1 team managers' heads as he won the title and 13 races. The following year, Piquet made his Formula 1 debut in the Dave Baldwin-Mo Nunn-designed Ensign N177 in the Grand Prix of Germany at Hockenheim, where he qualified 21st but retired with mechanical trouble.

He also competed in an ageing, privately owned McLaren M23 in 1978, when his best finish was ninth in the Italian GP. Then he was given a try-out by Bernie Ecclestone in one of his team's Alfa Romeo-powered Brabham BT46s in the Grand Prix of Canada, the last race of the season, when Nelson qualified 14th and came 11th. He joined Niki Lauda at Brabham in 1979, but the best he could do with the troublesome Alfa-engined BT48 was to come fourth at Zandvoort, qualify on the front row of the grid and set the fastest lap at Watkins Glen before retiring with mechanical problems for the ninth time that season.

Niki Lauda's abrupt but temporary retirement from the sport that same year meant Piquet inherited an early number one spot at Brabham and in 1980 that led to his first Grand Prix victory: it was in a BT49 – which was now powered by a Ford-Cosworth eight-cylinder unit – in the United States Grand Prix West at Long Beach, California, in typical fruit-and-nut-land weather of sun and warmth, beating Arrows' Riccardo Patrese by over 50 seconds. Nelson continued to score points with some high placings to make him a world title contender, a situation reinforced by two victories in succession in the Grand Prix of Holland at Zandvoort five months after breaking his duck, and the Italian GP at Imola. In the end engine trouble let him down, and he was beaten to the World Championship by Alan Jones with 67 points to Nelson's 54.

In 1981 it was Brazil versus Argentina on the Formula 1 front, as Piquet in the Brabham went toe-to-toe with Williams driver Carlos Reutemann, who beat Nelson on his home patch by winning the Brazilian GP. But Piquet was quick to return the compliment at Buenos Aires, where he won the Grand Prix of Argentina, with Carlos second in his Williams FW07C-Ford.

The Argentine led the championship for much of the season, although Nelson won at Imola again and Germany, but Carlos suffered a decline in his performance during the last race of the year in the car park of Caesar's Palace in Las Vegas. Carlos qualified on pole position, but only came eighth in the race to Nelson's fifth, which gave Piquet his first Formula 1 World Championship with 50 points to Reutemann's 49.

Now the reigning World Champion, Nelson was shrewd enough to stick with Brabham as the team switched to promising BMW turbo power and went through an extensive development programme. He paid the price, though, for he lost his title to Keke Rosberg in 1982. Piquet did not even qualify at Detroit, yet he managed to win the Grand Prix of Canada in the Brabham BT50-BMW a fortnight later, but still came a lowly 11th in the championship.

The whole Brabham-BMW-Piquet package immediately came good in 1983: Nelson won his home-town Grand Prix at the Jacarepagua circuit near Rio de Janeiro, continued to place well throughout most of the season and then won at Monza and Brands Hatch to take his title back with 59 points, two more than Alain Prost's tally. It was the first time a car with a turbocharged engine had ever won the championship.

A couple of lean years followed, mainly due to car unreliability, when Piquet won the 1984 Grands Prix of Canada and Detroit in the Brabham BT53-BMW and the 1985 French GP in a BT54. He was also frustrated by Ecclestone's reluctance to pay him what he considered he was worth, so in 1986 he left for Williams. He won the season's first race at Rio for his new team in the FW11-Honda and then again in Germany, Hungary and Italy to come third in the World Championship. That year Nelson suffered from a different kind of frustration – the team's unwillingness to at least try the impossible and persuade Nigel Mansell to help the Brazilian win the championship. The world title eventually went to Alain Prost in a close fight, with the Frenchman on 72 points, Nigel runner-up with 70 and Piquet third with 69.

Piquet and Mansell slugged it out in their Williamses again in 1987, Nigel winning six Grands Prix and taking eight pole positions – more than any of his opponents – but the wily Piquet was the steadier points scorer, and he ended up with his third Formula 1 World Championship. But Williams lost its Honda engine deal for 1988, as the Japanese manufacturer decided to supply its power units to McLaren and Lotus, so it was time for Nelson to move on again. He made the mistake of following the Honda V6s to Lotus, but Hethel's 100T was just not up to the mark and the Brazilian could finish no higher than third all season. And he lost his title again, this time to Ayrton Senna. The following year Honda decided to supply its engines to McLaren alone, so the best Lotus could do was cobble together a deal with Judd for 1989 – and that produced a worse year than '88. Nelson could not even qualify the car at Spa and his best placings were a couple of fourths and a fifth.

So Piquet moved to Benetton for 1990 and was reborn again. He won in Japan and Australia and came third in the championship: he scored his last F1 victory in 1991 in Canada, yet again driving the Benetton B191-Ford, by which time top team offers had all but dried up. Not one to sell himself cheap, Piquet left Formula 1 in 1992 and decided to have a go at the year's Indianapolis 500. Unfortunately he had a terrible accident during practice and suffered extensive foot injuries, which brought his distinguished motor racing career to an abrupt end.

Today the triple World Champion is closely associated with his son Nelsinho's career as an aspiring motor racing driver.

# Prost, Alain

ST CHAMOND IN THE Loire Valley of France was once known as a production centre of ribbon and rayon and for its railway works. Now it is best known as the birthplace of the little man who beat the world four times. For Alain Marie Pascal Prost, who was born in the French town on 24 February 1955, is third only to the great Juan Manuel Fangio and Michael Schumacher in the list of Formula 1's most successful racing drivers.

Those in the know, who witnessed the little Frenchman's performances in karts in the early '70s, had an inkling of what was to be. But even they had no way of knowing that the curly-haired youngster they were watching would win four Formula 1 World Championships and emerge victorious from 51 of his 199 Grands Prix to produce a career win-rate well in excess of 25%.

Prost's kart antics culminated in him winning the 1973 World Championship. Six years later he won the European Formula 3 title with a slew of victories in a Martini Mk27-Renault, soon after which Teddy Meyer of McLaren offered him a Formula 1 test drive in which he was so brilliant he was signed there and then. But the McLaren M29B, C and M30-Fords were not in such fine fettle in 1980 and the best Alain could do all season was to hustle one of them into fifth place in the Grand Prix of Brazil.

Renault were next to snap up Prost and they ran him alongside René Arnoux in 1981. Alain's first win in the RE30 was at home in the Grand Prix of France at Dijon, but the car was not all that reliable. So try as he might, Prost was unable to rack up enough points to win the World Championship, even though he did add victories in the Dutch and Italian GPs to his tally, all of which only got him fifth place in the title chase. The 1982 Renault 30B was not much better, although Prost did reel in wins in South Africa and Brazil. He put up with the unreliable car until the end of 1983, during which he also won in France, Belgium, Britain and Austria, but after leading the championship table for most of the season a late burst of success by Nelson Piquet snatched the title from Alain's grasp: the Brazilian scored 59 points that year to Prost's 57.

That was it. Alain's Renault sojourn came to a tempestuous end when he had a huge argument with the men from the Régie and then went back to McLaren for 1984, where Ron Dennis and John Barnard had transformed both cars and team. The new Porsche-designed TAG turbo engine sent the McLarens into the stratosphere. Prost won seven Grands Prix to teammate Niki Lauda's five, but the Austrian took the title by half a point, with 72 to Alain's 71.5 because only half-points were awarded for Alain's victory in torrential rain at Monaco.

The 1985 season turned out to be Prost's. He won five Grands Prix to become France's first Formula 1 World Champion, and then took the title again in 1986. Hampered by lack of TAG-Porsche engine development in 1987, Alain 'only' won the Grands Prix of Brazil, Belgium and Portugal, and lost his title to Nelson Piquet, but he did have the satisfaction of beating Jackie Stewart's long-standing record of 27 GP victories.

Ayrton Senna arrived at McLaren in 1988 via Toleman and Lotus and the team switched to Honda engines for the last year of the turbos. The Prost-Senna-Honda combination was dynamite. McLaren won an even more stratospheric 15 of the season's 16 races that year; only Gerhard Berger was able to stem the red and white tide in the Ferrari F187/88C. Inevitably, with two of the greatest drivers the sport has ever seen in the same team, relations were strained between Prost and Senna, and got steadily worse. The Frenchman became so fed up with their deteriorating relationship that he told team boss Ron Dennis he would be leaving at the end of the season. Dennis tried to talk Alain out of it and even offered him a year off with full pay, but Prost declined.

The wrangling between the two drivers rumbled on all season and came to a head in Japan. Ayrton needed to win the Grand Prix to take the title, but he tried an ambitious overtaking manoeuvre on Prost going into the chicane on the 47th of 53 laps and Alain simply slammed the door on him: both cars collided and went off. Prost called it quits there and then. Senna got going again, pitted and won the race, only to be disqualified for not rejoining the track where he had left it, which handed the World Championship to Alain on a plate.

As good as his word, Prost left McLaren and signed for a lacklustre Ferrari for 1990, when he helped transform the team to such a degree that it became a serious contender for the world titles. Alain went to the penultimate race of the season in Japan with a strong chance of securing his fourth World Championship, having won in Brazil, Mexico, France, Britain and Spain. But Senna had other ideas. He ran Alain's Ferrari right off the track at the first corner and the little Frenchman's title hopes evaporated there and then. The world was astounded at the Brazilian's vengeful manoeuvre and many thought his cold-blooded act of retribution should have cost him the title. But, for some unfathomable reason, FISA allowed him to get away with it and he was permitted to keep his second World Championship.

The Ferrari 642s and 643s did not work well in 1991 and neither Prost nor his teammate Jean Alesi won a race. Worse still, Alain was at loggerheads with team boss Cesare Fiorio and publicly criticised the cars, likening them to trucks! That severely dented the ego and image of Ferrari, riled its *tifosi* and, not unexpectedly, got Alain fired, so he didn't even compete in the last race of the season in Australia.

Prost tested a Ligier in 1991, but he was not impressed with the JS35-Lamborghini and decided not to compete in 1992: instead, he became an F1 TV commentator. But he was back in the driver's seat again in 1993, this time at the wheel of a Williams FW15C-Renault, in which he won seven Grands Prix and his fourth World Championship, a healthy 26 points ahead of second-placed Senna, which must have been satisfying. Then he hung up his helmet.

In 1996 Prost did a deal with Ligier owner Flavio Briatore to buy the team's material and established his own squad in premises close to the French Magny-Cours circuit. There were some promising performances in 1997: Olivier Panis came fifth in the Prost JS45-Mugen in the Grand Prix of Australia, the team's debut race. He even drove the car into third in Brazil and second in Spain. But then performance fell off and stayed that way. Alain stuck it out until the end of the 2001 season, when he closed the team down.

In 2003 the little champion decided to drive for Toyota in the Anderos Trophy, a kind of F1 championship on snow. He won the series for the first time in 2007 and gave a repeat performance in 2008, the year his son Nicholas began his motor racing career.

# Purley, David

DAVID PURLEY IS A hero you have probably never even heard of, but a hero he most certainly was. If you remember him at all, it will be for his one-man attempt to rescue his friend and fellow F1 driver Roger Williamson from a burning car during the 1973 Grand Prix of Holland.

Purley was driving a March 713G sponsored by Britain's biggest refrigerator manufacturer, Lec, a company owned by his father. He was dicing with Williamson when one of the tyres on Roger's March seemed to deflate; the car crashed, overturned and caught fire when the fuel tank contents leaked out and ignited.

David immediately stopped his car, ran to the burning March and tried to tip it back onto its wheels with his bare hands. Marshals with fire extinguishers but no fire-retardant clothing just looked on and, incredibly, the race was not even stopped. Purley could see Williamson was alive and heard the stricken driver pleading to be freed, but David just could not right the car. The flames were minimal at first, but spread and intensified after a couple of minutes. With no thought for his own safety, David kept straining to lift the blazing car and screamed for help, but no one came. In the end he snatched an extinguisher from one of the idle marshals, but the fire had become too intense for it to have much effect. The track fire engine eventually arrived and put out the flames, by which time Roger had died of asphyxiation.

The race was won by Jackie Stewart, his 26th GP victory, but on the podium he, Francois Cevert and James Hunt stood motionless after the avoidable death of their colleague.

Purley said later that if he could have righted the car he could have got Williamson out and the Briton would not have lost his life in such a horrific way. David was awarded the George Cross, Britain's highest civilian medal for valour, in recognition of his selfless rescue attempt.

A keen flier, Purley became Britain's youngest holder of a private pilot's licence in 1962, when he was 17. His father gave him a job as Lec's company pilot, but initially the lad was more inclined to buzz the beaches of his home town of Bognor Regis on Britain's West Sussex coast. Later he matured somewhat and ended up flying all over Europe and Africa for Lec. But after an argument with his father and a brief respite as a builder's labourer, Purley impulsively joined the exclusive Coldstream Guards, not long after which he was selected for an officer cadet course at the Sandhurst Military Academy.

On active service in Aden during the troubles there, Second Lieutenant Purley's armoured car hit a land mine. The vehicle exploded and six of its occupants were killed: Purley was the only survivor.

David did his jump training and qualified as a paratrooper. He narrowly avoided certain death when his army parachute failed to open after jumping from a Hercules. Incredibly, he managed to manoeuvre himself on to the top of his platoon sergeant's parachute below him and rode the billowing silk canopy down 10,000 feet to a safe landing.

Following his military service, in 1968 David went motor racing for the first time in his AC Cobra road car, soon moved on to a Chevron B8 and then got himself a Brabham BT28, in which he beat James Hunt and his Lotus 59 to win the 1970 Grand Prix des Frontiers at Chimay, Belgium. It turned out to be a hat trick, really, because Purley won the race again in 1971 in the Brabham and once more in 1972 in an Ensign.

After a brief spell competing in F2 with a March 722, in which he took third at Pau but not much else, Purley went into Formula 1 with a Lec-sponsored March 731G and made his heroic effort to save Roger Williamson at Zandvoort on 29 July 1973. His highest placing of the four Grands Prix in which he competed was a disappointing ninth in the Italian GP.

He did not have much stomach for motor racing for a while after the 1973 season, but he did win the 1975 F5000 race at Britain's Oulton Park in his Cosworth-engined Chevron B30. The following year he won the Shellsport Group 8 Championship in the same car. The final race in the series was a tribute to the new 1976 F1 World Champion James Hunt at Brands Hatch, in which Purley led from start to finish and put up the fastest lap to claim his championship in a blaze of glory.

David went back to Formula 1 with his own team in 1977. He drove a Ford-powered car called a Lec CRP1, designed by Mike Pilbeam. He briefly led the Grand Prix of Belgium at Zolder and stood his ground as Niki Lauda probed Purley's defences in a faster factory Ferrari 312T2. The Austrian eventually slipped through and went on to finish second, while David came in a lowly 13th.

After the race Lauda stalked off to Purley's pits at the head of a pack of journalists. Niki started wagging his finger at David, admonishing the Englishman for not moving over and called him a rabbit. But an unruffled Purley simply told the Ferrari driver that, if he had wanted the lead earlier, he should have taken it: then he returned the compliment and called Niki a rat. After that, Lauda raced with a rat painted on his car and Purley a rabbit.

Less than two weeks after the Lauda clash, Purley was out in the Lec at Silverstone qualifying for the British GP when his throttle jammed wide open as he was coming up to Becketts. The car hit the Armco at over 100mph and stopped dead within five feet. It was a miracle David was not killed. As it was, it took nearly an hour and a half to extract him from the wreckage and get him to hospital, where it was found both his legs were shattered and his pelvis was broken in three places. But the next day he started telling anyone who would listen that he would be back. And he was. But not before some agonising operations to regain the two inches his left leg had lost in surgery. The process consisted of breaking the leg again, letting it calcify and repeating the process until his two legs were the same length once more.

David's comeback was in the Aurora British Formula 1 series at Snetterton in 1979 in his Lec CRP1. He kept up with the leaders for much of the race and came fourth. But he was exhausted and had to be lifted out of the car by four men. He retired soon after.

On 2 July 1985, now 40, David Purley died the way he had lived: on the razor's edge. He was coming out of a roll over Bognor Regis when his aircraft lost power and crashed into the English Channel. Rescuers found his body a few hours later, still strapped into the sunken aircraft.

Purley's smashed Lec CRP1 and his spare car, which is in one piece, are part of the Donington Collection, silent reminders of one of life's true heroes.

# Resta, Dario

DARIO RESTA COMPETED IN the first race ever held at Britain's hallowed Brooklands circuit on 6 July 1907 and died there trying to set speed records on 3 September 1924. In between, his European career had its highs and lows, but his exploits in the United States were, without doubt, the stuff of heroes. He won the 1915 American Grand Prize, the 1916 Indianapolis 500 and, in that same year, became the only non-American to win the American Automobile Association Championship.

But who was Dario Resta? It's complicated. He was born in Faenza, Italy, in 1884, to an Italian cavalry officer and his wife. They moved to London when Dario was two years old and the boy was sent to all the right schools. That's why he ended up speaking English with such an upmarket accent, which caused a few jaws to drop in the States. He originally went to America on business in 1914, when a certain Alphonse Kaufmann, a Peugeot importer, prevailed on him to race the French cars in the US. That set the stage for Resta's remarkable American career.

Dario began racing in Britain in 1906. He competed in the 1907 Montague Cup, the first race ever held at Brooklands, and would have won it in his 1906 Mercedes Grand Prix but for a signaller's error. He ended up third, as he did in the same event in the same car in 1908.

He set his cap at Grand Prix racing and drove a heavy, underpowered 9-litre Austin in the French GP at Dieppe against such stars of the day as Camille Janatzy, Vincenzo Lancia and Fritz von Opel, but only came 19th in the unwieldy car out of 23 finishers. He improved his placing in France's Coupe de l'Auto in 1911 to finish eighth. The following year the regulations were changed to include Formule Libre and 3-litre cars with a maximum width of 1750mm. Dario drove a Sunbeam into fourth place in the 1912 Grand Prix of France, having initially led the 3000cc class. He stuck with that car for the next three years and managed sixth in the 1913 event at Amiens and fifth in the French classic in 1914 in the workmanlike Sunbeams that seldom distinguished themselves.

Next Dario competed in a Peugeot EX3 racing car, which had been brought to the States especially for him by the wealthy Kaufman. Before it was allowed to race, the entrepreneur had the brilliant engineer and future builder of Indy winners Harry Miller overhaul it to make sure it was really competitive, after which Resta took charge of it.

The EX3 made a dream debut in the United States on 27 February 1915, when Resta picked his way through the hazardous 3.84-mile San Francisco street circuit to win the American Grand Prize – a Grand Prix by any other name. He led almost from start to finish and couldn't even be caught by Howdy Wilcox and his ultra-powerful Stutz, which came second. The Anglo-Italian repeated that stirring performance a week later on the same treacherous corkscrew of a circuit, when he and his EX3 won the famed Vanderbilt Cup by covering its 104 laps in 7hr 7min 53sec. Second again was Howdy Wilcox, who came in seven minutes later in the mighty Stutz, with Hughie Hughes third 20 minutes down in an Ono.

Things didn't go quite so well for Dario and his 1913 Peugeot at the 1915 Indianapolis 500. He was strongly challenged by Ralph DePalma in a 1914 Mercedes. Both drivers made two pit stops, but DePalma's crew got their man back on the track slightly quicker. Dario's blue Peugeot started giving steering trouble in the closing stages of the event, which meant he was forced to slow his pace to keep going. But he managed to nurse the Peugeot into a well-earned second place behind winner DePalma.

It was to be a phenomenal year. Dario won the famous Vanderbilt Cup again, both the season's Chicago 500 races at the city's Maywood Speedway, and the first-ever race at the Sheepshead Bay Speedway, Brooklyn, in the wet, recording an average speed of 108mph in a new 4.5-litre Peugeot racer. That year Resta had the third highest win-rate of all drivers competing in the States: 31.5%, to top-scorer Frank Lockhart on 36.4% and Jimmy Murphy with 36%.

The 1916 season was a blur of victories and excitement for Resta, who moved his family to Bakersville, California, and on 30 May won the Indianapolis 500, which had been reduced to 300 miles in deference to the First World War. It was an easy victory, in part because DePalma was not there with his mighty Mercedes. But the Italo-American was at the Chicago 500 with the Merc 11 days later, when the two put on a fine display as they fought desperately for the win. In the end it went to Resta after DePalma's car slowed with plug trouble. Dario took 5hr 7min 26sec to cover the 500 miles at an average speed of 97.58mph – 8mph faster than the record for the Indianapolis 500 at the time.

Resta won again at the Omaha Speedway in July and Chicago in October. His last US victory secured him his second Vanderbilt Cup in 1916, no longer run through San Francisco but on an 8.4-mile circuit at Santa Monica. It looked an easy victory in the Peugeot with its new aerodynamic tail as he snatched the lead from Earl Cooper and his Stutz. The Anglo-Italian was going well in the American Grand Prize at Santa Monica two days later when he hit ignition trouble, which seemed to give the race to Howdy Wilcox after his EX3 misfired and was retired. One of Dario's chief rivals, Johnny Aitken, was out with a broken piston but, desperate to score points towards the AAA Championship, he took over the Wilcox Peugeot. With his sick EX5 sidelined, Resta offered to buy Earl Cooper's Stutz for cash there and then, but Cooper wasn't having any. So on they charged until the finish, where Aitken was first over the line and Cooper second. But Dario still won the title because the AAA disqualified Aitken and ruled that Wilcox was the real winner.

The Peugeots had had their day. They were being outclassed by more modern racing machinery like the Chevrolet brothers' Frontenacs, the Duesenbergs and, later, the Millers. Resta was no longer competitive in the US either, although he drove Frontenacs and Packards. He competed in Sunbeams in Europe, but the best he could do was win a couple of provincial hillclimbs and take second place to Kenelm Lee Guinness in the Grand Prix of Geneva.

Dario, now 39, was down to drive a Sunbeam in the 1924 Grand Prix of San Sebastian at Lasarte, Spain, in late September, but that was not to be. At Brooklands one of his Sunbeam's rear tyres blew at 120mph and a back wheel locked solid as he was trying to set new class records. His car writhed and jerked uncontrollably then crashed heavily, killing Resta and injuring his riding mechanic, Bill Perkins.

# Rickenbacker, Eddie

HERO IS FAR TOO modest a word to describe Eddie Vernon Rickenbacker. Racing driver, First World War ace, Medal of Honour winner, holder of no fewer than seven Distinguished Service Crosses, car manufacturer, Indianapolis Speedway owner, Pacific Ocean crash survivor and founder of Eastern Airlines.

What makes one man capable of achieving so much? Well, faced with a tough situation Eddie would often say, 'I'll fight like a wildcat.' That attitude of mind, tempered with enormous reserves of courage, determination, character and a penchant for taking risks, made him one of the greatest superheroes of all time – a definition that gets a little closer to summing him up.

Way before he joined the US army he was one of America's best racing drivers. He competed in a total of 42 top races, won seven and was ranked third in the 1916 AAA Championship.

Edward Rickenbacker was born to Swiss-German immigrant parents in Columbus, Ohio, on 8 October 1890. His father William was killed in a building site accident when Eddie was 13, so the boy left school, went to work and did a correspondence course in automotive engineering in his spare time. At 15 he marched into the Frayer-Miller car manufacturing plant in Columbus and asked for a job. Lee Frayer turned him down because of his age, but next morning Rickenbacker went to work for the company regardless and did such a good job cleaning its workshop that Frayer took him on.

Eddie got his first whiff of motor racing in 1906, when Frayer asked the boy to be his riding mechanic in the American Elimination Trial, from which five cars would be selected to compete for the Vanderbilt Cup. They practised for a couple of days and, true to form, Rickenbacker felt confident.

But he hadn't reckoned on a tyre that blew at 60mph. They replaced it, but when they got going again the engine started overheating and clattering, and its oil pressure went through the roof; so Frayer stopped the car, trial over.

Frayer-Miller went down the tubes soon after that, so Lee joined the Columbus Buggy Company in 1907 as chief car designer and took Rickenbacker with him. By that time Eddie was 17, and already running the test department and up to 15 men who worked in it.

The 1910 Red Oak, Iowa, dirt track race was Eddie's first taste of driving in a competitive event, but it didn't last long. His Firestone-Columbus flew off the track and smashed into a fence, leaving Rickenbacker bruised and badly shaken but still bent on becoming a racing driver. He jumped in at the deep end in 1911 when he became Lee Frayer's relief driver in the Indianapolis 500 Sweepstakes. He piloted the Red Wing Firestone-Columbus for over 350 of the race's 400 miles and brought it home 13th out of 40 starters.

The Columbus Buggy Company went bust in 1912 and that left Rickenbacker without a job, so he became a professional racing driver, fighting it out at Iowa country fairs until he had an argument with the AAA and his licence was suspended. So he went to work as a mechanic for the Duesenberg brothers in Des Moines, where they were building racing cars for the Mason Automobile Company and, after Eddie got his licence back, he competed in the 1913 Columbus Race. It was a 200-mile event, but the Mason only lasted 107 of them before its driveshaft broke and the youngster was out. He won his first major race in 1914 in a Duesenberg. It was the 300-mile Sioux City event, in which he beat some of the big names of the day, including Barney Oldfield and Vanderbilt Cup winners Harry Grant and Ralph Mulford.

Rickenbacker moved to Peugeot for the 1914 Corona Race, but that blew up in his face when a driveshaft went after 37 laps. The Peugeots didn't turn out to be the hyper-competitive cars Eddie thought they were, so he joined Barney Oldfield and Bill Carlson at the Maxwell Automobile Company. His first race for the new team was the 1915 American Grand Prize, but torrential rain eventually soaked through his ignition wires after only 40 laps and he retired again. Ironically, Dario Resta won the event in Eddie's old Peugeot. Same thing happened in the Vanderbilt Cup race: Rickenbacker dropped out with a broken engine and Resta won in a Peugeot.

Eddie continued to campaign the Maxwell, but the 1915 Indy slipped through his fingers; in fact he never did win that event, even though he tried five times. But he won the Sioux City for the second successive year and then went on to victory in the Omaha Derby. By this time Maxwell had had its fill of racing, so Rickenbacker scraped enough money together plus sponsorship to buy the four dormant Maxwells and completely rebuilt them. He won the 1915 Providence Race on the new one-mile Narragansett Park circuit in his newly named Maxwell Special to finish fifth in the AAA national ranking.

Rickenbacker still ran the Maxwell Specials in 1916, when he won the 150-mile Sheepshead Bay event at an average of 96.2mph, then he took the win in the Montamarathon-Potlach Trophy at the Pacific Coast Speedway in Tacoma by overtaking Tommy Milton's Duesenberg 26 laps from the end, and also went on to win the Ascot Derby near Los Angeles in a Duesenberg. He ended up third in that year's AAA National Championship, which was won by Dario Resta.

After training, Eddie joined the First World War American Expeditionary Force in 1917 and was attached to the new 94th Aero Pursuit Squadron after learning to fly in his spare time. He shot down his first German plane on 29 April 1918, and his fifth barely a month later to become an ace. He ended up with 26 'kills' – 22 German aircraft and four observation balloons – and that made him the Ace of Aces.

In 1930 Rickenbacker was awarded the Medal of Honour for conspicuous gallantry in the war, to which his seven Distinguished Service Crosses for extraordinary heroism also testified so eloquently.

After the war Eddie turned his talents to building his own cars. He founded the Rickenbacker Motor Company in 1921 and made stylish mid-range vehicles for six years until his company went under. In 1927 he bought the Indianapolis Motor Speedway and managed to keep that going through the harsh post-Wall Street Crash years. And he was the first to set up a live broadcast of the Memorial Day Indy 500, which he established as a national institution. But he closed the circuit in 1941 and it stayed that way for the duration of WW2. In 1945 he sold the Speedway to businessman Tony Hulman.

Rickenbacker had also founded Florida Airways in 1926, which he sold on to Pan-Am before becoming vice-president of the General Aviation

Corporation and later boss of its Eastern Air Transport division, which he moulded into Eastern Air Lines.

During the Second World War he toured US bases in the Pacific. On the way from one of them his B-17 ran out of fuel and crashed into the ocean, where he and the crew drifted for 22 days without food or water before being rescued.

In 1963 Eddie retired from Eastern, of which he had become chairman and CEO, and published his autobiography three years later: it sold a quarter of a million copies. He had a heart attack in October 1972 and died of pneumonia in Switzerland on 23 July 1973.

# Rindt, Jochen

JOCHEN RINDT LOOKED WILD, dishevelled, and had that devil-may-care swagger of a young person who didn't have to worry about money. But he was a spectacular racing driver, as anyone who remembers the 1970 Grand Prix of Monaco will confirm.

Rindt was lying fifth in his works Lotus 49C at Monte Carlo when he overtook Henri Pescarolo's Matra-Simca at the Gasworks hairpin to take fourth on lap 36, then slipped past Denny Hulme's McLaren 14A into third and stayed there. Four laps from the end, second-placed Chris Amon's March 701 lost a rear suspension bolt and that changed everything. Rindt was nine seconds away from race leader Jack Brabham in a BT-33 at the time and he went for it. After two laps of sheer brilliance, Jochen had chopped Black Jack's lead down to just over a second. As they shot out of the tunnel there were maybe a couple of car's lengths in it. Then Brabham braked too late going into Gasworks and sent the straw bales flying, and the dynamic Rindt flew past him to take his last-lap victory, the second F1 win of his tumultuous career. After that Jochen was on his way to becoming the 1970 Formula 1 World Champion driver – posthumously.

Born in Mainz, Germany, on 18 April 1941, Rindt was his family's only survivor of a 1942 Allied bombing raid. After that he was adopted by his grandparents in Graz, Austria, where he grew up, wild, rebellious and in love with motor sport. Jochen inherited the family spice business when he turned 18 so, with more than enough money to pay his way, he went motor racing and began his rather exuberant climb through the ranks, first in production cars, then Formula Junior and eventually Formula 2, where he really began to make his mark.

Jochen bought an F2 Brabham BT10-Cosworth that Ford of Austria entered for the 1964 London Trophy at Crystal Palace, which he won with a spectacular drive, beating established stars like Graham Hill, Denny Hulme and Jim Clark. After that he became a sort of F2 folk hero, putting in wildly entertaining performances to win both the British and French Formula 2 titles. He competed in the year's European Formula 2 Championship too, but he was an ungraded driver and so ineligible to score points; which was just as well, because Jochen won five of the championship's ten races and would have swept to the European title as well. Instead, it went to Jacky Ickx, who only won two races.

While all this was going on Rindt was paired with Masten Gregory to drive a NART-entered 3.3-litre Ferrari 275 LM in the 1965 24 Hours of Le Mans. The two didn't think they had much of a chance, because they were up against Carroll Shelby's mighty 7-litre Ford GT40 MkIIs. But the Fords had been hurriedly developed and their racing fuel consumption was anybody's guess. Sure enough the American big bangers took the lead, but as the race wore on they were plagued by overheating and also had to make constant refuelling stops. So their challenge faded, as did the works Ferrari P2s, which were all experiencing brake problems. That left the Belgian Pierre Dumay/Gustave Gosselen Ferrari 275 LM in the lead and the NART car second, reeling in the Belgians fast; at one stage the exuberant Jochen was clipping 12 seconds a lap off the front runner, which eventually capitulated to a puncture, leaving the Rindt-Gregory Ferrari a clear run to victory.

After sampling Formula 1 in a Rob Walker Brabham-BRM, Jochen signed a three-year contract with Cooper to drive its Maserati-engined T81, but although the spectators loved his balls-out driving style the results didn't really happen; a fourth in the 1965 German Grand Prix, a sixth at Watkins Glen. Things picked up a little in 1966 with a second in the Belgian GP, thirds in Germany and at Watkins Glen, but 1967 produced more gloom.

So Jochen joined Black Jack's team for 1968, but the four-cam Repco V8 in the Brabham BT26 was a failure, and the only reason the young Austrian scored a third at Kyalami was because he drove the 1967 BT24 instead. In August the soul-destroying BT26 took Rindt to third in the German GP, but just eight points and 12th place in the drivers' championship.

Colin Chapman came calling at the end of 1968, hoping to find a driver who stood at least a chance of filling the shoes of the late Jim

Clark. Jochen liked driving for down-to-earth Brabham, but Chapman's glittering record and Firestone's cash were too much of a temptation. Colin didn't quite know what hit him, though: the edgy, pushy, cigarette-puffing Rindt was sceptical too. And with good reason, because he began to lose confidence in Chapman's outfit after the British GP when a loose rear wing end plate on his Lotus 49B forced him into the pits to have it ripped off before rejoining the fray. He kept his second place and continued hounding Jackie Stewart's Matra, but on lap 71 he was forced into the pits again – for more fuel. Cursing what he considered the indifferent Lotus organisation, Jochen lost second to chase his pal Piers Courage, whom he overtook to end up fourth.

The 1969 Italian GP was another Stewart-Rindt dice and Jochen managed to snatch the lead at Lesmo until Stewart passed him, leaving him to fight Bruce McLaren for second, a battle he won. The USGP was yet another struggle between Stewart and Rindt, with lesser skirmishes between the Austrian, McLaren and Courage. Jochen held off Stewart for much of the race, but the Scot finally passed him so that the two eventually pulled out 20 seconds on third-placed Piers in the Brabham BT26. But Rindt repeatedly lunged at Stewart's Matra and succeeded in overtaking it on lap 21 to pull away from the spluttering, smoking Matra until the car faded from the race in a cloud of blue. Jochen was 42 seconds up on Courage at the halfway mark and won by almost 48 seconds from second-placed Piers.

Jochen would have liked to rejoin Jack Brabham, who was now dangling a pot of Goodyear gold in front of him, but he decided to stick with the money and technology Colin Chapman had at his finger tips. It seemed he wasn't wrong either, for Chapman unveiled a pre-season sensation called the Lotus 72, a car with a mass of new bells and whistles: unprecedented aerodynamics, torsion bar suspension, radiators at the sides. Jaws dropped across the F1 world as Colin began rewriting the F1 car design handbook.

Rindt used the Lotus 72 well and won the Grands Prix of Monaco, Holland, France, Britain and Germany as rumours persisted about his imminent retirement. Then came the Italian Grand Prix, by which time Jochen's championship domination was almost unassailable. But during the last practice session on the Saturday afternoon his rapid Lotus 72C swerved into the guardrail under braking just before the Parabolica, and he was killed outright.

Jacky Ickx went on to win the Grands Prix of Canada and Mexico in a works Ferrari 312 B after that, but he could only manage a drivers' championship total of 40 points by the end of the season. Rindt had amassed 45 before he was killed, making the young Austrian Formula 1's first posthumous World Champion driver.

# Rosberg, 'Keke'

KEIJO ERIK 'KEKE' ROSBERG was a kind of motor racing Cinderella Man for quite a while. He went from the drudgery of retiring or not even qualifying a stream of uncompetitive cars to becoming the 1982 Formula 1 World Champion the minute he had reliable machinery with which to lay his talent bare.

I first met Rosberg on a cool April day after he had beaten everybody in the 1979 European Formula 2 Championship race at Hockenheim, Germany. He was a no-nonsense straight-talker then and nothing was going to change him as he raced his way towards the 1982 world title and beyond. And he was just as decisive when he ran his own German Touring Car Championship (DTM) brace of Audis and steered his son Nico through the early stages of his young life and now his mightily successful career in the sport.

Keke was born on 6 December 1948 in Solna Municipality north of Stockholm, Sweden, but was brought up in Finland. His pushy driving style had shaken up Formula Vee, Formula Atlantic and F2 before he applied it to his first staccato year in F1 in 1978, during which he tried to compete in a succession of five ineffectual cars. The first of them was Teddy Yip's Theodore TR1, but after five Grands Prix in which the Finn either retired, did not qualify or did not pre-qualify, Yip decided to withdraw the TR1 and further develop it. So Keke switched to ATS for three races, but the best he could do with its uncompetitive HS1 was a couple of lowly finishes and a retirement. Then he moved to Wolf and did two Grands Prix in the WR3, in which he came tenth in Germany – his highest placing of the year. Then along came the new WR4 for the Dutch GP, but Rosberg had to retire it in Holland and was unable to pre-qualify it in Italy, so the Finn went back to ATS and competed in the last two races with its D1: he retired that at Watkins Glen and was not classified in Canada. Four finishes, three retirements, two not classifieds, four not pre-qualifieds and one did-not-qualify. Hardly the record of a future World Champion.

However, a glimpse of what Rosberg could do with competitive machinery turned the heads of the Formula 1 demigods in just his second race with the TR1, the non-championship BRDC International Trophy race at Silverstone. There was an almighty cloudburst during the event, which sent many a household name slithering off the track and into oblivion. But Keke, a latter day *Regenmeister* of the Rudolf Caracciola and Jacky Ickx stamp, drove with great panache and precision to win. But after that, pure frustration for the rest of the year.

Rosberg didn't take to the F1 stage again until the Grand Prix of France in July 1979, a year in which he drove a string of equally uncompetitive Wolf cars and scored no championship points at all. He was a surprise third in the 1980 Grand Prix of Argentina and came fifth in the Italian GP with the Fittipaldi F7, which not even 1972/4 F1 World Champion and team principal Emerson could turn into a winner. Keke stayed with Fittipaldi in 1981, but he was unable to qualify the car for five races and retired from six!

Mercifully, he eventually got his lucky break. Alan Jones retired at the end of 1981 and that left a seat free at Williams, so Sir Frank took a chance and signed the 32-year-old Finn for 1982.

Armed with a competitive car at last, Rosberg really went to town; he didn't win many of the year's Grands Prix but he kept up a steady flow of points with consistently high placings. His trademark aggressive driving style sent him marching steadily up the championship table, and for a moment it looked like he might take the title without winning a single Grand Prix. Then on 29 August he won the Swiss at the little 2.3-mile Dijon circuit and that, plus a couple of points from fifth at the Caesar's Palace Grand Prix in Las Vegas, made him the 1982 World Champion. A zero to hero performance if ever there was one.

Williams were late switching to the turbo engines that were now powering the likes of Brabham and McLaren, so Rosberg had an uphill battle to make an impression on the 1983 season with his normally aspirated FW08. In fact this was the first year that the World Championship ever went to a turbocharged car, the Brabham-BMW driven by Nelson Piquet. But Keke did pull off a brilliant win at the Monaco Grand Prix, where the circuit was wet. He took a risk and, unlike most other competitors, started the race on slick tyres: sure enough, the roads of Monte Carlo gradually dried out. Meanwhile the Finn put on a riveting display of car control to win from Piquet's Brabham and Alain Prost's Renault turbos, leading 75 of the 76 laps.

The brilliant Porsche turbo engine took the McLaren MP4/2 to victory no fewer than 12 times in 1984, while Keke and teammate Jacques Laffite were busy getting the Williams-Honda turbo package to work. A taster of greater things to come arrived when Rosberg led the Brazilian GP for nine laps before retiring and then actually won in Dallas. The Williams-Honda act was coming together nicely by 1985, when he took pole position at the British Grand Prix with an average speed of 160.9mph, which remained the fastest single lap in Formula 1 history for 16 years. And he won the Grands Prix of Detroit and Adelaide that season, while new signing Nigel Mansell took victory in Britain and South Africa.

But Keke moved to McLaren for 1986, just as the Williams-Honda package really came good: Sir Frank's team won nine of the season's 16 Grands Prix. To make matters worse, our Finnish hero was roundly beaten by his McLaren-Porsche teammate Alain Prost, who won the world title with 72 points to Rosberg's 22. After that Keke retired from Formula 1, which he openly admitted years later was too early.

Rosberg made his motor racing comeback in the 24 Hours of Spa in the Moneytron team's Ferrari Mondial, and he then spent a couple of years with the Peugeot sports car operation, for whom he won twice. He switched to the DTM series to drive Mercedes-Benz and then Opel before setting up his own Team Rosberg to compete in a string of different disciplines in Germany. He eventually went back to the DTM with his team, which ran the two Audis in 2006.

While all this was going on Keke became an effective manager, steering the careers of double Formula 1 World Champion Mika Häkkinen and 24 Hours of Le Mans winner JJ Lehto. And he closely follows his son Nico, who rose from successful campaigns in Formula 3 and GP2 to victory in his first Formula 1 race in the 2012 Grand Prix of China driving a Mercedes-Benz.

In 2013 Nico made the two of them the only father and son to have won the Monaco Grand Prix.

# Rosemeyer, Bernd

THIS SON OF A garage owner from Lingen, Lower Saxony, Germany, Bernd had never raced a car until 26 May 1935, yet 16 months later he was the king of Grand Prix motor racing – the 1936 European Champion, the equivalent of today's Formula 1 World Championship – with six wins to his credit. And all of them scored in a real handful of a car designed by Ferdinand Porsche, the rear-engined, supercharged, 4951cc Auto Union Type C, with its swing axles and skinny tyres, beating the likes of old hands Rudolf Caracciola, Hans Stuck and Achille Varzi.

Okay, so Bernd was used to competing in front of thousands of spectators, because he had won nine big-league motorcycle races for NSU and DKW in 1933 and 1934. But going from bikes to a skittish, tail-happy bundle of power like the Auto Union and becoming king of all he surveyed in less than 18 months just shows what a huge talent Rosemeyer was; definitely up there with Nuvolari, Fangio, Clark, Senna and Schumacher.

Germany was short of seasoned Grand Prix drivers in 1934 when the Nazi-backed Mercedes-Benz and Auto Union began their attack on European motor sport. That's why they imported experienced men like Luigi Fagioli and Achille Varzi to race their cars. Willy Walb, Auto Union's team manager, decided to look elsewhere and try out some successful German motorcycle racers, so he invited 12 of them to a test day at the Nürburgring. First, they drove the awkward Auto Union powerhouse on the 3.73-mile Sudschleife. Then Walb selected the fastest five, which included 25-year-old Rosemeyer, and sent them out on the full 14.17-mile track. In the end, he decided to sign Paul Pietsch and Bernd Rosemeyer, whose times were 11min 14.6sec and 12min dead respectively; to put that into perspective, Mercedes-Benz works driver Manfred von Brauchitsch set a fastest lap of 10min 32sec at the 'Ring during the 1935 Grand Prix of Germany.

Six Grands Prix slipped by before Walb gave Rosemeyer his chance at the ultra-fast Avus circuit in the Grunewald district of Berlin. Bernd was to drive a closed, aerodynamic version of the Auto Union, which looked more like a submarine on wheels. He was lying third until a tyre threw a tread and he had to drop out. Those promising four laps were a sign of good things to come at the next Eifelrennen at the Nürburgring three weeks later. Putting up an incredible performance to take second, this motorcycling new boy had the temerity to pass Caracciola's Mercedes-Benz and lead for two laps until the wily Rudolf first shadowed and then passed the young pretender on the last lap to win by 1.8 seconds.

It took Bernd the rest of the season to win his first Grand Prix, but with creditable placings along the way; he finished fourth in the German GP, second in Italy's Coppa Acerbo, third in the Grand Prix of Switzerland and fifth in Spain. The win came in Brno, Czechoslovakia, the last European Championship race of the season. At 18.10 miles, the Masaryk Circuit was the longest in use at the time and was made up of a network of dusty, narrow roads south of the city. But new boy Rosemeyer, helped by the fact that Mercedes-Benz didn't enter, outclassed the field, which included Achille Varzi at the height of his powers in another Auto Union, and Tazio Nuvolari in an Alfa Romeo 8C-35.

Next came a year of fireworks that started disappointingly for Bernd, with retirements in Monaco, Tripoli and Tunis. Things didn't look as if they'd improved much in Spain, either. Rosemeyer crashed in practice at the Lasarte road circuit near Barcelona when his steering broke. He started the race with an injured nose and knee, which may account for his lowly fifth place, but the music was about to change. Bernd was to win five of the next six Grands Prix.

The weather was lousy in the Eifel Mountains, where a huge slab of fog blanked the 14-mile Nürburgring, but the swirling mass eventually gave way to rain as the cars roared off to their destiny. Caracciola jumped into the lead in his Mercedes-Benz W25B and stayed there for the next couple of laps, until he was taken by Nuvolari in an Alfa 12C-36: then fog all but blotted out the circuit's 176 corners again. Most of the drivers slowed as an act of self-preservation, but not Bernd and his works Auto Union Type C. He had extraordinary eyesight that enabled him to see where the others couldn't, and gained a massive 30 seconds a lap on Tazio, who was not exactly a slow driver, to win the race from the Italian by over two minutes. That earned Rosemeyer the title *Nebelmeister* – 'Fog Master.'

The near miss that prevented him from winning six straight GPs was the Grand Prix of Hungary, in which Bernd came second to his new friend and arch-rival Nuvolari. A broken rear axle stopped Tazio from repeating that performance in the 1936 GP of Germany, which Rosemeyer won from teammate Hans Stuck by almost four minutes. The meteoric young German added victories in the Coppa Acerbo and the Swiss GP to his collection, all of which earned him the European Championship, the sport's top title, less than two years after driving a racing car for the first time. He also became the 1936 European Mountain Champion, with wins at Freiburg and Feldberg. An astounding year.

Rudolf Caracciola snatched his title back in 1937, although Rosemeyer won at Donington after nail-biting battles with Hermann Lang, Manfred von Brauchitsch and Caracciola. A remarkable achievement on a notoriously small, 2.4-mile track with 12 corners driving a tail-happy, mightily powerful Auto Union, slewing sideways more times than not. And Bernd won the year's Vanderbilt Cup race, 90 laps of the 3.4-mile Roosevelt Raceway on Long Island, USA, a chance to caress the huge Cartier challenge trophy, and take home a miniature version of the cup and $20,000.

During the 1937 season Rosemeyer also found the time to break no fewer than 22 Class B and C speed records in sexily-faired Auto Unions on the Frankfurt-Darmstadt autobahn between 16 July and 27 October, three of them world beaters.

It was record-breaking that killed 29-year-old Rosemeyer on 28 January 1938. He set off along the Frankfurt–Darmstadt autobahn in yet another slick new aerodynamic Auto Union with the objective of breaking Rudolf Caracciola's record of 268.7mph, set in a Mercedes-Benz Streamliner earlier that bitterly cold morning. Bernd had already recorded 268.7mph on a trial run and had reached 270mph during his record attempt as he roared through the third of his four checkpoints. Then his car seemed to go out of control due to either wind or a steering problem and put two of its wheels on the central grass strip, after which the Auto Union charged into a bridge embankment, then a clump of trees, and was smashed to pieces. The mangled bodywork ended up more than 500 yards from the grotesquely twisted chassis.

When the Auto Union officials got to Rosemeyer they found him lying motionless on the ground, dead.

A memorial was later erected marking the spot where Bernd crashed and died. It is still there to this day at the Bernd Rosemeyer Parkplatz on the A5 south of Frankfurt.

# Salvadori, Roy

TALL, HANDSOME AND CHARMING, Roy Salvadori was everything Hollywood ever wanted a racing driver to be. He was a 1950s–'60s swashbuckler and wouldn't have looked out of place swinging down from the rigging of a man o' war, sword in hand, alongside Douglas Fairbanks Junior.

Fantasy perhaps, but no less dashing than the profession he chose: motor racing. And he was good at it. Roy won 98 races and took 126 podium places during his 25-plus year career, because Salvadori was one of the old school: it seemed perfectly natural to him to compete in up to five races a day. That's what he did with such panache, for instance, at Goodwood on Easter Monday 1955. He won the F1 Glover trophy in a Maserati 250 F, then the Chichester Cup for F2 cars in a Connaught, and after that the sports car race in an Aston Martin; and he came second in the other two races. All in one day!

His may not be a household name, but that is probably because he never won a World Championship Grand Prix. He came close a couple of times, but that's all. Oddly enough, the moving parts in his GP racers all stayed together for the duration of non-title events. At those, Roy did well. He won F1 races at Snetterton, England, in 1954, those at Goodwood, Aintree and Snetterton in 1955, Snetterton again in 1956 and Crystal Palace in 1961.

His place of honour in motor racing, though, was earned by something completely different. He won the 1959 24 Hours of Le Mans with Carroll Shelby driving an Aston Martin DBR1, which also contributed to Aston winning that year's World Sports Car Championship, beating Ferrari and Porsche at their own game.

Roy was born in England of Italian parents in Dovercourt, Essex, on 12 May 1922. He started motor racing in 1947, driving a 2.9-litre Alfa Romeo, and worked his way up to his first Formula 1 race in 1952, when he qualified a Ferrari 500 19th at the British Grand Prix and drove Aurelio Lampredi's four-cylinder into eighth place. Salvadori spent the next year trying to knock unreliable Connaught A-Lea Francis cars into some semblance of competitiveness, but was only rewarded with a string of retirements. That was followed by 1954–56 in a Maserati 250 F run by Sidney Greene and his Gilby Engineering team, which produced much the same story.

Things were no better in 1957, when he had abortive rides in a BRM P25 in the Monaco GP and a Vanwall VW1 in the French. Then he was asked to join Cooper, and that was a whole new ball game. First time out in a Cooper T43-Climax, Roy qualified the car a cautious 14th and drove a hard race to bring the car home fifth. He stayed with Cooper in 1958 and took the T45-Climax to a resounding third in front of his own fans in the British GP, and an excellent second in the German. He ended the season in fourth place in the World Championship with 15 points, well ahead of teammate Jack Brabham in equal 18th on three.

Meanwhile, Aston Martin had been competing for the World Sports Car Championship since the series started in 1953, but had little to show for it. They brought out the DBR1, a major improvement over the DB3S that preceded it. The engine was uprated to 2.9 litres, a tad off the WSCC 3-litre limit. It had neutral handling with a minor tendency to understeer, which Salvadori liked. He said the car was better all round, with greater stability, especially in the wet, and had better brakes. But many cars have an Achilles heel and in the beginning the DBR1's was its gearbox, which a lot of additional development and a great deal of testing more or less sorted out before the 24 Hours of Le Mans.

Aston entered three cars, for Stirling Moss/Jack Fairman, Maurice Trintignant/Paul Frère and Roy Salvadori/Carroll Shelby. The Anglo/American crew knew they were in with a chance, but, with Stirling and Jack driving a slightly more powerful DBR1, they knew they had to box clever. For a start, they practised as little as possible and agreed a technique of extra-late braking and fast cornering during the race to save the gearbox and engine.

The minute hand on the big clock shuddered around to 4:00pm and they were off. Stirling charged into an immediate lead to tempt the Testa Rossa drivers into wearing out their cars early on. He lost the lead to Jean Behra's TR during the second hour, but the Salvadori/Shelby Aston had been playing a waiting game, having kept out of the initial cut and thrust. They were eighth at the end of the first hour, fifth after the second. The Behra/Gurney TR started to lose oil pressure and speed with much pit stopping, so after six hours Salvadori had little trouble in passing them to take command of the race.

Roy had been worried by a vibration problem for some time and pitted the DBR1, but the mechanics said the car was A-OK. So off he went again until the shake got so bad he had to slow and pit again. They found the trouble, a damaged tyre with a chunk of tread gone.

Shelby took the car out next, the Aston having been relegated to second, three laps down on the Olivier Gendebien/Phil Hill TR. By 11:00am on Sunday they had closed to within a lap of the Testa Rossa. Then the lead Ferrari called into the pits steaming like an old Dover to London express train, went out again, but retired after one lap. And that was the end of Ferrari's challenge.

Roy saw some of the drama and eased off, knowing he was in the lead, and started to worry about the creaks and groans he had not noticed for the other 20 or so hours. Shelby took over and drove the last stint to victory, a just reward for David Brown, who had invested so much in his company's non-stop British racing programme. Trintignant/Frère came second in another DBR/1 to drive home the great British win. Moss/Fairman, who had been the pacemakers drawing out the brittle Ferraris, retired on lap 70.

After first and second at Le Mans, Aston Martin decided to enter the Tourist Trophy at Goodwood, where Roy's car went up in smoke, but Stirling Moss won, so Aston Martin snatched the WSCC title from Ferrari's grasp.

That same year Roy and Carroll Shelby drove the ill-fated Aston Martin DBR/250 F1 car, but the best the Briton could muster in the under-developed machine were a couple of sixth places in the UK and Portugal. The car did another two races in 1960, but it was still uncompetitive.

It was a different matter with the Cooper T53-Climax in the United States Grand Prix at Watkins Glen, though. Roy had qualified 12th on the grid but drove a pushy race until he overtook Dan Gurney's Porsche and Bruce McLaren's Cooper to take second place. He was gaining on leader Innes Ireland's Lotus 21-Climax until there were just four seconds between them – then Roy's engine blew and he dropped out.

Roy Salvadori subsequently enjoyed a successful career in the motor trade before retiring to Monaco in the late 1960s.

# Scarfiotti, Ludovico

LIKE HIS UNCLE THE late Fiat boss Gianni Agnelli, Ludovico Scarfiotti was a suave, well-mannered gentleman who was no stranger to the privileges of wealth. He was, perhaps, no Grand Prix star – except on one glorious day in 1966 – but he turned himself into an immensely capable hillclimber and sports car racer.

Born in Turin in October 1933, this handsome aristocrat with a Tony Curtis hairstyle was drawn to motor racing at the age of 23, when he competed in the last Mille Miglia in 1957. He drove one of the family's products, a hot Fiat 1100, but didn't even make it as far as the halfway point in Rome. He had caught the motor racing bug, though, and soon bought himself a string of OSCAs, in which he put up some manly performances before having a go at hillclimbing, only to find he was really good at it.

Today, hill and mountain climbing are mere shadows of what they were during the first half of the 20th century, but when Scarfiotti began to make his name in this branch of the sport it was considered highly prestigious. That is borne out by the fact that Ferrari and Porsche regularly battled each other for the laurels at high altitudes on the Continent, where none other than Ludovico Scarfiotti won the European Mountain Championship in 1962 and 1965 driving a Ferrari Dino.

Scarfiotti made his Formula 1 debut in the 1963 Grand Prix of Holland at Zandvoort at the wheel of a factory Ferrari Dino 156, which he took over from an injured Willy Mairesse. The Italian gentleman qualified his 1.5-litre factory car 11th on the grid and actually won a World Championship point by coming home in sixth place behind some of F1's 'royalty,' like winner Jim Clark in a Lotus 25-Climax, second-placed Dan Gurney in a Brabham BT7-Climax and his teammate John Surtees in another Dino.

The 1963 season was really shaping up well for Ludovico, who also moved

into the World Sports Car Championship and won first time out by taking
victory in the 12 Hours of Sebring in a works Ferrari 250P, partnered by
British star John Surtees. But the injured Mairesse was back at the wheel
in time for the year's Targa Florio and found he had a new teammate –
Ludovico. So the two of them went off to Sicily with Lorenzo Bandini, where
their Ferrari Dino 196SSP was beaten into second place by no more than 12
seconds by Jo Bonnier and Carlo Abate in a Porsche 718 GTR. Almost six
weeks later Scarfiotti and Bandini made it an all Italian success when they
won the 24 Hours of Le Mans in a factory Ferrari 250P, that classic year in
which Ferraris monopolised the first six places. With his stunning debut
performances in those races, Ludovico made a major contribution to Ferrari
beating Porsche again for the championship by 39 points to the Germans' 34.

Enzo Ferrari didn't select Scarfiotti for Formula 1 again until almost
the end of the 1964 season, when he was given an outing in a Dino 156,
in which he qualified 16th and finished 9th – not the kind of result that
endeared him to the Commendatore, who was increasingly of the opinion
that this Turin gentleman was an endurance racer rather than an F1
combatant. But, as it turned out, the Great Man got it wrong, at least in part.

As if to back up Ferrari's theory, Ludovico continued to star in the
WSCC and took second in the 1964 12 Hours of Sebring with Sicilian school
headmaster Nino Vaccarella in a Ferrari 275P, and won the ADAC 1000
Kilometres at the feared Nürburgring in a 275P, partnered once more by
Vaccarella. He wasn't so successful in the 12 Hours of Reims, though, only
managing third in a 250GTO with Mike Parkes, but during the season he
had contributed plenty of points to Ferrari's routing of Porsche with 54
points to Stuttgart's 22.

Victory at the 'Ring followed again in 1965 with John Surtees in a
factory Ferrari 330P2, and Ludovico also came second in the 1000 Kilometres
of Monza with the Briton in a similar car. But Scarfiotti was canonised by
his countrymen in 1966 for pulling off something few other Italians have
been able to achieve. He won the Grand Prix of Italy at Monza in a Ferrari.

Ludovico's F1 appearances had been spasmodic, to say the least, until
John Surtees' controversial departure from the team in mid-1966. So the
line-up for the Italian GP was Lorenzo Bandini, Mike Parkes and Ludovico
in 312s and Giancarlo Baghetti in a 158/246.

Parkes took pole, but Scarfiotti was up there with him on the front row of the grid, having qualified faster than the other front-row sitter, Jim Clark in a Lotus-BRM. Ludovico and Mike led the field away, which set the crowd off in a cacophony of cheering, horn-blowing and bellowing. In a race that had four leaders in as many laps, Scarfiotti managed to move up to the front on lap 13, with Hulme (Brabham), Parkes (Ferrari) and Surtees (Cooper-Maserati) carving each other up for the slightest advantage. Meanwhile, Ludovico was still in the lead and building up a strong advantage of 15 seconds on the second-placed car, during which he set a fastest lap of 1min 32.4sec. And he held on to first place until the end, which sent the spectators into delirium. It was the first time an Italian had won the Grand Prix of Italy since Alberto Ascari in 1952. To complete the crowd's happiness, Parkes came second. The only blemish on the day appeared on lap 34, when Bandini's 312 went out with ignition trouble.

After that enormous high, Ludovico had a couple more Formula 1 outings in Ferraris in the Grands Prix of Holland and Belgium, but only managed a single point at Zandvoort.

But the Scarfiotti sports car bandwagon rolled on, with Ludovico and Mike Parkes winning the 1966 1000 Kilometres of Spa-Francorchamps round of the International Championship of Makes in a Ferrari 330P3, in which they also took pole position and set the event's fastest lap of 3min 46.4sec.

In 1967, his big moment came at the 24 Hours of Daytona, where he came second with Mike Parkes in one of the Ferrari 330P4s. That was that famous moment in motor racing history – and certainly one of the sport's most iconic images – when the winning Ferraris crossed the finish line three-abreast.

Ludovico came second with Mike Parkes in the 1967 1000 Kilometres of Monza and the 24 Hours of Le Mans in 330P4s before leaving Ferrari.

He drove the South African Grand Prix for Cooper-Maserati in 1968, but retired. Then he did the Spanish and Monaco GPs in Cooper T86B-BRMs and scored fourth places in both. Scarfiotti also signed with Porsche for World Championship sports car racing and came second with Gerhard Mitter in a 907 at the BOAC Six Hours at Brands Hatch before he came to grief practising for a European Mountain Championship event at Rossfeld, Germany, where the throttle of his Porsche Bergspyder is said to have stuck open and he died in the ensuing accident. A great loss of a great gentleman.

# Schell, Laury, Lucy and Harry

LAURY, LUCY O'REILLY AND Harry Schell were father, mother and son. They were all larger-than-life characters, who made their very distinct contribution to the colourful playboy image that some aspects of motor racing projected before the Second World War and immediately after it.

At first the main culprit was Lucy. She once announced that she wanted to be to France – where she was living at the time – what Enzo Ferrari was to Italy! Her American husband Laury went along for the extremely eventful ride. Both were completely in love with motor racing, but Lucy was the one who could do the most about it. She was the only child of an Irish-American multi-millionaire and her father doted on her. So she had virtually unlimited resources.

Lucy met moderately successful racing driver Laury, who had lived in France since he was a boy, on one of her trips to Europe after the First World War. The couple seemed a perfect match, as Lucy was just as crazy about the sport as Laury. So they married, and their son Harry was born on 29 June 1921.

The two were part of the gay Pareee upmarket French society set, and competed in international motor sport, with Lucy a regular competitor in the Grands Prix de la Baule and Marne. She even won the Coupe des Dames and came ninth overall in the 1929 Monte Carlo Rally.

In the mid-1930s, when it was obvious to the French that they could not beat the Mercedes-Benz-Auto Union Grand Prix steamroller, they created their own sports car series. Lucy knew Delahaye was developing its 135, so she pressed the manufacturer to produce a sports version of it called, not surprisingly, the Compétition Spéciale, which her Ecurie Bleue would race. But that meant more investment by the ailing French company, which looked unviable until Lucy strong-armed 12 of her rich friends into ordering a car apiece. All of a sudden Delahaye had a worthwhile proposition on its hands and had unwittingly entered the sports car championship. In the end they put up a two-car team themselves, while people of the calibre of René Dreyfus, Laury Schell, and René Carrière were competing as CS privateers. Major results came from René le Béguet, who won the 1937 Monte Carlo Rally in the car, and Eugéne Chaboud/Jean Trémoulet were winners of the1938 24 Hours of Le Mans in another.

In early 1936, Lucy persuaded Delahaye to design and build a Grand Prix car that complied with the 4.5-litre regulations and she underwrote the cost of them doing so. The result was a 230hp V12 magnesium engine – cutting edge technology at the time – in a more advanced 135 CS chassis. With wings, it could be raced in the sports car category: without them, it was a Grand Prix contestant and was, of course, called the Delahaye Type 145 CS *Grand Prix*.

But at the end of the 1936 season Delahaye dissolved its racing team, which meant Lucy O'Reilly Schell's Ecurie Bleue took over its Type 135S to be raced by Laury in 1937. He did well with the car and won the Prince Rainier Cup at Monaco, came third with René Carrière in the Mille Miglia and third in the Tunis Grand Prix. Meanwhile, as well as running the team, Lucy continued to compete.

Laury Schell was killed in an accident in November 1939, and after an almighty row with France's Fonds de Course over backing Lucy moved Ecurie Bleue to Monaco and refused to compete in the French Grand Prix. By then she was running Delahaye 155s, but she became fed up with their uncompetitiveness, so she switched to Maserati 8CTFs and took them to the USA to compete in the 1940 Indianapolis 500. It was not a happy experience. René Dreyfus blew the engine of his car. René le Béguet qualified, but his Maserati was in a sad state afterwards and it looked like he would not make the start. None other than Luigi Chinetti, who was to become famous as a 24 Hours of Le Mans winner and owner of the American NART team, worked on the 8CTF until dawn of race day. Surprisingly, the car lasted the 200 laps and Le Béguet came 10th.

With the Nazis carving up Europe, Lucy decided to stay in the US, and continued her motor sport interest through the Indianapolis 500. Harry, meanwhile, went to war after the Germans occupied France, first as an aircraft tail gunner before being commissioned into the US Tank Corps.

After the war, Harry raced 500cc Coopers in F2 and F3 and, like his mum and dad before him, became a playboy. He lived in Paris and wintered with the smart set on the Riviera. Handsome, 6ft 1in tall and a racing driver to boot, he was a regular 'wine, women and song' sort of chap. He was certainly a ladies' man and was married three times.

Schell made his Formula 1 debut in the 1950 Grand Prix of Monaco driving a Cooper T12-JAP, but retired after crashing on lap one. During his career he raced a succession of cars as a works and gentleman driver – some under his mother's Ecurie Bleue team name – but never won a championship Grand Prix, although he competed in 56 of them and racked up a total of 32 points. He did win the non-title F1 events at Snetterton and Castle Combe in 1955 and Caen in 1956. And he took a Maserati 250 F to third in the Grand Prix of Pescara and a BRM P25 to second in the 1958 Dutch GP.

But Schell's most heroic drive was in the 1956 Grand Prix of France, where he showed the world the Vanwalls would become a force to be reckoned with. He over-revved his VW1's engine on the sixth lap and retired, but not for long. Mike Hawthorn was tired after competing in the preceding 12-hour sports car race, so Harry took over his car. The American must have been under some divine influence or something, because he started lapping the Vanwall faster than race leader Juan Manuel Fangio in a Lancia-Ferrari D50. Schell got to within 30 seconds of the Argentine's car, outbraking and overtaking eventual winner Peter Collins and Eugenio Castellotti in their D50s on the way. Harry then set off after Fangio and was closing on him when his car began to lose power and he had to pit for a new injection pump. That dropped him way down the order and he finished tenth after putting on a great show.

Schell was also a fair hand at sports car racing. He won the 1956 1000 Kilometres of the Nürburgring with Stirling Moss, Piero Taruffi and Jean Behra in a Maserati 300 S and, put in three fine performances in the 12 Hours of Sebring: he came second with Luigi Musso in a Ferrari 860 Monza in 1956, second again with Stirling Moss in another 300 S in '57, and third sharing a Porsche 718 RSK with Wolfgang Seidel in '58.

Harry Schell was killed while practising for the 1960 International Trophy race at Silverstone in his Ecurie Bleue Cooper T51-Climax, eight years after the death of Lucy.

# Schumacher, Michael

HE WOULD PROBABLY HATE being called a prodigy but, like it or not, that's what he is. How else can you describe a kid who won his first motor racing *championship* at six years old? A man who became the Formula 1 World Champion *seven times* and in doing so won *91* F1 world title Grands Prix and stepped on to the podium no fewer than *155 times*, as well as setting *77 fastest laps* and taking pole position *68 times*, all in 17 years?

Rolf and Elisabeth's son Michael was born in Hürth, Germany, on 3 January 1969. Schumacher Senior built his son a kart from spare parts and Michael drove that to win the Kerpen-Horrem Karting Club championship when he was six. He won his country's Junior Kart Championship in 1983, but that was just the beginning; in 1987 he won the German and European Kart Championships, in 1988 the Formula König title with nine victories out of a possible ten. Schumi, or Schuey – just two of the nicknames with which the press lumbered him – signed with his future mentor Willi Weber's F3 team in 1989 and won the German Championship a year later, as well as the prestigious Macau and Mount Fuji F3 Grands Prix.

Peter Sauber signed Michael to compete for the 1991 World Sports-Prototype Championship in the new Mercedes-Benz C291. The car was troublesome for much of the season – except during the last race at the Autopolis circuit near Kumamoto, Japan, where Schumacher and Karl Wendlinger shared the winning C291.

Formula 1 soon beckoned in the form of Eddie Jordan, who gave the German his F1 debut in the 1991 Grand Prix of Belgium. Then Schumi moved to Benetton, whose B192-Ford was competitive in 1992, so he won the Grand Prix of Belgium and came third in the Formula 1 World Championship. Another Benetton victory followed in the 1993 Portugal Grand Prix, a season in which Michael stepped on to the podium another eight times.

The road to Michael's first Formula 1 World Championship was spectacular. He won the season's first four Grands Prix – in Brazil, Aida, Imola and Monaco – driving a Benetton B194-Ford. But Damon Hill, Graham's son, was making his mark in F1 too, and he brilliantly won the Spanish GP in a Williams FW16-Renault, with Schumi second.

Michael snatched the initiative to win in Canada and France, with Hill second at both, but Damon fought back and did something his father never managed – he won the British Grand Prix. That was a turning point, because Schumacher was disqualified from that race's results and banned from the following two GPs for ignoring a black flag. Then he was disqualified for a technical infringement concerning his car's stepped bottom. By the Australian Grand Prix, Hill had made up his 36-point deficit and just one point separated them. On the race's 36th lap Schumi hit a guardrail with his two left wheels. Hill tried to pass as the Benetton limped back on to the track and the two collided, so both had to retire. That meant Michael kept his one point lead and won his first F1 world title, with Damon runner-up.

Schumacher and Hill battled for the championship again in 1995, but Michael kept a grip and swept to the title again with nine wins and a massive 102 championship points to Damon's four victories and 69 points.

The great Ferrari saga began in 1996, Michael's first year at Maranello. He had been tempted with money, certainly, but the great allure was the seductive prospect of restoring Ferrari to its former glory for the first time in 17 years. Schumacher was up against some tough nuts in Damon Hill, Jacques Villeneuve and their Williams FW18-Renaults. But he took the Ferrari F310 to victory in Spain, Belgium and Italy, although poor car reliability put him third in the World Championship, while Hill became World Champion.

Damon was no longer 'the enemy' in 1997, Jacques Villeneuve was; Gilles' son breathed down Michael's neck in the Williams FW19-Renault most of the season. The Canadian won seven GPs to Schumi's five, with the title showdown set for the season's finale at Jerez. The Ferrari was slowing by lap 48, so Jacques passed Michael to take the lead. According to a later FIA hearing, Schumacher responded by deliberately driving his F310B into Villeneuve's car in an effort to eliminate it and conserve his championship points lead. But Jacques still managed to finish third and win the title, while Michael and his 78 points were excluded from the championship.

The next man to thwart Schumi's World Championship ambitions was Mika Häkkinen, the 1997 Jerez race winner. The Finn eclipsed Michael's six victories with eight of his own in 1998. Yet again, it all came down to the last race of the season, this time at Suzuka, Japan. But the Ferrari F300 stalled on the starting grid, meaning Schumacher eventually got away in 21st place. He sliced through the field and into third until one of his tyres punctured and he retired. Mika went on to win his first F1 World Championship.

The 1999 season looked like it would be a straight fight between reigning World Champion Mika Häkkinen and Michael Schumacher; by the British Grand Prix at Silverstone the German had three victories to the Finn's two. But Michael's Ferrari F399 just seemed to charge straight on at Stowe and thudded into the trackside barrier. Schumi's leg was broken and that put him out for most of what was left of the season, although he did make a major contribution to Ferrari winning the F1 Constructors' Championship for the first time in 16 years.

The new millennium started well for Schumacher and his Ferrari F1-2000, with three consecutive wins in Australia, Brazil and at Imola; but then McLaren-Mercedes-Benz drivers David Coulthard and Michael's arch-rival Mika Häkkinen stepped in and things suddenly looked a lot harder. But with eight victories to his credit Schumacher did eventually bring the Formula 1 World Championship for drivers back to Maranello for the first time since Jody Scheckter 21 years earlier. And for good measure Ferrari won the constructors' title too.

After that, Michael was crowned World Champion driver another four times before he retired in 2006. With 16 of the 2006 Grand Prix of Japan's 53 laps to go, Schumacher was leading when his Ferrari's engine broke for the first time in *six years* and he was forced to retire. Fernando Alonso won and went to the top of the drivers' championship table with 126 points to Schumi's 116. And there was just one more race to go, the Brazilian.

Michael conceded the championship to Alonso. He could only qualify tenth at Interlagos, but worked his way up to sixth in true Schumacher fashion, until he was forced to pit with a puncture. That dropped him to 19th, but still Michael was able to climb to fourth place, where he stayed until the end. And he set the race's fastest lap getting there, at 1min 12.162sec.

After that Schumacher became a Ferrari advisor. He competed on two wheels in the IDM Superbike series, but injured his neck in an accident. He did try to replace an injured Felipe Massa after the Brazilian's Hungaroring accident in 2009, but opposition from other teams put a stop to that.

At 41 years old, Michael returned to F1 with Mercedes-Benz from 2010 until 2012, but the cars weren't up to expectations, the magic had gone, Formula 1 had become too much of an effort.

A great champion had had enough.

# Scott-Brown, Archie

THIS IS THE STORY of a hero who was more heroic than most. You may not have heard of Archie Scott-Brown, but that shrewd judge of racing talent Juan Manuel Fangio, who won the Formula 1 World Championship five times, called this diminutive Scot phenomenal and said he showed uncanny car control.

Why more heroic than most? Well, William Archibald Scott-Brown was born deformed on 13 May 1927 in Paisley, Renfrewshire, Scotland, because his mother had contracted measles during her pregnancy. When she did give birth, doctors said Archie would never walk. His legs had no shin bones, both his feet were clubbed and he had no right hand. As a child he underwent 22 operations that partly corrected his leg problems and he was eventually able to walk.

But even with such disabilities, he became known in motor racing as the 'king of the four-wheel drift,' because he was one of his day's greatest balancers of cars, with all four wheels losing their grip while the car was on full opposite lock.

Scott-Brown had his first taste of speed at 11 years old in a small car powered by a lawnmower engine built by his father in 1938, and it soon became clear that the lad loved going fast. He had little time for schooling, so he went out to work and joined Dobie's Tobacco Company in 1949 and they soon sent him off to its East Anglia territory. His mother had divorced his boozy father by that time, so she accompanied Archie east: mother and son set up house in Cambridge.

Two years later Archie came into a little money, and with it he bought an MG TD and cut his teeth on that in club racing, in which he did well despite, as the 5ft Scot once joked about his disabilities 'a certain shortage of essential equipment.' The young man caught the eye of Brian Lister, who raced a Tajeiro-JAP in local events but was not really very good at it. So they eventually did a deal whereby Brian would be the entrant and return to his family's engineering firm and Archie would be his driver, all expenses paid. The remarkable Scott-Brown took over Lister's seat in the Tajeiro and proved he was an exceptionally gifted driver who normally won if the JAP engine held up.

Brian built his own Lister-MG in 1954. Don Moore tuned the engine and the car was entered for the Empire Trophy race at Oulton Park, where Archie qualified it first in his class. A protest from another competitor over his disabilities meant his entry was quashed by the RAC and his racing licence was revoked for a couple of months while the situation was sorted, thanks to a lot of press support.

But sorted it was, and Scott-Brown scored his first big-time success driving a 2-litre Lister-Bristol in the Curtis Trophy over 27 miles of the Snetterton circuit in May 1955, when he led briefly before settling for second place. Amazingly, the one-handed Archie – his right arm ended at the elbow – was invited to drive a works Connaught B-Alta Formula 1 car at Goodwood during Easter 1956, which made him the first disabled driver to compete in Formula 1. Even more surprisingly he challenged Stirling Moss' Maserati 250 F and Mike Hawthorn's BRM for the lead, which he snatched with the prowess of a real professional. He stayed in command until his brakes started to go and a stub axle gave up the ghost on lap 17 of the 32-lap race. Three weeks later he took pole at the Aintree 200 with a lap that was 2.2 seconds quicker than Hawthorn's BRM, then led the race from the start until piston trouble took him out once more on lap 13, when he was a clear six seconds ahead of anybody else.

He retired from the British Grand Prix but impressively took pole position in the Grand Prix of Italy and Europe at Monza, but was not allowed to race 'on medical grounds,' a decision he took in his stride but which outraged British motor racing fans. Meanwhile, the Connaughts continued on their unreliable way before the team was sold to one Bernie Ecclestone. After a disappointing seventh behind Moss at Silverstone in the International Trophy event, Archie won a great victory in the BRSCC's F1 race in October 1956 from Stuart Lewis-Evans in another Connaught and Roy Salvadori in Gilby Engineering's Maserati 250 F.

Brian Lister decided to have a go at the 3.5-litre class in 1957, so he acquired a Jaguar engine, which he had spent the previous winter installing into his own chassis to create the famous Lister-Jaguar, a 300hp rocket that was to be campaigned by Archie: the pairing was immediately successful, with Scott-Brown and the Lister-Jaguar winning the British Empire Trophy at Goodwood. He was entered for 14 races that year and won in 12 of them before taking a busman's holiday down under. There he won the 1958 Lady Wigram Trophy in the car at the Wigram Airfield near Christchurch, New Zealand.

Briggs Cunningham had Scott-Brown drive his 3.5-litre Lister-Jaguar with Walt Hansgen in the 1958 12 Hours of Sebring, and the Scot was going well until Olivier Gendebien tried to shove his way past in a Ferrari 250 Testa Rossa, rammed the rear end of the Lister and then climbed up over the back of it. The Belgian managed to get back to the pits for lightning repairs, got going again and eventually came second, but a downcast Archie and his Lister Jaguar retired.

With so much success to their credit, there was even talk of 5ft-tall disabled Archie and the renowned Lister-Jaguar entering the 1958 24 Hours of Le Mans, which would have made the world sit up and take notice. But that was not to happen.

Archie had been beaten by Masten Gregory in another Lister Jaguar just before the Sports Car Grand Prix at Spa-Francorchamps came round on 18 August 1958 when, notably, Jim Clark was making his first Continental appearance in a D-Type Jaguar. By this time, Scott-Brown, who had a friendly rivalry going with Gregory, had won an incredible total of 71 races in four years and was out for revenge against his Kansas nemesis. The Scot certainly impressed the spectators with a fine display of car control in the rain at the notoriously fast Belgian circuit. Maybe he was trying a little too hard, because he was leading on lap six when he hit a huge puddle just where Dick Seaman had had his fatal accident in a Mercedes-Benz in 1939. Scott-Brown's car aquaplaned, its right front wheel hit a road sign that shouldn't have been there, broke its axle, left the circuit, slammed into a clump of trees and burst into flames. Two courageous policemen dragged Archie from the blazing wreckage and he was rushed to hospital, but he was too badly burnt and died soon afterwards. Le Mans was not to be.

At the Snetterton circuit there is a plaque dedicated to Archie Scott-Brown's memory that says simply, 'Despite his disabilities, he won many races in Lister Jaguars built in Cambridge by George Lister and Son.'

# Seaman, Richard

IT MAY SOUND CORNY, but Dick Seaman's short life really was the stuff of Hollywood movies. He was tall, handsome, Britain's top racing driver, married to a BMW heiress, needed Adolf Hitler's personal approval to join Mercedes-Benz motor racing team and then poked the Nazis in the eye by daring to win the *German* Grand Prix in a *German* car. And that is not the half of it.

Richard John Beattie-Seaman was born into a wealthy family on 4 February 1913 and at 20 years old was hell-bent on a motor racing career. Early efforts in a two-litre Bugatti came to nothing. In fact they riled his father William so much he threatened to disinherit Dick unless he buckled down to studying. But the only thing the youngster was interested in at Cambridge University was its flourishing motor club, where he met a well-to-do American named Whitney Straight. Dick bought Straight's old MG Magnette and decided the only way to make money from racing was to compete in Europe. His first victory was in the voiturette race at the 1934 Grand Prix of Switzerland. Raymond Mays scored ERA's first win in the Nuffield Trophy handicap race at Donington the same year, but Seaman came second in the MG.

At the end of 1934 Dick negotiated a deal with ERA: he would buy one of its new cars at cost price and enter races as part of the works ERA team. He wished he hadn't bothered. First, ERA missed three delivery dates in April and May and eventually gave him his car in early June. As if that wasn't bad enough, one of the wretched car's pistons burnt out while Seaman was leading the Grand Prix des Frontiéres at Chimay, Belgium; oil pressure disappeared as he led the voiturette race at the Nürburgring; a locked brake bent the front axle at the Kesselberg hillclimb; the same thing happened practising for the Nuffield Trophy at Donington; and the supercharger broke at Dieppe.

Dick was livid. He'd had enough of ERA and its slipshod car maintenance, so he took a lock-up garage in Kensington and formed his own small team. His mechanic was none other than Giulio Ramponi, ex-Scuderia Ferrari, who rode with Giuseppe Campari when he won the 1928 and 1929 Mille Miglias. Giulio sorted the ERA so well that Seaman won the 1500cc race at the Coppa Acerbo near Pescara with the revitalised car and, more satisfying still, he beat all the ERAs in the Prix de Bern, including Raymond Mays in the factory car! But Seaman broke one of his own car's hubs practising for the Masaryk GP in Czechoslovakia and telegraphed ERA to send him another one. Of course, it didn't arrive, but Ramponi improvised a repair that was so good Dick won that event too.

Seaman bought Lord Howe's ten-year-old, eight-cylinder, 1500cc Delage and everyone said he was crazy. But Ramponi wielded his magic spanner again and Dick won the 1936 British Empire Trophy, the voiturette races on the Isle of Man, the Coppa Acerbo, the Prix de Bern and the JCC 200 at Brooklands. And he famously won the Donington Grand Prix with Hans Ruesch in the Italo-Swiss driver's Alfa Romeo 8C-35.

Then, out of the blue, Seaman received a telegram from Alfred Neubauer at Daimler-Benz inviting him to a driver selection session at the Nürburgring. And that is when his inner conflict began. Should he accept an invitation from a country in which the Nazis were building up to a war with Britain? After polling his closest motor racing friends, including Lord Howe, he took their advice and accepted, did well and was invited to more tests at Monza. At the end of it all Seaman signed a provisional contract, which would be confirmed if Adolf Hitler approved it; the Führer did so in February 1937.

Seaman's first race for Mercedes-Benz was the 1937 Tripoli Grand Prix on the superfast but sand-covered Mallaha circuit in a W125, and he did well. He was second to winner Hermann Lang at the halfway mark, when he retired with a broken supercharger. His was the top Mercedes to finish in the Vanderbilt Cup, coming second to winner Bernd Rosemeyer's Auto Union, and the Englishman finished the season with fourths in the Italian and Czech GPs.

Half of 1938 slipped by before Dick got to drive another Mercedes-Benz in anger. Cars, Mercedes claimed, were thin on the ground, but they fielded no fewer than seven W154s for the Grand Prix of Germany, one of them for Seaman. Dick set the third fastest time in practice at the Nürburgring and that put him on the front row of the grid. He was holding a strong second place in the race when he pitted for more fuel. He stopped his W154 behind the von Brauchitsch car, which suddenly burst into flames. Deciding that the mechanics could deal with the blaze, Seaman coolly punched a hole in the smoke with his Mercedes and sped off into the lead and victory over the great Rudolf Caracciola, who came second.

There was a stunned silence from the half a million spectators at the 'Ring as the significance of the Englishman's *coup d'état* began to sink in. On the winners' dais a po-faced Korpsführer Hühnlein, the Nazi boss of German motor sport, half-heartedly presented Seaman with Hitler's *Siegerpreis* and knew he would have a lot of explaining to do at a decidedly tense meeting with the Führer afterwards. Seaman rounded a unique year off with a second in the Swiss Grand Prix at Bern where he also set the fastest lap of 95.34mph, and a third in his old stomping ground of Donington, the race famously won by little Tazio Nuvolari in an Auto Union.

Dick married the daughter of a BMW director, Erica Popp, in London on 7 December and later signed a contract for 1939 with Daimler-Benz. He retired from the Eifel GP with a broken clutch, after which he and Erica travelled to Spa-Francorchamps for the Grand Prix of Belgium. The race was run in pouring rain and that, many thought, gave *Regenmeister* Caracciola a decided advantage. But Seaman wanted to take that title away from Rudy and he gave chase. Ironically, Rudolf lost it at the La Source hairpin on lap nine, spun off and was out of the race. Dick took the lead from Hermann Lang on lap ten, by which time the rain had eased off and patches of the notorious track started to dry out. So Seaman increased his speed until his car lost adhesion, charged off the circuit and slammed into a tree. The impact broke Seaman's arm and knocked him out. It also fractured the car's fuel pipe and, with the Mercedes on almost full tanks, masses of fuel gushed out on to the red-hot exhaust and ignited. Seaman was severely burnt by the time rescuers eventually dragged him from the blazing wreck and he died later in Spa Hospital. He was 26.

After his death Daimler-Benz ordered each of its Mercedes dealers worldwide to display a photograph of Seaman, who was buried at Putney Vale Cemetery in London. Hitler sent a wreath but it was not taken to the cemetery, where Dick's grave is still beautifully maintained by Mercedes-Benz to this day.

# Segrave, Henry

KING GEORGE V THOUGHT it was very funny. 'You're late, my boy,' he guffawed. The world's fastest human being had *tried* to get to Buckingham Palace on time for his investiture, but he turned up half an hour late. He had been delayed by a slow goods train huffing and puffing across not one but three level crossings that stood in his way. The king was most amused, and could barely contain himself as he tapped the Grand Prix winner and land speed record holder on both shoulders with his ceremonial sword and said with all the decorum as he could muster, 'Arise, Sir Henry.'

Henry Segrave earned his knighthood at the Daytona Beach Road Course, where he became the first person to break the 200mph barrier driving *Mystery*, the fire-breathing 1000hp Sunbeam, to set a speed of 203.79mph. That was his most recent exploit, because his short life was crammed with incredible acts of courage and daring dating back to his childhood.

Henry O'Neil de Hane Segrave was born in Baltimore, Maryland, on 22 September 1896 of an American mother and an Irish father, which made him a British national. At nine years old he would sit enraptured listening to his father's chauffeur, John Wilson, explain how the combustion engine, brakes, suspension and just about everything about a car worked. He was entranced, and even browbeat poor Wilson into allowing him to drive some of his father's cars, which thrilled little Henry but often frightened the life out of Wilson.

Henry went to Eton before he was commissioned into the Royal Warwickshire Regiment soon after the outbreak of the First World War and ended up commanding a machine-gun platoon in France at the age of 19. But his left foot was so seriously wounded that the surgeons were tempted to amputate it, which would have nipped Segrave's racing ambitions in the bud there and then. Happily, they didn't

Henry hadn't fully recovered when he was transferred to the Royal Flying Corps school in Britain, from which he received his wings on 1 January 1916. That was a time when fighter pilots had something like a three-week life expectancy. After a spell at the War Office in London, Captain Segrave married British musical comedy star Doris Stocker.

Following more promotion, Major Segrave was seconded to the British Mission in Washington, where he bought a 60hp Apperson. Soon afterwards he was introduced to Bill Brown, the great David Bruce-Brown's brother, who quickly brought back all Segrave's old craving for speed. It was not long before he drove the Apperson down to Sheepshead Bay Speedway to give the car a run. At first he drove gingerly over the two-mile board track, but eventually managed to work the car up to 82mph, which was quick in 1918.

Back in Britain after the war, Henry began to race an Opel Grand Prix at Brooklands and gradually established himself as a master of the world's first racetrack. That attracted the attention of the cynical Sunbeam designer Louis Coatalen, the man behind the firm's Wolverhampton-based racing effort. Coatalen eventually invited Henry to drive one of his cars in the 1921 Grand Prix of France. His aim was to become the first Briton to win a Grand Prix in a British car, previously the preserve of the French, Italians, Americans and Germans.

Segrave became the first Briton to finish a Grand Prix, even if he didn't win it. The 30-lap French GP was over a 10.72-mile Le Mans circuit and was won by American Jimmy Murphy in a Duesenberg, while Segrave came ninth in his 1998cc straight-six works Sunbeam just over an hour later.

It took Segrave another two years to achieve his ambition, partly because only two Grands Prix were held each year at the time. But on 2 June 1923 three of the straight-six Sunbeams were on the Tours starting grid for the 35-lap, 496.3-mile Grand Prix of France, with Henry, aspiring French ace Albert Divo and Brooklands racer Kenelm Lee Guinness sitting in their respective cockpits. There was some stiff opposition, but Segrave made his 102hp count to win from Albert Divo's Sunbeam in second and Ernst Friedrich third in a Bugatti T30.

Next, Sunbeam took its new supercharged car to Lyon for the 1924 French GP, but the British team's high hopes were dashed by faulty magnetos and the best Segrave could do was fifth, although he did put in the race's fastest lap of 11min 19sec for the 14.38-mile circuit.

But the Grand Prix of Spain at Lasarte was an entirely different story. Admittedly Segrave and the supercharged Sunbeam were hounded by Bugatti racing boss Meo Costantini in a T35, but Henry got the Wolverhampton car home after 35 laps of the 11.029-mile circuit in 6hr 1min 19sec, a minute and 41 seconds ahead of second-placed Costantini.

After that the Sunbeams faded from the Grand Prix scene, although Segrave continued to race until 1926, by which time his attention was focusing more on record breaking. He started out on 21 March by setting a new land speed record of 152.33mph on the compacted sand of Southport, England, in a 4-litre Sunbeam Tiger he called the *Ladybird*. His time stood for nearly a year before John Parry-Thomas beat it in *Babs*, a 27,059cc Liberty aero-engined monster, with which he reached 169.30mph on Pendine Sands.

A year later Segrave snatched his record back with a mighty 203.79mph in a 1000hp Sunbeam called *Mystery* on the Daytona Beach Road Course, making him the first man to exceed 200mph.

But that didn't last long. A young upstart named Ray Keech from Coatesville, Pennsylvania, took Sir Henry's record away from him on 22 April 1928 in the 81-litre White Triplex *Spirit of Elkdom* at Daytona, with a speed of 207.55mph. Segrave wanted his record back, so he got JS Irving to design a sensation. It was called the *Golden Arrow*, a front-engined record car powered by a 23.9-litre, 925hp Napier Lion W12 aero motor originally meant for the Schneider Trophy air races. The car was long and slender with a snap-down chisel of a nose and an all-aluminium body by Thrupp and Maberly. Sir Henry took the brand new car to the Daytona Beach Road Course on 11 March 1929, it having covered only 19 miles previously, and gave it a practice run before a massive crowd of 120,000 spectators. Soon afterwards he went for the record in his graceful howling monster and set a new flying mile speed of 231.45mph to become the fastest man on four wheels again.

American Lee Bible tried to beat Segrave's shiny new record just two days after it had been established, but he crashed and killed a photographer, a rude awakening. Sir Henry quickly became disillusioned with land speed records and left the sport. His *Golden Arrow*, which is now on display at Britain's National Motor Museum at Beaulieu, Hampshire, never ran in anger again.

Sir Henry switched to breaking speed records on water. He broke one on Britain's Lake Windermere on 13 June 1930 but crashed on his return run. He was dragged unconscious from the wreckage, but came round long enough to be told he had set a water speed record before dying from his injuries. He was just 33 years old.

# Senna, Ayrton

TWENTY YEARS AFTER HIS death, Ayrton Senna is more active than ever. Through his foundation, which he and his sister Viviane discussed before his tragic death in the Grand Prix of San Marino at Imola, Italy, on 1 May 1994. To date the project has raised upwards of $80 million towards schemes to help underprivileged children develop the skills and opportunities they need to achieve their full potential.

A long way from the man whose 'war' with McLaren teammate Alain Prost made the Frenchman leave for Ferrari at the end of 1989. And the man who had no qualms about driving Prost's Ferrari off the track in the 1990 Japanese Grand Prix to win the year's Formula 1 World Championship. And the man who unwisely lambasted FISA president Jean-Marie Balestre because he felt he had been wronged, but had to withdraw his unflattering remarks for fear of not being licensed to race in 1990.

Senna's career was packed with controversy, but he was a brilliant driver who won the 1988, 1990 and 1991 Formula 1 World Championships, 41 Grands Prix and took 65 pole positions, a record until one Michael Schumacher broke it a decade later.

It all started with a homemade 1hp kart powered by a lawnmower engine built by his father. Ayrton was 13 when he started in his first kart race – from pole, of course – and won the 1977 South American Kart Championship. In 1981 he left for the UK, where he joined Van Diemen and won two British Formula Ford 1600 championships. After that he announced his retirement and went back to Brazil to join his father's business – until he was offered a Formula Ford 2000 drive, so he went back to the UK and won the British and European FF 2000 titles.

In 1983 Ayrton won the British F3 Championship with West Surrey Racing, then the Macau F3 event in November for Theodore Racing.

Meanwhile, Ted Toleman, a British businessman, had put together a Formula 1 operation, but the team was struggling. Ayrton had tested for many teams, including Lotus, whose sponsor said no; Brabham under Bernie Ecclestone was a runner, but they eventually went for Roberto Moreno. That left Toleman-Hart, so in 1984 Ayrton joined them to partner Venezuelan motorcycle superhero Johnny Cecotto. And that led to a drive that shook the world. It was at the Monaco Grand Prix, where Senna started 13th. The skies opened up, yet Ayrton still charged on until he was right on the tail of leader Alain Prost's McLaren MP4/2. Many thought the 24-year-old would win, but race director Jacky Ickx decided the wet conditions were was just too dangerous and had the GP red-flagged on lap 31 of 78, so victory went to Prost.

Lotus-Renault boss Peter Warr got his way in 1985, when Senna was recruited to partner Elio de Angelis, and that's when the Brazilian really laid his claim to greatness. He took pole and then put on a display of perfect car control in the pouring rain to win the GP of Portugal by over a minute. Ayrton and the hardly competitive Lotus still managed fourth in the World Championship that year. Derek Warwick, a known charger, was due to join Lotus for 1986 but Senna opposed the move, certain the team couldn't prepare winning cars for two top drivers. So the chosen one was Johnny Dumfries (aka the Earl of Dumfries), but even one winning car was not on. Senna took pole and led at least half the year's events before unreliability stepped in, so wins in Spain and Detroit weren't anything like enough to win the title.

Honda power in 1987 took Ayrton to victory in Monaco and Detroit, but three years of indifferent car reliability meant Senna was off to McLaren for 1988.

And that's where the Senna-Prost war began. The two clashed throughout the season after Ayrton swerved to stop the Frenchman overtaking him in the GP of Portugal and almost put Prost into the pit wall at 180mph. The result: a fuming Prost and an FIA warning for Senna. The two were neck and neck with seven victories apiece when the F1 circus reached Suzuka for the GP of Japan, where Senna stalled on the grid and bump-started his McLaren to get away in 14th and win the race and the World Championship.

Things worsened in 1989, when Senna and Prost were often at each other's throats. But Ayrton led every lap of the San Marino, Monaco and Mexican GPs to win them plus another three. Still not enough to stop Alain from winning the championship, with Ayrton runner-up.

They clashed yet again at Suzuka in 1990 after each had won five Grands Prix, Prost driving a Ferrari 641 and Senna a McLaren MP4/5 B. Ayrton took pole, but Prost got away best; and then, in a clear case of retribution, Senna drove Prost off the track to take the title – an action that Prost later defined as 'disgusting.'

In 1991 Ayrton drove the McLaren MP4/6-Honda but was not convinced of the car's competitiveness. Yet he still won the first four races of the season, then added another three wins to his tally to become the youngest driver ever to win three Formula 1 World Championships.

At Honda's request an unhappy Ayrton stayed with McLaren in 1992, but the car was unreliable and the 12-cylinder engine had had its day. Yet his gritty talent still won him the Grands Prix of Monaco, Hungary and Italy – but no title.

After a lot of press speculation Senna eventually decided to stay with McLaren for 1993. Honda had left F1, Renault wouldn't supply its V10, so McLaren ran an obsolete Ford V8 engine. Ayrton had agreed to drive the South African GP for McLaren-Ford to see how the combination worked: he came second, so he stayed on. He won the next race in Brazil and then put in a really courageous, thinking man's drive in heavy rain in the European GP at Donington. He passed four cars on the first lap and beat the superior Williamses, Benettons and Lotuses to win. He went on to take Monaco, Japan and Australia, but the challenge of Alain Prost in the Williams FW15C-Renault was still too strong. Alain took the title with 99 points to second-placed Ayrton's 73.

Senna joined Williams-Renault for 1994 for the princely sum of $1 million a race, his teammate Damon Hill. In Brazil, Ayrton took the pole but lost time to a pit stop, got back into the race, pushed hard but spun out. He was on pole again at the next Pacific GP at Aida, but Mika Häkkinen's McLaren-Peugeot hit the back of his car and Nicola Larini's Ferrari crashed into him. Race over.

Senna was leading the San Marino GP at Imola as he went into the ultra-fast Tamburello corner at about 200mph, but his car seemed to go straight on until it hit the barrier and stopped abruptly. Ayrton didn't move.

The medics got him out, tried to treat him at the trackside, then rushed him to hospital in Bologna, where he later died.

The Brazilian government announced three days' mourning. Ayrton Senna's body was flown back to São Paolo and escorted to the city by a vast motorcade led by 16 police outriders over a 20-mile route lined by 2500 policemen. His grave is still one of the most visited in the world.

# Shaw, Wilbur

ONE WAS BORN IN Shelbyville, Indiana, in 1902 and the other in a cramped workshop in Bologna, northern Italy, 35 years later. Yet when the two came together they astounded the world by becoming the first to win the Indianapolis 500 twice in succession, in 1939 and 1940.

Warren Wilbur Shaw built his first car at 18 years old and by the time he was 22 he had won America's National Light Car Championship in his RED Special. After that he raced on just about every half-mile track in Indiana, Ohio and Illinois. In 1927 he was invited to drive the rebuilt Miller in which Jimmy Murphy crashed and died in 1924 in the Indianapolis 500. Unnerved by the Jinx Special, as the car had been renamed by its rather cynical sponsor Fritz Holiday, Wilbur came fourth in his rookie year.

Months later tragedy struck when Shaw lost his wife and baby during childbirth. For some time after that he had little stomach for racing. He remarried in 1929, after which he went back to the Speedway to score an outstanding second in 1933 driving a Stevens Miller. There was no joy in 1934, but Wilbur came second at Indy again in 1935, this time in his own Shaw-Offenhauser. Two years later he was the toast of the Brickyard in 1937 when he won the first of his three Indianapolis 500s in his Shaw-Offy. He came second in the same car in 1938.

That same year Ernesto Maserati was well on the way to developing a potent front-engined car called the 8CTF (*8-Cilindri a Testa Fissa*, or 8-Cylinder Fixed Head). He expected at least some European success with it but many thought he was kidding himself, and they were right. The mighty Mercedes-Benzes and Auto Unions were still crushing everything in their path, and had been doing so since 1934. They won eight out of a possible nine European Championship Grands Prix in 1938 and nothing was going to get in their way in 1939, least of all an untried car from the middle of nowhere in Italy.

Still, Ernesto was a gifted designer with a string of successful racecars to his name, like the 4CS/CM 1500, the 4C 2500, the twin-engined V5, the 8C 3000, the 8CM and the 6CM. His new creation had an eight-cylinder, 3-litre supercharged engine made of two separate cylinder blocks cast into a single in-line unit with one sump and cylinder head. Fuel feed was independent for each four-cylinder division and there were two superchargers, one operated by the driveshaft and the other by the valve gear, both turning at the same speed. The system was completed by two Memini carburettors, all of which put out a respectable maximum of 365hp at 6300rpm.

The car made its debut in the 1938 Grand Prix of Tripoli but was trounced by three Mercedes-Benz 154s driven by Hermann Lang, who won, Manfred von Brauchitsch, second, and Rudolf Caracciola, third. The best an 8CTF could do in Europe after that was third in the year's Grand Prix of Germany, driven by Nürburgring expert Paul Pietsch.

Only three Maserati 8CTFs were built. Two of them ended up with Ecurie Lucy O'Reilly Schell, run by Harry's mother. Wealthy American businessman Mike Boyle had been impressed by the performance of the little Maserati 6CM he had bought for Mauri Rose to drive in the 1938 Indianapolis 500. So he sent fabled mechanic Cotton Henning to Bologna to buy an 8CTF. Few expected the car would have much impact on Indy. But they had not reckoned on Mike Boyle's considerable financial backing and the utter professionalism of his team, especially Henning, who meticulously went through the 8CTF in the US to make sure it was in perfect mechanical order for the race.

It needed to be. Because Shaw's first victory in the Maserati 8CTF was no walkover. It was a 200-lap brawl between Wilbur, Jimmy Snyder in an Adams-Sparks, Louis Meyer in the Bowes Seal Fast and Cliff Bergere's Miller Ford-Offenhauser. Wilbur's victory in a car that failed in Europe – mainly due to poor pre-race preparation – was the biggest possible shot in the arm for Maserati. And the American driver sent Maserati a photograph of himself sitting in the 8CTF at the Brickyard with the inscription, 'To the Maserati brothers, for building such a marvellous car.'

Three Maserati 8CTFs were entered for the 1940 Indianapolis 500, two of them by Lucy Shell for Rene Dreyfus and René Le Béguet. Hope of doing well was nearly dashed when practice almost reduced Le Béguet's car – the only one of the two to qualify – to being a non-starter. None other than

Luigi Chinetti worked until dawn on race day to get the 8CTF into racing condition. Surprisingly, the car lasted the 200 laps and came tenth.

Shaw's Maserati was immaculately prepared once more by Cotton Henning, Wilbur having qualified second at 127.065mph. He won at an average speed of 114.277mph from poleman Rex Mays driving a Stevens-Winfield and Mauri Rose in a Wetteroth-Offenhauser.

Just before the 1941 Indy fire broke out in the Speedway garages, but the 8CTF and its spares were saved. They included a suspect wheel, which had been marked OK but to be used last. At the end of lap 138 Wilbur was well ahead of the rest of the field and likely to become the race's first hat-trick winner, when he pitted for more fuel and tyres. The questionable rim was mistakenly fitted to his Maserati and, with a record fourth Indy win in his sights, the wheel gave way, the Maserati crashed and Wilbur was hospitalised.

Shaw retired from racing during the Second World War, having won the race three times – twice in succession – and led it for a total of 508 laps.

A senior executive with Firestone during the Second World War, Shaw was told by the chairman of the Indianapolis Speedway, First World War ace Eddie Rickenbacker, that the Brickyard, which had been closed during the hostilities and was in a bad way, would be demolished and turned into a housing estate. There was no way Shaw wanted the glorious Speedway to come to such an ignominious end, so he went looking for money with which to revive the circuit. He found wealthy businessman Anton (Tony) Hulman, told him of the circuit's plight, and Hulman negotiated with Rickenbacker and bought America's motor racing temple. He made Shaw president and general manager of the circuit and their joint aim was to turn it and the American public holiday Memorial Day into what they dubbed 'The Greatest Spectacle in Motor Racing.'

Wilbur Shaw was being flown back from a business meeting in Michigan with two other people on 30 October 1954 when his aircraft crashed near Decatur, Indiana. There were no survivors.

For many years Shaw's winning Maserati 8CTF has graced the Indianapolis museum. Wilbur himself was inducted to the International Motorsports Hall of Fame in 1991, together with Ralph DePalma, Phil Hill, Bruce McLaren and Tony Bettenhausen.

In 2013, about 100 of Wilbur Shaw's personal possessions were put up for auction, including his diamond-studded chequered flag gold ring and the three trophies with which he was presented for winning the Indianapolis 500 in 1937, 1939 and 1940.

# Siffert, Jo

AT THE END OF 1969, during the height of the Ferrari-Porsche World Sports Car Championship 'wars,' Jo Siffert was wined and dined at Maranello by Enzo Ferrari, who offered him a deal for 1970. But it was not only the bravura of the Swiss in a racing car that interested the wily old Commendatore. After 17 years of trying, the German manufacturer had taken the championship away from Ferrari, which had hogged it for 12 of those 17 seasons.

The Swiss driver was thrilled that he had been asked to join the most prestigious team in motor racing, especially because of his modest origins and his hard slog to reach the top. But if he signed for the Prancing Horse he would be put to work immediately in an effort to win back the world sports car title for the Italians. And Porsche would lose the man who had won them six WSCC races in 1969 alone! An astute move by Ferrari, but it didn't work.

The German manufacturer was doing well selling its expensive road cars, in part on the back of its championship exploits – it had been runner-up seven times before winning the 1969 title – and the slightest danger of losing its top driver to the 'enemy' was the stuff of boardroom heart attacks. So Porsche *paid* for Siffert to compete in F1 at the wheel of an STP March. That is how good the little Swiss was in sports cars and how much Porsche wanted to keep him driving theirs.

Jo also did well in F1 and even beat Jim Clark in two consecutive years of the non-championship Mediterranean GP. But his talent was only rewarded with two world title Grand Prix wins, while he scored 14 memorable victories in Porsche's big bangers.

The Siffert story is literally one of rags to riches. His parents in Fribourg barely earned enough to keep the family going, let alone pay for money-gobbling pastimes like motor racing. So Jo was on his own. He left school at 15 and became a rag merchant (no pun intended), but soon discovered that repairing and selling crashed cars was more to his taste, and later qualified as a coachbuilder before doing his military service.

Siffert painstakingly saved up for a 125cc Gilera bike he wanted to race in 1957, salting away money from additional jobs like picking flowers and selling them to passers-by, and collecting Swiss Army bullet shells from shooting ranges and selling them back to the lean-budgeted military. A couple of years later he won his national 350cc championship.

Always with an eye on the cost of it all, Jo scraped together 13,000 Swiss Francs to buy a Stanguellini Formula Junior single-seater in 1960. He worked as a coachbuilder during the day and laboured on his racing car at night, and in 1962 his dream came true: he had amassed enough money to buy a Lotus 24 Climax.

He made his F1 debut during practice for the 1962 Grand Prix of Monaco, but was unable to qualify. He drove a Lotus 24-BRM for Switzerland's Ecurie Filipinetti for a while in 1963, when he racked up his first major victory in the non-championship Syracuse Grand Prix in Sicily. Soon after that he went out on his own, and scored his first F1 point with a dramatic drive into sixth place in the Grand Prix of France at Reims. Dramatic, because Jo's driving style was, shall we say, hard-nosed and unconventional. He would slash his braking distances to the bare minimum, hurl his car into each corner on the ragged edge (again no pun intended) and obscure the racing line.

Siffert acquired a Brabham BT11 chassis into which he lowered a BRM V8 power unit for 1964 and won the non-title Mediterranean Grand Prix with it at Enna-Pergusa. Jo's big break came in 1965 when he was invited to join Jo Bonnier in Rob Walker's private team and drive the Scot's second Brabham-BRM. The arrangement worked out well for both of them, because Siffert won at Enna again with that car and gave Walker his first victory since the halcyon days of Stirling Moss. Among the drivers Jo beat at Enna was Jim Clark, who said the Swiss was so sideways the Scot never knew whether try to take him on the right or the left!

Walker bought a Cooper-Maserati T81 for the first 3-litre season in 1966 and chopped his driving staff in half, releasing Jo Bonnier and retaining Siffert. The car was not really up to it, though, and the best Siffert could do was a couple of fourths at the 1966 and 1967 US Grands Prix at Watkins Glen.

Meanwhile, Siffert was playing himself into sports car racing and came fourth in the 1967 24 Hours of Le Mans in a Ford GT40 with Bruce McLaren and Mark Donohue. After that he became a Porsche man and started his career with the Stuttgart firm by winning the 1968 Daytona 24 Hours in a 907 with Vic Elford, Jochen Neerpasch, Rolf Stommelen and Hans Herrmann. His next sports car win came a month later at the 12 Hours of Sebring, in a 907 again with Hans Herrmann, followed by wins in a Porsche 908 in the Nürburgring 1000 Kilometres with Elford and a solo victory at Zeltweg.

Walker dug deeper into his pocket and bought an updated Lotus 49 for 1968, but the car was almost throttled at birth when Jo crashed it badly in the wet practising at Brands Hatch for the non-title Race of Champions. Worse still, Rob's UK base was burnt to the ground soon afterwards and, with difficulty, he eventually managed to buy a Lotus 49B, with which Jo promptly won the '68 British GP at Brands Hatch, beating the works Ferraris of Chris Amon and Jacky Ickx. Siffert stayed with Walker and the 49B for an undistinguished 1969, and his Porsche-financed 1970 in the March 701 was much the same.

Compensation came from his victories in sports car racing, first the Targa Florio with Brian Redman driving a 3-litre, eight-cylinder 908/3, although its car had to slow for a bit after an old poster clogged most of its front air intake. Siffert and Redman had become quite a team, for they also scored their second successive victory in the 1000 Kilometres of Spa in 1970, driving a Porsche 917K with almost three minutes in hand over second-placed Ickx and John Surtees in their works Ferrari 512S. The duo struck again in the 1000 Kilometres of the Österreichring in a similar car, with Porsches taking five out of the race's first six places. All of that success helped give Porsche the championship again.

Jo won the 1000 Kilometres of Buenos Aires with Derek Bell driving a Porsche 917K in 1971, the year he moved to BRM, with whose P160 he won the Grand Prix of Austria. The Swiss was entered for the end-of-season 1971 Victory Race at Brands, but after a coming together with Ronnie Peterson's March the P160's suspension broke; the car careered wildly off the track at Hawthorn Hill and burst into flames. Siffert, who was trapped in the BRM, died of asphyxia.

# Stewart, Jackie

THREE WEEKS AFTER HE had won the 1966 Grand Prix of Monaco in an ageing works 2-litre V8 BRM P261, Jackie Stewart lay trapped in the wreckage of his car after having flown off Belgium's Spa-Francorchamps circuit in the pouring rain at 165mph. His BRM smashed into a telegraph pole, hit a shed and ground to a halt in a farmer's outbuilding. Fuel flooded his cockpit and soaked him as Stewart lay there – a potential Roman candle – for 25 minutes. His leg was trapped by the car's distorted steering column, and he hoped against hope that a rogue spark wouldn't ignite the fuel and turn him into a human torch.

Eventually his teammates Graham Hill and Bob Bondurant freed him, but his problems weren't over by a long chalk. There was no doctor or medical staff on the scene so Jackie, who had suspected spinal injuries, was eased on to the back of a pickup truck to await an ambulance. The vehicle eventually turned up and took him to the circuit's first aid centre, where his stretcher was unceremoniously dumped on to a dirty floor, which was strewn with cigarette butts and other rubbish. Precious minutes later another ambulance showed up, Stewart was loaded aboard and off he went to Liège hospital with a police escort. But the police lost the ambulance or vice-versa, and Jackie's driver did not know the way to the hospital. Mercifully, after that string of disasters, a United Kingdom Air Ambulance flew him back to Britain for treatment, without which Stewart may well have died.

So it is little wonder that John Young Stewart, born in Dumbarton, Scotland, on 11 June 1939, became a powerful advocate of motor racing safety after that sordid affair. His three F1 World Championships and a record 27 Grands Prix victories – not to mention five non-championship wins and six Tasman Series successes – gave him a lot of clout. So he used it to campaign for improved emergency services, medical facilities, trackside safety barriers where there were none and better ones where they were inadequate, improved racing cars – the removable steering wheel is down to him – crash barriers in front of the pits, obligatory safety harnesses, full-face helmets, run-off areas ... the list is a long one, and it made him unpopular with a lot of track owners, race organisers and even some of his fellow drivers, but his popularity among race fans was huge, and that shielded him from excesses of vengeance.

Jackie's father Bob had been an amateur motorcycle racer and elder brother Jimmy was a promising Ecurie Ecosse driver until a series of accidents in the early 1950s forced him into premature retirement. Meanwhile, Stewart the Younger was an apprentice mechanic in the family's Jaguar dealership and became a clay pigeon marksman of Olympic standard. Early sports car successes in 1961–63 soon reached the attentive ears of Ken Tyrrell, who invited Jackie to Goodwood for a try-out. The young hopeful stepped into a T72-BMC Formula 3 car Bruce McLaren was testing and soon bettered the New Zealander's times. Bruce went out again and beat the Scot, after which Jackie took to the track and beat Bruce again, so Ken offered the young Scotsman a place in his F3 team. And that was the beginning of an outstandingly successful relationship, which would last until Jackie's retirement in 1973.

Stewart began to dazzle in Formula 3 and, soon after winning at an extremely wet Snetterton in 1964, he was offered two Formula 1 rides, first by Cooper and then by Lotus as fellow Scot Jim Clark's number two. He declined both and signed for BRM. His third place at the 1965 Grand Prix of Monaco was fair warning that he was on his way, and victory in the BRM P261 at the year's Italian GP at Monza announced that he had arrived. Then came the Monaco win for BRM in May 1966 and the Spa debacle, which meant Jackie missed the French GP but was back in the BRM for the British in July, but retired. That was to be the way of things for the rest of the '66 season, as Stewart and teammate Graham Hill struggled to make the notoriously unreliable H16 engine work.

The two put on an incredible show in the 1966 Indianapolis 500, though. Stewart was leading the race until eight laps from the end when mechanical problems with John Meecom's Lola T90-Ford forced his retirement. The race was won by teammate Graham Hill, while Jackie was accorded Rookie of the Year honours. Five years later Stewart did win in North America, at Canada's Ste Javite and America's Mid-Ohio circuits in the Can-Am Challenge, driving Lola T260-Chevrolets

By the end of the 1967 season Stewart had joined Ken Tyrrell's brand new F1 team for the following year and drove Cosworth DFV-engined French Matras. A move that won him the Dutch, German and US Grands Prix that season and was to make him World Champion for the first time in 1969.

In 1970 Ken bought a new March 701-Ford for Jackie while the Englishman was developing his own F1 car in the greatest secrecy. Stewart did well in the March too, taking the win in the Grand Prix of Spain and battling it out with the mercurial Jochen Rindt – who won the title posthumously in his Lotus 49Cs and 72s – a gifted Jackie Ickx and Clay Regazzoni in their Ferraris. He came equal fifth in the championship with Jack Brabham.

The new Tyrrell was an immediate success for its speed and reliability and Jackie won the Spanish, Monaco, French, German and Canadian GPs plus his second World Championship in the car in 1971. But he lost his title to Brazilian Emerson Fittipaldi in 1972, even though he won in Argentina, France, Canada and the USA.

By 1973 Jackie was thinking of retiring from the sport, but first he set out to keep his title and did so by wining in South Africa, Belgium, Monaco, Holland and Germany, ending up with 73 points to Fittipaldi's 55. His Tyrrell teammate François Cevert was tragically killed practising for the US Grand Prix at Watkins Glen, so the Tyrrells were withdrawn as a mark of respect. Stewart retired one Grand Prix short of his 100th.

But Jackie had done it all. He had won three world titles and 27 Grands Prix, breaking Jim Clark's record of 25 victories. Stewart's was a record that was to stand for 14 years before diminutive Frenchman Alain Prost came along and broke it with an eventual career tally of no fewer than 51 title victories.

After retirement Jackie kept hyper-busy campaigning for safer motor racing, as a consultant to the Ford Motor Company and as a television commentator.

He got back into Formula 1 with his own Stewart Grand Prix team in 1997, partnered by his son Paul. It fielded SF1-Fords for Rubens Barrichello and Jan Magnussen for its first event in Australia, but both retired with various problems. Its best result of the year was Barrichello's second place at a rainy Grand Prix of Monaco. Victory eventually happened for the fledgling team at the 1999 Grand Prix of Europe at the Nürburgring, where Johnny Herbert won with Rubens Barrichello third in their SAF-3-Fords. The team was sold to Ford at the end of the 1999 season and was renamed Jaguar Racing, which was sold on to Red Bull six years later.

Jackie was knighted by Queen Elizabeth II in 2001.

# Stuck, Hans

HANS STUCK FIRST MET Adolf Hitler in 1925, when a mutual friend brought the budding Führer to the racing driver's farm near Munich, Germany, for a day's hunting. Hitler never forgot his day out and, after taking power on 30 January 1933, telephoned Stuck, who had been bemoaning the lack of a decent German car to race since both Austro-Daimler and Mercedes-Benz had dropped out of the sport.

The *Reichskanzler* said that Stuck, then 32 years old, would get his car, and asked for a list of his needs. Hans immediately contacted Professor Ferdinand Porsche, who had designed both the Austro-Daimler and the Mercedes-Benz SSKL he was racing at the time, and the two arranged to meet in Berlin together with Baron Klaus von Oertzen of Auto Union. They had an audience with the Führer during which Hitler agreed the state would part-fund German motor racing, but the money was to be divided equally between Auto Union and Mercedes. And so the foundations were laid for the birth of the famous 'Silver Arrows.'

Stuck was born into a wealthy family of landowners in Warsaw, Poland, on 27 December 1900, and as a young man helped them run a dairy farm near Munich. He bought himself a four-cylinder Dürkopp car and used that to deliver milk to his family's customers in record time. He set his cap at motor racing and struggled until he won his first 'official' race in 1923, then a string of national hillclimbs, which attracted the attention of Austro-Daimler. After a trial period he became an A-D factory driver, and won the 1929 mountain championships of Germany, Austria, Switzerland, Italy, France and Hungary for them: he was so good at that branch of the sport that he was eventually dubbed 'King of the Mountains.' But Austro-Daimler pulled out of racing in 1931, leaving Stuck without a ride.

One of his friends from way back was Crown Prince Wilhelm, the

Kaiser's son, who convinced his contacts at Mercedes-Benz to sell Hans one of its huge but 'extra light' SSKLs at a special price, a car the lanky star drove for the next three years. He first appeared in it at a Czech hillclimb, in which Rudolf Caracciola was also competing in a Mercedes. Both won their respective classes and struck up a rather wary friendship that was to last a lifetime.

Stuck won his first Grand Prix in Lemberg, Poland, in 1931, then entered the SSKL for the Grand Prix of Argentina, scheduled for February 1932. But when he saw the 'roads' on which he would be racing he withdrew: in some places there wasn't even enough ground clearance for his big Mercedes. So he took the car to Brazil, where he won the national hillclimb title.

Back in Germany, Hans won six top mountain climbs in the SSKL to make him the 1931 Alpine Champion.

After their audience with Hitler in early 1933 Professor Porsche got down to work, and had a prototype of the big V16 Auto Union ready by November, when Stuck tested the car on the Nürburgring. Four months later Hans set three new world speed records in the swing axle, rear-engined 175mph monster. The new car had its first race on the Avus circuit near Berlin on 27 May 1934, when Stuck and the 'P-Wagen,' as the car was called by the *cognoscenti*, led for 11 laps until clutch trouble forced its retirement.

August Momberger was the first to distinguish himself in the new, tail-happy V16 Auto Union by coming third with it at Avus, but the P-Wagen's first victory was by Stuck in the Grand Prix of Germany at the Nürburgring, which made the Mercedes-Benz W25As, Alfa Romeo P3s and Maserati 8CMs look pretty sick, especially as he set the fastest lap of 10min 43.8sec over the notoriously difficult 14.167-mile circuit.

That win really turned Hans into a national hero, eulogised by everybody from Adolf Hitler down. To mark his great victory, Stuck had to drive his racing car on the public roads for hundreds of miles from Berlin to the Auto Union headquarters in Zwickau! All the schools along the route were closed that day so that the kids could line the roads in their thousands to wave and cheer Germany's new idol.

Hans was having the year of his life. He also won the Grands Prix of Switzerland at Bern and Czechoslovakia at Brno in the Auto Union A and recorded the fastest lap at both. His GP successes should have made Stuck the European Champion driver – if there had been one. The AIACR (the International Association of Automobile Clubs) had failed to create the championship when they introduced its new 750kg minimum weight regulations. So Hans had to be content with his 1934 European and German mountain titles.

Deprived of his title by officialdom's shortcomings, Stuck was back for another try in 1935, when the drivers' championship belatedly came into being. But it was Rudolf Caracciola's year: he won the Monaco, Tripoli, Eifel, French, Belgian and Swiss GPs, a performance that swept him to the title. Hans won the Italian Grand Prix and took second in the German for Auto Union and the first heat of the Avus GP, came second in the Grand Prix of Germany at the Nürburgring and consoled himself with the 1935 German Mountain Championship.

Then 1936 was the year of the startlingly gifted newcomer Bernd Rosemeyer, who became the year's champion, while Hans was unable to score a single Grand Prix victory, although he did come second in the German Grand Prix again and won the German Mountain Championship once more.

Auto Union fired Stuck at the end the 1937 season claiming that he was no longer competitive, which was a lie. The truth was that Hans' wife Paula was accused of being a Jew, and hateful slogans aimed at her began to appear on the walls of the Zwickau factory and elsewhere in Germany. Stuck considered retiring, but did not do so. Anyway it was Paula's grandfather who was Jewish: she was a Christian.

When it emerged in 1938 that Auto Union had fired Stuck, the SS investigated. The matter of Paula Stuck's Jewishness went all the way up to the big boss of both the SS and the Gestapo, Heinrich Himmler, and then on to Hitler himself. The Führer was livid and ordered that Paula's Jewishness should be forgotten and not be allowed to hinder Hans' career. Himmler demanded Stuck's reinstatement as an Auto Union driver, after which Hans was back in business in time for the German GP at the Nürburgring in July. He did well by taking third, and his was the highest-placed Auto Union. He also won five major mountain climbs that year and earned himself both the European and German Championships. So much for being 'uncompetitive.'

Hans Stuck was just as at home driving Professor Porsche's V16 swing axle monster as he was Professor Robert Eberan Eberhorst's less volatile V12 of later years. By the time he retired in 1957, having become Germany's mountain champion again at the age of 60 in a 700cc BMW, Stuck had won five European Championship Grands Prix, the non-championship GP in Bucharest, 17 mountain championships – including two European titles – and set 13 world speed records.

# Surtees, John

HOW DO YOU GET to be the only man to have won both the motorcycle and Formula 1 World Championships in a single lifetime? Perhaps Mauro Forghieri, the man whose Ferraris won 11 world titles, got it right when he said John Surtees was a classy driver, a complete tester and a good technician.

Surtees was certainly blindingly fast, which, added to his engineering and design prowess, meant he understood why and how things worked: a marvellous stock in trade with which to cross swords with the world's best.

Born in Tatsfield, Surrey, on 11 February 1934, John was just a kid when he started out in grass-track events, but soon worked his way up to circuits where he gave even established stars like Geoff Duke a hard time. He first got his toe in the door of the motorcycle World Championship in 1952, when he came sixth on a 500cc Norton in the Ulster Grand Prix; he won the 250cc class of the 1955 race on an NSU and came third on a Norton in the 350cc segment. That year he was given a Norton factory-sponsored ride and proved he was definitely a star in the making by beating the then reigning World Champion Geoff Duke twice. After that he got the call from Italy's MV Agusta, for whom he won an incredible 68 of his 76 350cc and 500cc races and no fewer than seven World Championships between 1956 and 1960. In all, John started in 49 motorcycle races, won an incredible 38 – a win rate of around 77% – and climbed on to the podium after 45 of them!

At 26 years old and with those seven World Championships under his belt – three 350cc and four 500cc – John switched to racing cars and joined Lotus, for whom he drove an 18-Climax into second place at the British Grand Prix, beating the team's number one Innes Ireland in a similar car by 40 seconds. Surtees took pole in the next GP in Portugal and set the fastest lap, but the Lotus 18's radiator split on lap 37 and he was forced to retire. Then followed a couple of low placings in the Yeoman Credit Cooper T53 in

1961, although things looked up in '62 with seconds in Britain and Germany aboard the Bowmaker V8 Lola MkIV, which helped take him to fourth in the Drivers' World Championship table.

In 1963 John moved to Ferrari, where his Italian (learnt at MV Agusta) helped him fit in straight away. He won the year's 12 Hours of Sebring with Ludovico Scarfiotti in a 250P, his first victory for Ferrari, and that was soon followed by him winning the 1000 Kilometres of the Nürburgring with Willy Mairesse a couple of months later. In 1965 John and Scarfiotti drove a 330P2 to a convincing win in the German event again and he turned in a stunning victory in the 1000 Kilometres of Monza in a P3 with Mike Parkes.

John won his first Grand Prix at the tricky Nürburgring in a Dino 156 and also set the race's fastest lap of 8min 47sec over the 14.167-mile circuit in what was Ferrari's first F1 victory for two years. But it was in 1964 that Surtees made history by also winning the Formula 1 World Championship for drivers to achieve his unique double. He won the German GP again that year and sent the thousands of adoring Italian fans into delirium in September by winning the Grand Prix of Italy at Monza in a Dino 158, after a mighty tussle with Graham Hill's BRM, to take the Formula 1 World Championship by one point, John's 40 to Hill's 39.

In September 1965 John was testing a Lola T70 sports racer at Mosport, Canada, when the car suffered a structural breakdown and crashed. Surtees nearly died from his injuries and was out of racing for the rest of the F1 season as he slowly recovered. But he started the 1966 season in good enough form to take the new Mauro Forghieri-designed Ferrari 312 into battle. He took pole position in the Monaco Grand Prix, the first race under the new 3-litre regulations, and led the race for the first 14 laps before his rear axle gave him ever-worsening trouble and he had to retire. It was a different story at the next GP at Spa-Francorchamps, which John won after a freak rainstorm, but internal strife came to a head soon afterwards in a clash between Ferrari motor sport director Eugenio Dragoni and Surtees. It was over the Briton's post-accident fitness, as he was down to drive for Maranello in the 24 Hours of Le Mans. Even though he was Ferrari's lead driver, John was forbidden to compete in the event, which didn't sit well with him at all, so he left.

But Surtees was soon back in F1, although in a different car. He joined Jochen Rindt in the Anglo-Swiss Racing Team to drive a Cooper T81 powered by the big V12 Maserati engine originally designed for a Maserati 250F that never happened. After a short time spent getting his feet under the table, he brought the car home third in the United States Grand Prix at Watkins Glen, where he also recorded the race's fastest lap. Better was to come in the Mexican GP: he won the race and leapt right up to second place in the Formula 1 World Championship behind winner Jack Brabham, and way ahead of Ferrari's Lorenzo Bandini, Mike Parkes and Ludovico Scarfiotti, which must have been satisfying.

With the Cooper-Maserati adventure over, John joined Honda to drive its RA 273 and later the RA 300 for 1967. Reliability was the initial problem with the car, in which Surtees took a fine third place in the South African Grand Prix at Kyalami and then battled through a string of retirements until the Italian GP. He won the race in the RA 300 after a dramatic series of scraps with Jackie Stewart's BRM and especially Jack Brabham's BT26-Repco, the two constantly overtaking each other, with last blood going to John by just 0.2 of a second.

In 1966 Surtees became Cam-Am's first champion, beating Americans Mark Donohue, Dan Gurney and Phil Hill at their own game. He won three of the six counters at Ste Jovite, Riverside and Star Dust, Las Vegas, in a Lola T70-Chevrolet, and would go on to win Star Dust again the following year.

Unreliability still dogged the Honda in 1968, with Surtees manfully struggling to make his mark with the RA 301, but the retirements continued, although John did manage to bring the car home second in the French GP and took pole in Italy before he crashed trying to avoid Chris Amon's spinning Ferrari 312 at Lesmo. Still, third in the USGP, the season's penultimate Grand Prix, took the Briton to equal seventh in the championship with Jo Siffert.

Surtees switched to BRM for 1969, but its P139 was uncompetitive. So he formed the Surtees Racing Organisation, which competed in F 5000, F2 and F1 as a constructor for nine seasons. John retired from driving in 1972, the year Mike Hailwood scored the team's best result by winning the European Formula 2 Championship in a Surtees TS10-Ford.

John is still seen at special events driving priceless vintage racers, like the ex-Rudolf Caracciola Mercedes-Benz W125 belonging to the Stuttgart manufacturer's museum.

# Szisz, Ferenc

UNLIKE THOSE OF JIM Clark, Ayrton Senna, Michael Schumacher or Sebastian Vettel, Szisz is not a name at the forefront of all our minds. Yet it was one that had been hovering about in my subconscious for years, but I never took the trouble to find out who the hell he was. Then Renault did it for me: to mark Fernando Alonso's win in the 2006 Grand Prix of Canada driving its R26, the company issued Szisz's report on his landmark victory in the world's very first Grand Prix 100 years earlier. The report is a must-read for every Grand Prix fan and I shall reproduce it here later, word for word.

But who was the winner of the world's first Grand Prix? Well, he was born in Szeghalom in the Austro-Hungarian Empire on 20 September 1873 and originally trained as a locksmith. But he became fascinated by motor cars, so he studied engineering and made his way to France. There he joined the Renault brothers' firm in 1898, when they were building De Dion-Bouton-engined cars for a rapidly expanding market; his engineering knowledge got him a job in the company's test department.

In 1900 Szisz was selected to become Louis Renault's riding mechanic, but with the death of the latter's brother Marcel in the horrific 1903 Paris–Madrid race Louis decided to withdraw from the sport. He relented in 1905 and authorised the construction of the 105hp Renault AK, powered by a 13-litre inline-four that had a top speed of 91.9mph, and he appointed Szisz as one of its drivers.

The Hungarian did fairly well in the car from the outset, coming fifth in the 1905 Gordon Bennett Cup elimination race at the Auvergne circuit near Clermont-Ferrand. He did the same again in the year's Vanderbilt Cup on Long Island, where he was up against the likes of David Bruce-Brown, Felice Nazzaro, Eddie Rickenbacker and Vincenzo Lancia. The event was won by Frenchman Victor Hémery in a Darracq.

With the world's first Grand Prix scheduled to take place on a public road circuit in the countryside around Le Mans on 26 and 27 June 1906, Louis Renault decided to enter a team of three cars for Ferenc, Claude Richez and a Jean Edmond, with Szisz as team leader. Organised by the Automobile Club of France, the race was run over two days for a total of 12 anti-clockwise laps of a 64.12-mile triangular road circuit outside Le Mans for a total of 769.440 miles, with the 33 cars setting off at intervals to cover six laps a day. The winner was Ferenc Szisz with his riding mechanic Marteau, who covered the distance in a total of 12hr 14min 7sec, an average of 62.887mph.

This is Szisz's verbatim report on how he won the world's first Grand Prix:

'I was held up on the first lap by a defective tyre. In this contest, one had the choice of one of two evils: either to use solid tyres and slide, or round tyres with less rubber and risk a puncture. Which do you prefer: to be hung or shot? To be sure we had removable rims, but we weren't the only ones. While other competitors had them on all four wheels, we only had them on the two in front.

'Nonetheless, my car ran not only with excellent consistency but also with extraordinary speed. The only exceptions were the changing of a spark plug at the start and the stop to change the tyre. I lapped faster than virtually all the competition, including Lancia, Baras and Jenatzy. None of them overtook me on the track except when I had to stop to change tyres.

'On the second lap I was overtaken by Baras when I burst another tyre. Around the middle of the lap, though, I managed to overtake him to put myself back in the lead. When I drove past my team I saw the index fingers of all hands uplifted to show I was leading. On my fourth lap I stopped in front of the stands at my pit to take on supplies and learn my lap times.

'The race was exceptionally hard. Whenever I passed one of the competitors who was struggling – which happened at least 30 times during the race – the tar thrown up almost burned my eyes. With our short wheelbase, we had the front wheels virtually in front of our eyes and suffered awfully. My hour of desperation came late on the first day. At five that evening, my eyes were so inflamed I couldn't see anything. A thick fog seemed to have descended before me.

'That whole night the Renaults and Hugé Grus made efforts to look after me. By eleven it finally got a bit better and by midnight M Renault was racing around Le Mans trying to find a pair of safety goggles for me.

'At one in the morning, needle and scissors in hand, he took on the role of tailor and cut me a face mask to fit around my goggles. My distressed condition had been well nigh critical. To have been the victor on the first day and then perhaps on the second to have to watch another winning: Inconceivable!

'When I finally got started again everything went well. Knowing that no competitor was in front of me and with the aim of profiting as much as possible from the clear road, on the second day I set my fastest lap. I lingered eleven minutes at my pit for recuperation and started off again at 5.45 am. I was back at 6.47 am after completing the lap in 51 minutes.

'I drove the final laps in a state of tremendous excitement. Victory was to be mine and as I drove past M Giradot I couldn't keep from shouting to him "We've done it!" The honest Martaud is the best tyre fitter I know. While we reckoned on four minutes to change a removable rear rim, he could fit a fresh tyre on a non-removable front rim in five.

'And then came the finale, the Marseillaise, the minister, the ovations. All very gratifying – as was the return journey to Paris and the factory where our colleagues awaited us.'

After that, Szisz's motor racing career more or less fizzled out. He and the Renault AK did come second to Felice Nazzaro in the 1907 French GP, they retired with mechanical problems in the 1908 ACF GP and the American Grand Prize at Savannah, Georgia, after which he left Renault to open a garage of his own in Neuilly-sur-Seine. He was enticed out of retirement by his old friend Fernand Charron to drive an Alda in the 1914 GP of France at Lyon and was honoured by being granted the number 1 for his car. But he had to stop to change a wheel on the 11th of 20 laps and, as he did so, his left arm was hit by Carl Jörns' Opel and badly broken, so he retired.

After the First World War, in which Szisz was head of the transport troops in Algeria, he returned to Renault and worked there before retiring at the end of the 1930s. He lived in Auffargis south of Paris until his death in 1944. He and his wife are buried in the town's churchyard.

A memorial to Ferenc Szisz and the Renault AK stand at the main entrance to the Hungaroring, home of the Hungarian GP.

# Taruffi, Piero

BORN ON 12 OCTOBER 1906 in Albano Laziale in the province of Rome, Italy, Piero Taruffi drove with brains, not brawn. He was a qualified mechanical engineer and that helped him keep his finger on the pulse of his racing cars, carefully pacing himself and his machinery until the very end: either of the race or the car. And he was one of the best car sorters of his day, never satisfied until his charge was perfectly set up. A nitpicker, some would say, a full-blown professional – with the huge added plus of an engineering degree – according to others. He was so good at sorting out a racing car's problems that Enzo Ferrari, with whom he had a prickly relationship, often asked him to thoroughly test his Scuderia's racers when their malaise baffled Ferrari's own men.

Taruffi drifted in and out of Ferrari's life for the best part of 30 years. He was a motorcycle racing champion when the Commendatore recruited him in 1931. For four years from 1931 to 1934, Scuderia Ferrari raced 500cc Rudge and Norton motorbikes as well as cars. Never one to miss a trick, Ferrari's idea was to have Taruffi race his motorbikes while he weaned the Roman engineer on four-wheel competition. Taruffi's idea was to phase out his motorcycle racing and branch into cars. Piero won three major motorcycle races for Ferrari, including the 1932 Grand Prix of Europe in Rome on one of the Scuderia's 500cc Nortons: he also competed in modest provincial car races to hone his four-wheel skills.

So the two engineers suited each other, but were often at loggerheads. Later in life, Taruffi said 'Ferrari asked me to drive his cars when he needed me. I agreed to do so when it suited me.' Sparks often flew.

Piero eventually graduated to Grand Prix racing and competed in 13 events between 1933 and 1949, but did not win any of them. To his credit, he refused to be roped in on the 1933 Nuvolari-Varzi-Borzacchini Grand Prix of Tripoli lottery scam, a race in which Taruffi came fifth in his Alfa Romeo 2300, his highest GP placing in those 16 years. He was a more accomplished road racer; a driver with the tenacity of a pit bull, a trait born out by the fact that it took him almost 30 years to win the Mille Miglia, but win it he eventually did.

He began his Mille Miglia odyssey at 23 years old in 1930, driving a Bugatti Tipo 23 with his friend Lelio Pellegrini, but the car overheated and kept misfiring so they finished a lowly 40th. He made equally unsuccessful attempts in 1931 driving a supercharged Itala Tipo 61 and a Scuderia Ferrari Alfa Romeo 8C 2300 in 1932. But his fourth attempt at the race in 1933 in one of Ferrari's Alfas went much better, because he and Count Carlo Castelbarco took third place in an 8C 2300 Monza. That was followed in 1934 by fifth overall and the 1100cc class win with Guerino Bertocchi in a Maserati 4CS.

After that Piero was plagued by years of Mille Miglia mechanical failures and accidents – but no lack of determination – in a variety of cars: in 1940 his works Delage D6-3L dropped out with engine trouble; the same went for the Cisitalias of '47 and '48; transmission trouble put his works Ferrari 166 MM out in 1949; he retired his factory Ferrari 340 America in '52; same again in the 3-litre Lancia D20 in '53; in '54 his Lancia D24 was run off the road by an inept back marker; in '55 he passed the entire Mercedes-Benz team – including eventual winner Stirling Moss – in his Ferrari 118 LM to lead at Pescara but by Rome oil pump and transmission trouble cost him that race; in '56 the brakes of his Maserati 300 S stopped working but then he crashed.

He did it in the end. It was in a Ferrari Tipo 335 in the 1957 Mille Miglia. By Rome, Taruffi was four minutes ahead of his teammate Wolfgang von Trips in a similar car, although Englishman Peter Collins' Ferrari led the way into the capital. But transmission trouble was gnawing away at Peter's car until he had to retire it. Taruffi's 335 was none too healthy either, but he stroked it along towards Brescia and victory with the German a close second. That was Piero's last race and also the last Mille Miglia, brought down by an horrendous accident at Guidizzolo, where the De Portago-Nelson Ferrari crashed, killing both men plus nine spectators, five of them children.

Taruffi peaked as a racing driver in the 1950s, but was less successful at circuit racing. After little joy with an Alfa Romeo 158, he moved back to

Ferrari in 1951, when he drove the 373 into second place in the year's first championship Grand Prix on the Bremgarten circuit in Switzerland. His road-racing skills scored big time that same year when he and Luigi Chinetti won the Carrera Panamericana, a mad dash along the length of Mexico from the Guatemala border to the Texas state line. The pair drove the works Ferrari 212 Inter the 1931 miles to victory in 21hr 57min 50sec – an average of just under 88mph – to give the Commendatore his first-ever win on North American soil.

The Roman engineer's finest year in GP racing was in 1952, the first coming of the Ferrari 500 F2. He won the Swiss GP at the Bern circuit and the non-championship Grand Prix of Paris at Montlhéry in this car, plus the Ulster Trophy at Dundrod in a 375 Thinwall Special, came third in the Grand Prix of France, second in the British, fourth in the German in the 500 and third in the 1952 World Championship, the closest he ever got to the title.

A no-no year followed in 1953, except for his fastest lap of 53.94mph on the murderous 44.64-mile Piccolo Circuito della Madonie in the Targa Florio before his somewhat delicate Lancia D23 gave up the ghost. But Taruffi's horizons were greatly brightened by his 1954 Targa Florio win for Lancia. His mount was Vittorio Jano's 3.3-litre, V6 Lancia D24 with its flowing Pininfarina body, a beast as elegant as it was effective. Luigi Musso in a Maserati A6GCS gave 'the Silver Fox,' as the Italian press had dubbed the now white-haired Taruffi, a run for his money. But Piero was first across the finish line at an average speed of 55.76mph, a substantially quicker average time for the entire race than his fastest lap of the previous year.

In 1954 Taruffi designed and built TARF, a sort of twin torpedo, four-wheel machine powered by a 500cc Gilera engine, in which he became the first to exceed 200kph at Montlhéry, near Paris.

Taruffi began 1956 driving the dud Ferrari 555 Supersqualo, which he qualified 15th at the Monaco Grand Prix and finished eighth. But towards the end of the season he was drafted in by Alfred Neubauer to give the Silver Arrows a helping hand. And he did brilliantly, coming fourth in the W196 in the British Grand Prix and a stunning second to World Champion Juan Manuel Fangio on his home territory at Monza. He also won the 1000 Kilometres of the Nürburgring with Stirling Moss, Jean Behra and Harry Schell, all driving a Maserati 300 S.

Taruffi died on 12 January 1988.

# Trips, Wolfgang von

HOW WILL HISTORY REMEMBER Count Wolfgang Alexander Albert Eduard Maximillian Reichsgraf Berghe von Trips? 'Von Krash,' as the dimwitted sniggeringly called him? As a journeyman? Or as a true gentleman who all but won the Formula 1 World Championship for drivers?

The last, I believe, would be a fair entry for the history books. OK, so he had a number of accidents, the last of which took his life. But he was no journeyman, rather a World Champion in the making. When he died he was leading the F1 World Championship table by 33 points to Phil Hill's 29.

After a charmed adolescence riding off-road motorcycles on the family's estate near Cologne, Germany, von Trips competed in a number of minor national car races and worked his way up to being a reserve driver in the 1955 Mercedes-Benz sports car team. He was on the sidelines at the horrific 24 Hours of Le Mans that year, when teammate Pierre Levegh's SLR crashed at 155mph. The car disintegrated and its various components scythed through a crowd of spectators, killing over 80 people and injuring more than 120. Three months later von Trips was a fully-fledged member of the Mercedes team and drove his SLR into third place in Ireland's Tourist Trophy, together with André Simon.

After a couple of outings for Porsche, von Trips was snapped up by Ferrari for 1956 to join other greats including Peter Collins, Juan Manuel Fangio, Phil Hill and Olivier Gendebien. He and Collins drove a 290 MM into second place in the Swedish Grand Prix at Kristianstad in August and contributed a hefty bunch of points that year to Ferrari's zillionth World Sports Car Championship.

Mike Hawthorn joined Scuderia Ferrari in 1957 and for some unfathomable reason christened the German nobleman 'Taffy.' But despite that encumbrance, the '57 season started well for von Trips. He came third with de Portago, Collins and Castellotti in the 1000 Kilometres of Buenos Aires in a Ferrari 290 MM and was about to win the last Mille Miglia in a 315 S when Enzo Ferrari had a word in his ear at the Bologna service area: the Commendatore said it would be pleasant if Piero Taruffi won the race, as it was his 16th attempt and he had promised his wife, Isabella, he would quit racing if he emerged victorious. In reality, Taruffi was exhausted and his car was giving transmission trouble, so von Trips went in for a bit of play-acting and eased off, which gave the win to Taruffi by 2min 59sec.

An anticlimactic Formula 1 debut followed at Monza, where the Count was entrusted with a Vittorio Jano designed and modified Lancia-Ferrari D50: his steering broke going into the Curva Grande during practice, so von Trips didn't even start the race. But there was better news on the sports car front: Trips and his countryman Wolfgang Seidel drove their Scuderia Ferrari 250 TR into third place in the Grand Prix of Venezuela to give the team yet another world sports car title.

Tragedy bit deep into the heart of Scuderia Ferrari in 1958, though. Both Peter Collins and Luigi Musso were killed in racing accidents. Meanwhile, Wolfgang was almost always on the podium in World Championship sports car races, with a second in the 1000 Kilometres of Buenos Aires, a third in the Targa Florio and the ADAC 1000 Kilometre Rennen at the 'Ring to bring another world title home to Maranello. The *Reichsgraf*'s highest placing in just six Formula 1 outings was a fine third in the Grand Prix of France in a Dino 246.

Count Wolfgang switched sides for 1959, but a lot of good it did him. For instance, he was driving a 1498cc F2 Porsche at Monaco but went out on lap two after skidding on oil that gushed from Cliff Allison's terminally sick Dino: it sent the German slithering into the back of Harry Schell's BRM and that was that. There was a glory famine at Maranello in 1959. The team was beaten into equal second place in the WSCC, which it shared with its rival Porsche, while Aston Martin won the title. The Count contributed to that surprising humiliation by sharing the second-placed Porsche 718 RSK with Jo Bonnier in the RAC Tourist Trophy.

Hard-up for regular points scorers, Enzo Ferrari charmed von Trips away from Porsche for 1960 and he was glad he did. The blond German took second place in the 1000 Kilometres of Buenos Aires on 31 January, driving a 250 TR with Californian Richie Ginther. He came second again in the

Targa Florio in a Dino 246 S co-driven by Phil Hill and helped Ferrari take back its World Championship, relegating the previous year's winner, Aston Martin, to fourth place. Things were also looking up on the F1 front, with Trips a regular points scorer in the Ferrari Dino 246 and 156 P, ending up equal sixth in the drivers' championship with Olivier Gendebien.

The 1961 season looked like it was going to be a Wolfgang von Trips year. He was an experienced campaigner, who had earned his spurs in both Formula 1 and world sports car racing. Sure enough, he won the Grand Prix of Holland by less than a second in an exciting tussle with American Phil Hill in their shark-nosed Ferrari 156s. Hill won Belgium with Wolfgang a close second, but von Trips won the British Grand Prix with Hill almost a minute down on the German in second place.

By that time, even with Phil snapping at the Count's heels, the smart money was on von Trips to win the Formula 1 World Championship.

He was doing well in sports car racing too. Wolfgang, Willy Mairesse, Giancarlo Baghetti and Richie Ginther took second place in the 1961 12 Hours of Sebring in a 250 TR; then the Count and Olivier Gendebien won the Targa Florio in a Dino 246SP.

Wolfgang led the F1 drivers' title table as the circus descended on Monza for the Italian GP. Trips qualified his Ferrari Dino 156 on pole just 0.01 of a second faster than Pedro Rodriguez in a similar car. At the end of the first lap, Jim Clark in his Lotus 21-Climax and Jack Brabham in a Cooper-Climax were just ahead of von Trips as the 33 cars streamed noisily past the main stand. But tragedy struck on the second lap as Clark and Wolfgang shot into the braking area for the Parabolica: von Trips' Dino hit the back of Clark's Lotus and the red car flew off the track, throwing the hapless German driver out as it did so, fatally injuring him. But the Dino charged on through the protective fence like a wild thing and killed 11 spectators. Clark's Lotus went into a series of spins before it came to rest and the Scot stepped out unhurt.

As the race ground on, four of the remaining Ferraris had pulled out a 20-second lead on Stirling Moss and the rest. Phil Hill won the race by more than 30 seconds, ahead of second-placed Dan Gurney in a Porsche 718. That gave Ferrari enough points to secure the World Constructors' Championship and Hill the single point to narrowly win the 1961 World Drivers' title.

The score line read Phil Hill 34 points, Wolfgang von Trips 33.

# Varzi, Achille

HISTORY HAS NOT BEEN kind to Achille Varzi, even though he won 16 Grands Prix, the Targa Florio twice, the Mille Miglia and three Italian motor racing championships for Scuderia Ferrari, Bugatti, Maserati and Auto Union – an outstanding record which should have earned him a place up there with his great antagonist, Tazio Nuvolari.

But he became addicted to morphine, which began to eat away at his career when it was at its peak.

Stern, unsmiling, hollow-cheeked, brilliantined hair plastered down flat, some believed he was pathologically shy and over-compensated with excessive severity. To most he was a cold-blooded, humourless individual who was tough on his friends and even tougher on himself.

Achille was the youngest of three brothers born to a rich family from Galliate, 20 miles west of Milan, Italy, on 8 August 1904. When still a boy, his father gave him a motorcycle with which to commute to and from school. One day he borrowed his elder brother's Garelli 350 and promptly won the 1922 Circuit of Tigullio. He later graduated to a 500cc Norton and won the 1924 Grand Prix Reale of Catalunia, Spain. He became one of Italy's top stars, like Tazio Nuvolari, who was 12 years his senior. The two crossed swords for the first time in '24 and went on doing so until Achille was killed in 1948. Nuvolari the unpredictable fireball; Varzi calm, precise, relentless.

Varzi' first car race was the 1928 GP of Tripoli, won by Nuvolari with Achille third, both in Bugatti Tipo 35C 2000s. Then he came second in an ex-Giuseppe Campari Alfa Romeo P2 at the 1928 GP of Italy at Monza. In 1929 he was invited join Alfa Romeo and took third in the Mille Miglia in a six-cylinder 1750, and won in Alexandria, Rome and Livorno plus the GPs of Spain and Monza in the P2.

Alfa's Vittorio Jano employed both Nuvolari and Varzi in 1930. Each drove a supercharged Alfa Romeo 1750 in the Mille Miglia. At Ancona, the Alfa bosses told both men – who were lying first and second – to slow down: there's no sense in the two cars having accidents or breaking down and losing the victory. But Nuvolari went on to win and Varzi believed his teammate had not respected the team's orders: his pride was dented and a rift developed between them.

Three weeks later, galvanised by the Mille Miglia slight, Varzi won the Targa Florio with a masterful performance in his works P2. He didn't even stop when spilt fuel ignited and started to burn the car away from under him. Next four races, four retirements. Achille needed a faster mount so he joined Maserati in mid-season and started to win immediately: the Coppa Acerbo, the Grands Prix of Monza and Spain.

For 1931 Varzi joined Bugatti and drove for them until late 1933, winning the Grands Prix of Tunis twice, France (with Chiron), Monte Carlo and Tripoli as well as the Circuit of Alessandria, Susa-Moncenisio and Avus. Slim pickings for almost three years and a star like him.

At the end of 1933 Nuvolari left Ferrari, so Varzi took over from him. In 1934 Tazio raced Alfas for Jano. Come the Mille Miglia, and both turned up in 8C 2300 Monzas. This time, though, Varzi took his revenge. And he continued to win for the rest of the season: the Italian national championship (his third), the GPs of Tripoli, Spain and Nice, the Targa Florio, Circuit of Alessandria and the Coppa Ciano, but due to an argument at the Mille Miglia his relationship with Enzo Ferrari went from bad to worse. At the end of the year the pair separated acrimoniously.

Meanwhile, Hitler's PR machine got into gear with Mercedes-Benz and Auto Union. And Achille met Ilse Pietsch, all wispy blond hair, astoundingly beautiful face and voluptuous figure. They began an affair that was laced with morphine, the beginning of his decline.

Varzi signed with Auto Union for 1935 and first competed in its 4951cc, 375hp, 180+mph car in the Tunis GP, which he won. His 1936 opened with a second at Monaco, after which came the Grand Prix of Tripoli; and that is when the Italian first took morphine.

He won the race with help he didn't need. Auto Union team boss Karl Feuereissen waved a green flag at race leader Stuck, the team's secret order to slow down. Achille took the chequered flag and became the first three-times winner of the GP of Tripoli.

Stuck was furious, Varzi delighted and Feuereissen embarrassed, but the matter was out of their hands. The Nazi and Fascist governments had agreed that, where possible, Italian drivers should win Italian races, and German drivers should win German races: Libya was an Italian protectorate, so victory had to go to Varzi.

A week later Achille's Auto Union flew off the track during the Grand Prix of Tunisia, somersaulted through the air and landed in a field of cacti. It was his first racing accident and he was shaken to the core. After that he deteriorated rapidly: puffy face, deeper lines, once immaculate hair ruffled, unpressed clothes. And instead of his normal icy reserve, he became a nervous talker, subject to violent mood changes.

After a string of poor results Achille just disappeared. The team doctor found him in Rome days later and convinced him to return. He still competed for AU in the Swiss Grand Prix, where he drove at a furious pace and came second to Rosemeyer.

After that Varzi couldn't race any more and didn't see a circuit again until July 1937: he just continued his free-fall into the destructive arms of morphine. In a determined cry for help, he entered a clinic to kick the habit: ten months later he had improved sufficiently to go back to racing, this time in a little Maserati 6CM at the 1937 Circuit of San Remo. He won and recorded the fastest lap. The old talent was still there, struggling up through the corrosive bile of morphine.

After the San Remo success Varzi, looking much older but in reasonable health, told Feuereissen that he was cured, had left Ilse, and wanted to race again. The AU boss eventually came round and Varzi managed sixth at Livorno: but due to his condition the mechanics had to lift him from the car afterwards. Achille was slow qualifying for the next event at Brno and asked to be excused from the race. Demoralised, he went in search of Ilse again but couldn't find her: he felt unwanted, so he sought the solace of morphine again.

Disgusted with himself, Achille checked into a Modena clinic in yet another attempt to kick the habit and, at the end of 1938, he had been cured.

He failed to qualify for the 1946 Indianapolis 500 in a Maserati 4CL, but scored a spectacular victory driving an Alfa 158 in the Grand Prix of Turin. For many reasons, it was a stirring comeback.

Achille raced an Alfa in 1947 and did well – second in the Coppa Perón at Buenos Aires, the winner at Rosario and São Paolo. Back in Europe he took second in the Grands Prix of Switzerland and Spa and won the GP of Bari.

On 2 July 1948 Varzi went out in pouring rain driving an Alfa 158 to practise for the Swiss GP. Inexplicably, his Alfetta went straight on at a corner, jerked violently, spun twice and overturned slowly into a ditch, killing Varzi immediately.

# Villeneuve, Gilles

ENZO FERRARI DOTED ON Gilles Villeneuve, the only driver the iron-willed Italian Commendatore ever embraced. The diminutive Canadian reminded him of Tazio Nuvolari, another of his favourites who, like Gilles, would race his car until it literally fell to bits rather than give up. They were tenacious racers of a singular audacity, whose staggering talent could grab hold of a car by the scruff of the neck and make it do what they wanted.

But Gilles, born Joseph Gilles Henri Villeneuve on 18 January 1950, wasn't always like that. When he joined Ferrari in late 1977 he test-drove a 312 T2 so that Enzo Ferrari and Mauro Forghieri could see what he had to offer. Completely ruined brakes, was the answer. They saw that Villeneuve was full of natural talent but was always on ten-tenths. He didn't know how to manage his driving. So they taught him between the autumn of 1977 and the following winter. Forghieri says they literally 'constructed' Gilles Villeneuve the Grand Prix racing driver.

Villeneuve was fearless in a racing car, his incredible courage coming from his tranquil acceptance of the risks he was running. He nearly always drove flat out and could take his car to the absolute limit while miraculously keeping it under control. He was smoothish and precise when his car was working well, but he was a tyre-smoking, opposite-locking demon when it was less than perfect.

A small, doll-like man, Gilles attracted a huge following, many of his fans women who knew nothing about motor racing. To them he was a romantic hero, who became such a huge star that *Time* magazine gave him its coveted front cover.

If a driver can be summed up by his performance in a single race, the one that best defined Gilles Villeneuve is the 1979 French GP at Dijon. He battled lap after lap in a markedly inferior Ferrari 312 T4 with René Arnoux in a state-of-the-art Renault RE10 turbo. Villeneuve pushed his car way over the limit that day and wouldn't give an inch. The two fought so hard they even got into an incredibly dangerous wheel-banging war, their cars lurching from side to side after each nerve-jangling blow. Gilles seemed to regard every foot of the small circuit as a hand-to-hand battleground, braking impossibly late for every corner on badly worn tyres as he and his off-song Ferrari tussled with Arnoux for the smallest advantage. Gilles literally threw his car into corners, tugging his steering wheel to the left and right with fanatical determination until he eventually passed the wide-eyed Frenchman, but could do nothing to catch winner Jean-Pierre Jabouille, who scored F1's first turbo car victory in his Renault.

At the end of it all the elated Gilles and René laughed about their wheel-banging warfare and, back at Maranello, Enzo Ferrari – who was not given to exaggeration – said, 'I believe Ferrari has found a great driver.'

Villeneuve had done all his previous racing in North America, starting with 95mph snowmobiles, which gave him his uncanny sense of balance. He served his motor racing apprenticeship in Formula Ford and then Formula Atlantic, in which he became the 1976 and 1977 champion. He drove an old McLaren M23-Ford in the 1977 British Grand Prix at the invitation of Teddy Meyer. After qualifying an excellent ninth, he finished 11th in a far from competitive car.

Ferrari, that shrewd judge of driving skill, insisted on recruiting baby-faced Gilles to replace the departed Niki Lauda for the last two Grands Prix of 1977. But before that Villeneuve tested at Fiorano, initially lapping at 1min 30sec, got down to 1min 18sec after 15 minutes and was doing 1min 14.38sec at the end of the afternoon, having shattered the T2's brakes.

Gilles crashed heavily in Japan, one of those last two 1977 races. Enzo Ferrari said at the time, 'Forget it. If he wasn't like that, he wouldn't be Villeneuve.'

Villeneuve scored his first GP win before his adoring home crowd at Montreal in the 1978 Canadian GP in the Ferrari 312 T3, with his future Maranello teammate, Jody Scheckter, second in a Wolf WR6-Ford.

In 1979 Gilles drove what many feel was one of the most heroic laps in Formula 1 at the 1979 Dutch GP. His left rear tyre had a slow puncture and suddenly collapsed. But after a brief 'agricultural excursion' he wrestled the car back on to the track and drove like a wild thing on three tyres – often on full opposite lock. His tyreless wheel fell off before he got to the pits, where he insisted a new unit be fitted. It took time, but eventually Ferrari were able to convince him that the car was beyond repair: race over. That year he still won the South African, the USGP West at Long Beach and East at Watkins Glen, but he knew he was expected to defer to Scheckter. His time would come, he reasoned. Gilles was an honourable man, a fact he demonstrated in no small measure at Monza, where the '79 World Championship was within his grasp. But he did what was expected of him and allowed Jody to win the Italian GP and the title, instead of passing him and taking the race and title for himself. Points: Jody 51, Gilles 47.

The 1980 Ferrari 312 T5 was one of the least competitive cars Maranello had ever campaigned. It never went beyond fourth place all season and only racked up a total of eight points, six of which were scored by Gilles. But 1981 was a different story altogether, as Ferrari changed its tune and went for a 1.5-litre turbo engine, which powered Gilles to two spectacular victories at Monaco and in Spain.

FOCA boycotted the 1982 Grand Prix of San Marino, which reduced the field to just 14 cars. On Thursday 22 April a secret dinner took place at Imola at which only French was spoken. The diners agreed to make sure that the spectators and TV viewers would still enjoy an exciting race on the Sunday, despite the depleted entry. Among other things, it was agreed that Arnoux's Renault and the two Ferraris would make a show of it during the first half, but the surviving cars had to be conserved during the second half to get as many as possible to the chequered flag. The winner would be the driver who led the last ten laps. On lap 44 of 60, Villeneuve and his Ferrari 126 C2 took over the lead from René when the Frenchman retired and, just to make sure everyone would stick to the agreement, the Ferrari pits held out a 'slow' signal. But Gilles' teammate Didier Pironi had different ideas and overtook the Canadian five times, the last on lap 59, and won. Villeneuve was furious at Pironi's duplicity and refused to speak to the Frenchman again.

Two weeks later Gilles was killed at Zolder towards the end of qualifying for the '82 Belgian GP, his feud with Pironi still unresolved.

Villeneuve's millions of fans were distraught. Hundreds of tearful girls hung around the front gate of the Maranello factory to grieve together on the hallowed ground over which he had walked. They flooded the team's press office with written prayers and epitaphs. Italian roads – including one in the Ferrari factory complex – squares and circuit corners were named after him. Gilles had become a legend, and remains so to this day.

# Villeneuve, Jacques

THIS SELF-CONFIDENT CANADIAN IS one of the elite. Only he, Mario Andretti and Emerson Fittipaldi have won motor racing's grand slam: the CART Championship, the Indianapolis 500 and the Formula 1 World Championship.

A son of the art, you might say, because his dad Gilles Villeneuve was a sort of reincarnation of Tazio Nuvolari to Enzo Ferrari, and came within an ace of winning the F1 world title himself. Jacques wrested his World Championship from another son of the art, Graham Hill's son Damon, at the end of 1996.

Jacques was born in Saint-Jean-sur-Richelieu, Quebec, Canada, on 9 April 1971 to Gilles and his wife Joann, but grew up in Monaco, which his parents had made their home. Gilles, a star Ferrari driver, was tragically killed qualifying for the 1982 Grand Prix of Belgium when his son was just 11.

Like many recent F1 stars, the young Villeneuve began in karts and showed so much promise that his Uncle Jacques, the 1983 Can-Am champion, enrolled the lad in the Jim Russell Racing Driver School in Quebec, from which he qualified with honours. But at 17 and showing all that promise he was still too young to qualify for a racing driver's licence in Canada or Italy, so he qualified for one in Andorra.

Still 17, Villeneuve cut his teeth on the Alfa Cup and came tenth, mixing it with Formula 1 pros like Riccardo Patrese and Mauro Baldi. Then he tried the 1989 Italian Formula 3 Championship, and after that the Japanese F3 series in 1992 and won three races. That led to the Trois Riviéres Formula Atlantic in Canada and a third place in the series, followed by the North American Toyota Atlantic championship for the following season, where he scored seven pole positions and won five races in 15 events to come third in the title table.

In 1994 he moved up a notch with his Forsythe-Green squad to do the Indy Car Championship, and made everyone sit up and take notice: he came second in the Indianapolis 500 and won his first race in the series at Road America. That and other placings took him to sixth in the championship and earned him the title Rookie of the Year.

But 1995 was a year to remember. Villeneuve won four races in the championship, including the biggest of them all, the Indianapolis 500. They even gave him a two-lap penalty in that race, but he still came roaring up through the field to win with a two-second lead over yet another son of the art, Christian Fittipaldi, to become the '95 CART Indy Car World Series Champion. And he was just 24.

Frank Williams had been eyeing the sensational young Canadian for some time, so he offered the lad a seat in a Williams FW18-Renault for 1996. Villeneuve promptly won pole position in the season's opener in Australia, but an oil leak slowed him enough to let his teammate Damon Hill win the race, with Jacques just holding on to second; not bad for an F1 beginner.

An F1 victory wasn't long in coming. It was in the Grand Prix of Europe at the Nürburgring, where he kept his head as ex-World Champion Michael Schumacher in a Ferrari 310B pressured him to get out of the way. Jacques went on to win in Britain, Hungary and Portugal to become runner-up to Hill in the World Championship.

Damon left Williams for Tom Walkinshaw's resuscitated Arrows team, so Villeneuve became the Williams number one in 1997 and was up for the title yet again: this time, the opposition a ruthless Michael Schumacher. Jacques took ten pole positions that season, won two out of its first three Grands Prix and then added Spain, Britain, Hungary, Austria and Luxembourg to his haul. So by the time it came to the last race of the year, Schumi was just a single point ahead of Villeneuve in the championship table as the circus descended on Spain's Jerez circuit for the Grand Prix of Europe. Jacques took pole, but Michael was leading him on lap 48 when the Canadian braked late going into the Dry Sac corner and took the inside line to overtake the German. The two collided – the FIA later ruled that Schumacher had responded to the challenge by deliberately driving into Villeneuve in an attempt to eliminate his rival and protect his points lead – and Michael went off and retired. Jacques continued more slowly with a badly bent sidepod to come third in the race and win the Formula

1 World Championship at only his second attempt. Later the FIA stripped Schumacher of all the points he had scored that season and his second place in the championship.

The Williamses were underpowered in 1998, so Villeneuve's title defence soon went up in smoke as he tried to fight it out with the faster Ferraris and McLarens. Mika Häkkinen took the championship from the Canadian with 100 points to Jacques' meagre 21 down at fifth place in the table.

Title gone, Villeneuve joined British American Racing (BAR) – part-owned by his personal manager Craig Pollock – for 1998, but that went badly, with Jacques retiring from the first 11 races, and he didn't score any points all season. Same again in 1999, but the team acquired Honda engines for 2000 and things became marginally better. Well, at least he was able to score 17 points in the BAR 02-Honda – Michael Schumacher took the title in his Ferrari F1-2000 with 108 – with a smattering of fourths and fifths. In 2001 Jacques even managed a couple of podium finishes with thirds in Spain and Germany, but his total number of championship points dipped to 12. Things got worse in 2002 as the BAR 04-Honda staggered through the season, enabling Villeneuve to score just four championship points. Another disastrous year followed in 2003, when Jacques only managed six points as car unreliability meant he had to retire eight times.

Villeneuve had no contract for 2004, so he had to take the best part of a year off, except for the last three Grands Prix of the season in which he drove a works Renault for Flavio Briatore, but 11th in China and 10th in both Japan and Brazil were the best he could do. Villeneuve signed with Peter Sauber for 2005, but all he could do for the Swiss team was come fourth in the Grand Prix of San Marino and score nine championship points. Then BMW bought Sauber and it seemed Villeneuve's days with the team were numbered, extracting just seven points from the first 12 Grands Prix. Soon after his crash at the German GP he and the team parted company.

Jacques did well at the 2007 24 Hours of Le Mans, where he helped put the diesel-engined Peugeot HDi V12 5.5-litre turbo into fourth place on the starting grid. The car was in second for much of the race, but it started to develop engine trouble and was eventually retired 2hr 28min before the end. In 2008 Villeneuve, Marc Gené and Nicolas Minassian went the distance and took their Audi HDi to second place at Le Mans, which spurred Jacques on to promising he would be back at the Sarthe until he won the race.

Since then he has competed in various NASCAR series and other championships without much luck.

Jacques has long been a keen amateur musician and lyric writer and has released both a single and an album in Canada.

# Villoresi, Luigi

VILLORESI WAS MILAN'S DRIVER. He was born there, lived there all his life, had a Maserati dealership there, his most devoted fans were there. For decades the names of Milan and Luigi Villoresi were synonymous. And he did the city proud.

He won 26 Grands Prix, the 1939 and 1940 Targa Florios, the 1951 Mille Miglia and three Italian national championships.

Born in Milan on 16 May 1909 Luigi, nicknamed 'Gigi' – an Italian diminutive rather like Bob is to Robert in English – started competing in the sport in 1932 with his brother Emilio, campaigning their Lancia Lambda in minor rallies. Their talent began to emerge in 1935, when they won the 1100cc unsupercharged class of the Mille Miglia in a Fiat 508 CS Balilla Sport.

Luigi's first encounter with Maserati, which would be a major influence on his life, was when he and Emilio bought a Tipo 4CS, in which Gigi came sixth in the 1937 Prince Rainier Cup at Monaco. His drive caught Ernesto Maserati's eye and he invited Luigi to join the works team, all of which led to his first victory for Maserati in the 1937 Grand Prix of Brno. The following year he won the Coppa Acerbo in a Maserati 6CM, a tragic year because Emilio, just as talented as his elder brother, had been taken on by Scuderia Ferrari but was killed testing an Alfa Romeo 158 at Monza.

Luigi felt Enzo Ferrari was generally insensitive and showed insufficient concern towards the Villoresi family after Emilio's death, and bore a grudge against the Commendatore for decades afterwards.

But Gigi continued racing, and Targa Florio victories were scored in Grand Prix-like circumstances. Politics forced the event out of the Madonie Mountains and on to a 3.5-mile track made up of a network of roads in Palermo's Real Favorita Park. The locals didn't like it; they far preferred a day out in the mountains rather than a park they could visit any time. And this Grand Prixified Targa kept competitors away in droves. There were only 14 starters in 1939 compared to the 40–50 the event used to attract in its heyday; but Gigi in a Maserati 6CM beat Piero Taruffi to the win that year. The number of entries went up to 16 in 1940, every single one of them in Maseratis. But Luigi, this time in a 4CL, won again before the event closed down for the duration of the Second World War, after which it was combined with the Giro di Sicilia for a while.

Villoresi became Maserati's star driver the moment Grand Prix racing resumed after the Second World War, when he won the first GP to be held after the hostilities, run through the streets of Nice on 22 April 1946: his car, a Maserati 4CL. A month later he drove a Maserati into seventh place in the Indianapolis 500 and would have done much better but for persistent magneto trouble.

In 1947 he won Nice again, the GP of Nîmes, the General Perón and the Eva Duarte Perón GPs in Buenos Aires, all of them in Maserati 4CLs. A year later Gigi was still on the rampage, winning both the Argentine GPs again plus those of Comminges, Albigeois and Peña Rhin, Naples, this time all in Maserati 4CLTs.

For 1949 Villoresi and his protégé Alberto Ascari joined Scuderia Ferrari, and Gigi just kept on winning. He took the GPs of Brussels, Luxembourg, Rome and the Circuit of Garda in Ferrari 166s and the Grand Prix of Holland driving a Ferrari 125 F1. A few months later he won the Grand Prix of Eva Perón in Buenos Aires, the Rosario Cup at the wheel of a Ferrari 166 C plus another three key races for Ferrari.

After he won the 1950 Grand Prix of Marseilles for Ferrari he was involved in a tragic accident at the 1950 Grand Prix of Nations at Geneva on 30 July, when his Maserati 4CL skidded on oil, smashed through the trackside barrier and killed three spectators. Gigi broke his left leg and suffered head injuries, which put paid to his motor racing for the remainder of the season.

In 1951 Luigi formed Scuderia Ambrosiana with Giovanni Lurani and Franco Cortese, a team that continued until 1954. That same year Villoresi kicked off the 1951 season with victory in the Grand Prix of Syracuse in a Ferrari 375, which led him to the race of his life: the 1951 Mille Miglia.

To begin with he was one of a crowd, because 26 Ferraris were entered for the race, one of them driven by Villoresi and Ferrari mechanic Pasquale Cassani. It was a smart looking 340 America Vignale coupé, which proved remarkably resilient in the pouring rain as all the other works Ferraris dropped out due to accidents or breakdowns. Even Gigi went off the road at Ravenna and severely bent the left front wing, the suspension and half the radiator grille of his car, but he was able to get going again and shot into Florence in the lead, with Giovanni Bracco and Umberto Maglioli two minutes behind him in their Lancia Aurelia B20 GT. But Villoresi really opened up the big V12 on the straight roads across the Padania Plain to Brescia, to win by a sizeable 20 minutes.

Many years later Gigi was reintroduced to his perfectly restored Ferrari 340 Vignale America at a press event in California and drove a relay of journalists around the state in it. Almost 80 by then, he was exhausted at the end of the day and asked under his breath, 'How on earth did I win the Mille Miglia in that piece of agricultural machinery?'

The usual bag of gold plus an exciting challenge attracted 41-year-old Villoresi and his young friend Ascari, now the reigning Grand Prix World Champion, to Lancia in 1953. Gianni Lancia was determined to break into Formula 1, so he had the brilliant veteran Vittorio Jano design and build the eight-cylinder D50. And he wanted a sort of 'dream team' to drive it, so he spirited the highly experienced Gigi Villoresi and Alberto Ascari away from Ferrari, added Eugenio Castellotti and – for one race – Louis Chiron to the line-up. The car certainly showed promise when Ascari took pole position for its very first race, the 1954 Spanish GP, for which Gigi qualified fifth. Both dropped out with mechanical ills. But after Ascari's death in May 1955 Gianni Lancia retired from motor sport and he and his family gradually withdrew from the company, which had become financially unsound.

After the 1951 Mille Miglia victory Gigi won the 1953 Giro di Sicilia, in which he covered the 676 miles at an average speed of 61.06mph in a Ferrari 340 MM, and then went back to the beginning: rallying. He was one of over 300 entrants in the 1958 Monte Carlo Rally and among just 75 that crossed the finish line; he won the over 2000cc class in a Lancia Aurelia B20 coupé with Ciro Basadonna.

Villoresi and Basadonna also won the prestigious 1958 Acropolis Rally outright in a Lancia Aurelia B20 GT, which turned out to be Gigi's last victory.

After that Luigi retired from the sport, but stayed in touch, especially with Maserati for whom he became a roving ambassador. He was a member of the Maserati Register's executive council for many years and ran his Milan dealership until he was almost 80.

He died in 1997 at the age of 88.

# Watson, John

JOHN WATSON IS ONE of those rarities: an Irish Grand Prix winner. It was a feat pulled off by as many of his countrymen you could count on the fingers of one hand, and when you add to the equation the fact that he was also a successful World Sports Car Championship driver his rarity sky-rockets.

John's dad Marshall raced a Citroën Light 15 in his youth and became a well-to-do motor trader in Belfast. He did everything he could to help his son into motor sport and he even stumped up the necessary cash to get the youngster's racing career off the ground. The young Watson began in club events and worked his way up to Formula 2, in which he drove machinery financed by dad between 1969–71 without exactly setting the world on fire. He moved up to Formula 1 and had a go at World Championship sports car racing in 1973, eventually turning out to be good at both. I say eventually, because John made his F1 debut in a Brabham BT37 in the British Grand Prix at Silverstone, qualified 23rd on the grid and retired. But he was mildly encouraged by a solid fifth place in the World Sports Car Championship Watkins Glen Six Hours driving a Mirage M6 in partnership with motorcycle wunderkind Mike Hailwood.

In 1974 the fresh-faced, extremely enthusiastic Watson drove a BT42 then a BT44 for the Hexagon Brabham team, bankrolled by London motor trader Paul Michaels, and scored his first Formula 1 point at the Monaco GP in the company of men like winner Ronnie Peterson, Jody Scheckter and Emerson Fittipaldi. Having broken his duck, as the cricketers say, Watson went on to a well-deserved fourth place in the Austrian Grand Prix that year as well as fifth in the USGP at Watkins Glen.

The following year he drove a TS16/4 for the great John Surtees but the car was uncompetitive, so he signed for American millionaire Roger Penske before the season was out, taking the place of Mark Donohue, who had died of head injuries after a crash in the warm-up for the year's Austrian Grand Prix. John made a solid but unspectacular debut in the PC1 at the USGP at Watkins Glen, where he put the car on the grid in 12th place brought it home safely in ninth.

After a slow start in 1976, Watson began to make his mark in F1 when he came third in the Grand Prix of France after first being disqualified and then reinstated in the outcome of a wrangle over the height of his PC4's wing. John knew he had arrived when he won the Grand Prix of Austria in the car at the Österreichring, beating the likes of Jacques Laffite, Mario Andretti and Ronnie Peterson. A sixth followed at the Glen again so that, when the scores were totted up at the end of the season, Watson was equal seventh with Laffite in the 1976 Formula 1 World Championship. A long way from Northern Ireland clubbing.

Roger Penske withdrew from Formula 1 at the end of the year, so Watson moved to Bernie Ecclestone's Brabham-Alfa Romeo set-up, where his teammate was Niki Lauda. He did no better than second in the French GP at Dijon in 1977, but he did put the Brabham-Alfa BT45 on pole for the Monaco GP before retiring with mechanical woes. The 1978 season held little magic for John, with just a second in the Italian GP in the disappointing BT46, his highest placing of the season. So after two years of mediocrity he moved to McLaren as the team's number one after the death of Ronnie Peterson, who was due to be McLaren's lead driver, at the Italian Grand Prix at Monza in September. But there was not much magic to be had there for the next couple of years either. The McLaren M28, its B and C versions plus the M29 B and C were incredibly uncompetitive and brought just a single podium place to the Irishman in those 24 months – third in the 1979 Grand Prix of Argentina. But partway through the season Ron Dennis and John Barnard took the team in hand and Watson responded in spades almost immediately, with a fine victory in the 1981 British GP at Silverstone.

After winning the 1975 and 1977 Formula 1 World Championships, Niki Lauda came out of retirement and joined McLaren for a small fortune, which John found psychologically hard to take. Nevertheless, Watson buckled down to driving the best way he knew how. Lauda may have won the 1982 Long Beach GP in the MP4/1B in April, but the Irishman bounced right back a month later with victory in the Grand Prix of Belgium in a similar car, and on 6 June he did it again by winning the Detroit GP for McLaren. Together with other points-scoring places, including seconds in Brazil and the Caesar's Palace car park in Las Vegas, Watson was equal second with Didier Pironi in the 1982 World Championship standings with 39 points, five behind the new F1 title holder Keke Rosberg of Williams.

The 1983 season started well for John with victory in the second Grand Prix of the year at Long Beach. He qualified a lowly 22nd but sliced his way up the field to take an incredible win, almost 30 seconds ahead of his teammate Niki Lauda in second. After that came thirds in Detroit and at Zandvoort and little else, which did not exactly thrill Mr Dennis, so Watson was replaced by the diminutive Alain Prost at season's end. The Irishman's unpredictable swings in driving form – brilliant when his car was sharp, to lacklustre when it was not – were too much for the team boss, so that apart from a single outing a couple of years later in an MP4/2B-TAG Porsche at Brands Hatch, where he came seventh, Watson never competed in Formula 1 again.

In fact, the only time John ever laid a finger on a Formula 1 car after that was to give Eddie Jordan's budding F1 car a thorough shakedown in 1991.

Formula 1's loss was the World Sports-Prototype Championship's gain. In 1984 Watson and Stefan Bellof drove a Porsche 956 to victory in the Fuji 1000 Kilometres, which helped provide the Stuttgart constructor with the year's title. Three years later Watson agreed to drive the XJR-8 for Jaguar and he almost won the 1987 World Sports-Prototype Championship. Paired with Dutchman Jan Lammers, he won first time out in the Gran Premio Fortuna at Jarama, repeated that success in the 1000 Kilometres of Monza and did so again in the last event of the season at Fuji, with a second in the Silverstone 1000 Kilometres and the 1000 Kilometres of Spa. Lammers and Watson tied for second place in the championship with 102 points apiece, the title going to Raul Boesel in a sister car with 127. John's success meant that Jaguar won the Constructors' World Championship with a crushing 178 points to second-placed Brun Motorsport's 91, a source of great satisfaction to the Irishman.

When he retired John ran a motor racing school at Silverstone and then turned to TV commentating, first on Formula 1 and later on sports car racing.

# Zanardi, Alessandro

ALESSANDRO ZANARDI IS AN inspiration to us all. Here is a double CART champion who lost both his legs in a devastating motor racing accident in 2001, nearly bled to death, underwent more surgery in which his legs were further shortened to allow them to heal and fought back through a long, painful and exhausting rehabilitation course. As if that were not enough, he made his motor racing comeback in 2004 with BMW Italy-Spain, won his first World Touring Car Championship race in 2005, goes handcycling, is a Paralympics double gold medallist and deftly presents his own Italian TV programme.

In May 2003 he even went back to the EuroSpeedway, 80 miles south of Berlin, Germany, where the accident happened 13 laps from the end of the 2001 CART race, and covered those uncompleted laps in a ChampCar using hip- and hand-operated brake and accelerator controls. He recorded almost 193mph, and that would have been enough to put him in fifth place on the grid in the 2001 event!

Alex was born on Bologna, Italy, on 23 October 1966 and began racing when he was just 13. He competed in the Italian F3 Championship in 1988 and moved on to Formula 3000 in 1991 to win his debut race in Rome driving the Barone Rampante team's Reynard 91D Mugen. He did three F1 races for Jordan that year, drove a number of events for Minardi-Lamborghini in 1992, tested for Benetton in 1993, then joined Lotus but crashed badly in the Belgian GP at Spa-Francorchamps. He returned to Lotus in time for the 1994 Grand Prix of Spain, but the Lotus-Mugens were unreliable and then the team imploded, so Alex went sports car racing for a while.

He crossed the Atlantic in 1995 and signed for Chip Ganassi Racing as number two driver to Jimmy Vasser before winning his first race on 23 June

1996 at Portland in the team's Reynard 961-Honda. He also won at Mid-Ohio and Laguna Seca that year to come equal second in the championship with Michael Andretti and took five pole positions, all in his first US season. For that Zanardi was named 1996 CART Rookie of the Year.

Much was expected of Alex the following year, when he delivered the goods: and how. He won the 1997 CART Championship, fencing mainly with reigning champion Jimmy Vasser, Gil de Ferran and Paul Tracy and turning in victories at Long Beach, Cleveland, Michigan, Mid-Ohio again and Elkhart Lake plus some strong placings, setting six fastest laps and scoring four pole positions in the process. He ended the season with 195 points against second-placed de Ferran's 162. Alessandro won his second championship in succession in 1998 with seven wins and five second places and recorded three fastest laps to pile up a total of 285 points, almost twice as many as his nearest rival and best friend Vasser's 169.

To mark his two successive CART Championships, Honda built a special commemorative version of their upmarket Acura NSX and named it the Alex Zanardi Edition of which 51 were produced, all in the same red as his Chip Ganassi car. The manufacturer presented the first of the series to Alex and sold the remaining 50 to members of the public.

Sir Frank Williams liked what he saw so he signed the young Italian to drive for his Formula 1 team from 1999. Pre-season testing went fine, but Alessandro's teammate Ralph Schumacher was often faster than him in Grands Prix and Zanardi's race performances were patchy, so he was replaced by Jenson Button for the 2000 season.

Alex fancied a return to CART and signed for Mo Nunn's team in 2000, but it seemed the old flare had gone – or at least it had dimmed – as the Italian was unable to score a top-six place all season. He drove his Reynard 001-Honda into fourth place in the 2001 Molson Indy Toronto, but his most competitive race was in the American Memorial 500 at Germany's EuroSpeedway, in which his horrendous accident happened. Alessandro was leading the event when he made a late pit stop. He was just leaving pit lane and trying to get back into contention when he accelerated hard and the car spun right in front of Patrick Carpentier's Reynard. The Canadian was able to avoid the gyrating Zanardi car, but not so Alex Tagliani, whose Reynard sliced into the side of the double champion's racer and split the monocoque in two. The Italian lost both his legs and a great deal of blood and it was only the fast, efficient work of a medical team at the circuit and later in hospital that saved his life.

After a long spell in hospital, Alex began a tough rehabilitation programme with racing still very much in mind. He soon dispensed with the unambitious standard prosthetic legs and designed his own, which he considered were more suited to racing. His road back to the sport included the honour of flagging off the 2002 CART race at Toronto, and a year later he lowered himself into a ChampCar for the first time since the accident to complete those 13 unfinished laps at the EuroSpeedway.

Fittingly, Alex competed in his first post-accident race in his own country, at the Monza circuit, driving a specially adapted BMW touring car, and finished an extremely creditable seventh. He kept at it, driving for Roberto Ravaglia's BMW Team Italy-Spain, and on 24 August 2005 won his first World Championship race against a whole grid full of door-handling hard-chargers. Later that year he also won the Italian Touring Car Championship: feats that earned him the Laureus World Sports Award for Comeback of the Year in 2005. He continued to reinforce that born-again success when he won the WTCC races in Istanbul in 2006 and Brno in both 2008 and 2009, at the end of which he decided to retire from world level competition.

Alex got back behind the wheel of a Formula 1 car again in November 2006. He went to Valencia, Spain, where BMW-Sauber let him test one of their cars, its hand controls on the steering wheel. It was a bit of a lash-up, because he could only steer with his right hand while he used his left to accelerate, but he was still elated by the experience and said driving an F1 car again was 'just incredible.'

And now to handcycling. Zanardi actually entered the 2004 New York Marathon's handcycling division and came fourth. He was so inspired by the experience that he took up the sport seriously. That led to him competing in the 2009 Para-Cycling Road World Championships and winning two gold medals for his hand-bike victories in the 2012 Paralympic Games in London.

And as if that were not enough, Alessandro has a company that builds a range of kart chassis – and, of course, they are winning. Martin Plowman became the Asia-Pacific Champion driving a Zanardi in 2004, and between 2006 and 2008 Zanardi karts also raced for the CIK-FIA World Championship and the ICA World Cup.

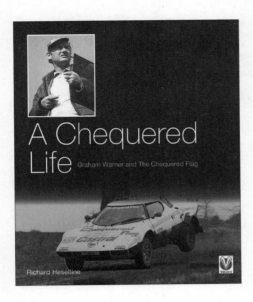

# Also from Veloce Publishing ...

# TT Talking - The TT's most exciting era

## As seen by Manx Radio TT's lead commentator 2004-2012

Charlie Lambert

Foreword by John McGuinness

The 2007 centenary of the Isle of Man Tourist Trophy launched the TT into a new era of success. In this book, Charlie Lambert – Manx Radio TT's lead commentator – tells the story of this sensational upturn, from his own role behind the microphone, to the pressures, controversies, laughs and sadness that go with being the man at the heart of the world's most famous motorcycle road race.

- A colourful and entertaining take on the world-famous TT races
- Inside stories from the TT paddock
- Characters and quirks of the most famous motorbike races
- Behind the scenes at Radio TT
- Foreword by the TT's fastest rider, John McGuinness
- Personal view of the TT by the man with the microphone, Charlie Lambert
- Crises, cock-ups, controversies ... and worse!
- Two-wheel aces McGuinness, Hutchinson, Donald, Anstey, Martin, Dunlop, Cummins, Farquhar
- Sidecar stars Molyneux, Crowe, Klaffenbock, Sayle, Holden
- Intelligent discussion of the most controversial motor sport event

V4750 • Paperback • 22.5x15.2cm • £14.99* • 160 pages • 45 pictures
ISBN: 978-1-845847-50-0 • UPC: 6-36847-04750-4

For more info on Veloce titles, visit our website www.veloce.co.uk, email: info@veloce.co.uk or phone +44(0)1305 260068  * Prices subject to change, P&P extra

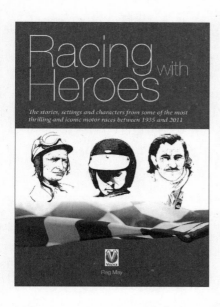

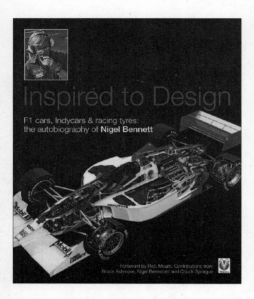

# Index